THE
COMMUNIST MOVEMENT

D1525631

FERNANDO CLAUDIN

THE
COMMUNIST MOVEMENT

FROM COMINTERN TO COMINFORM

✻

PART TWO
THE ZENITH OF STALINISM

Translated by Francis MacDonagh

MONTHLY REVIEW PRESS
NEW YORK AND LONDON

Originally published by Editions Ruedo Ibérico,
copyright © 1970 by Editions Ruedo Ibérico

Library of Congress Cataloging in Publication Data
Claudín, Fernando.
    The Communist movement.
    Translation of La crisis del movimiento comunista.
    Includes bibliographical references and index.
    1. Communism—History. I. Title.
HX40.C59813   335.43   74-25015
ISBN 0-85345-366-7

First Printing

Monthly Review Press
62 West 14th Street, New York, N.Y. 10011
21 Theobalds Road, London WC1X 8SL

Manufactured in the United States of America

CONTENTS

Contents

PART TWO:
THE ZENITH OF STALINISM

5

REVOLUTION AND SPHERES
OF INFLUENCE

Support the liberation movement in China? But why? Wouldn't that be dangerous? Wouldn't it bring us into conflict with other countries? Wouldn't it be better if we established 'spheres of influence' in China in conjunction with other 'advanced' powers and snatched something from China for our own benefit? That would be both useful and safe ... Support the liberation movement in Germany? Is it worth the risk? Wouldn't it be better to agree with the Entente about the Versailles Treaty and bargain for something ourselves by way of compensation? ... Maintain friendship with Persia, Turkey and Afghanistan? Is the game worth the candle? Wouldn't it be better to restore the 'spheres of influence' with one or other of the Great Powers? And so on and so forth.

Such is the new type of nationalist 'frame of mind', which is trying to liquidate the foreign policy of the October revolution ...

That is the policy of nationalism and degeneration, the path of the complete liquidation of the proletariat's international policy, for people afflicted with this disease regard our country not as a part of the whole that is called the world revolutionary movement, but as the beginning and end of that movement, believing that the interests of all other countries should be sacrificed to the interests of our country.

STALIN, 1925

FROM COMINTERN TO COMINFORM

The four years between the dissolution of the Comintern and the creation of the Cominform[1] were a period of spectacular expansion for the Communist movement, particularly in the main theatres of the war, Europe and Asia. The world which emerged from the great upheaval included, at the end of 1945, fourteen million organized Communists beyond the Soviet frontiers, as against a million at most on the eve of the war and many fewer – it is impossible to name a figure, but the fall was very heavy, especially in Europe – during the period of the German–Soviet pact.[2] Within this general increase, to which the most striking exception was the United States, certain parties stand out sharply. In addition to the party in the Soviet Union (and the Vietnamese and Cuban parties in recent years), they were to be the sensitive points of the world Communist movement; these were the Chinese party, the parties of the European 'people's democracies', and the French and Italian parties.

The Chinese party increased its membership during the war against Japan from 40,000 in 1937 to 1,200,000 in 1945, and strengthened its position as leader of the great Asian revolution. By the end of 1947 it had 2,700,000 members, and during the summer of the same year, a little before Stalin decided to set up the Cominform, the liberation army went over to the offensive against the Kuomintang. The decisive turn in the civil war had been taken and the victory of the revolution was taking shape on the horizon.[3]

At the outbreak of the war all the Communist parties in the future 'people's democracies' were operating in secret and, except for the Czechoslovak party, had for years led a precarious existence. Their organized forces were reduced to a few thousand militants, and in Romania and Hungary their political influence was tiny. The Polish party had been almost destroyed by the Stalinist purges and repressions of the late thirties, and the same purges had also, though to a lesser degree, affected the Yugoslav, Hungarian and Romanian parties (see p. 670 note 18). In 1947 these parties together had a total membership of over seven million and power was either already in their hands or within their reach.

France and Italy contained the two senior Communist parties in the developed capitalist world. The Italian party shot from 5,000 members in 1943 to 2,000,000 in 1946. On a more modest scale, the French party grew from 300,000 at the outbreak of the war (of which only a minute proportion remained during the period of the Nazi–Soviet pact) to almost a million in 1946. Both became the hegemonic parties within the working class, and extended their influence into other social sectors, especially among intellectuals. Both took part in the governments which followed the liberation in 1947.

The numerical growth, and even more the political influence, of other Communist parties remained well below the levels we have just mentioned, but is worth noting in a number of cases. In seven small European countries within the developed capitalist zone (Sweden, Norway, Denmark, the Netherlands, Switzerland, Austria and Finland) the total number of active Communists rose from under 100,000 at the outbreak of war to around 600,000 in 1946–7. And even the always tiny British party, which had had 18,000 members in 1939, touched 50,000 in 1944.[4] The Communist parties of Austria, Finland, Belgium, Denmark and Norway joined the governments of the immediate post-war period.

During the war the Greek Communist Party (17,500 members in 1935, 72,500 in 1945) became the main organizer and leader of the National Liberation Front (EAS) and the people's army (ELAMS). Only the last-minute intervention of the British expeditionary force in December 1944 (covered by the secret Stalin–Churchill agreement signed in October of that year)[5] prevented the triumph of the revolution. In 1946 the Greek Communist Party organized armed struggle, which reached a climax in the last months of 1947, at the same time as the creation of the Cominform. At the other end of the Mediterranean the Spanish Communist Party was rebuilding its organization under Fascist terror and supported a large guerrilla movement.

In Asia, the Indian Communist Party increased its membership from 16,000 in 1943 to 90,000 in 1948. The Japanese party, which before the war had been underground, severely persecuted and had had at most a thousand organized militants, won 2,000,000 votes and five seats in 1946 and in 1949 3,000,000 votes and thirty-five seats (there are no statistics for party membership). The same phenomenon can be found in almost all the Asian countries: small Communist cells grow and parties are formed where none existed. The Vietnamese Communist Party began its heroic struggle. On a smaller scale Communist influence also grew in some Middle Eastern countries (Iran and Syria). The Iranian Communists took part in the government for a short period in 1946.

The Latin American parties combined had 90,000 members in 1939. Around 1947 they had nearly half a million. Outstanding among them were the Communist parties of Brazil, Chile and Cuba, with approximate membership figures for 1945–7 of 200,000, 60,000 and 40,000. The Chilean and Cuban Communists took part in governments during one period, and the international Communist movement built great hopes on the Brazilian party. 'Brazil may soon become the American Russia', was a favourite saying.

The most important exception in this general growth of the Communist movement in the first years after the war was, as has already been said, the United States. The world capitalist super-power remained impermeable to Marxism, and the tiny Communist Party experienced no more than a short burst of growth in 1944, when its general secretary, Earl Browder, decided to transform it into an ambiguous 'Communist Political Association', ready 'to collaborate in order to ensure the efficient functioning of the capitalist regime in the post-war period'.[6] Nevertheless, even in the United States, in spite of the crisis in the Communist Party, a slight leftward shift could be seen in the labour movement. The American Federation of Labor refused to join in setting up the World Trade Union Federation, but the other large trade-union grouping of the American proletariat, the Congress of Industrial Workers, joined the WFTU with the Soviet unions and other trade-union groups led by the Communists.

Trade-union unity was widely restored at national level, and with the creation of the WFTU in February 1945 unity on a world scale was achieved for the first time since the October revolution. Another sign of the radicalization of the labour movement was the growth of the left wings within the Social Democratic parties and the tendencies favourable to common action with the Communists.

At the centre of this world-wide array of labour-movement forces and of Communist party growth stood the state and society born of the October revolution, now enhanced with a new prestige. The Soviet system had refuted Trotsky's pessimistic predictions and had emerged stronger from the great trial, and world opinion recognized the decisive contribution made by the USSR to the defeat of Hitler's imperialism. The effect produced by the Soviet military victories on the workers and peoples of every continent can be compared with the echo produced in its day by the October revolution, but with one difference. The Soviet

Union now appeared as more than the exemplary incarnation of the socialist revolution. For broad sectors of society far removed from Communism, the U S S R was the supreme champion of all progressive causes, of the independence of peoples and peace between states. The Communist parties benefited from this renewal and increase of the Soviet Union's prestige. Together with the important role they had played in the struggle against Nazi occupation, it was one of the main causes of their development in this period.

The Communists, and with them the most radical groups of the labour movement, were filled with euphoric optimism about the prospects for revolution throughout the world. The impressive demonstration of Soviet military power gave them unlimited confidence in the eventual success of the struggle for socialism, both in the countries where it took the form of armed struggle (China, Greece) and in those in which it developed under the protection of the Red Army (the countries of Eastern Europe), and also in those in which it seemed about to take a new path, the conquest of the state by the use of the machinery of bourgeois democracy (France and Italy). Communists were convinced that any revolutionary action, armed or peaceful, would receive the firm support of the 'invincible fortress' of socialism. It was true that the impunity with which the Anglo-American intervention against the Greek rising had developed was not a good sign, but this discordant note was not enough to darken the overall picture. Eveyone knew that Yugoslavia was helping the Greek partisans, and who could doubt that behind Yugoslavia was the action of the great Soviet power? Was not this the rallying cry of international reaction?

In short, after the setback of the inter-war period, the world revolution seemed to have resumed its march with irresistible force. It is true that, for the moment, it had stopped once more before the developed capitalist countries (excluding the tiny eastern zone of Czechoslovakia and East Germany). Once more its path did not resemble that described by Marx. But were not the spectacular growth of the Communist parties of France and Italy, the left-wing tendencies which were developing in the Social Democratic parties and the labour movement, and the overwhelming Labour victory in Britain all signs that socialism would soon burst into the cradle of capitalism? 'I guess the whole world is on a leftward march,' Vandenberg noted in his diary when he heard of Churchill's defeat in the election.[7]

The real or apparent successes of Communism during these years naturally helped to give plausibility to the apologetic picture of its growth under Stalin's leadership which had been spread by the Stalinist party leaders of the thirties. Trotsky's criticism seemed to have collapsed. Who could believe that the Soviet system was a degenerate bureaucracy in the face of the vitality, heroism and fighting qualities shown by the Communists and people of the USSR during the war? The theory of socialism in one country and its strategic implications, the Soviet Communist Party's role of world leadership, a monolithic structure as the optimum condition for fighting effectiveness in any Communist party, had not all these and other theses maintained in the time of the Communist International been fully confirmed by the 'judgement of history'? Had not the crushing of Trotskyism and Bukharinism, the Moscow trials, all the examples of Stalinist repression, the German–Soviet pact, the systematic subordination of the revolutionary movement to the supreme interest of the state, the holocaust of the International for the sake of the 'grand alliance', had not they all been inexorable demands of 'historical necessity', wisely interpreted by Stalin's genius? The great-power nationalism which permeated the whole of Stalin's world policy was sufficiently concealed by the liberating content of the victories of the Soviet armies.

This empirical 'verification' of Stalin's theses and decisions had an immense impact on the new army of Communists, built up on the foundation of the cells formed by the International. In the veterans it strengthened the reflexes developed during the time of the 'world party', giving them new and successful ideological justifications for their previous behaviour; in the neophytes it facilitated the rapid assimilation of the same reflexes and the axiomatic acceptance of the received heritage. In this way the uncritical and dogmatic mentality cultivated within the Comintern during the Stalinist period was transmitted to the new formations, which after 1945, as the figures we have quoted show, formed the immense majority of every party. The whole world was entering the atomic era. A new technical and scientific revolution was beginning. New problems were about to be raised by the development of capitalism and the emancipation of the former colonies, and by the 'building of socialism' in new countries. And yet the theoretical ideas of the Communist movement had never been as poor as in the decade which followed the Second World War. In this period the clericalization of the movement reached its highest point. Stalin was deified, and the textbook *The History of the Communist Party of the Soviet Union (Bolsheviks): Short Course* became the Communist's bible. The good Communist had no need to blow his mind on the works of Marx or Lenin, because Stalin had distilled the essence of Marxism, all it was really necessary to know, into this little book written in a way that was at once 'accessible' and 'profound', to enable all men, be they scholars or 'simple men', to follow unhesitatingly the high road to Communism. From 1945 onwards this gift of 'the father of peoples' went through numerous editions of millions of copies in all languages.

The great Soviet victory in the Second World War provided new ideological and political justifications for Stalinist uniformity and dogmatism, but the war and Stalin's own policy nevertheless gave rise to factors and processes which worked against this.

The war against Fascism had swollen the national feelings of peoples and their aspirations to an independent national life; it had made them sensitive to any attack on their national rights. Given their role in the struggle against the Axis, the Communist parties could not avoid being 'contaminated' by this resurgence of national feelings and aims. Stalin's policy, too, directed as it was to saving the 'grand alliance' led them in most cases to relegate aims of social revolution to a lower rank, when they did not stop formulating them completely. The result was that 'national' and 'patriotic' ingredients acquired an extraordinary weight in the attitudes of the parties and the formation of their militants (it should not be forgotten that the new members soon formed a large majority of the membership of all Communist parties), and often took on an openly nationalist tone.

This stress on 'nationalism' logically contained the germ of a contradiction with the Great-Russian chauvinism on which Stalin's policy was based. However, as long as this combination of nationalism and opportunism favoured the preservation of the alliance between the USSR and the capitalist states which had fought Hitler, the contradiction remained buried. It showed itself immediately, however, when Communist parties combined in themselves national aspirations and revolutionary aims, as in China, Yugoslavia and Greece, because this revolutionary national policy created difficulties for Stalin's grand strategy.

The 'nationalization' of the Communist parties, formally sealed by the dissolution of the Comintern, gradually took on aspects which were worrying for the Stalinist monolith. All the parties, in most cases sincerely, in some in a 'Machiavellian' spirit, continued to consider themselves as under the leadership of Moscow. They did not question the leading role of the Soviet party or Stalin's infallible wisdom, but were obliged, by the force of events and the diversity of national situations, to act for their own benefit and take a larger initiative.

The first signs of indiscipline and 'heterodoxy' now appeared. The Chinese Communists pretended to give way to Stalin's pressure to reach agreement with Chiang Kai-shek, but steadily continued their revolutionary war. At the end of 1946 the Vietnamese Communists began a war of liberation from French colonialism which was equally in contradiction with Stalin's policy of the moment. The Communist parties of France and Italy began to talk about an original road to socialism, not Soviet but 'French' and 'Italian'. In the United States Earl Browder, followed by a considerable group of the party, openly went over to reformism, and was excommunicated in 1946. But the most disturbing feature for Stalin were the events which took place in his European camp, in particular the developments in Yugoslavia.

The resulting internal situation of the Communist movement, in the period from the dissolution of the Comintern to the setting-up of the Cominform, was complex and contradictory. The ideological and political foundations of the Stalinist monolith were mutually reinforcing and the prestige and authority of Stalin and the Soviet Communist Party reached unheard-of proportions, but at the same time centrifugal tendencies began to grow and hostile attitudes appeared which were a threat to the monolithic cohesion of the movement. The 1948 Yugoslav rebellion made the first wide breach in the world-wide structure of the Stalinist monolith and revealed the fundamentally opposed character of the contradiction between Russian nationalism and revolutionary movements with their roots in their national situation. The Yugoslav rebellion, by the total isolation it experienced within the Communist movement, also revealed the immense force which the monolith's ideological and political grip still exercised on the movement as a whole. The struggle against the Yugoslav 'heresy' had the further effect of tightening this grip and giving it for a time an increased aggressiveness.

Even before the Yugoslav incident, the monolithic cohesion of the movement which emerged from the war had already stood up to a test on ground more familiar to veterans of the Comintern. This was the great 'switch' of 1947, caused by the crisis in the anti-Fascist alliances. This crisis exposed the whole element of opportunism in Stalin's policies since 1941, both at the international level, with regard to the 'grand alliance', and on the national level, in the policies of the majority of Communist parties. The 'switch' took place, however, without the parties holding any serious discussion about the policy followed so far, about the crucial period of the war and the period immediately following it, or about what should be done after that. It was decided by Stalin and his immediate assistants and then imposed on the whole Communist movement, without a single voice being raised to protest against the procedure followed and without any indication that there was the slightest divergence from Soviet theses and instructions.

Among these instructions was the constitution of the Cominform. The Communist movement found itself from one day to the next with a new centre of leadership without having had the slightest part in its creation. Everything was decided at a secret meeting in Poland in 1947 attended by representatives of the nine parties which, at Stalin's wish, were to form the new body, those of the Soviet Union, Poland, Czechoslovakia, Hungary, Romania, Bulgaria, Yugoslavia, France and Italy.[8] Not even the central organs of these parties had discussed in advance the subjects dealt with at this meeting – the new international situation, the policy to be followed by the Communist movement in this new situation, the setting-up of the Cominform, etc.

In the following chapter we shall discuss the problems arising from the Communist movement's new line, adopted at the meeting which set up the Cominform. Before that, however, it is appropriate to analyse the process which led to the 'switch' of 1947. We must start with the problem which the meeting in Poland found itself obliged to discuss, though it did it in a truncated fashion, avoiding the main element – Stalin's policies – and without being willing to recognize openly its true nature: the problem of the frustration of the revolution in France and Italy. The Polish meeting had to deal with this difficult problem, however, even if it was in a half-hearted manner, since it was a main element in the political process which inevitably produced the situation of 1947, in which the grand illusions prompted by the 'grand alliance' melted to reveal the 'cold war' and the hopes of a peaceful, democratic and parliamentary road to socialism in Europe revealed their emptiness.

THE REVOLUTION FRUSTRATED (FRANCE)

It is clear that, in the conditions of 1945, with the Red Army on the Elbe, the confirmation of the 'revolutionary possibility' created in France and Italy would have meant the victory of the revolution in continental Europe and a radical change in the world balance of power to the detriment of American imperialism, the only large capitalist state which had come out of the war strengthened. Correspondingly, it is impossible to exaggerate the negative effect of the frustration of this possibility on the further development of the world revolutionary movement. Without any exaggeration, it can be compared to the consequences of the defeat of the German revolution in 1918–19.

'Where would the world be,' asked Dimitrov in November 1937, 'if after the October socialist revolution, in the period 1919–20, the proletariats of Germany, Austria–Hungary and Italy had not stopped half-way in their revolutionary thrust? Where would the world be if the German and Austrian revolutions of 1918 had been completed and if, after the victory of the revolution, the dictatorship of the proletariat had been established in the centre of Europe, in the highly developed industrial countries?'[9] Practically the same can be said of the rising tide of revolution in France and Italy in 1944–5. Dimitrov naturally does not fail to identify, as the cause of the proletariat's 'stopping half-way in their revolutionary thrust', the leaders of Social Democracy, who 'united with their bourgeoisies'. Who was it, then, that checked 'half-way' the revolutionary thrust of the French and Italian proletariats in 1944–5?

At that time the vast mass of the proletariat was under the leadership of the Communist parties. And not only the proletariat, as Togliatti said later: 'The vast majority of the working class, and a considerable part of public opinion outside the working class, took their stand with the advanced workers' parties which were inspired by the Marxists, and this distinguished the situation in our country, as in France, from that of other Western European countries.'[10] In other words, in 1944–5 only the Communist parties could halt the revolutionary movement of the proletariat, and in practice this is what they did. The real question is therefore not 'Who applied the brake?' but 'Was the behaviour of the Communist parties in France and Italy legitimate from the point of view of the interests of the proletariat and of the revolution?' To answer that question requires an analysis, even if only a quick one, of the policies of the two parties in the resistance and the liberation. We shall start with the French party.

The German-Soviet Pact and the French Communist Party

The French Communist Party is the only Communist party which went into the war in a state of legality; it had 300,000 militants and majority influence within the working class. It entered the war with the banner of anti-Fascism flying. Hitler's Germany, *violà l'ennemi!* The party denounced the capitulationist policy of Daladier and the French right as an integral part of the struggle against Hitler. The most reactionary elements called vehemently for the banning of the Communist Party because they saw it as a major obstacle to an agreement with Germany. These were the conditions in which the bomb of the German–Soviet pact exploded, taking the leaders of the French party totally by surprise. (Naturally, Stalin had paid no attention to the Communist leaders of other countries, even to those of the country most directly affected.) As an immediate reaction, the party leadership justified the pact as a supreme effort to preserve peace, but it fully maintained its support for national defence against Hitler's aggression. On 1 September 1939 the Communist parliamentary group unanimously proclaimed 'the unshakeable determination of all Communists to stand in the front line against Hitlerian Fascist aggression', and on 1 September the Communist deputies voted for war credits.[11]

The government banned the Communist press and, on 26 September, the party itself. With the bourgeois parties incapable of organizing the defence of the country, when they were not looking purely and simply towards capitulation, the PCF could have turned this persecution to its own use and recovered its influence by keeping firmly to its line of resisting aggression by Hitler and connecting this with the struggle against the impotence or treachery of the bourgeoisie, clearly distinguishing between its own policy and Soviet policy.

But the party's position was soon brought into unconditional alignment with that of Moscow. After proclaiming that France was right to support Poland and voting for the military credits asked for by the government for any intervention in support of Poland, the party announced that 'the Poland of the landowners does not deserve support', and welcomed the occupation of Eastern Poland by the Red Army. It used similar arguments to justify the occupation by the USSR of the Baltic states. Both actions could be defended as military measures directed against Germany, but the leadership of the PCF took over the mystifying version given by Soviet diplomats. When Molotov described France and Great Britain as the aggressive states and Germany as inspired by the most peaceful of intentions, the party adopted this view, although apart from totally falsifying reality, it was suicidal in French conditions. The PCF gave the forces of reaction ideal arguments with which to present it as the party of national betrayal. This gave the French bourgeoisie two advantages: it could increase the isolation of the Communists and make repression easier, and at the same time conceal its own policy of capitulation.

Once the national disaster was complete and the occupation had begun, the party persisted in its attitude. It attacked Vichy but did not lead the cause of national liberation, or organize a national revolutionary and anti-Fascist war, like the Yugoslav and Greek Communists. It left the banner of national liberation in the hands of typical representatives of bourgeois nationalism, like de Gaulle. The blind docility with which the French Communist Party obeyed Moscow during the period of the

German–Soviet pact ultimately left it under three serious disadvantages. First, it prevented it from taking advantage from the beginning of the collapse of the French state and channelling the main stream of national sentiment in the direction of revolution. Second, it left the initiative in the struggle for national liberation in the hands of the bourgeois nationalists. Third, and as a result of the factors just mentioned, it made repression against the party easier.[12]

It is important to point out that at this period the party advocated as the solution to the unprecedented crisis which had overtaken bourgeois France the only solution which a revolutionary party could consider, a socialist revolution. In a policy document entitled *Pour le salut du peuple français,* distributed in March 1941, minor struggles are said to be preparing the way for 'the great social battles which will produce the people's republic, the new France, the France freed from capitalist exploitation, the socialist France in which there will be bread, freedom and peace for all'. But to talk about a socialist revolution in a France occupied by Hitler's armies without calling for a war of liberation was nonsense. And yet the party implied the possibility that a 'people's government' could emerge from the struggle against the Vichy state alone. The document, without a word on the organization of the struggle against the occupier, called on the workers, peasants, middle classes, intellectuals and the rest to

devote all their energies to the methodical organization of a vast fighting front in preparation for the everyday action and mass movements which will sweep away the capitalist clique in Vichy and make way for the people and the government of the people.

The first point of the programme included with the document implies that national independence would then be negotiated by this government:

National liberation and the freeing of prisoners of war: in order to complete this task the people's government will take all necessary steps to establish peaceful relations with all peoples. It will reply on the power given it by the trust of the French people, the sympathy of other peoples and the friendship of the Soviet Union.

The second point announces:

> The establishment of fraternal relations between the French and German peoples in the memory of the action taken by the French Communists and people against the Versailles Treaty, against the occupation of the Ruhr basin and against the oppression of one people by another.

The document says nothing about the need to overthrow Hitler's regime in order to make such relations possible. What meaning could this policy have apart from the acceptance of a lasting global arrangement between Nazi Germany, which at this period controlled the whole of Europe, and the Soviet Union? Was not the position of the PCF closely related to that of the Soviet government's attempts at this time to strengthen its compromise with Nazi Germany, a policy admitted, as we have seen, by Soviet historians? A final detail is in place here: the document quoted was drawn up by Maurice Thorez in the USSR[13]

The struggle for a socialist France was, no doubt, the aim which the revolutionary party of the proletariat should have adopted in the situation of historical crisis in which France was placed, but for the leadership of the French Communist Party it served as a 'leftist' cover for a policy which, in order not to conflict with the policy of the Soviet government, rejected the only course which could have led to a socialist solution of the crisis, a national, anti-Fascist and revolutionary war against the Nazi occupation. Not only does the document quoted above not call for such a war, but it is also fairly easy to read between the lines its opposition to this course. The French people, it says, 'firmly reject the calls of all warmongers ... and will not take part in another imperialist war'.[14]

The rejection of the socialist alternative

From the moment when Nazi soldiers crossed the Soviet frontier the French Communist Party also crossed the impalpable frontier separating it from the 'warmongers' and placed itself firmly 'at the head of the struggle' for national independence. But obviously its delay in taking this step and the repercussions of its former policy inevitably removed much of its credit in the final balance. Now, after 'waiting' for two years, the party criticized the caution of de Gaulle's headquarters, which advised against any armed action for the time being. The PCF called for immediate armed action, and organized it without counting the risks and sacrifices. The initiative and courage of the Communists, and their capacity for organization, gradually won the sympathy of the people. Those who were most eager to fight among the workers, students and intellectuals returned to the party.

On the political level, however, the party fell into the opposite error to the one it had made at the beginning of the war. Whereas, during the first period, Great Britain and the United States were described as enemies of the French people, from 22 June Communist propaganda immediately stopped all criticism of those who had now become great democratic states and allies. Until 22 June de Gaulle had been a mere agent of the City, and Gaullism had been described as 'a fundamentally reactionary and anti-democratic' movement whose aim was to rob France 'of all her freedom in the event of an English victory'.[15]

After 22 June de Gaulle naturally became an ally, and criticism of the 'reactionary, anti-democratic essence' of Gaullism disappeared from PCF documents. The party, however, for a long time maintained an attitude of reserve towards the General. In May 1942 Molotov had a discussion with de Gaulle in London. In return for de Gaulle's assurance that he would support the Russian demand for the opening of a second front, Molotov announced his agreement with the General's claim that all Frenchmen, and the peoples of the French colonies, should unite under his leadership.[16] In the following months the PCF joined the London committee and appointed Fernand Grenier as its representative on it. In a letter of 10 January 1943 to the Central Committee of the PCF, de Gaulle took note of their joining the committee and laid down, in a way which left no room for ambiguity, the principle of the subordination of the party to the Gaullist leadership. The letter said:

The arrival of Fernand Grenier, the Communist Party's decision to join the national committee, which he brought in your name, its readiness to place at my disposal, in my capacity as Commander-in-Chief of the French forces, the units of courageous irregulars which you have formed and inspired, these are all signs of French unity ... I am sure that the representatives whom I have appointed will find in the leaders of the PCF a readiness to co-operate in achieving a spirit of sacrifice and the same loyal discipline which already exists within your organizations.

And on the 21st of the same month Grenier wrote in *L'Humanité:* 'We are reflecting the feelings of Frenchmen in proclaiming our confidence in General de Gaulle, who was the first to raise the standard of the resistance.'[17] In February, the Communist deputies detained by Vichy in Algiers prison were released; they had remained in prison even though Algeria had been in the hands of Anglo–American troops since 11 November 1942. And in June of the same year – by apparent co-incidence it was a few days after the disbanding of the Comintern – the French Committee for National Liberation (CFLN), which had just been formed and had its headquarters in Algiers, revoked the decree of September 1939 by which Daladier had declared the Communist Party illegal. The composition of the CFLN, with Generals de Gaulle and Giraud at its head, could not have been more reactionary. It grouped together 'the men sent by the bourgeoisie to obtain their credentials as "resistance fighters" and to ensure the safeguarding of their interests', according to the *Histoire de la Résistance* produced by a commission under the chairmanship of Jacques Duclos. But this did not prevent the leadership of the PCF from greeting the formation of the CFLN with the following statement:

All Frenchmen look to the French Committee for National Liberation to organize France's active participation in the war against Hitler by mobilizing all the resources, energy and will of France overseas, for the material and moral support of the patriots who are successfully waging a difficult and glorious struggle on the soil of the fatherland.[18]

At this period the PCF saw entry into the CFLN as fundamental to its policy, and imposed as a condition the committee's acceptance of a platform of which the following was the most progressive demand: 'the development of democratic and social policies which will galvanize all French energies and create enthusiasm for the participation of all in the war of liberation'. Although this general declaration was hardly compromising, and would even have helped the representatives of 'the upper bourgeoisie to obtain credentials as resistance fighters', de Gaulle rejected any conditions, no doubt as a firm demonstration of the principle of his absolute leadership, just as he refused to allow the party's representatives to the CFLN to be appointed by the party itself. Only de Gaulle could appoint them. In the end the party joined the CFLN without agreement by the General to any compromise.[19]

It is true the party at the same time was very active in developing its own forces in the national front (a unified movement, directed by the party, which in time acquired some strength). It advocated the coordination of the different organizations and tendencies in the internal resistance. The spring of 1945 was an important stage in this process. The MUR (Mouvements Unis de la Résistance) united Combat, Franc-Tireur and Libération, the CGT re-formed underground, and on 27 May the National Council of the Resistance (CNR) was set up, representing all organizations and tendencies. During the discussions which led up to the formation of this body a particularly interesting problem arose. The only organized party existing in the resistance was the Communist Party. In the beginning de Gaulle did not want the party represented as such on the CFLN. Faced with the impossibility of imposing this wish, however, he looked for another solution, which is described in Duclos' history as follows: 'In order not to let the Communist Party be the only party to have the title "party of the resistance", [de Gaulle proposed] that other political groups should be represented on the committee.' The reconstitution of the old parties would both 'reinforce the Gaullist cause in the eyes of the allies' and form 'the only effective barrier to Communist influence'. Duclos continues:

This move, however, met violent opposition from the resistance movements. The Vichy regime had discredited many politicians. Although there were individuals in all parties who were members of resistance organizations, no party except the Communists had re-formed underground . . . The resistance movements vigorously opposed this reappearance of the parties.

The underground newspaper *Défense de la France* wrote:

It seems right and proper that the Communists should be represented on the liberation committee because they are actively engaged in the common struggle, but it would be hard to accept the presence of representatives of the old movements.

The question was, without any doubt, a vital one. It raised the fundamental problem of what sort of result the struggle should have. The alternatives were to return to the traditional political system which had brought the country to a national catastrophe or to create a new, unified force inspired with the spirit of the resistance, in which the Communists would be given a leading position. This was a unique opportunity offered to the party to put itself at the head of a reforming current and guide it towards a radical transformation of French society. But the party turned the scales in favour of the past and supported the Gaullist proposal. Duclos explains this action as follows:

> It is a fact that political life in France is traditionally expressed in broad currents which are one of the characteristic features of French bourgeois democracy. Political apathy and the condemnation of parties have always in France been weapons in the hands of reaction. In view of all this and of the need to reach rapid and effective unity in the national struggle, the Communist Party agreed to the formation of the CNR on the principles proposed by Jean Moulin. In a report to the London committee Moulin paid tribute to the Communist Party's desire for unity.[20]

The 'characteristic features' mentioned by Duclos did indeed constitute an indisputable 'fact'. A second and equally indisputable 'fact' was that reaction had more than once exploited the impotence of Social Democratic and radical petit-bourgeois political parties. But a third, and again indisputable, fact which Duclos' arguments ignore is that the traditional political parties, 'French bourgeois democracy', had just suffered the greatest collapse in their history, and it was not now reaction which disowned them, but the new revolutionary forces which had come into being in the resistance; reaction, on the other hand, was clutching desperately at the 'characteristic features of bourgeois democracy'. The fourth indisputable 'fact' – which later events were to demonstrate – was that by supporting the Gaullist solution the PCF was preparing the way for the restoration of French capitalism. The tribute paid to it by the London committee was fully justified. It was indeed necessary to secure

rapid and effective unity in the national struggle, but everything depended on the way this struggle was understood and, secondly, on the
direction it should take. If it was to lead to the restoration of traditional
bourgeois democracy, the 'unity' chosen by de Gaulle, with the support
of the PCF, was certainly the most 'effective'. With this type of 'unity' –
which Stalin in fact tried to impose on them – the Yugoslav Communists would have led their resistance towards the restoration of the traditional monarchy, and the only European revolution which did not
result from the demarcation of 'spheres of influence', and which triumphed in spite of these divisions, would not have taken place.

During 1943, and especially during the early months of 1944, the
unified resistance network grew strongly throughout France, and in this
network the Communists occupied key positions which gave them an
opportunity for leadership in organizational matters. But the ability to
lead in the decisive battles which lay ahead and to lead towards revolution, and success in French society, did not depend merely on positions
within the resistance apparatus or on ability to organize armed struggle
(in which the party, as the Spanish Communist Party had done, gave
excellent proofs of its ability), or even on a spirit of sacrifice and courage
in the fight, where the Communists were equally exemplary. (The PCF
deserved its title of 'party of the martyrs' – *parti des fusillés* – but less so,
unfortunately, that of 'party of the revolution'.) All this was not enough.
What was needed in addition, and in the first place, was a political line
and the will for such a revolutionary transformation within the party
leadership.

The national uprising, followed by the allied landings in Normandy,
gave reality to the problem of power. The greater part of France, including Paris, was liberated by the armed forces of the resistance with
the help of the masses, without the direct intervention of the allied
armies. The liberation committees almost everywhere became organs of
power, and the patriot militias proved themselves genuine mass organizations.[21] The Communist Party was the main force in this great popular rising. In prestige and influence it had no rivals in the trade unions
and factories, in liberation committees and patriot militias, among intellectuals and the young, or among the armed forces created during the
resistance.[22] This fact alone shows the revolutionary character of the

situation. Even if this character was not to be borne out by events, the Communist Party was, in the eyes of the masses, the party of revolution. Once the Vichy state and the power of the occupier had collapsed, the majority of the proletariat and broad sectors of other wage-earning social groups placed their hopes in the party which they associated with the idea of revolution and with the Soviet Union, whose prestige – this is another fundamental element of the situation – now reached an intensity among the French people which it never afterwards regained.

As his *Memoirs* show, de Gaulle was well aware that 'the leadership of the fighting elements was in the hands of the Communists'. He believed that the PCF wanted to take advantage of the moment of the liberation to lead the resistance forces in a seizure of power, and long afterwards, in the face of all the evidence, he continued to attribute that intention to it.

Benefiting by the confusion of battle; overpowering the National Council of the Resistance, many of whose members, aside from those already committed to the party, might be accessible to the temptation of power; taking advantage of the sympathy which the persecution they had suffered, the losses they had endured and the courage they had displayed had gained them in many circles; exploiting the anxiety aroused in the people by the absence of all law and order; employing, finally, an equivocation by publicizing their adherence to General de Gaulle, they intended to appear at the insurrection's head as a kind of Commune which would proclaim the Republic, answer for public order and mete out justice. Furthermore, they meant to be careful to sing only the 'Marseillaise', and to run up no flag but the tricolour.[23]

The plan attributed by de Gaulle to the Communists had no existence in reality, but it must be admitted that it was an excellent plan; de Gaulle clearly saw the cards in the party's hand and the skill with which they could be used. What a true revolutionary party in this situation should have been concerned with was not an abstract plan for the seizure of power by the proletariat, but the seizure of power by the resistance, the real resistance, not the resistance in London or Algiers. This did not mean a direct challenge to de Gaulle, but forcing de Gaulle to challenge the resistance. It did not mean a clash with the 'liberating' Anglo-American armies, but facing these armies with the *fait accompli* of the power of the resistance and mobilizing against any attack on this power the national feelings which had been intensified by the liberation. Such could have been the first steps to socialist revolution in the France of 1944. De Gaulle understood it perfectly. Unfortunately he was not the Secretary General of the French Communist Party.

Aware of the seriousness of the situation, de Gaulle manoeuvred skilfully. He began to install his machinery and limit the powers of the liberation committees. He advanced more confidently when he realized that the Communists were giving way without much resistance, and finally made the surprising discovery that in the Communists he had the great 'patriotic' force capable of co-operating more effectively than any other in the restoration of the 'eternal France'. The process was rapid.

In the early months after the establishment of the de Gaulle government the leadership of the PCF, under the pressure of the spontaneous mass movement and the vigorous revolutionary currents in its own ranks, followed an ambiguous political line, defending the committees of liberation and the patriot militias but doing nothing to promote firm mass action or raise the basic problems of the democratic-socialist transformation of French society. On 27 October 1944 Duclos declared in a party assembly: 'The patriot militias must remain the watchful guardians of the republican order while at the same time taking active charge of the military education of the popular masses.' He added that in each area the militia should include the thousands of 'citizen-soldiers' and should be placed under the authority of the committees of liberation, with a permanent position and a stock of arms and ammunition.

The next day de Gaulle replied by signing a decree dissolving the militias. The two Communist ministers protested, but remained in the government. The party leadership gave internal instructions to maintain the organization of the militias, not to surrender arms, to form secret stores, etc., but it did not mobilize the people against the direct attack on the powers of the Resistance clearly visible in the General's intentions.[24] De Gaulle took with one hand what he offered with the other. On 6 November a decree announcing an amnesty for Thorez appeared in the *Journal officiel*. Discussing this action in his memoirs, de Gaulle wrote: 'Thorez has made many requests to me. I have decided to perform this act of clemency after very careful thought. Bearing in mind the circumstances of the past, the events which have taken place since and the needs of the present, I believe that the return of M. Thorez to the leadership of the Communist Party may in fact have more advantages than disadvantages.' The needs of the present, as described by the General, were to 'trim the Communists' claws' and 'deprive them of the powers they are usurping and the arms they are displaying'. His calculation of the 'advantages' the return of Thorez might have proved correct. The general secretary of the party returned to France on 27 November. His first major slogan was, 'One state, one police force, one army'. De Gaulle commented, 'From the moment of his return to France Thorez has been helping to clear up the traces of the "patriot militias". He has opposed attempts at usurpation by the liberation committees and the acts of violence on which over-excited groups have embarked.'[25]

And in fact, as soon as Thorez arrived, the party organizations received internal instructions to disband the militias and surrender their arms. In the report he made before the Central Committee on 21 January 1945, Thorez publicly advocated the disbanding of the militias and all 'irregular' armed groups. While these might have been justified before and during the rising against the supporters of Hitler and Vichy, he said, law and order should now be guaranteed by the regular police forces. In the same report Thorez advocated (as he had already done on 14 December 1944 at a speech to a meeting organized by the party in the Vélodrome d'Hiver) that local and departmental committees of liberation should make no attempt to take the place of the official administrative bodies.[26]

The moment chosen by de Gaulle to pardon Thorez was not determined only by motives of domestic politics. The General was preparing to visit Moscow, and to have had to turn up there with the 'Thorez case' still on his hands would have been annoying. On the other hand, granting an amnesty to Stalin's influential disciple would be an excellent introduction. Everything was very well arranged. On 6 November the decree was published, on the 27th of the same month Thorez arrived in Paris and on 2 December de Gaulle met Stalin in Moscow. The General's aim was to strengthen his position *vis-à-vis* Great Britain and the United States by the signature of a bilateral pact with the USSR, and he succeeded in this after laborious manoeuvres. If the amnesty granted to Thorez eased agreement between de Gaulle and Stalin, the Franco–Soviet pact eased agreement between de Gaulle and Thorez. The cogent arguments put forward at the Central Committee meeting on 21 January 1945 against any limitation of the authority of the new French state cannot have been totally unconnected with the happy outcome of the Moscow negotiations.[27]

The Restoration of 'la France éternelle'

At the same time as it was efficiently cooperating in the elimination of the 'usurpatory tendencies' of the committees of liberation and the 'last survivals of the patriot militias', the party placed the armed forces of the resistance, which were under its control, at the full and complete disposal of the Gaullist and allied high command, and merged them in the French 'grand army', for the formation of which Thorez had argued passionately from the moment of his arrival on French soil. In other words, the party liquidated the popular armed forces built up during the resistance. At the same time as this general destruction of the political and military foundations for a new popular power which had been created during the resistance and liberation, the party threw itself into another battle for the restoration of *la France éternelle* – the notorious 'battle for production'. This began immediately after the liberation of Paris.

In a report presented to a meeting of trade-union militants on 10 September 1944, Benoît Frachon called on the workers to 'rebuild our large industry on *more rational* foundations and ensure its *full return*'. Reconstruction, he explained, 'should not benefit the financial and industrial oligarchies', but that was a problem which would be solved 'when the time comes for the people to be consulted about the form of government they wish to adopt'; at that time 'we shall give our opinion about the disappearance of the trusts and the appropriate methods for replacing their domination by an economy at the service of the nation'. But for the moment, and without waiting for the last word from the ballot boxes about who should benefit from the 'reconstruction', the workers must work hard. The secretary of the CGT, who was also a leader of the Communist Party, suggested that they should form 'patriotic production committees'. On 24 March 1945 he presented his report to the CGT national committee.

In the meantime the workers had received a small increase in wages, less than the modest 50 per cent demand made by the CGT while it was still underground – and prices had risen. 'During this time [between the liberation and March 1945],' said Frachon in his report, 'justified discontent has spread in the ranks of the working class. If, in spite of this, strikes have been practically non-existent, this is due entirely to the workers' strong sense of *national* duty and to the authority of the CGT and its militants.'[28] It was indeed true that the party, under the leadership of Thorez, had worked hard to instil 'a strong sense of national duty' into Communist or CGT workers. In the early stages the main justification offered was 'the war effort' and the fact that Germany's defeat was not yet complete. In fact the outcome of the war was already settled, as Stalin had implied in his speech of 6 November 1944, and French arms production could have little influence. What was not yet settled was the question whether the struggle and sacrifices of the French workers would result in the consolidation of French capitalism 'on more rational foundations' or in 'an economy at the service of the nation'. The 'war effort', in the context we have described, could only help to paralyse and demoralize the forces capable of imposing the second alternative. The defeat of Germany brought no break in the 'battle for production'; instead it reached its peak.

Thorez found another argument which was not spectacularly new, having been used by all the Social Democratic parties every time they took part in a bourgeois government, as the Communists were now doing. The workers, then and now Thorez said, should not make excessive demands or strike, but increase production, because it was in the interest of the rich bourgeoisie to create difficulties for a government with socialist ministers. In his report to the Tenth Party Congress in June 1945 Thorez did as well as if not better than his Social Democratic predecessors and contemporaries:

Where does the mortal danger for our country lie? It is in the field of production ... If the trusts and their agents oppose the effort for reconstruction and production, this means that it is in the interest of the people, of the working class, to work and produce, in spite of and against the trusts.

It was of course no part of the intention of 'the trusts and their agents' to oppose the workers' desire to 'work and produce', and Thorez was unable to give the Congress a single convincing piece of evidence for this alleged intention of the trusts. What could hardly have delighted them, on the other hand, was the idea of 'democracy with the trusts removed', which Thorez presented as the party's long-term aim. But then again, there was no need for it to worry them too much either, since it was an aim which was to be reached by means of parliamentary legality, in conditions of authority and stability: 'The most hopeful prospect for our country,' declared Thorez in the same report, 'is the maintenance for a considerable time of a government of broad national and democratic unity, which will ensure the best conditions for authority and stability.' Only in this way could the 'greatness of France' be guaranteed, because only in this way could production develop successfully, and, in Thorez's own words, 'Today the extent and quality of our material production and our place in the world market are the measure of the greatness of France.' The people must 'steel themselves for the battle for production as they steeled themselves for the battle of the liberation. The task is to rebuild the greatness of France, to secure in more than words the material conditions of French independence.' The remark was directed at those, inside or outside the party, who used 'revolutionary phrases' to criticize the line followed by the leadership of the PCF: 'We must fight the leftist ideas of a few sectarians who think, even if they do not always put it clearly into words, that we may have abandoned the revolutionary line.' Fortunately the Central Committee, under the far-sighted leadership of Thorez, had shattered 'the plan of reaction, which was trying to push the most advanced elements of democracy and the working class into adventures in order to divide the people'. Throughout the report Thorez mentions the concepts 'revolution' and 'revolutionary' only in a pejorative sense. He had already, in his January speech to the Central Committee, reached the stage of criticizing the use of this concept by making an indirect parallel between it and the concept of 'national revolution' used by the Vichy regime:

331

We who are Communists should not at the moment make explicitly socialist or Communist demands. I say this at the risk of appearing lukewarm in the eyes of those who are forever using the word 'revolution'. It has a certain popularity, but four years of 'national revolution' under the auspices of Hitler have warned the people against the demagogic misuse of certain terms emptied of their meaning.

Thorez put into circulation the term 'Hitlero-Trotskyites', and called for vigilance to expose and expel from the party all 'disruptive elements, troublemakers, agents of the enemy, Hitlero-Trotskyites, who usually hide behind left-wing phrases'.[29]

The 'battle for production' reached its climax with Thorez's visit to the mining areas in the *département* of the Nord. In spite of the campaign by the party and the CGT, the miners had sometimes resorted to strikes, and Thorez rebuked the Communists who had taken part in them. In a speech on 21 July 1945 to an assembly of Communist miners at Waziers, he said:

My dear comrades, I am now putting the problem to you as responsible men. In the name of the Central Committee and in the name of the decisions of the Party Congress I tell you quite frankly that we cannot approve the smallest strike, especially when it breaks out, like the strike last week in the Béthune mines, on the fringe of the union and in opposition to the union.

As a result of the strike 30,000 tons of coal had been lost, and Thorez exclaimed, 'It's a scandal, a shame. It does great harm to the union and the interests of the miners.'[30] A year after the 'Waziers appeal', Thorez was congratulating himself on the results achieved:

Coal production has increased by over 50 per cent. With over 160,000 tons a day, we have beaten the pre-war level by 8 per cent. It is a marvellous success. France is the only country, with the exception of the Soviet Union, which has such a result to be proud of ... We should congratulate our miners, who have not spared their sweat and their toil.[31]

(To read Thorez's speeches at this period gives the impression that France was in the middle of building socialism and that the central task for the workers was to get under way an economy which they controlled.)

In December the Association of Public Service Workers decided to organize a warning strike, and a monster meeting was held in the Vélodrome d'Hiver to prepare it. The speakers, even those of the SFIO, insisted on the need for a general strike. It was opposed only by Henry Raynaud, a Communist leader of the CGT. 'In present circumstances,' said Raynaud, 'a general strike would be catastrophic. By shutting down the railways, it would starve the country.' Two days later Thorez told the Council of Ministers that it would be wrong to give way to intolerable pressures and said that, with a few corrections, the Finance Minister's proposals should be adopted.[32] Referring to this year, 1945, which the French Communist Party might have called, using the language of the Cuban Communists today, 'the year of production', de Gaulle wrote in his memoirs:

As for Thorez, even in his efforts to advance the Communist cause, he will serve the national interest on a number of occasions. His constant call is for the maximum of work and production at any price. I shall not try to understand him. I am satisfied if France is served.[33]

It was soon to become clear that 'the Communist cause' was not making much progress, but that France, or rather the French bourgeoisie, was indeed being well served.

In June 1946 Thorez found himself obliged to make the following statement to the Central Committee. (The situation in question was the rejection in a referendum of the draft constitution supported by the Communists and Socialists and the result of the legislative elections of 2 June, which showed a clear move to the right on the part of the electorate.)

The situation is very serious. It was to reach this position, and if possible to make us retreat even further, that the rich French bourgeoisie, in the strength of its long experience and great capacity for manoeuvring, has made skilful use of all its resources and all its men in turn. At the moment of the liberation the bourgeoisie made no direct assault on the popular movement, but tried to divert it, to loosen it and break it up. They prevented the union of the forces of the resistance and gradually reduced the influence of the National Committee of the Resistance and the local and departmental committees of liberation.[34]

This statement was revealing, because what it meant was:

(a) Two years after the liberation, two years in which the Communists had formed part of the government, what had made progress in France was not the popular movement which emerged from the resistance but the rich bourgeoisie, which had strengthened its economic position and had recovered its political influence. Thorez's original tactic of fighting against the trusts by making the workers work harder and longer and tighten their belts had led to the strengthening of the trusts. The checks on the mass movement and the decision to refrain from actions which could have attacked the legal order so as to avoid any risk to the 'national union' had led to the restoration of the dictatorship of the bourgeoisie in the nation. The soft-pedalling of proletarian demands in order to avoid frightening the middle groups had had the effect of making these very groups swing to the right, towards the parties of the bourgeoisie, which now displayed an increasing determination which contrasted with the cowardice and weakness of the party of the proletariat. Thorez himself admitted this in his report. The path to a 'new democracy' exclusively through the winning of a parliamentary majority had led to the restoration of the worst form of the 'old democracy', the traditional democracy of bourgeois France. Communist parliamentary cretinism was now yielding the same fruits as Social Democratic parliamentary cretinism.

The PCF leadership's attempt to offload on to the SFIO the responsibility for the failure to form a Socialist–Communist government based on the parliamentary majority enjoyed by the two parties was useless. Everyone knew that right-wing Socialists would never accept such a possibility without being forced into it by a powerful mass movement, and Thorez's leadership had seen to it that the mass movement which emerged from the liberation was strangled at birth. Even the left-wing Socialist and union militants who might have sincerely supported a Socialist–Communist government expressed justified reservations about the future which such a formula might hold in store for them. It is true that Thorez did make several references at this time to a possible French road to Socialism, differing from that followed by the Bolsheviks, but these occasional remarks were not supported by any serious theoretical work and amounted in fact to extrapolating from the experience of the Eastern European people's democracies, with the omission of the small detail of the part played there by the Red Army and other instruments of Soviet power. For the rest, the French Communist Party's enslavement to Stalin and his dogmas was so plain that it was hard to regard Thorez's timid toying with heresy as anything more than a tactical manoeuvre.[35]

(*b*) By admitting that 'at the moment of the liberation the bourgeoisie made no direct assault on the popular movement', but had 'tried to divert it, to loosen it and break it up', Thorez was accepting the arguments of those, inside and outside the party, who had at the time demanded an offensive revolutionary policy, capable of developing the powerful popular and workers' movement which the national rising had brought into being. If the 'rich bourgeoisie' had not dared to make a direct attack on this movement, that was because they had felt its revolutionary potential. But who had 'gradually reduced the influence of the National Committee of the Resistance and the local and departmental committees of liberation'? The 'rich bourgeoisie' or the policy argued for and imposed by Thorez from the moment of his return from Moscow? In another part of his report Thorez again referred to the 'devious tactics [of the forces of the bourgeoisie], of which they now feel strong enough to boast, which were designed to contain and divert the people when they could not attack them directly in August 1944'.[36] What could be more logical than for the bourgeoisie to boast? It was less logical for the Secretary General of the Communist Party also to claim credit for a policy which had been so marvellously adapted to the 'devious tactics' of bourgeois reaction.

Nevertheless Thorez defended the line followed since the liberation, which he considered completely correct. If some small faults had appeared they could be traced to the work of the sections and federations. With all the unconcern in the world, as if he had no responsibility in the matter, Thorez criticized 'certain comrades who are not free from parliamentary illusions'. In the context of the report, however, this criticism has no other function than to act as a formal balance to the real attack, which is directed at the left. Discontent with the existing line had become widespread in the party, and Thorez found himself obliged to recognize it, even while minimizing it. He quoted specific cases, a resolution from a cell in the Yonne which criticized the leadership for 'cooperating in the government and making one concession after another', and another from the Hautes-Pyrénées which charged it with 'collaborating with reaction and giving support to anti-democratic laws'. Thorez invited the party to oppose these positions strongly. Those who defended them had not understood 'that we have become a party of government; they are calling in question our general line'. To convince the recalcitrant, Thorez produced (for the first time in public, as far as I am aware) the great argument, the unanswerable argument, which was to continue in use for years to justify the policy of the PCF at the liberation. Those who criticized this policy, said Thorez, 'have not even learnt from the article of the American journalist Walter Lippman, who wrote in *Le Figaro* that Anglo-American troops were ready to intervene if the Communists should come to power in France.'[37] We shall return later to this supreme, and at first sight so solid, justification. For the moment it ends our quick examination of PCF policy up to its exclusion from the government.

Neither the 'serious situation' which had been created nor the discontent among the party membership – which anyway was easily crushed by the traditional methods of ideological intimidation and administrative measures – were enough to make the party leadership introduce changes in its policy. Shortly after the Central Committee meeting just mentioned, Thorez made the statement which was quoted above praising the increase in coal production, which had been achieved thanks to the 'sweat and toil' of the miners, and the party resigned itself to the wage freeze ordered by the government of which its ministers were members.

The most scandalous aspect of this policy, however, if one can talk of degrees in such a context, was the attitude of the PCF to the struggle of the peoples oppressed by French colonialism. Since Molotov, at his meeting with de Gaulle in May 1942, had accepted that all the peoples of the French colonies should submit to de Gaulle's leadership, the policy of the PCF had been to demand the retention of the colonies within the French Union, with a degree of autonomy or formal independence. In this it was doing no more than taking up the policy it had pursued at the time of the Popular Front. In his report to the Tenth Congress (June 1945), Thorez defined this part of the party's policy in these terms: 'to create the conditions for a union in freedom, trust and brotherhood between the colonial peoples and the people of France'. The party maintained the principle of free determination, but 'the right to divorce does not mean the obligation to divorce'.

The practical result of this colonial policy – which could have been accepted without hesitation by Van Kol and the other leaders of the Second International who advocated a 'socialist' colonial policy at the Stuttgart Congress – was that the party was associated with all the acts of colonialist repression practised by successive French governments from the liberation until 1947. After the savage repression in May 1945 in the Constantin district of Algeria, in which thousands of Algerians were killed,[38] the Communist ministers stayed in the government, and at the Tenth Congress, a month after the butchery, Thorez made this statement:

When we talk of democracy we cannot forget that one of its demands is a broader and more comprehensive attitude towards the people of the colonies. As at Arles, we say that we must recognize the legitimate demands of the peoples of the colonies, first, in the interests of these poor people themselves, and second, in the interests of France. In Algeria, after the painful events of last month, the most urgent task is to improve the food supply, lift the state of siege, dismiss the officials appointed by Vichy and punish the traitors who have provoked hunger strikes after feeding the enemy for two years. We must demobilize and send home the Algerian soldiers, NCOs and officers who belong to the age-groups not called up in France, and, finally, we must apply the order of 7 March 1944 on the extension of democratic freedoms in Algeria.

That was all, apart from this conclusion: 'A democratic France must help in the development of the Algerian nation which is in the process of being formed.' The PCF did not recognize the existence of an Algerian nation. Until it 'formed', the Algerians, like the Moroccans and the

Tunisians, must, according to Thorez, remain united to France: 'We have never stopped pointing out that the interests of the peoples of North Africa lay in union with the people of France.' (The meaning of this statement becomes even clearer when one realizes that it followed immediately on the remark quoted above, 'the right to divorce does not mean the obligation to divorce'.) Thorez also regretted the recent acts of repression against the peoples of Syria and Lebanon, who had demanded independence. The party supported their right to self-determination, but reminded them of what it had said about divorce. It is for this reason, said Thorez, referring to the repression practised in these countries, that 'we regret all the more the blow struck at our traditional prestige and the interests of our country in the Near East'.[39]

And then, at the end of 1946, came Vietnam. After the French army had in effect re-established the colonial regime in the south of the country (without the organization of the slightest protest action by the PCF), the fleet shelled Haiphong on 23 November 1946 and French imperialism's war against the Vietnamese people began. The PCF persisted in its passivity and even, for a while – according to Communist sources – wondered whether to attribute responsibility for the war to 'Vietnamese troublemakers'. In any case, the colonial war against the Vietnamese people continued for six months under Communist leadership, pursued by a government which included five Communist ministers, one of them the General Secretary of the party, who was Vice-President of the Council of Ministers. For four months, from January 1947, the Minister of Defence in this government was a Communist. When the National Assembly in March voted military credits for the colonial war, the Communist group abstained, but the ministers voted in favour, in order to maintain 'governmental solidarity', and they ratified the instructions given to the new High Commissioner appointed by the government to conduct the war on the spot.[40] Duclos, according to Jacques Fauvet, used a weighty argument in favour of maintaining 'ministerial solidarity': the four-power conference (between the USSR, the USA, Britain and France) was about to begin in Moscow, and 'our foreign minister will be defending the cause of France'.[41] The cause of Vietnam could wait.

While the conference was in session French troops put down an insurrection in Madagascar with the same methods which they had used two years earlier in Constantin.[42] The party did no more than make a few formal protests and demand that the parliamentary immunity of the Madagascan deputies who had been imprisoned should be respected. The main thing was to preserve 'ministerial solidarity', since in order to plead 'the cause of France' at the Moscow conference, Bidault had to be able to speak in the name of a united nation. The cause of Madagascar, like the cause of Vietnam, could wait.

The 'cause of France' so dear to Thorez and Duclos had in this case a clearly defined content, the demands of a victorious France against a defeated Germany. All the PCF's flexibility in its dealings with the French bourgeoisie turned into inflexibility when it dealt with the 'German problem'. Thorez's policy on this question was based on a 'principle': 'The German people bears the crushing responsibility for having followed Hitler in his war of extermination against other peoples . . . It must bear the consequences; it must pay.'

The other 'crushing responsibilities' seem to have been erased from history: the responsibility of the peoples of France and Great Britain for tolerating the Versailles Treaty and the policies which led to Munich, the responsibility of the two Internationals for a policy which made Hitler's rise to power possible, Stalin's responsibility for a policy which missed the great opportunity of 1936 to change the course of events in Europe and led to the defeat of the Spanish republic, etc.

Thorez's anxiety at this moment was that the Versailles Treaty had made the mistake of demanding reparations in money from the Germans, when it was much more effective to demand 'reparations in kind and, in the first place, to use German labour'. The PCF demanded the internationalization of the Ruhr and the integration of the Saar into the French economy. Ruhr coal should help the economic reconstruction of France. All this was to be guaranteed by 'a long-term occupation of Germany'. But there is no need to exaggerate. Thorez was realistic in his patriotism: 'We are not opposed,' he explained, 'to the development of some heavy industries in Germany. We are not children. We know that you cannot reduce Germany to the level of a primitive tribe, but we want some assurance.' On the other hand, Thorez was inflexible in his insistence on the use of 'German labour'. During his tour of the mining areas of the Nord, he had already recommended that more work should be got out of German prisoners. In an interview with Reuter, published in the *Daily Mail* of 15 December 1946, he sharply criticized the English for their softness in this respect: 'We have the impression that the British are soft-hearted with the Germans, instead of making them work.'[43]

For the first time since Thorez had become the General Secretary of the PCF, a public difference with Stalin appeared. This sensational event was not connected with any problem of the revolutionary struggle in France, nor did it derive from the French Communists' shock at the cavalier fashion in which Stalin, like Roosevelt and Churchill, had settled the fate of each European people and decided that France should stay in the capitalist zone. The difference was about the Ruhr. In the Reuter interview mentioned above Thorez admitted it publicly: 'Our Soviet friends say, "Inter-allied control of the Ruhr". We say, "Internationalization of the Ruhr". We must find a compromise formula.'

The dispute had broken a few months earlier, at another four-power conference, when Molotov had firmly opposed the dismembering of Germany and the placing of the Saar under French control. The PCF held to its positions, and earned Léon Blum's barbed compliment: 'Our Communist comrades very legitimately took this opportunity to show by their actions that their nationalism was indeed a French nationalism, genuine, solid and deeply rooted – sufficiently deep-rooted to stand up even to this blast.'[44] In fact the difference between the 'foreign policy' of the PCF and that of the Soviet Union was of limited importance; it was a disagreement about the methods of preventing a resurgence of German imperialism which did not affect the substance of the question. Even on the question of methods, what was common to the two positions was that both of them had nothing in common with an internationalist revolutionary view of the problem. This in no way detracts from the significance of the fact that the son's first gesture of independence from the father took place in the area of nationalism. In any case, disputes of much greater importance soon banished this small seed of conflict between the emerging 'Communist' nationalism of the French and the all-powerful 'Communist' nationalism of the USSR.

The truth was that the 'grand alliance' had in practice ceased to exist.

American imperialism had launched itself firmly on the establishment of its world dominion. It offered the European bourgeoisie the manna of dollars in return for submission. It also offered them its military protection – and it was then the sole possessor of the atom bomb – against the 'red peril'. And while Thorez and Duclos were free with concessions – what sort of concessions we have already seen – to maintain 'ministerial solidarity', to allow Bidault to 'defend the cause of France' with the support of 'national unity', the French Foreign Minister signed a separate agreement with Bevin and Marshall about the Ruhr coal. In return for the manna which became known as the 'Marshall Plan', the French bourgeoisie abandoned its 'German demands' and turned firmly towards integration into the American bloc. But before they would part with their dollars the United States insisted that the Communist parties should leave the bourgeois governments of Europe.

In practice the operation went off briskly, without meeting serious difficulties. In each case a different pretext was used to conceal the new master's orders, but everywhere the result looked the same. On 19 March Spaak formed a government without the Belgian Communists. On 5 May Ramadier dismissed their French counterparts, and on the 30th of the same month De Gasperi reconstituted his government without the Italian Communists.

In the case of France the pretext was the big strike in the Renault factories. After three years of the 'battle for production' and of anti-strike policies on the part of the CGT and the Communist Party for the greater good of 'national unity' and 'the greatness of France', at the end of these three years, which had resulted in a wage freeze under a government in which Socialist and Communist ministers were a majority, the idea began to take root in the consciousness of the workers that they could fight a 'battle' of their own. The CGT tried to neutralize the discontent by presenting a series of modest demands in March 1947, but it took no real action and discouraged others from taking any. On 25 April the Renault workers joined a strike, which had apparently been started by the Trotskyists and immediately supported by members of the Socialist and Christian unions. In government circles the PCF were accused of being the instigators, and Ramadier put the question of confidence in the government's economic and social policy to the

National Assembly. Confronted with thousands of striking workers and deep and increasing unrest among those who were not yet on strike, the party could not approve the extension of the wage freeze in such an ostentatious way without doing severe damage to its reputation with the workers and making the position of its left wing, which was involved at Renault, much weaker. Just as Ramadier took advantage of the opportunity to obey American orders under cover of domestic pressures, the PCF also was not going to miss the chance of striking two blows at once. It hoped, on the one hand, to bring about a crisis in the government which had just taken a dangerous step towards accepting American policy (the party leadership thought that its attitude would bring about a ministerial crisis), and, on the other, to refresh its image as the party of the defence of proletarian interests.

The first plan failed. Ramadier did no more than reorganize his government without the Communist ministers (thereby confirming that the basic problem was not one of domestic, but of foreign, policy). But the vote against the government's economic policy did not mean that the party intended to mobilize the masses against that policy. In parliament, Jacques Duclos removed Ramadier's fear of an extension of the strikes: 'Only fools talk about a general strike now.'[45] More than ever, the party presented itself as 'a party of government'. It continued to think that the agreement between Bidault, Bevin and Marshall on Ruhr coal was only a dangerous, but not irreparable, episode. Even after Moscow's refusal to join the Marshall Plan in late June, the PCF leadership obstinately persisted in entertaining illusions about continuing the 'grand alliance' whose happy influence had allowed it to become a 'party of government' for nearly three years. And right up to the Cominform meeting at the end of September, it still did not realize that the time for change had come.

In the meantime Thorez never tired of repeating the irrefutable proofs which the party had given for nearly three years that it was a real 'party of government'. He never stopped complaining that its merits were despised by the other Republican parties. The following is one example, from 8 June 1947:

In 1944 the general production index stood at 35, compared with 100 before the war. At the end of 1946 it was 90. And after the first war? In 1919 the production index was much lower; it stood at 57. In 1920 it was 62, in 1921 55, in 1922 78; in 1923 it reached 88. In other words, thanks to the working class the country has recovered in two years, whereas five years were needed to achieve the same result after the last war, although the difficulties were less.

The great merit of the working class and of our party is that we, the Communists, were the ones who went and told the working class what had to be said. Without rhetoric, we told the railway workers, the miners. But when we talked about unity at a socialist congress the present Minister of Labour said, 'Unity to produce coal? Is that socialism?'

But after the 1914–18 war the standard of living of the working class rose. In 1921 the retail price index stood at 337, compared with before the war, and the wage index was 472. This meant a 40 per cent increase in the purchasing power of wages. The trend was not reversed until after the financial crisis of 1925. What is the position today? In October 1944 prices had risen to 291 and wages to 321. In October 1946 prices had reached 851 and wages 417. This means that there has been a 50 per cent reduction in the real purchasing power of wages compared with 1937.[46]

In other words the Communist Party's cooperation in the government from 1944 to 1947 had had effects more favourable to the restoration of the capitalist economy, and less favourable to the material conditions of the masses, than those produced by the reactionary government of the horizon-blue chamber of 1919–21.[47] There is nothing mysterious about the contrast when one remembers that in 1919–21 the working class put up a fierce struggle, including strikes, to defend its living conditions, whereas in 1944–6 it meekly accepted the slogans against strikes and for increased production which poured from the PCF. The bourgeoisie had done a gross injustice to the Communist Party, and it is easy to understand the ageing Cachin's question at the Eleventh Congress (June 1947), referring to Thorez, 'What madness made them get rid of such a statesman?'[48] Indeed, such 'madness' had required all the ignorance of European affairs characteristic of American politicians and all the servility towards American politicians revealed by their French counterparts.

THE REVOLUTION FRUSTRATED (ITALY)

As regards its general line, the policy of the Italian Communist Party (PCI) during the resistance, the liberation and the early post-war years did not differ in any important way from that of the French party. It was the Italian version of the line dictated to the Communist parties by Stalin's grand strategy and reflected in the final resolution of the Comintern. Some important differences did appear, however, in the way in which it was applied; these were determined partly by the nature of the objective problems in Italy and partly by the special features of the Italian party and its ruling group.

The PCI's inevitable subordination to Moscow never had that absoluteness which marked that of the PCF under the leadership of Thorez. The PCI was the party of Gramsci and Bordiga, both of whom, in spite of their different political positions, were united in the struggle for the autonomy and individuality of the party in the face of the Moscow centre. Even though Togliatti brought the party into the Comintern system, this tradition, and above all the stamp of Gramsci, was never totally effaced. Togliatti's intellectual formation and his complex personality made it difficult for him to adapt to the Stalinist model. Thanks to his highly individual capacity for compromise and manoeuvre, and also making use of his high position in the Comintern, Togliatti succeeded in maintaining a difficult balance between subordination to Soviet leadership and the demands – as he saw them – of the Italian situation. In the period we are examining the preservation of this balance was made easier by the basic harmony between Stalin's grand strategy and Togliatti's vision of Italian problems. The divergences came later, although a few 'dissonances' did appear even in this period.

The German–Soviet pact and the PCI's acceptance of the Comintern's positions cost it its working agreement with the Socialist Party, but the repercussions on its policies and situation in the country were less than those on the French party. The PCI had adapted itself to underground work several years previously and, above all, it did not yet have to face the problem of German aggression. There was no break in its line on domestic policy; its 'Vichy' was the Fascist state and the party's activity continued to be sharply anti-Fascist. When Italy entered the war in June 1940, the party accused Mussolini's government of 'selling the people to German imperialism'. In May 1941 another party document violently attacked German imperialism and declared that neither Great Britain nor France was a threat to Italy; it called for the breaking off of the pact with Germany and the departure of German troops from Italy.[49] It will be seen from this that its position with regard to German imperialism, on the one hand, and the Allies, on the other, was different from that of the French Communists at the same period.

The Salerno switch

The Soviet Union's entry into the war made possible the rapid restoration of the pact on unity of action with the Socialists (October 1941) and its extension to the anti-Fascist 'Justice and Freedom' group (which shortly afterwards changed its name to the Action Party). During 1942 the anti-Fascist struggle grew mainly in northern Italy. In the spring of 1943 the workers of Turin took an initiative which led to a powerful wave of strikes stretching to Milan and Genoa and involving over 100,000 workers. The German defeat before Stalingrad, the Anglo–American landings in Sicily and the strikes in the north made it clear to the dominant groups of the Italian bourgeoisie that the time had come to get rid of Mussolini and to place themselves under the protection of the Allies. Their chief aim, naturally, was to forestall a revolutionary solution to the crisis of the regime, and the Badoglio government showed its true face from the start. A government circular gave the following instructions:

Any movement must be ruthlessly crushed at the start ... Troops will act in combat formation and open fire at a distance, using mortars and artillery, without warning, as if in the face of the enemy. No shots are to be fired in the air for any reason, but at the body, as in combat, and if any act of violence, even an isolated one, is committed anywhere, those responsible are to be immediately executed.[50]

But the fall of the dictator had removed the last restraints on the mass movement. The anti-Fascist parties came into the open, the official unions passed into the hands of commissars appointed by the united anti-Fascist committees which formed everywhere. Strikes in support of the release of political prisoners multiplied. In the factories workers' commissions were elected, the first elected bodies to appear in Italy after the fall of Mussolini.

During this time the Germans, who already had seven divisions in Italy, dispatched another eighteen and occupied the north and centre of the country, while the Badoglio government took no defensive measures. It seems that the King and the Marshal, and the rich Italian bourgeoisie, had hopes of leaving the war in order to devote themselves to the enemy at home, using the apparatus of the Fascist state. They thought that both the Germans and the Allies, equally concerned to avert the 'red peril', would agree to the operation.[51] The German reaction destroyed this hope, and the government had no choice but to seek refuge in the south of the country, under the protection of the allied armies, and leave the Germans to crush the anti-Fascist movement in northern and central Italy. On 9 September, after announcing the armistice secretly concluded with the Allies, the King and the royal family, with the Marshal and a distinguished retinue of generals and high officials, fled from Rome without making any arrangements for defence against the invaders. A month passed before Badoglio declared war on Germany; he took the step on 13 October under pressure from the allied High Command. Italy now split into two zones, that occupied by the Germans, which until the spring of 1944 included the north and centre of the peninsula and was reduced in the summer of that year to the north, and the zone occupied by the Allies, which, conversely, until the occupation of Rome at the beginning of June, included only the south (the front ran just north of Naples), and began to spread into the centre in the summer.

From November 1943 the mass movement and armed action began to assume great importance in the northern zone. Serious strikes broke out in Piedmont, Lombardy, Liguria and Tuscany. On the initiative of the Communist leadership in the north, and with the support of the Committee of National Liberation of Northern Italy (which included the Communist, Socialist, Liberal and Christian Democrat parties, and the Action Party), a general strike was called in March 1944 over all the territory occupied by the Germans. The Communist Party and the

Socialist Party issued a common appeal. Over a million workers took part in the movement, the most important of its kind in occupied Europe during the Second World War. In Turin the strike lasted a week. Simultaneously with the strikes and other forms of mass struggle, the partisan movement grew very fast. During the summer of 1944 there were already about 100,000 men in combat units. Luigi Longo gave the following description of the situation in northern Italy:

Given the extent of the mass movement, there existed in many regions a *de facto* duality of power, the organs of the Fascist authorities, which were becoming increasingly discredited, and the anti-Fascist executive organs, existing illegally but enjoying great popularity among the people. And in addition to these regions where a duality of power existed, there were, during the whole period of the Nazi occupation, other areas of northern Italy totally liberated from the Fascist authorities, both German and Italian. They were controlled by democratic bodies, freely elected under the protection of the partisan forces.[52]

The Communists and the Socialists – the first heavily predominant – made up the controlling nucleus of this powerful movement, whose principal strength was the working class of industrial Italy and whose revolutionary spirit was noted by many non-Communist historians or participants in the events.[53] But while this popular power began to take shape in the industrial north, in the agricultural south the Italian bourgeoisie's new political power structure was being planned.

Shortly after the fall of Mussolini, the left-wing leaders had tried to come to terms with Badoglio on a number of points in order to organize the struggle against the German occupation, but the tacit complicity of King and Marshal with the Nazis, and the Marshal's policy of antipopular repression, made any agreement impossible. After the abandonment of Rome the problem of the formation of a government representative of the anti-Fascist forces and willing to conduct a vigorous fight against the German troops became urgent.

Meanwhile the 'Big Three' gave *de facto* recognition to the Badoglio government, and in their *Statement on Italy,* published at the end of October 1943, after a few generalities on the democratization of the Italian political system, they explicitly recommended the entry into the

347

government of 'representatives of the sectors of the people who have always opposed Fascism'. On 12 November *Pravda* published an article by Togliatti (who was still in the Soviet Union; he began his return to Italy at the end of February 1944 and landed in Naples on 27 March) which included the following: 'The measures proposed in the statement correspond exactly to the interests and aspirations of the Italian people. They form a programme around which all the democratic anti-Fascist forces of the country must rally to secure their rapid implementation.'[54] It was useless to point out that the essence of this 'programme', which had been signed by the representatives of Churchill and Roosevelt, was the setting-up of a bourgeois democracy in Italy. To begin the reconstruction the 'programme' required a compromise between the anti-Fascist parties and the Badoglio government, which these parties with reason regarded as a survival of Fascism.

Togliatti's position, which followed very closely the arrangement reached by the foreign ministers of the 'Big Three' at their Moscow conference, was markedly different from the position maintained at that point by the PCI in Italy itself. According to an internal document of the party leadership active in occupied Italy, dated October 1943:

The mission and function of the working class in the present events are to put itself at the head of the struggle for national liberation and, through that struggle, to win an influence among the Italian people which will enable it to become the leading force in the creation of a genuine popular democracy. This should be the party's policy.

The document mentioned two mistakes to be avoided. One was to identify the aims of the resistance with those of proletarian revolution, which meant falling into 'infantile extremism'.

But an ever more serious error, on the side of opportunism, would be to underestimate the importance of the problem of political leadership in the complex of forces within which the working class is active, and to accept the demands of the reactionary forces represented by Badoglio and the monarchy in the name of a misunderstood unity. These representatives may be allowed an auxiliary role, but not a leading role, in the fight against Fascism and for national liberation.[55]

It is symptomatic that this document should have been published as an article in the party's illegal publications in December, that is, after Moscow radio had indicated Togliatti's position. The Socialist Party's policy at this period was not to the right of that of the PCI – far from it. Even the Action Party announced that the aims of the resistance could not be limited to the establishment of a bourgeois democracy.[56]

In the south of Italy the PCI, the Socialist Party and the Action Party led a vigorous campaign against the King and the Marshal. Towards the end of January 1944 a joint congress of the anti-Fascist parties, attended by delegates from the Committee of National Liberation, met at Bari. (The CLN had been set up in Rome in September 1943 after the fight of the King and the Badoglio government, and continued to have its underground headquarters in the city until the liberation, though its practical activity was very limited.)[57] The Action Party put to the Congress a series of measures which were supported by the Communists and Socialists, as well as by the CLN delegates. These included a demand for the immediate abdication of the King, the suggestion that the Congress should constitute itself a representative assembly for the country until the election of a constituent assembly and the appointment of an executive junta to be responsible for relations with the United Nations. The liberals, led by Benedetto Croce, manoeuvred skilfully. The philosopher admitted that the King was the 'surviving representative of Fascism', but stressed that the Action Party's proposals could only be carried out by an act of force, an impossibility in view of the presence of the allied forces. The only solution, he said, was to bring pressure to bear on the King to force him to abdicate. The Congress hesitated. It appointed an executive junta, but did not constitute itself as a representative assembly and took no steps to mobilize the people.

Nevertheless, the left-wing parties did not abandon their position. In response to a speech on 22 February in which Churchill mocked the anti-monarchist and anti-Badoglio resolutions of the Bari Congress, the workers of Naples called a strike. As a result of the opposition of the military authorities, this was replaced by a big popular meeting at which only representatives of the left-wing parties spoke. This meeting took place on 12 March. On the 14th, when agitation against the government was at its height, Badoglio announced the recognition of his government by the USSR and the re-establishment of diplomatic relations between the two countries. (The Western allies had not yet taken this step.)

Such were the general features of the situation when Togliatti landed at Naples on 27 March. He arrived ready to apply the Italian policy of the 'Big Three'. It is not surprising that his judgement on the policy of the left-wing anti-Fascist parties, his own in particular, was severe. Years later, he told his biographers that the PCI at the time had taken 'a dangerous path, which could lead nowhere', by going so far as to 'organize meetings against Churchill and to study, with the other anti-Fascist parties, the possibility of organizing a popular consultation, not on the initiative of the government but on that of the parties'.[58] In the twinkling of an eye Togliatti extricated the party from the impasse in which it had been caught and set it on the road to success and national unity. On 29 March the party leaders of the southern zone met, and Togliatti, 'taking the bull by the horns', proposed 'the postponement of the problem of institutions until it was possible to call the constituent assembly, and the unity, as a priority, of all political tendencies to take part in the war against Germany, in other words, the immediate setting-up of a government of national unity'. 'At first,' according to the same biography, 'most of those present were astounded,' but Togliatti 'expounded his proposals so clearly and so convincingly that no one could object'.[59] According to other sources, some old party leaders were not so easily convinced, but Togliatti, apart from his talent as a polemicist, had behind him all the prestige of the Communist International and the Soviet Union. He had just returned from Moscow. Who should know better than Stalin what was good for the Italian people? If the Soviet Union had recognized the Badoglio government, there could be no doubt that the cause required it so.[60]

The Italian Communist Party's switch of policy – the *svolta di Salerno*, as it was later called in the history of the PCI – finally made it possible to overcome the resistance of the Socialists and the members of the Action Party. The 'sacrifice' of Victor Emmanuel III, who – yielding to pressure from Benedetto Croce and Roosevelt – announced his intention to abdicate and appoint his son Umberto as Regent once Rome was liberated, made the compromise easier. But still the birth of the government of national unity proved very difficult. At the last moment

the Liberals and the Action Party were about to ruin the whole undertaking, but Togliatti 'led the counter-attack with the support of
Badoglio, the Socialist Lizzardi and the Christian Democrats Rodino
and Jervolino; and in order to find a solution to the situation he had to
agree to join the government himself'. Jervolino said later that, if the
question of religion had not been raised, he could have become a Communist himself, and he welcomed the spirit of sacrifice shown by the
Communist leader in accepting a ministerial post. 'If you had refused to
join the government,' he told Togliatti, 'it would have been said that you
regarded it as a government of fools and that that was the reason why you
didn't want to take part in it.'[61] It is not clear whether this is a reference
to the undistinguished role the anti-Fascist leaders were engaged in
playing. Having up to the very last moment denounced the King and
Badoglio as survivals of Fascism, and denounced their tacit sabotage of
the war against Germany, they now agreed to be ministers of this King,
under the leadership of Marshal Badoglio, in the name of the 'war effort'
against the invader and to eliminate the last traces of Fascism. It was not
too much to ask of the key man of the operation, the man whom the
proletariat regarded as their representative and the representative of the
Soviet Union, that he should guarantee by his presence the sincerity of
the anti-Fascist and democratic ideals of the brand new government,
which would take office once it had sworn its collective oath to the
King.

In PCI documents and historical accounts influenced by the party's
official point of view, the formation of this government of national unity
under the leadership of Badoglio has been presented as an essentially
Italian operation, directed mainly by Togliatti. In reality, it was a 'Big
Three' operation, and, according to Soviet sources, the credit for the
idea belongs to the Soviet Union. The *Soviet Encyclopedia* puts it very
clearly: 'On the initiative of the USSR, which had established direct
relations with the Italian government on 11 March, the Badoglio cabinet
was reorganized on 22 April 1944 to include representatives of the six
parties of the anti-Fascist coalition.'[62]

The 'initiative' is easy to understand from the Soviet point of view. In
spite of the presence of a representative of the USSR on the consultative
commission for Italy (set up at the Moscow Conference of the three

foreign ministers), which had its headquarters in Algiers, it was the allied military commission (which included no Soviet representative) which in practice held the real power. Diplomatic recognition of Badoglio gave the USSR an opportunity of direct intervention, and the 'reorganization' of the Badoglio government, with the entry of the Communists, increased those opportunities. For Stalin the problem was not to get the PCI to adopt a strategy capable of giving a revolutionary resolution to the crisis of Italian capitalism. Stalin had ruled out that solution in advance immediately it became clear that Italy would be 'liberated' by the allied armies. The problem was to place on the Italian political chessboard pawns which could check the influence of the Allies. (In 1947, at the founding meeting of the Cominform, the Italian Communists were to be severely criticized by Zhdanov, not because they had lacked a revolutionary policy which could put all its force behind the great proletarian and popular movement which had come into being on the fall of Mussolini, but because they had been unable to prevent Italy's accession to the American bloc.) Of course, Stalin's 'initiative' for the reorganization of the Badoglio government could be implemented only with the agreement of the British and Americans. When one remembers that exactly at this time, in order to give satisfaction to Churchill and Roosevelt, Stalin was bringing pressure to bear on Tito to come to a *modus vivendi* with King Peter, it is not surprising that Churchill and Roosevelt should have brought pressure to bear on King Victor Emmanuel to reach a *modus vivendi* with Togliatti.[63] The game was the same.

From National Unity to Christian Democrat Monopoly

Thus 'national unity' was created. The Communist Party, in the glory of its twofold prestige as the 'party of revolution' and the 'party of order', began to grow rapidly. Equally fast, if not faster, the new political forces of the old ruling classes began to organize. For this purpose they could make use of the magnificent guarantee provided by the left-wing parties, which meant a unique opportunity to combine traditional ideology, the drug of religion, with the new, fresh aspirations to liberty and democracy, even with Socialism (Christian Socialism of course). These new political forces of the old ruling classes grew rapidly, absorbing the remains of Fascism, the old and experienced civil bureaucracy, the even older and even more experienced clerical bureaucracy, the armed forces of the old state, etc. It was an unquestionably just development, since the sun of national unity, of the *secondo risorgimento,* was to shine equally on all Italians, independently of their religious beliefs and their political sympathies (only the Fascist, as the just reward of his wickedness, was excluded from the community, and even he only needed to change his skin to get back).

After the liberation of Rome the government of national unity demonstrated its anti-Fascism and democratic spirit by substituting Bonomi for Badoglio at the head of the government. A reformist Social Democrat in his youth, Bonomi was expelled from the Socialist Party in 1911 because of his excessive social chauvinism, and in 1921 became leader of one of the governments which left the way open for Fascism. In the biography of Togliatti which he himself revised there is the following appraisal of Bonomi:

In spite of all the time that had passed, there could still be seen in him traces of the period in which he had been active in the working-class movement and had known its problems and successes. It was probably this that led him to see in Communist policy a new form of his old reformist possibilism. This was the source of his sympathy for Togliatti and the excellent relations between the two men, but also of the frequent serious disagreements. His dominant fault was his excessive concern for the fate of the old state apparatus and the outward forms of government.[64]

Indeed, Bonomi took jealous care of the old state apparatus, and systematically built its main components into the 'new' structure. On the other hand the condition of the mass of the workers caused him little concern. Their duty was to support the 'war effort' with stoicism, in a spirit of national unity. The *rinnovamento sociale,* which all the parties as a matter of course had included prominently in their programmes, would be carried out once the enemy were beaten, when the guns had fallen silent and the electorate had spoken. As Togliatti had unambiguously said in his first public speech after his return from the USSR, 'The problem for the Italian workers today is not to do what was done in Russia.' The problem for 'today' was the defeat of Hitler's Germany, and to succeed in that task, which Togliatti described as 'the most revolutionary task of all' at that time, 'we must guarantee order and discipline in the rear of the allied armies'. Basic social problems would be considered when the constituent assembly met. For the time being, the party had a programme which included 'thorough agrarian reform' and other economic, social and political reforms which, when they were carried out in the 'new democracy', would prevent 'a small group of greedy, selfish and corrupt men from once more concentrating in their hands all the wealth of the country and using it to suppress freedom and impose a policy in conflict with the national interest'. To those who accused the party of 'abandoning revolution', Togliatti replied, 'Leave us alone. It's our business, and we know a bit more about it than you.'[65] And, indeed, it was rather presumptuous to give lessons in this 'business' to a man who had been one of the highest leaders of 'the world party of the revolution'.

In fairness, it should be emphasized that the party called for immediate measures to improve the situation of the masses and stop the uncontrolled speculation which was enriching a minority at the expense of those who worked and fought. But the principal speculators were well protected, as Togliatti pointed out:

> The forces of big capitalism, the large organizations of the industrialists, landowners and bankers, are in their places. They were not damaged by Fascism, and they are trying to lead the political and economic life of the country in a direction which will not serve the interests of the workers in a spirit of national solidarity, but will benefit the interests of this class of owners at the expense of the people and the nation.[66]

Improving the condition of the masses, in the country's situation of economic ruin and chaos, was only possible through a determined attack on the interests of these castes which lacked 'the spirit of national solidarity', but this was precisely what the policy of national unity made impossible. The unions were growing furiously, a powerful peasant movement had been created in the south, and the Communist Party, the Socialists and the whole anti-Fascist left was daily growing stronger. But the policy of national unity meant that their action could not go beyond certain limits; if it did, 'governmental solidarity' – and class solidarity – would be threatened. As early as the end of 1944, the disillusion of the masses with the Bonomi government was clear.

Battaglia's and Garritano's *Storia della Resistenza italiana,* which never questions the correctness of the PCI's policy of national unity, but does record the facts, notes that: 'One of the arguments used by neo-Fascist propaganda to make the partisans and the masses abandon opposition and resistance was the disillusion with the democratic government which began to appear south of the Gothic Line.' (The 'Gothic Line' was the name given to the Apennine front, running just north of Florence, which remained stable from September 1944 to April 1945. The neo-Fascist propaganda referred to is that of Mussolini's puppet regime, 'the republic of Salo', set up in the region occupied by the Germans.) The same work continues:

> The disillusionment was due mainly to the fact that the government had not fulfilled the Italian people's hopes of renewal. The Bonomi government was to have been the government of the CLN and the anti-Fascist parties, instead of the Badoglio government, which was the government of the generals loyal to the King. But the generals, though under the stimulus of defeat, were willing to contribute to the military effort against the Germans; their influence in Rome was replaced by that of the senior state bureaucracy and the remnants of the Fascist ruling class, which began to undermine the unity of the CLN and the government itself, and paralysed democratic action.[67]

In reality, however, it was not just the influence of the senior state bureaucracy and the 'remnants' of the Fascist ruling class which was paralysing the 'democratic action' of the government. The main factor was that the ruling classes, grouped behind Christian Democracy, supported by the whole apparatus of the Church and by the Allies, considered it possible – and also necessary, as a precaution against the entry on to the political scene, when the north of Italy was liberated, of the powerful popular forces organized in the resistance – to reinforce their political control over southern and central Italy and place the masses under even greater pressure to be passive.

In November the leadership of the Christian Democrat Party made a violent attack on the Communist Party, accusing it of fomenting 'violence', 'disorder' and 'anarchy'.[68] Bonomi submitted his resignation. After a difficult crisis the second Bonomi government was formed. The Socialist Party and the Action Party refused to take part in the new government, which continued, less successfully, the policies of its predecessor. The Communist Party agreed to take part, along with the Liberals and the Christian Democrats. Togliatti was appointed Vice-President of the government, a post, according to his own biography, 'mainly honorary and symbolic', but he regarded this solution to the crisis as a victory for the policy of national unity. To realize this, he said, it was enough to remember one fact: the purpose of the crisis was the formation of a government without the CLN parties, and in the new government all the members were from these parties.

> In the first battle which they tried to wage, [the anti-democratic forces] were completely defeated, and in the battle we played an outstanding part ... If they had allowed themselves to be removed from the government, the CLN parties, and particularly the most advanced, would have compromised the rare conquests they had made. They would have left the new state apparatus once more in the hand of conservative and reactionary forces.

In following this course, 'we remained faithful to the line of war, national unity and constructive democratic action, a line which will determine the fate of the working class and of our party itself.'[69]

The anti-democratic forces, as Togliatti describes them in the same place, 'are hidden forces which dare not come into the light of day', and it is true that they were seen only in the guise of allies, churchmen, Liberals, Christian Democrats, or employees of the state (the civil bureaucracy, the armed forces, the police). Their tactics at this period were not to exclude the working-class parties from the government; they were intelligent enough to realize that the 'honorary and symbolic' presence of a man like Togliatti among the ministers gave them an excellent alibi with the people, thanks to which they could continue to strengthen their positions in all the structures of state and society. They had no desire at all to see the anti-Fascist parties 'abandon' the state apparatus the integrity of which Bonomi so jealously guarded.

(Bonomi's ministers – that is the left-wing ministers, since the Christian Democrats and the Liberals had the same religious reverence for the immovable state apparatus, quite apart from the fact that they were 'rejuvenating' it with new elements which made no difference at all to its essence – the left-wing ministers therefore either gave way to this punctilious conservation of the state machine or endangered government unity, the keystone of the sacred structure of national unity.) The interest of the conservative and reactionary forces was precisely that the 'new state', which was still their state, should certainly not be abandoned by the working-class and popular parties until it had recovered sufficient strength, until the country had got over the dangerous political crisis. On that basis and it was the fundamental problem behind the crisis of the first Bonomi government – the working-class parties and the anti-Fascist left must strictly respect the contract of national solidarity concluded at Salerno. This was not easy, because the discontent of the masses, and their spontaneous initiatives, constantly tended to break this contract.

It required all Togliatti's capacity for manoeuvre, all his dialectical apologetics with the Communist Party and the Italian masses, all his experience in high political circles, and, above all, all the revolutionary prestige of the Communist Party – all its anti-reformist virginity – to succeed in holding the balance between the demands of governmental solidarity (which included especially submission to the allied authorities) and solidarity with the mass of the workers. The virulent attack on the Communist Party by the leadership of the Christian Democrats was obviously an 'enormous slander', as Togliatti's biography describes it. To accuse of fomenting 'violence', 'disorder' and 'anarchy' the party which constantly preached the need to maintain order and discipline, which spread among the Italian people a belief in the liberating, democratic and peaceful intentions of the Allies, which developed in the proletarian masses an awareness of their national mission, explaining that it was not to be confused with the mission of the Russian proletariat in 1917 – to make such an accusation against such a party was not only an 'enormous slander', but also seemed to make no sense.

But politics is politics. The Christian Democrat leadership had no wish to offend its ally, but simply wanted to see it restrain the popular masses still further. The committees of liberation, for example, showed an irritating tendency, at local and provincial level, to try to increase their power, to take initiatives without consulting the government, in short, to create a situation of dual power. But that was the Russian way, not the one it had been agreed should be followed in Italy. These tendencies appeared increasingly dangerous as the moment approached for the liberation of northern Italy, with its partisan army and the weight of its committees of liberation and its working-class parties. Shortly before the government crisis the Communist Party had explained its position on the committees of liberation:

The committees of national liberation, instead of being kept at a distance, as they tend to be by some authorities, should have their functions recognized and widened. *Any duplication of powers must be avoided*, but the active participation of all the democratic and anti-Fascist forces in the organized effort now required of the country must be ensured.[70]

The Christian Democratic attack on the PCI and the government crisis were intended to ensure a political development in which tendencies towards a 'duplication of powers' would be firmly checked and the 'active participation' of the democratic and anti-Fascist parties would remain strictly within the limits set by the government itself. In contrast with the victory chant he proclaimed immediately after the solution of the ministerial crisis, Togliatti shortly afterwards found himself forced to admit that 'the events of the last government crisis mean, from different points of view, a setback to the movement towards a new democracy arising out of the need to continue the war and maintain national unity'.[71]

The political concessions made by the party in order to remain in the government were not limited to the south of the Gothic Line; the concessions it made north of that line were even more serious. As has already been mentioned a number of times, the greatest worry of the Italian ruling classes and the Allies was the possibility of a revolutionary explosion in the north after the defeat of the Germans.

The first move aimed at destroying the partisan movement was the halting of the allied advance in autumn 1944, which left the German and the Italian Fascist troops free to devote the whole winter to fighting the resistance. General Alexander, the Commander in Chief of the allied forces, ordered the partisans to cease all operations until the spring, to bury their weapons and concentrate on listening to the radio broadcasts from the allied headquarters. (These orders were repeated on the radio, so that the German command was fully aware of them.)[72] The CNLAI (the National Liberation Committee for Northern Italy) and the general staff of the partisan army decided to ignore Alexander's orders and to continue the struggle. But the CNLAI also acted in accordance with the national unity line. (The north Italian leadership of the PCI had accepted the *svolta di Salerno*, and in spite of the Socialists and the Action Party, who tried to oppose it within the CNLAI, the position of the Communists, Liberals and Christian Democrats prevailed.)[73] In order to reach an agreement with the allied command and the Bonomi government, the CNLAI sent to the capital a delegation which, on 7 December, signed what was called the 'Rome protocol'. The partisans undertook to obey British and American instructions on the conduct of the war, to appoint as military leader of the partisan army an allied 'secret officer' and follow his instructions until the territory was liberated. According to the previously quoted *Storia della Resistenza italiana*,

It seems as if the liberation movement was forced, with this agreement, to make heavy concessions; in reality the Allies simply obtained confirmation that the partisan movement 'would not make a revolution', which, obviously, was worrying them.

These Communist historians continue:

In reality, this was not a success for the Allies, but for the Italians. The CNLAI saw itself officially recognized as not only the *de facto*, but also the *de iure*, government in northern Italy ... as a result of the Allies' recognition the Bonomi government in its turn recognized the CLNAI as its 'delegate' in the occupied territory, and a bridge was thus established between the two Italies, a situation which the forces hostile to the resistance, already organized in southern Italy, had until then tried to prevent.[74]

And so we see the democratic and working-class forces, with the support of the powerful symbol of national unity, going from success to success.

After 'completely defeating' the anti-democratic forces which were trying to exclude them from the government, they then succeeded – by 'simple confirmation' of the fact that they did not intend to make a revolution – in getting themselves recognized as the 'legal government' of the north. The Allies and the Bonomi government generously allowed them to exercise their power as the 'legal government' by fighting the Germans and the supporters of Mussolini, and the Allies in their turn gave the latter complete freedom to destroy this 'legal government' and its brave partisan units.

All parties made efforts to carry out faithfully the explicit or tacit compromise which had been made. The German troops, with the support of the neo-Fascists, launched one offensive after another against the partisan army, while the Allies scrupulously observed the truce they had granted until the spring. South of the Gothic Line, the Bonomi government and the anti-Fascist parties did nothing to mobilize the people against this criminal complicity of the Allies. The partisan army and the fighting working class of the north held out on their own against the Fascist offensives during the long hard winter of 1944–5. In this trial they not only showed themselves to be the 'legal government', but demonstrated the real power of industrial Italy.[75] Towards the middle of April 1945, when Germany was already practically defeated, the Allies went over to the offensive on the Gothic Line. The partisan army and the working class took the lead with a general rising. By a combination of military actions and strikes against the authorities they liberated all the large towns and the greater part of the territory before the arrival of the allied forces. The situation was described by Luigi Longo, who was one of the chief leaders of the resistance and the rising in northern Italy:

At the beginning of April more than 300,000 partisans began fighting in northern Italy and liberated one after another the towns of Bologna, Modena, Parma, Piacenza, Genoa, Turin, Milan, Verona, Padua and the whole region of Venice before the allied troops arrived. The partisans saved the industrial installations and lines of communication which the Germans were preparing to destroy, took tens of thousands of prisoners, and succeeded in capturing considerable quantities of arms. Everywhere the partisans set up national liberation committees as the authority and

executed the main leaders of Italian Fascism . . . For ten days, until the
arrival of the allied troops and authorities, the national liberation committees directed the whole political, social and economic life of northern
Italy. The police forces were taken over by the partisan units which were
not involved in military operations against the German troops.[76]

So for ten days the working class and the mass of the people of northern
Italy had controlled the power and the main industrial enterprises of the
country. They had 300,000 organized fighters (a number which could be
rapidly increased), and possessed a considerable quantity of weapons
taken from the Germans. On the eastern frontier was the Yugoslav
army, in full control, on the Austrian border the Soviet army. But there
was also the 'Rome protocol', the policy of national unity – and Yalta.
The end of this part of Longo's report to the founding meeting of the
Cominform is brief:

When the allied authorities reached the north with their troops, they
began to remove from important posts the men of the resistance appointed
by the national liberation committees, and replaced them with officials
from the old administrative apparatus. And the Rome government, as
soon as the Allies handed over to it control of the whole country, speedily
replaced all the people appointed to responsible positions by the national
liberation committees with alleged 'specialists', i.e. officials of the old administrative apparatus.[77]

A Soviet historian gives a more complete account of what happened:

The Anglo-American military administration declared a state of war in
the north of Italy. It abolished all the democratic arrangements made by
the national liberation committees and dismissed from the administrative
service all those who enjoyed the confidence of the people, replacing them
with reactionary officials. It returned to the capitalists and landowners the
goods which had been confiscated from them. The occupiers disarmed the
partisan detachments and went on to dissolve the National Liberation
Committee for Northern Italy.[78]

The only omission from the Soviet historian's account is that the
consultative commission for Italy included a Soviet representative, and
that, as far as I know, not a single Soviet protest was made, either within

the committee or elsewhere, against the behaviour of the 'occupiers' in northern Italy. There was also no mention of the fact that the PCI was the first to encourage the disarming of the partisans, as Togliatti reminded it at the party's Fifth Congress (December 1945): 'We are all united by our agreement to have no recourse to violence in the struggle between the parties. This agreement calls for the disarming of all, and we were the first to carry it out by taking measures towards this end with the partisan units.'[79]

The rising in northern Italy aroused enthusiasm and hope in the people. It was said at the time that the 'south wind' – the reactionary policy of the traditional ruling classes, camouflaged under anti-Fascism – was opposed by the 'north wind', the desire on the part of millions of workers, peasants and intellectuals for far-reaching social and political changes. In the course of 1945 all the left-wing anti-Fascist parties became mass parties. The Communist Party increased its membership from 400,000 in April to 1,700,000 in December. The Socialist Party had 800,000 members by the end of the year, and the Action Party, which expressed the views of the radicalized petty bourgeoisie, and in particular of important groups of intellectuals, had about 250,000 members. Even within Christian Democracy – which, as Togliatti said, was two parties in one, with 'two contrary souls' – the left-wing tendencies, particularly among the party's youth, were growing considerably in strength. The trade-union confederation (CGIL), which combined all the political tendencies within the working class, had rapidly acquired over five million members. In the south a powerful movement of peasants and casual workers was growing. The management committees set up in all the big northern factories under the protection of the rising still functioned, in spite of being no longer legally recognized, and, most of all, the workers were conscious of their strength and in a mood to fight.[80]

In spite of government and allied moves to purge the committees of liberation and prepare for their abolition, these united organs of anti-Fascism, in which, on local and regional levels, the left-wing tendencies were in the majority, firmly fought for survival. In spite of all attempts at disarmament, many weapons had been hidden, and the possibility of building para-military self-defence organizations on a large scale on the basis of the partisans was beyond doubt; it depended entirely on the will of the left-wing anti-Fascist forces. In addition, the catastrophic economic situation of the country made it objectively necessary – at least if economic restoration was to benefit the workers – to carry out urgently radical structural reforms and make a ruthless attack on the rights of the big industrialists, bankers and landowners. The national element was also involved; the colonialist behaviour of the new occupiers wounded national feelings which had been stimulated by the war against the German occupiers.

Political, economic, social and organizational considerations thus favoured a break by the anti-fascist working-class left with the compromise policy of the 'anti-Fascist' right, the political instrument of the traditional ruling classes, and a transition of an offensive strategy involving the mobilization of millions of manual workers and intellectuals in support of an advanced democracy with a socialist content. The 'north wind' symbolized the underlying possibility of organizing a vigorous mass struggle to defend and strengthen the multiplicity of new forms of the new democratic power which had grown up during the war of liberation and under the protection of the April rising. The slogan launched by the Action Party – 'Finish the CLN revolution' – reflected the willingness of a large sector of the petty bourgeoisie, and especially of the intellectual and professional classes, to go forward with the working class to a democratic socialist transformation.

In June 1945, under pressure from the 'north wind', a new anti-Fascist coalition government was formed. It was led by F. Parri, the most striking leader of the Action Party and the President of the northern CLN, but even the vaguely socialist positions of the members of the Action Party were regarded by the leadership of the PCI as excessively leftist. The PCI, without which the left-wing coalition and a transition to an offensive strategy were clear impossibilities, continued to hold strictly and firmly to the policy of national unity introduced by the Salerno switch. Those of its members who called for another switch, this time to the left, found themselves accused of being 'leftist adventurers'; according to the official diagnosis, they had caught the 'infantile disease' and understood nothing about the 'relation of forces'.

No PCI document of this period or later provides the least analysis of this 'relation of forces'. The view that it made it impossible for the crisis of Italian capitalism to lead to socialism was handled by the PCI (just as the PCF dealt with French capitalism) like a metaphysical principle or a mathematical axiom which justified all the party's policy, which, of course, was based on a rigorous study of 'objective reality'. We shall come back later to this famous question of the 'relation of forces' in France and Italy in 1944–5. For the moment we shall simply note that for the leadership under Togliatti this 'relation' called for the acceptance of two imperatives, failure to accept which would risk bringing down the direct catastrophes on the working class and the party. These were the continuation of the coalition with the bourgeois wing of the anti-Fascist movement and the avoidance of any conflict with the Allies. (Each of these two imperatives of course implied the other, since it would have been impossible to maintain the coalition with the anti-Fascist right if a conflict with the Allies took place, and *vice versa*.)

From the moment when it accepted this framework, the party surrendered the initiative to the right, condemning itself to inability to do more than exercise pressure. It demanded, insisted and made proposals, but it did nothing to bring into play the powerful working-class and popular movement which was in ferment in the country. Italy was passing through a 'democratic revolution', Togliatti wrote during the summer of 1945, after the formation of the Parri government, and the working class 'insisted on' a leading role:

> The working class and the mass of the workers *demand* the chance to put their stamp on the democratic transformation which is now taking place, and, in view of the bankruptcy of the old reactionary ruling classes, *insist* on taking a decisive leading role in solving all the problems raised by the democratic revolution and, in general, in the running of the country. This implies, as *an inevitable consequence,* that the problems of the *economic and social emancipation* of the workers and all related questions should receive *the beginnings of a solution,* in accordance with the wishes of the people, *even before the democratic revolution is complete.*[81]

By what magic mechanism would the working class's 'demand' that the democratic revolution should bear its 'stamp', and its 'insistence' on playing a leading role, have as an 'inevitable consequence' the beginning of a socialist solution ('the economic and social emancipation of the workers')? Togliatti did not explain this mystery in this text or in any other. But in December of the same year he explained what was happening in practice, what the fate of the working class's 'insistence' was and how their economic and social emancipation was being brought about:

It is not possible [said Togliatti in his report to the Fifth Congress of the PCI] to move forward in a system where the government is paralysed because every time it is necessary to take effective measures in any field the left-wing parties which are working out a logical democratic programme face constant blackmail, which forces them to submit to the inertia of the government and even to accept anti-democratic measures in order to avoid crises which would lead the country to chaos.[82]

It emerges from this passage that the 'paralysis' affected only the 'logical democratic programme'; anti-democratic measures were applied, but democratic measures got no further than the resolutions of the left-wing parties or their leaders' speeches. In the face of 'blackmail' – the threat of the break-up of the coalition government or allied intervention – the PCI and with it the other left-wing parties resigned themselves to the reactionary policy of the right and accepted compromises which it would have been hard to classify among those which Lenin regarded as admissible for a revolutionary party. And following a logic which is always demonstrated in social crises, in the absence of a party capable of placing itself firmly at the head of the masses the floating groups in the middle began to drift towards the right.

The crisis of the Parri government took place in December. While the working class was 'insisting' on playing a leading role, the bourgeoisie – its old and new 'castes' reunited – consolidated its positions within the state and put De Gasperi at the head of the government. The *Cronache di vita italiana* of Togliatti's biographers described it thus: 'The north wind suffered a decisive check. All political discussion centred on the question "monarchy or republic?", and the social pressure produced by the April rising was contained. The north and south winds compromised.'[83] In fact, in place of the disturbing topic 'capitalism or socialism?', which in some form had occupied the centre of the political struggle since April, all parties reached a tacit agreement to give priority to the question 'monarchy or republic?', which was much less dangerous to the ruling classes and particularly good for inflaming the imaginations of the south. During this time the dismantling of the committees of liberation and the elimination of the resistance at all levels went ahead systematically. The real centres of bourgeois power and the Allies wasted no time. The 'purges' made no progress, but the General Secretary of the Communist Party continued to run the Ministry of Justice with exemplary competence.[84]

On 2 June 1946 the voters chose a republic, and at the same time ratified the dominance of Christian democracy in Italian politics. At the time of the Salerno meeting the Christian Democrats had been one – and far from the most influential – of the parties of the anti-Fascist coalition which joined the Badoglio government. After two years of 'national unity' they had become the leading party in Italy. The elections for the Constituent Assembly, held on the same day as the referendum on the Constitution, gave them 8,000,000 votes (35·2 per cent of the votes cast), compared with 4,300,000 votes (18·9 per cent) for the PCI and 4,700,000 votes (20·8 per cent) for the Socialist Party. These eight million votes represented the majority of the peasants and the urban petty bourgeoisie, and even a proportion of workers. This social mass voted for the party manipulated by the big industrialists and landowners because it saw no essential difference between it and the working-class parties, as far as social aims were concerned, and it had the advantage, on the other hand, of reconciling them with the church and religion. According to a PCI leader, the Christian Democrats presented themselves at the elections for the constituent assembly 'with a social programme of structural reforms which corresponded to the aspirations of the Catholic workers and *was substantially identical with that of the Communists and Socialists*'.[85] Togliatti stressed this point immediately after the elections, and admitted that the Communists and Socialists had made a mistake in not distinguishing themselves sufficiently from the Christian Democrats; in reply to the statements they made almost everywhere 'that their economic and social programme was no different from that of the Communists and Socialists, the left did no more than call on the Christian Democrats to declare clearly in favour of a republic.'[86]

But this was nothing new. Ever since the fall of Mussolini, throughout 1945, when the 'north wind' was blowing through the country, the PCI, in its anxiety to preserve 'national unity' at all costs, had helped this new instrument of the ruling classes in its political demagogy. It had reduced its own 'social programme' to reforms which were perfectly compatible with bourgeois democracy, and, more important, it had not tried to stimulate a real struggle for these reforms. This was the decisive factor; the party neglected the struggle to assert and extend the new demo-cratic power brought into being by the resistance, which could have been the beginning of a real advance to socialism. In other words, the policy of the PCI made it possible for the masses not to put the Chris-tian Democrats' 'economic and social programme' to the test.

It was true that the elections to the Constituent Assembly emphasized the vast force which the two working-class parties together represented. The 40 per cent of the electorate which had voted for them included a large majority of the industrial and agricultural proletariat, and con-siderable sections of the peasantry and urban middle classes and of the intellectuals. But after the elections the role of this force in the political process continued to be that of a brilliant second rather than of the star. The comment of Maurice Vaussard, one of the historians of European Christian Democracy, was well justified: 'Basically, though they jibbed at times, as long as the policy of tripartism lasted Togliatti and Nenni always gave way before the leader of the Christian Democrats.'[87] The 'structural reforms' were once more postponed. According to the same writer the leaderships of the anti-Fascist parties had agreed before the elections that the functions of the Constituent Assembly should be lim-ited to drafting and voting on the Constitution. He adds:

In short, everything went off as though a tacit agreement had been made from the beginning between the two big mass parties [the PCI and the Christian Democrats] to allow De Gasperi to surmount the two main difficulties he would have to face after the liberation, the vote on the peace treaty and that on the new constitution, which would, in particular, have to choose between ratifying or not the Lateran Treaty ... De Gasperi secured the support of his own party and the Communists, who between them formed a majority of the assembly, for the ratification of the peace treaty, while the same majority, against the opposition of the Socialists, the

Action Party and many Liberals, included in the new constitution the substance of the Concordat which had been inseparable from the Lateran Treaty and proclaimed the Catholic religion the state religion, granted legal validity to religious marriage, banned divorce and guaranteed clergy salaries.[88]

(The severity of the peace terms imposed by the 'Big Three' had aroused general indignation in Italian public opinion, and without the strict subordination of the Christian Democrats to the British and Americans and of the Communists to the Russians ratification would have created serious difficulties. Everything went off as though the explicit or tacit compromises mentioned by Vaussard really existed. It is hard to believe that the PCI's acceptance of the constitutional ratification of the Church's traditional role in Italian society and the Christian Democrats' concessions with regard to the 'social content' of the Constitution had nothing to do with a bargain.[89] This did not prevent the PCI from hoping to benefit from concessions to the Church – justified as concessions to the religious feelings of the Italian people – through which it expected to acquire influence among the Catholic masses, or the Christian Democrats from hoping to benefit from the 'social' principles and provisions of the Constitution, which provided an excellent popular, and almost socialist, façade for the restoration of Italian capitalism.[90]

'The democratic revolution which is in progress in our country will lead, in its first stage, to a constituent assembly,' Togliatti had said in his report to the Fifth Congress. In the following stages progress towards socialism would be made in the framework of a 'republic organized on the basis of a representative parliamentary system' in which 'all reforms of the social content will be carried out with respect for democratic methods'.[91] But, in fact, what the Constituent Assembly symbolized was the end of the great political operation begun by the Italian ruling classes with the elimination of Mussolini. With reference to the situation created at the beginning of 1947, the *Cronache di vita italiana* says: 'The worst was over; the revolution and the north wind had been contained. Now a firm swing of the rudder was needed to point the ship firmly in the right direction, which ruled out any participation in government by left-wing forces.'[92]

In May 1947, shortly after his visit to Washington, De Gasperi dismissed his Communist ministers. To Togliatti's biographers this decision seemed unjust and mistaken, in view of the fact that the presence of the Communists in the government had proved to be 'an element of security and stability':

> Togliatti had been Minister of Justice, and instead of the bloodshed predicted by reaction an amnesty had been granted which made a notable contribution to pacification ... Scoccimarro and Pesenti were Finance and Treasury Ministers, and the lira, instead of collapsing, stood up very well. Gullo was Minister of Agriculture, and the only people who were dissatisfied were the famous barons of the south, against whom, for the first time, measures against large landholdings were applied, measures which had been called for for decades, long before Fascism, called for even by some of the south Italian bourgeoisie.[93]

Togliatti commented on the action as follows:

> An intelligent and capable adversary would not have removed us from the government. Quite the opposite, he would have taken us at our word as regards our declared aims, and would have dared us to stick to them. He would have worked to create a situation in which we would have been overwhelmed with no hope of escape and from which we could only emerge crushed. To understand that, and do it, would mean being intelligent, whereas De Gasperi is a mediocrity, perhaps even less than a mediocrity.[94]

This admission tells a lot about the party's aims and declarations, and the outburst about De Gasperi's intelligence was rather inelegant. It is possible that without Truman's brutal intervention he would have been able to get even more benefit from the PCI's 'policy of national unity', but it is flagrantly unjust not to admit that he made very good use of it to carry out the task entrusted to him by the Italian bourgeoisie. De Gasperi did not disappoint the trust and the hopes placed in him by the old Italian ruling classes. Can as much be said of the trust and the hopes which the Italian proletariat had placed in its representatives at the time of the greatest national catastrophe of modern Italy, of the most serious political social and economic crisis of Italian capitalism? Was it the historical mission of the revolutionary party to contribute to preparing the economic and political conditions of the 'Italian miracle'?

It is true that the Italian workers gained a series of victories which cannot be underestimated. Instead of Fascism bourgeois democracy, instead of an anachronistic monarchy a democratic republic with a constitution as advanced as a bourgeois constitution could be, and a whole series of social improvements. It was something like what the German proletariat obtained from the 'democratic revolution' led by the Social Democrats. All of that is certainly not eligible, but it makes it reasonable to ask 'in that case, why the Livorno split?', and in the case of France, 'Why Tours?'

REVOLUTIONS WITHOUT PERMISSION: CRITICISMS OF FRENCH AND ITALIAN OPPORTUNISM

At the founding meeting of the Cominform the policy of the Communist Parties of France and Italy was severely criticized as opportunist by the representatives of the seven other parties. Duclos and Longo found themselves before a tribunal which accused them of 'governmentalism', 'parliamentarism', legalism and other 'isms' characteristic of 'right-wing opportunism'. To judge from the attitude of Duclos during the meeting, the French leaders were taken unawares. Togliatti, on the other hand, must have suspected something, because he gave the following advice to the PCI delegation: 'If we are accused of having been unable to take power or having let ourselves be removed from the government, tell them we couldn't turn Italy into another Greece, not only in our own interests but also in the interests of the Soviets themselves.'[95]

These were in fact the two criticisms the French and Italians had to face. The first was made by the Yugoslavs, whose criticisms had sincerely revolutionary motives. The second came from the Soviets, whose annoyance was not caused by the fact that the policies of the French and Italian parties had spoiled the chances of the revolution, but that they had proved incapable of preventing the incorporation of their countries into American imperialism's new anti-Soviet strategy. Stalin even feared that Thorez and Togliatti had become too fond of office, to the

Revolution and Spheres of Influence

point of making concessions to the other parties of the former anti-Fascist coalition in order to get back into the government. Nor was this fear without foundation, since after what a Western historian has picturesquely labelled 'the defenestration of the Communist ministers' Thorez continued to present the PCF as a party of government and Togliatti proposed the formation of a new government of the left-wing parties and the Christian Democrats,[96] when what Stalin needed was a firm struggle by these parties against the Marshall Plan and the other aspects of the integration of France and Italy into the American bloc.

The Soviets were not in a particularly good position to act as the judges of the French and Italians. Fundamentally, Thorez and Togliatti had done no more than literally apply Stalin's instructions at the period of the 'grand alliance'. If they had sinned, it was only by excess of zeal. Yet that was probably not why Zhdanov and Malenkov suggested that the Yugoslav delegates should take the main role in criticizing the opportunism of the French and Italians. According to the later statements of Kardelj and Djilas, the Soviets 'wanted to create a gulf between the Yugoslav party and the parties of France and Italy'.[97] Later events seem to confirm this version, but in any case two more powerful motives encouraged the Soviets to adopt this procedure.

First, everything indicated the need for prudence; they could not be sure of the reactions of the leaders of the two big parties of Western Communism, who were already full of their own prestige and national importance, and it would serve no purpose to come into conflict with the two most powerful Communist parties of the capitalist world, from which the Soviets hoped for an important contribution in the struggle against American plans.

Second, the Yugoslav party was the ideal candidate for the role of prosecutor in virtue of the authority it had won by its exemplary revolutionary action. In addition, the Yugoslav leaders needed little pushing in this direction. During the war and in the immediate post-war period they had many times urged the PCI to change its policy. The setback suffered by the revolution in Italy was a serious danger to the Yugoslav revolution, which was threatened at the same time in the south by Anglo-American intervention in Greece.

Before going on to the criticisms made against the French and Italians

371

at the founding meeting of the Cominform, it will be useful to insert a schematic description of the main features of the policy of the Yugoslav Communist Party during the war of liberation and after it, and of the opposition it met from the Soviet leaders. Information about both is necessary for a better understanding of the significance of the Yugoslav criticism and to appreciate the skill of the Soviet leaders' manoeuvres. The Soviets used the positions of the Yugoslavs, who had had to carve out their own path in opposition to Stalin, to correct the opportunist positions of the French and Italians, which had been the direct result of the Stalinist line. The correction, of course, was in the direction required by Stalin's new international policy, the result of which was – as we shall see later – a move from one form of opportunism to another. In addition we must take account of Yugoslav and Greek experience (the latter can only be referred to incidentally) to complete our analysis of the reasons which brought about the frustration of the revolution in Italy and France.

The Revolution Victorious (Yugoslavia) and the Revolution Throttled (Greece)

From the first day of the German occupation, the leadership of the Yugoslav Communist Party worked out and applied a policy in which national liberation and the revolutionary transformation of the country were closely linked.[98] The second aim was regarded as one to be achieved, not after the victory over the invader, but in the course of the war itself. As each piece of territory was liberated, the power of the people was established there, based on bodies set up with the direct participation of the people and the resistance fighters.

The most characteristic aspect of this revolutionary orientation was the construction of this new popular power, rather than the radicalism of the programme. The programme was, on the whole, moderate, though directed towards the transition to socialism; its immediate objective was agrarian revolution, which was carried out as the line of battle moved on. Anti-Fascist unity, unlike that of France and Italy, was conceived on the following basis: it included all the parties, groups, tendencies and individuals who declared themselves in favour both of the aims of the programme and the methods by which it was to be carried out, excluding not only collaborators with the invader but also those who favoured the restoration of the monarchical system, and even those who wanted to preserve the capitalist system in the political framework of a bourgeois parliamentary democracy.

For this reason the war of liberation inevitably took on at the same time the form of a civil war against the bourgeoisie and the big land-owners. A struggle on this scale required resources on a level with its revolutionary ambitions. Small partisan detachments and local surprise attacks and campaigns of attrition against the enemy proved insufficient to determine the fate of the revolution. They would have been enough to prepare the ground and facilitate the operations of the armies of the great powers, as in France and Italy, but not to allow the people to decide its own future. The Yugoslav Communist Party therefore tackled, from the very beginning, the problem of forming a regular revolutionary army, capable not only of defeating the invaders but also of winning the respect of the allies. This approach, which was carried out in spite of enormous difficulties, was one of the key factors in the victory of the Yugoslav revolution.[99]

In the unitary logic of men like Thorez and Togliatti, the Yugoslav Communists' policy seemed pure adventurism, and this is in fact how it was regarded in the leading circles of the Comintern until its abolition, that is, during the most difficult period of the struggle in Yugoslavia. Instead of uniting the greatest possible number of allies against the enemy, did it not mean flinging part of them into the arms of the enemy? Colonel Draža Mihailović and his Chetniks, the military arm within the country of the royal government in-exile in London (in January 1942 Mihailović was appointed Minister of Defence by King Peter), recognized by the 'Big Three', followed this course towards collab- oration. This was not because the Yugoslav Colonel was less opposed to Hitler or less patriotic than de Gaulle or Badoglio, but because the Communist Party had right from the start pursued revolutionary objec- tives, which the Communist Parties of France and Italy, also right from the start, had abandoned. Tito made a number of attempts to agree with Mihailović on common action against the invaders, but on a political basis which guaranteed the revolutionary aspirations of the masses, which King Peter's Minister of Defence naturally did not accept. This clash between the emergent popular power and its army of liberation on the one hand and, on the other, the right-wing forces which a Salerno-type policy of national unity might have kept as allies of the Communists (or rather would have made the Communists their allies) did not isolate the Yugoslav Communist Party and the Popular Liberation Front (as the united anti-Fascist movement was called). The opposite happened: it isolated Mihailović and his Chetniks, who were obliged to reveal before the people their reactionary aims, the preservation of the old exploitative social system which they held out as the reward of the sacrifices and heroism of the resistance fighters.

The strengthening of the revolutionary army and the establishment of the new power in the liberated areas increasingly pushed Mihailović into a tacit – and sometimes open – alliance with the occupiers, which only further increased his discredit and isolation. Another result was that the royal government-in-exile in London (to which the main bourgeois liberal and Social Democratic leaders had attached themselves) lost its military base in the country. So did Churchill.

This policy of the Yugoslav Communists had from the start a disturbing effect on the 'grand alliance', and for this reason was firmly opposed by Stalin. The allied leaders could not imagine that the Yugoslav Communists were carrying out such a policy without obeying instructions from Moscow, and they continually pressed the Soviet government to order Tito to come to terms with Mihailović. Stalin tried to satisfy them. Although the Yugoslav Communist leadership regularly informed Moscow about the situation of civil war which existed between the liberation army and the Chetniks, Soviet propaganda described Mihailović as the commander of all the forces of the Yugoslav resistance and ignored the role of the Communists and the Popular Liberation Front and the appearance of a new revolutionary power in the liberated areas. Obeying Stalin's orders, Dimitrov sent messages to Tito urging him to change his policy. The following example is dated 5 March 1942:

Study of all the information you sent gives one the impression that the adherents of Great Britain and the Yugoslav government have some justification in suspecting the partisan movement of acquiring a Communist character and aiming at the Sovietization of Yugoslavia. Why, for example, did you need to form a special Proletarian Brigade? Surely at the moment the basic, immediate task is to unite all anti-Nazi currents, smash the invaders and achieve national liberation.

How is one to explain the fact that supporters of Great Britain are succeeding in forming armed units against the partisan detachments? Are there really no other Yugoslav patriots, apart from the Communists and Communist sympathizers, with whom you could join in common struggle against the invaders?

It is difficult to agree that the London and Yugoslav governments are siding with the invaders. There must be some great misunderstanding here. We honestly request you to give your tactics serious thought, and your actions as well, and make sure that on your side you have really done all you could to achieve a true united front of all enemies of Hitler and Mussolini in Yugoslavia in order to attain the common aim – the expulsion of the invaders and would-be conquerors. If anything remains to be done, you should urgently take measures and inform us.[1]

Tito was also asked to consider his struggle not 'solely from the national point of view, but also from the international point of view, from that of the British–Soviet–American coalition'. In reality there was no misunderstanding; there were two totally different policies. One was Moscow's, according to which the war against Nazi Germany should have no aim other than national independence and, at the most, bourgeois democracy. The other was that of the Yugoslav Communists, who combined the struggle for national independence and democracy with socialist revolution. This did not make their policy any less 'national', but, on the contrary, more deeply national – which explains its results – than that of the French and Italian Communists.

At the same time the Yugoslav Communist Party certainly looked at the struggle 'from the international point of view, from that of the British–Soviet–American coalition'. But this 'point of view' differed from Stalin's; it was the Yugoslav Communists' point of view. As they were very soon to show, they were capable of intelligent manoeuvres in the face of the manoeuvres of the British and Americans; they succeeded in obtaining their aid while at the same time forcing them to face the reality of the Yugoslav revolution. In this sense they taught the great leader a brilliant lesson in revolutionary tactics – but we shall return later to this Stalin–Dimitrov document, which tells us so much about much more than the Yugoslav problem.

Another form of pressure used by Moscow was to refuse the Yugoslav fighters' requests for arms and ammunition. The excuse given was technical difficulties, which were certainly considerable, but – as was discovered later, when the royalist government archives were transferred to Belgrade – at precisely the same time as they were refusing to send arms and ammunition to the liberation army, the Soviets were offering military supplies to the Chetniks and were willing to send a military mission to Mihailović's headquarters.[2] For over two years, without receiving any outside help, the liberation army fought simultaneously against the German and Italian armies – which launched six large offensives against them – against the troops of Nedic and Pavelić (the Serbian and Croatian quislings) and against Mihailović's Chetniks.

In the autumn of 1942, when the liberation army already had a strength of 150,000 fighting men, divided into two army corps of nine divisions (a total of thirty-six brigades and seventy batallions), the Anti-Fascist National Liberation Council of Yugoslavia (AVNOJ) decided to meet in Biihac, the capital of newly liberated Bosnia, and form a provisional government. Moscow strongly opposed the idea. This time the Yugoslavs gave way, but a year later they decided to go ahead. In October 1943, when the conference of the Foreign Ministers of the USSR, Great Britain and the USA was to meet in Moscow, Tito sent the three governments a memorandum informing them that the AVNOJ recognized neither the King nor the government-in-exile in London, that it regarded itself as the only representative of the Yugoslav people and intended to establish a democratic republic based on the committees of liberation. The conference ignored the message, and continued to recognize King Peter's government as the sole legal representatives of Yugoslavia. In reply the Yugoslav revolutionaries called a second National Assembly of the AVNOJ and legalized the establishment of the new state.

While Stalin, Roosevelt and Churchill were in conference at Teheran and began the great division of the world into 'spheres of influence', the delegates from the committees of liberation from every corner of Yugoslavia gathered at Jajce, the old capital of the kings of Bosnia, and declared the London government in exile deposed. King Peter and the members of the Karageorgević dynasty were condemned to 'perpetual exile' (the Assembly unanimously forbade their return to Yugoslavia in any capacity). The problem of the choice between a monarchical or republican system, however, was left for after the war. (It will be seen that the Yugoslav Communists were also well able to manoeuvre in the face of the Allies, but, unlike the Italians, they began by securing the new popular power; negotiation could come later.) The Assembly decided to give the new state a federal structure, and elected a provisional government.

When news of these decisions reached Moscow, Stalin's rage exploded. Manouilsky sent a message to Tito that 'the chief' was 'extremely annoyed and was saying that it was a stab in the back for the USSR and a manoeuvre against the Teheran conference'. Radio 'Free Yugoslavia', which broadcast from Soviet territory, immediately lost its freedom and was unable to broadcast the Jajce Assembly's resolution forbidding the return of King Peter. Broadcasts prepared by the Yugoslav Communist representative in Moscow were censored.[3]

But meanwhile London and Washington, having obtained on-the-spot information about the real balance of forces, the discredit and impotence of Mihailović and the power of the liberation army, decided to yield to facts and try to reach a compromise with Tito. Only then did the Soviet government recognize the decisions of the Jajce Assembly. Molotov made a statement which brought this position out sharply:

The events in Yugoslavia, *which have already been accepted by Great Britain and the United States*, are regarded by the Soviet government as capable of contributing to the success of the struggle of the Yugoslav peoples against Hitler's Germany. These events are a sign of the remarkable way in which the new Yugoslav leaders have been able to unite all the forces of the country.[4]

This 'remarkable way' in fact bore no relation to the method Moscow had been trying to impose for two and a half years.

The Soviet government decided at the same time to send a military mission to Tito's headquarters – which the British and Americans had already done – and in the early months of 1944 the Yugoslavs finally began to receive Soviet arms, including a few planes. The British and Americans had started sending arms to Tito by the end of 1943. But this aid had a price. Churchill on the one side and Stalin on the other increased their political and diplomatic pressure to make the Communists reach a compromise with the government-in-exile. To smooth the path, Churchill arranged for Bozidar Purić to be replaced as leader of the government-in-exile by Šubašić, who was regarded as 'more democratic'. Mihailović ceased to be Defence Minister, and the British government announced that it was suspending all aid to the Chetniks. Faced with this combined pressure from the British and the Soviets, the Yugoslav party leadership manoeuvred. In August 1944 Tito reached an agreement with Šubašić to provide for collaboration between the government-in-exile and the government established in the country, with a view to forming a 'mixed' government. Tito said of this later: 'We decided on this agreement because we knew our strength, we knew that the vast majority of the people were with us ... What was more, we had a strong army, the size of which our rivals could not even imagine.'[5]

At the end of November Stalin met Tito and pressed him again to accept the restoration of King Peter and make concessions to the Serbian bourgeoisie, but he did not succeed in altering the Yugoslav leader's attitude. 'What will you do if the British land in Yugoslavia?' asked Stalin. 'Resist with every possible means,' replied Tito. Stalin greeted this vigorous reply with an icy silence.

A few days later there took place the famous Churchill–Stalin meeting at which the cynical division of 'influence' in the Balkans was made. Without a word to Tito, Stalin made an agreement with His Majesty's Prime Minister to divide influence in Yugoslavia equally.[6] At Yalta this agreement was not only confirmed, but put into more detail. On 12 February 1945 the Russian and British military missions in Belgrade informed the Yugoslav leaders that at the 10 February session the three heads of government had decided to make the following 'recommendations' to Marshal Tito: (*a*) the Tito–Šubašić agreement was to come into force immediately, with the formation of a new government; (*b*) once formed, the government would announce: (1) that the A V N O J would admit members of the Yugoslav National Assembly who were in no way compromised in collaboration with the enemy, and that the new political body thus formed would take the name of Provisional Assembly; (2) that legislation promulgated by the AVNOJ would be submitted for further ratification by the Constituent Assembly.[7]

This decision provoked fierce indignation among all wings of the partisans, in particular the obligation to admit to the Provisional Assembly members of the 1938 Assembly which had been elected under the pro-Axis Stojadinović regime. But once more the Yugoslav leaders manoeuvred skilfully. They saw very clearly the need to combine firmness with prudence, to make no concessions on essentials but compromise on details in order to gain time in which to consolidate the revolution and, above all, strengthen the army. In particular, from the end of 1944 the total passivity of Moscow in the face of the war operations against the Greek resistance undertaken by the British Expeditionary Force filled out the sinister meaning of the silence with which Stalin had greeted Tito's reply to his question, 'What will you do if the British land in Yugoslavia?' The leadership of the Yugoslav Communist Party therefore decided to 'apply' the Yalta 'recommendations', but in such a way that the popular forces did not have to give up anything of their real power and Churchill and the Yugoslav bourgeoisie could keep their hope in the possibility of restoring the old social order. It should be borne in mind that an important group of Yugoslav bourgeois politicians (from which Social Democratic leaders were not absent) did not accept the Tito–Šubašić compromise and, with the support of the most reactionary circles of British imperialism, called openly from London for the sending of an Anglo-American army to restore order in Yugoslavia.[8]

The tactics adopted by the Yugoslav Communist leadership proved effective, and the Yugoslav revolution consolidated itself during 1945. When Šubašić and the other representatives in the 'mixed' government of the old ruling classes – and of the 50 per cent of influence reserved for Britain under the Churchill–Stalin agreement – realized that the Trojan horse method would not work, they resigned their ministerial posts. But it was already too late for the British and Americans to apply the 'Greek' remedy to the Yugoslav problem.

As has already been said, within the scope of this study we cannot give the case of Greece the attention its importance deserves. We shall do no more than note the following facts. The Greek resistance had the same revolutionary character as that in Yugoslavia and obtained comparable support in the country. At the end of 1944 it was practically in control of the country. But the leadership of the Greek Communist Party was unable to resist the pressure of Moscow with the firmness of the Yugoslav party. It made serious concessions to the policy of 'national unity' and accepted compromises with the allies which facilitated the British army's intervention against the Greek resistance. The October 1944 Stalin–Churchill agreement did the rest. On 7 November 1944 Churchill sent the following instructions to Eden:

> In my opinion, having paid the price we have to Russia for freedom of action in Greece, we should not hesitate to use British troops to support the Royal Hellenic Government under M. Papandreou . . . I fully expect a clash with EAM, and we must not shrink from it, provided the ground is well chosen.[9]

The battle between the British troops and the resistance forces lasted from the beginning of December 1944 until 12 February 1945, when an armistice was signed which led to the Varkiza agreement. This was later regarded by the Greek party as 'an unacceptable compromise and, basically, a capitulation in the face of the English imperialists and Greek reaction'.[10]

On 22 December Churchill, protected by British tanks, was able to enter Athens, and at a meeting with the leaders of the resistance announced – in order to make them capitulate – that 'the British had gone into Greece with the agreement of President Roosevelt and Marshall Stalin'. The head of the Soviet mission (who, while the people of Athens were fighting the British troops, stayed in the British headquarters, which was surrounded by partisans) was present at this meeting and confirmed Churchill's statements. Two days later, when negotiations between the resistance and the royal government had broken down and British aircraft were strafing the inhabitants of Athens, the Soviet government appointed an ambassador to the royal Greek government. And at the Yalta Conference, although the fighting between the British intervention forces and the forces of the resistance was barely over,

Stalin declared, 'I have confidence in the British government's policy in Greece.'[11]

The Varkiza agreement was used by the British imperialists and Greek reaction to re-establish royal power and begin a process of brutal repression against the working class and democratic forces. At the end of 1946 the Greek Communist Party and other resistance groups decided to reopen armed struggle, and the civil war began. Feeling too weak to cope with the situation, British imperialism gave up its role of police-man to American imperialism, and on 12 March 1947 Truman announced that the United States was undertaking the 'protection' of Greece and Turkey as the first application of the 'Truman doctrine'.

Yugoslav Criticisms of French and Italian Opportunism

The Communist leaders in Belgrade saw the armed intervention of Yankee imperialism in Greece as a direct threat to the Yugoslav revolution. They took the same view of the reactionary development of the political situation in France and Italy, accompanied by American military implantation in both countries. This is the context of the criticisms made by Kardelj and Djilas of the policies of the French and Italian Communists at the conference which set up the Cominform. The precise formulation of these criticisms is still a secret, but it is possible to get a fairly accurate idea from the later disclosures of the Yugoslavs and especially from the notes taken by Reale (who, with Longo, represented the PCI), which were published in 1957. In addition, this information can be compared with the indirect references contained in the published reports and documents of the conference, especially in Kardelj's report on the activities of the Yugoslav party.[12] These are the sources on which the account which follows is based.

The Yugoslavs felt that during the war and after the victory over Nazism there had grown up in the international Communist movement a tendency to revise Marxism–Leninism, which found its most complete expression in 'Browderism'. According to this view the end of the war was the beginning of a period of peaceful development and slackening of the class struggle, both nationally and internationally. The policies of the Communist Parties of France and Italy, the Yugoslavs implied, were a particular expression of this tendency. Its starting point was the belief in the possibility of a peaceful, legal and parliamentary road towards the seizure of power by the working class. To some extent it was a repetition of the view accepted by the Social Democrats after the First World War. The Italian and French Communists had regarded the governments in which they took part as the beginning of a people's democracy, which, according to the Yugoslavs, was a serious mistake.

While these views were being maintained the conspiracy to expel the Communists from the government was already being formed. It had been in the interests of the bourgeoisie to collaborate with the Communists because the bourgeoisie felt their weakness, and the Communists should have used this situation to occupy key positions, but they did not do so. On the contrary, with their theory that governments of collaboration with the bourgeoisie meant the beginning of popular democracy, which would now develop from this basis by legal and parliamentary means, they had achieved nothing but the disarming of the masses and the spreading of illusions about Christian Democracy and other bourgeois parties, and about Social Democracy. The French and Italian Communists should have realized that their honeymoon with the bourgeoisie and Social Democracy could not last. It could be no more than a struggle in which victory would go to those with the greatest boldness, the clearest vision and the fewest illusions about parliamentary coalitions, and who were able to win the support of the masses in order to seize power.

We maintained very close relations with the Italian comrades during the war, said the Yugoslavs. We invited them to study our experience, the approach which enabled us to liberate a great part of our territory and to build an army. But they were unwilling to take the path of insurrection. They said that it was necessary to curb the revolutionary developments in the north of Italy to avoid cutting it off from the south. Togliatti believed that the Communists would have been able to seize power only in part of the country, and that this would result in the division of the country and the loss of its unity and independence.

Instead of creating anti-Fascist unity from below, by setting up organizations with mass support, composed of all the tendencies genuinely prepared to take part in armed struggle and the establishment of a genuinely popular power, the French and Italian Communist leaders made the mistake of forming an anti-Fascist front from above, based on equal representation of the different parties, working-class and bourgeois, even though the aim of some of these parties was to restrain or stop armed struggle and to prevent any real transformation of the country. The published text of Kardelj's report on the activities of the Yugoslav party contains the following passage, which is a clear reference to the French and Italian Communists:

Some people have claimed that the formation of national liberation committees and the implementation of the democratic and revolutionary demands of the majority of the people would in the end alienate certain social sectors and certain political groups from the anti-Fascist front. The Communist Party of Yugoslavia has firmly fought these views. If the Yugoslav popular front had adopted these views, it would not have had the support of the masses, or rather, the majority of the people would not have been willing to take up arms and fight with the selflessness they have shown. If they fought with such zeal, it was because they knew that they were fighting for their democratic and social ideals as well as for national liberation. Practice has shown that the close association between the national liberation movement and the process of the people's democratic revolution, far from weakening the fighting spirit of a national uprising, gave it an exceptional attraction for the majority of the people.[13]

The Yugoslavs sharply criticized the PCF for allowing and even helping in the disarming and disbanding of the resistance forces at the end of 1944 and the beginning of 1945. They refused to accept the French leaders' arguments that the war was not over and any firm action against de Gaulle's policies would have meant a confrontation with the allies, which in turn would have produced a deterioration in the relations between Britain and the United States and the Soviet Union. This argument was false, the Yugoslavs insisted, because the most effective help to the Soviet Union would have been to reduce American influence among the French people. Similar criticisms were directed at the Italians for their policy in the months after the uprising in northern Italy. Kardelj and Djilas contrasted the behaviour of the Greeks, who had opposed the British by force of arms even though the war against Germany was not over, and their own action, the Yugoslav Communists' fight against the allied-supported government of King Peter and its Chetniks. The Yugoslavs criticized the general attitude of the French and Italian Communist leaders towards the British and Americans. They criticized their failure in practice to condemn Anglo-American policy openly, which made it easier for imperialism to recover its position. They criticized their illusions about 'democracy', imperialism and the 'improvement' of imperialism, and the way they spread these illusions among the masses.

The French and Italian Communist Parties were also accused of failing to give effective support to the armed struggle which the Communists and other left-wing forces had been waging in Greece since the end of 1946. They did not support the struggle, the Yugoslavs claimed, because the leaderships of these parties believed that the Greek civil war was a lost cause from the point of view of the popular forces, and would very soon be over. The French and Italian leaders' argument, that the imperialists wished to create a situation of the Greek type in their countries to give them a better chance of crushing the forces of democracy and the working class, was false, Kardelj said. The situation was the opposite: the Americans were afraid of the development of a similar struggle in France and Italy because that would be a serious threat to their position. The Yugoslav Communist Party delegates proposed that the founding meeting of the Cominform should study ways of providing effective help for the struggle of the Greek people, but they received no support.

This, in essence, was the Yugoslav Communist Party's criticism of the policy followed by the Communist Parties of France and Italy in the period 1941–7. To judge from the information available, it appears that Gomulka was the only other member of the conference to express a view close to that of the Yugoslavs. He maintained that the French and Italian Communists had had an opportunity to press for radical change in their countries at the moment of the liberation and had not used it. The stage during which 'the invader's administration was destroyed in the same process that forced his expulsion' was a 'decisive period' for 'the creation of a new state apparatus', said the Polish Communist; if there existed 'more favourable conditions in the countries liberated by the Soviet army than in those entered by the Anglo-Saxon armies', there were nevertheless even in these countries 'serious possibilities of bringing about essential changes in the organization of the new state, especially where the working-class parties had been active in organizing the struggle for national liberation and controlled armed partisan units', in other words, France and Italy.[14]

Zhdanov and Malenkov, as we have seen, stayed discreetly in the background, concentrating their criticism on the fact that the two parties, after being excluded from the government, continued to adopt a governmentalist and parliamentarist attitude instead of mobilizing the masses against the pro-American policy of their respective governments. The other participants in the meeting modelled their attitudes on that of the Soviet delegates. None of them made any objections to the criticisms of the Yugoslavs, but nor did any of them deal with the crucial problems which these criticisms raised.

The French and Italians, of course, realized that they were faced with two critiques from very different standpoints, and that only the one put forward by Stalin's spokesmen need be taken seriously. There was no need for a fundamental analysis of the reasons why the revolution had failed in France and Italy; all that was required was approval of the 'switch' proposed by Zhdanov. Once Longo and Duclos did reverence to self-criticism by recognizing in a general way that their parties had committed a number of opportunist errors by not sufficiently combining governmental and mass action, once they admitted their failure to realize in time the scope of the new American policy and the fact that the removal of the Communists from the government was the result precisely of the new anti-Soviet course of Washington's policy, once they promised to carry on a vigorous struggle against the Marshall Plan and scrupulously apply the new policy insisted on by Stalin, Zhdanov ended the 'discussion' and the next question was taken.

Having achieved this result, the Soviets no longer had the slightest interest in a deeper analysis of French and Italian opportunism. No more had the others. All the participants in the meeting were sufficiently aware of the problems to realize that the Yugoslavs' criticisms implicitly entailed a criticism of the policy imposed by Stalin on the Communist movement during the period of the 'grand alliance', and they all knew that this aspect of the question was taboo. Longo and Duclos could have used this argument to defend themselves and to accuse the Yugoslavs of criticizing Stalin's policy through them. But since it was obvious that Kardelj and Djilas were acting in concert with Zhdanov and Malenkov, such a 'defence' would have rebounded on themselves. In a private interview, Longo explained to Kardelj and Djilas that the Italian party's policy during the war had been dictated by Moscow, but in the official sessions no one stepped out of his role,[15] that of expiatory victims on the one side and that of prosecutor and judge on the other.

To the extent that the break-up of the 'grand alliance' progressed, the motives for friction between Moscow's policy and the interests of the Yugoslav revolution seemed to disperse. While the honeymoon between the 'Big Three' lasted, the Yugoslavs' revolutionary intransigence was regarded at Moscow as a 'negative' factor, but once London and Washington began their new anti-Soviet crusade it was suddenly transformed into a 'positive' one. The Yugoslavia of the partisans, with its not inconsiderable army and its strategic geographical position, became an important link in the European defence system which Stalin had begun to construct. And, *vice versa,* in the face of the threat implied by the 'Truman doctrine' to the Yugoslav revolution, Soviet protection seemed all the more necessary to Tito and his colleagues.

It was soon to appear, however, that the foundation of this political convergence was weak. Yugoslav intransigence was useful to the Soviets to the extent that it complied with the demands of the new Soviet policy. But the Yugoslavs had aims of their own in the Balkans which did not coincide with those of Soviet diplomacy. Moreover, Stalin's plans for his European outposts clashed with the Yugoslav desire to maintain national independence. Nevertheless, at the time of the setting-up of the Cominform the Yugoslavs had no interest in a clash with the Russians – quite the opposite. The implicit criticism of Stalin's previous policies contained in their attacks on the policies followed by the French and Italian Communist Parties was probably not deliberate (if it had been, the Yugoslavs would have said so after their break with Stalin). This critical content was simply the objective result of the fact that the policy of the French and Italian Communists had been no more than a faithful echo of Stalin's grand strategy.

It was one of the weaknesses of the Yugoslav criticism of the French and Italians that it avoided this key question of Stalin's policy during the period of the 'grand alliance', although without an analysis of this it was futile to claim to be revealing the reasons for the failure to make use of the revolutionary potential which had been created in France and Italy. This policy has been mentioned several times in the course of this study, but always in a fragmentary way. The preceding sections, which have examined the policies of the Communist Parties of France, Italy and Yugoslavia and looked briefly at the situation in Greece, have recorded the specific, local effects of the advice and instructions which issued from Moscow. Our study of the reasons for the dissolution of the Comintern and other passages in the first part of this book have also referred to some general features of this policy of Stalin's.[16] We have not yet, however, attempted the comprehensive examination which is indispensible if we wish to obtain an equally comprehensive understanding of the reasons and process of the failure of the revolution in Western Europe. The following section will attempt this examination.

FROM THE 'GRAND ALLIANCE' TO THE 'TWO CAMPS'

Stalin's policy during the Second World War was based on two main strategic rules, which have already been mentioned in previous chapters.[17] The first, which was formulated towards the end of the 1920s after the check to the revolutionary movement which began with the Russian revolution, and derives from the theory of 'socialism in one country', can be stated as the subordination of revolutionary action in any part of the world to the interests of the Soviet state. The second, which came into being in the thirties after the defeat of the German proletariat by Nazism, was the result of the loss of confidence in the revolutionary capacity of the Western proletariat, and called for giving priority to the exploitation of contradictions between the imperialist powers, and the subordination of any revolutionary action to this priority. The second rule is no more than the practical application of the first, in view of the inability of the Western proletariat to create a revolution. Given that the main object was to guarantee the security of the Soviet state and that revolution outside the USSR seemed unlikely, the only course open was the exploitation of inter-imperialist rivalries.

A typical example of the application of this twofold golden rule was Stalin's policy towards the Spanish revolution and the French Popular Front. Its first large-scale application, however, was Stalin's policy during the opening phase of the Second World War, when it was taken to its ultimate conclusion and did not stop at the monstrous step of signing an important pact with Fascism and restraining popular struggle against it, precisely in order to facilitate that pact.[18] The same principles continued to dominate all Stalin's policy after the invasion of Soviet territory by the Nazi armies. The way in which the anti-Hitler coalition was conceived, the political motives which dominated collaboration in military operations, the content of the political aims given to the war, the role assigned to the Communist parties, all the main aspects of Stalin's policy in the context of the 'grand alliance' adhere strictly to these two rules.

During the ten years between the 1935 Franco-Soviet pact and the Yalta agreement the supreme aim, the security of the Soviet state, also took on a significance far removed from that which it had had in Lenin's time. In the second half of the 1930s it meant essentially the maintenance of the *status quo* in Europe, in other words, the system of the Versailles Treaty. During the period of the German–Soviet pact it began to include territorial expansion, the revision of frontiers, annexation and the winning of 'spheres of influence'. In the war against the Axis powers this new content – the imperialist and colonialist substance of which was not completely revealed until many years later, with the invasion and occupation of Czechoslovakia – completed its domination. The 'supreme aim' took a specific form in Stalin's policy, the search for a durable compromise with American imperialism which would allow joint control of the world.

The war against the Axis powers took on a progressive and liberating content from the moment at which it began to lead to the destruction of the Fascist regime and of the form of national oppression which Nazi and Japanese imperialism had established in a series of countries and was trying to spread to others. The war tended to turn into a revolutionary war once the movement of the struggle against Fascism led to a conflict with the ruling classes which had used Fascism to maintain their domination, once the war brought into action the proletarian classes or they acquired arms and a consciousness of their power. But Stalin's policy, and still less that of Roosevelt and Churchill, was not the faithful expression of this content. If Roosevelt and Churchill, in spite of their declarations and promises about the freedom and independence of peoples, pursued essentially imperialist aims (and Roosevelt's more liberal position did not neutralize the imperialist essence of American policy), Stalin, with his similar promises and declarations, was pursuing the aims of the bureaucratic class which had replaced the revolutionary October proletariat in the leadership of the Soviet state. The new autocrat of all the Russias and the conservative bureaucracy whose symbol he was could not carry the revolution to other peoples after castrating it in their own country; they could not encourage in other countries the freedom and democracy they denied to the workers of the USSR. Stalin's foreign policy could be no more than the reflection of his domestic policy. The Soviet armies, like those of the Allies, performed a liberating function in so far as they destroyed the Fascist regimes and crushed Nazi imperialism, but at the same time they established a new form of oppression. The British and Americans brought with them support for capitalism, the establishment or the claim to establish their world dominion and the continuation of colonialism under different forms. The Soviet armies brought with them the establishment of a new social order, a copy of the Stalinist model, in which the abolition of capitalist private property did not mean the taking over of the means of production by the workers themselves, but their exploitation by a new privileged social group, whose bureaucratic domination was based on ideological mystification, the abolition of political liberties and the most enormous police apparatus in history. The Soviet armies also carried among their equipment Great-Russian nationalism's plans for domination and expansion. The time had come which confirmed Lenin's fear of the reappearance of Great-Russian nationalism under the banner of October.

The great mystification

Of course, while the liberating and anti-Fascist aims of the war could be openly proclaimed, the 'other' aims of the British and American capitalists and the Stalinist bureaucracy had to be carefully concealed. In the art, old as history, of disguising the most dishonourable actions under the noblest ideals, each of the three leaders drew on his own experience, and Stalin's was as rich as that of his eminent colleagues. They immediately found a 'common language'. The inevitable differences which arose between them had nothing to do with principles; all three always agreed in praising them at the very moment that they were trampling them underfoot. The differences stemmed from their very natural inclination to get the greatest advantage from the new division of the world. Of course, immediately one of the three felt himself injured he would brandish the sacred principles fiercely and accuse the others of wanting to infringe them. But when they reached agreements satisfactory to all three parties, each of them bore witness with all the weight of his prestige to the noble intentions of his colleagues.

In this respect Stalin's role was by far the most important. His enormous credit among the masses of workers throughout the world as the symbol of socialism and the October revolution rendered an invaluable service to the representatives of imperialism during the second great global crisis of the capitalist system. During the first, Wilson, Clemenceau and Lloyd George did not have such luck. Stalin's public interventions during the war and the accounts given by Soviet propaganda about the relations and agreements between the three great powers made a large contribution to the fostering in millions of human beings of illusions about the democratic and liberating intentions of the capitalist and imperialist allies of the USSR. The propaganda of the Communist parties, with rare exceptions, had the same effect, and the same can be said of their policy of alliances. This deception of the peoples was the necessary condition which enabled the great demarcation of 'spheres of influence' between British and American capitalism and the Soviet bureaucracy, the bartering of economic, political and strategic interests to be carried out with the maximum of docility on the part of the victims.

When, in his report to the founding meeting of the Cominform in 1947, Zhdanov announced that the world had split into two camps, and described the Allies of yesterday as 'rapacious imperialists', he could not avoid giving some explanation for such a radical change. Only the day before, as it were, Stalin had still been expressing his confidence in a world-wide understanding with the other super-power. (In December 1946 he described a wide-ranging agreement between the USA and the USSR as 'perfectly feasible'.)[19] The division of the world into two blocs and the transformation of the Allies whom five years of Soviet and Communist propaganda had presented as collaborators in building a new, just, democratic and peaceful world into rapacious imperialists or agents of American imperialism (in the case of the Social Democrats or the European bourgeois parties) could not have come about by magic in the summer of 1947. The division and the transformation must have had a history. Stalin's spokesmen now therefore found themselves obliged to produce a new version of the period of the 'grand alliance'. It was equally mystifying, but revealed a little of what previously had been carefully concealed. Now the true aims of the imperialist powers allied to the USSR were revealed, but the objectives pursued by Stalinist policy continued to be concealed.

The declaration adopted by the nine parties said, in effect, that during the war 'there had existed in the camp of the anti-Hitler coalition a difference about the aims of the war and the definition of the tasks involved in the organization of the world after the war'. While the Soviet Union intended to guarantee democracy, national independence and peace for all peoples, and was guided by the purest respects for the principle of the self-determination of peoples, the aims of the United States and Great Britain were 'the elimination of competitors [Germany and Japan] from markets and the establishment of their own domination'. These powers intended to 'strengthen imperialism and throttle democracy'.[20]

This 1947 account contradicted the version current during the war. Then Stalin insisted that there was a fundamental identity between the aims of the three great powers. In November 1944, when the defeat of Germany was within sight and the problems of 'the organization of the world' became immediate, Stalin formulated the following thesis, which was to be the pivot of the whole strategy of the Soviet government and the Communist parties in this crucial period: 'The alliance between the USSR, Great Britain and the United States of America is founded not on casual, transitory considerations, but on vital and lasting interests.'[21]

If the aims of the two western powers during the war were those defined in the Cominform declaration – and there can be no doubt about that – Stalin's 1944 thesis was false, unless the 'vital and lasting interests' of the USSR were understood in the Kremlin to mean very different things from those proclaimed during the war and repeated in the Cominform declaration.

An alternative to this hypothesis is the possibility that Stalin had made a serious mistake in 1944–5 about the real interests and aims of the imperialist powers. But Stalin's Marxism was not that rudimentary. As we shall see later when we examine the actual situation in which this statement was made, Stalin was expressing a reality; the secret agreements between the 'Big Three' had gone a long way. The grand strategist's mistake was to believe that these agreements provided a solid basis for the alliance between the ruling bureaucracy of the USSR and Anglo-American capitalism, and in particular for the alliance with the American super-power.

Once the international situation in 1947 had been explained as the result of the contradictions between the pure intentions of Moscow and the evil intentions of London and Washington, the Cominform meeting was faced with the task of also explaining why the baddies had been able, with such remarkable speed, to consolidate the old bourgeois forces, the very forces which had led to war and, in one way or another, encouraged Fascism in Western Europe. The explanation had to cover the smooth dismissal of Communist ministers from governments in Paris, Rome and Brussels, the ability of the imperialist powers to undertake new colonial wars, to show, in other words, why the forces of capitalism throughout the world, under the leadership of American imperialism, were in a position, two years after the great victory over Fascism, to go over to the offensive against the forces of the working class and democracy. According to Zhdanov, the results of the Second World War constituted 'an abrupt change in the relation of forces between the two systems – the capitalist and the socialist – to the advantage of socialism ...; the world capitalist system has suffered another sharp blow ... the prestige and influence of the working class have increased incomparably among the people ... the Communist parties have been considerably strengthened'.[22] But if this was the situation, why had the Communist ministers been removed, and not the bourgeois ministers? Why was it the world-wide forces of capitalism, and not the revolutionary forces, which had taken the initiative in extending the results of the anti-Fascist victory?

As we have seen, the way out of this awkward situation which was taken at the secret part of the Cominform meeting was to use the French and Italian Communist Parties as scapegoats. In the published documents, however, apart from some very discreet allusions by Longo and Duclos to the presence of the Allied armies as preventing their parties from going further, an answer to the question why the high tide of the working-class and democratic movement gave way so quickly and so easily to the counter-offensive of the bourgeois and imperialist forces, the crucial problem, was more or less ignored. Nevertheless, Zhdanov's report and the statement adopted by the meeting refer to one fact of major importance. Zhdanov said that during the war the Anglo-American imperialists 'did not dare to intervene openly against the Soviet Union and the democratic forces because they fully realized that the sympathies of the popular masses throughout the world were totally on their side; but in the months immediately before the end of the war the situation was already beginning to change'. And the statement, referring to the post-war period, says that, in order to achieve their aims, the imperialist forces 'adopted a mask of liberalism and peace in order to deceive and ensnare men without political experience'.[23] But in noting this fact – without which the course of events between 1945 and 1947 would certainly be inexplicable – the Cominform documents completely avoid the question which immediately comes to mind: what was done by the Soviet leaders, who enjoyed the full support of 'the popular masses throughout the world', the 'considerably strengthened' Communist parties and the working class, with its 'incomparably increased' prestige and influence, to prevent the imperialist forces from making their cunning plans for revenge? What did they do to stop reaction from putting on the mask of liberty, democracy and peace, and being able to deceive a sufficiently large proportion of the masses to enable it to recover and go over to the offensive when the defeat of Fascism was barely achieved? If it had been possible to quote some remark of Stalin's, one of his instructions, from the period of the 'grand alliance', which had attempted to warn the peoples of the true aims of the allied imperialist powers, if there had been the slightest hint of this in the policy followed by the Communist movement in agreement with the Stalinist line, it would obviously have been emphasized in the documents of the founding meeting of the Cominform and in the years that followed as irrefutable proof that Stalin and the Communist movement had foreseen the course of events and done all they could to check the plans of imperialism. But it was utterly impossible to find any such sources.

There can be no doubt that the 'mask' was very important. By presenting themselves as the defenders of democracy and enemies of Fascism, the supporters of the independence of peoples and of a just peace, the bourgeois and imperialist forces did indeed succeed in deceiving 'men without political experience', and many who regarded themselves as experienced. During the great world crisis, under the impact of the horrors of war and the crimes of Nazism, millions of men 'without political experience' became active in the hope of creating a new social system without wars and without oppression. In them the Communist parties possessed a revolutionary potential without precedent in history, provided that they could raise their level of political consciousness during the course of the war, help them to understand the reality of society and politics and show them in time the forces which, behind the famous 'mask', were pursuing goals very different from those of popular aspirations. This however would have made no sense unless the strategy of the Communist movement had, from the very first day of the war, taken as its main objective to give a revolutionary outcome to the second general crisis of the capitalist system.

In such a strategy the decisive factor could only be the strength of the popular masses, their political consciousness and their organization. In this strategy the whole activity of the Communist parties and the Soviet state would have had to be devoted to bringing this factor into play. This indispensable exploitation of inter-imperialist contradictions, or of contradictions within each country between the Fascist forces and the 'democratic' bourgeoisie, would have had to be seen as accessory to the development and constant reinforcement of the proletarian and popular forces. But Stalin's strategy, the strategy of the Soviet bureaucracy, to which the policy of the Communist movement subordinated itself, was completely the opposite. It was based, as we have said, on giving absolute priority to the exploitation of inter-imperialist contradictions and on the subordination of the actions of the popular forces to the requirements of that priority. During the period of tacit alliance with Hitler's Germany this strategy was reflected in a limitation of the struggle against Fascism and the abandonment of the standard of democracy, anti-Fascism and national independence to the bourgeois and imperialist enemies of Germany. During the period of alliance with the anti-Nazi powers it was reflected in a limitation on the action of the popular masses, in order to contain it within limits acceptable to these powers. This attitude necessarily entailed concealing from the masses the true aims of Anglo-American imperialism and tacit collaboration with it to deceive the peoples.

But this was not all. The fundamental aim of the Soviet leaders – the division of the world into 'spheres of influence' and the consolidation of the division through a compromise with the Washington government – required something more than concealing from the peoples the true aims pursued by the imperialist powers; it required endorsing the credibility of their apparent aims, since this was the only way in which the apparent aims of the U S S R itself could be made credible. In other words, this was the only way of justifying the identity of the 'vital and permanent interests' of the three great powers. Since the fact that the U S S R was beginning to employ imperialist methods had to be concealed at all costs, if the myth which sheltered the Stalinist bureaucracy was not to collapse, it was also necessary to pretend that these methods had been abandoned by the United States and Great Britain.

Earl Browder's theories, which were put forward immediately after the Teheran Conference, were only a clear and extreme formulation of what Soviet and Communist propaganda was saying hardly more discreetly at the same time. The common background shared by Browder's position of January 1944 and the views of more important Communist leaders is clear: 'Capitalism and Communism have begun to march together towards the peaceful society of tomorrow' (Browder); 'Our meeting here in the Crimea has reaffirmed our common determination to maintain and strengthen, in the peace to come, that unity of purpose and of action which has made victory possible and certain for the United

Nations in this war' (the Yalta declaration signed by Stalin in February 1945); 'The democratic great powers must guide the reorganization of the whole world in such a way as to guarantee peace and justice to all' (resolution of the Fifth Congress of the Italian Communist Party, January 1946).

It is a significant detail that not until a year after they had been uttered were Browder's extreme expressions (especially concerning the abolition of the 'instrument', the party – this was his mortal sin) condemned by Stalin, through Duclos. And it is even more significant that the condemnation was made shortly after Roosevelt, a few days before his death, had threatened Stalin with a deterioration in relations between their two countries if the Soviet leader did not moderate his demands with regard to the Polish government.[24]

The setting-up of 'spheres of influence'

Discussion still continues about whether the division of the world into 'spheres of influence' took place at Yalta or at previous negotiations between the 'Big Three', or whether it was the result of a *de facto* situation created by military operations and crystallized during the 'cold war'. (The fact itself is denied only in official Soviet versions, in the face of a whole series of documents which Moscow was obliged to make public as a result of their publication by the Western powers – correspondence between Stalin, Churchill and Roosevelt, records of the Teheran and Yalta Conferences, etc. – which amply prove its reality.)[25] In my opinion the abundant information available on this period supports the conclusion that the famous 'division' took place gradually, through a series of actions and decisions spread over the period from the beginning of the war to the break in 1947. During the 'cold war' the situation in Europe took on the stability which still characterizes it. (The situation was quite different in the third world, where the plans of the 'three' collapsed, mostly in the face of the assaults of the national revolutionary movement.) The division was a policy, implemented by means of military operations and diplomatic negotiations, the activities of parties and secret services. As far as the Soviet Union is concerned, the beginning of this policy can be precisely dated: it begins with the secret clauses of the German–Soviet pact. After the Nazi attack on the USSR the problem of 'areas of influence' was immediately raised in the nego-tiations between the 'Big Three', and was equally quickly accompanied by mystification about the real aims of the three powers spread by propaganda.

When Nazi Germany attacked the USSR and so removed the check placed on the activities of the Communist parties and popular masses by the German–Soviet pact, Roosevelt and Churchill realized the political urgency of competing with Stalin, who had announced in his speech on 3 July, 'Our war for the defence of our fatherland will merge with the struggle of the peoples of Europe and America for their independence and for democratic freedoms.' ('America' here means the United States.) In the declaration of principles known as the Atlantic Charter, issued on 14 August 1941, the leader of the largest colonial empire and the leader of the largest capitalist power solemnly proclaimed that

... their countries seek no aggrandizement, territorial or other;
... they desire to see no territorial changes that do not accord with the freely expressed wishes of the peoples concerned.
... they respect the right of all peoples to choose the form of government under which they will live; and they wish to see sovereign rights and self-government restored to those who have been forcibly deprived of them.
... they will endeavour with due respect to their existing obligations, to further the enjoyment by all states, great or small, victor or vanquished, of access, on equal terms, to the trade and to the raw materials of the world which are needed for their economic prosperity,

and promised 'a peace ... which will afford security that all the men in all the lands may live out their lives in freedom from fear and want'.

'The democratic emblem of the Atlantic Charter,' the very Stalinist Soviet historian Deborin was to write years later, 'was intended to con-ceal the true imperialist aims of the North American and British govern-ing circles.'[26] This was perfectly clear to Stalin and the Deborins from 14 August 1941, but did not prevent the Soviet government from pub-lishing, on 24 September, a declaration of adherence to the Atlantic Charter. Even if it is admitted that this gesture was necessary to obtain assistance from the United States, and that the time was not right to

397

reveal the real aims of imperialism, the Soviet government could very well have suggested in the friendlest way to its new allies that, simply to collect the greatest number of allies against the common enemy, they should grant, or at least promise, national independence to the colonies. This would have been all the easier since it was the direction in which Roosevelt's policy was moving, not, obviously, from anti-imperialist feeling, but to facilitate the penetration of North American capitalism into the colonial world, which had hitherto been a European reserve. But the Soviet government did not take this opportunity of putting to the test, even discreetly, in the eyes of the peoples of the world, the 'democratic emblem' of the Anglo-Saxon imperialists. The Stalin–Eden interviews of December 1941 enable us to understand why.

With no attempt at concealment – no doubt regarding this distinguished representative of British imperialism as an ideal partner in discussions about a share-out – Stalin explained his first ideas for changes in the map of Europe. East Prussia would have to be taken away from Germany – in order to compensate Poland for the territories which Russia had annexed – and also the Rhineland and perhaps Bavaria. Independence could be given to Austria, and the Sudetenland restored to Czechoslovakia. The 'area of influence' acquired by Italian Fascism should be divided between Yugoslavia, Greece and Turkey (from which Stalin hoped to obtain bases in the Dardanelles), and should France not re-emerge as a great power Great Britain might well keep bases at Boulogne and Dunkirk, as well as in Belgium, the Netherlands, Norway and Denmark. In return for this gracious concession to His Majesty's Government, Stalin asked for only one thing – which he made the essential condition for the signature of the treaty of Anglo-Soviet alliance proposed by Eden: Great Britain was to recognize immediately the Soviet frontiers as they had been established by the division of 'areas of influence' between Stalin and Hitler under the secret clauses of the 1939 pact. The Anglo-Soviet treaty of alliance, Stalin explained could consist of two public parts, one dealing with the military alliance during the war and the other with the setlement of European problems after the victory. There should also be added to these two public documents a secret protocol recording Great Britain's recognition of the Soviet frontiers of 1941. Eden opposed these suggestions, and invoked the Atlantic Charter. Stalin replied, 'I thought that the Atlantic Charter was directed against those people who were trying to establish world dominion. It now looks as if the Charter were directed against the USSR.'[27]

Commenting on this edifying scene in his *History of the Cold War*, André Fontaine remarks that Eden could have reminded Stalin of the first decisions of the Soviet power, repudiating secret diplomacy and publishing the secret treaties negotiated by the Tsars. Eden, of course, was not so indiscreet. He could only welcome Soviet diplomacy's unambiguous return to the time-honoured methods of which Tsarism was a past master, as Marx noted more than once. It was the first essential for an understanding. Stalin's interpretation of the Atlantic Charter was in fact in perfect accord with the views of its authors. It was directed solely against new aspirants to world dominion, but not against the oppression of peoples by British colonialism or American imperialism, or against the subjection of the peoples of the former Tsarist empire to Great-Russian nationalism. Eden's use of it was not more than a polemical feint, and Stalin's severe reprimand was perfectly understood by the English minister, who was completely unconcerned at the fact that the peoples of Finnish Carelia, the Baltic states, the eastern territories of Poland, Bessarabia and Bukovina were not to be free to choose their destiny. His only concern was to safeguard the traditional interests of British imperialism in Eastern Europe.

As has been seen, the negotiations on the sharing-out of 'areas of influence' between the 'Big Three' began on the first day of the 'grand alliance' and were carried out in careful synchronization with the public activities designed to camouflage them and deceive the peoples. Shortly after the conversations between Eden and Stalin the United Nations declaration was published (1 January 1942), which ratified the Atlantic Charter and carried, as well as the signatures of Great Britain, the United States and the USSR, those of other countries whose names alone are eloquent proof of the fidelity of the first two signatories to the principles proclaimed in the document: India, Panama, Haiti, Cuba, the Dominican Republic, etc. We shall not follow all the twists and falterings of the secret negotiation on the one hand and the public mystification on the other, with its close connections with the policies imposed by

Moscow on the Communist movement. We shall limit ourselves to pointing out some of its more important episodes.

In May 1942 the Anglo-Soviet treaty of alliance, for a period of twenty years, was signed. It did not include recognition by Great Britain of the Soviet frontiers of 1941, but this did not mean that the Russians had abandoned their demands. They had simply been postponed. The difficult military situation is the likely explanation of this apparent and temporary concession on Stalin's part. His real concession was in another area, as can be seen from the policy of the Communist Party of India.

On the outbreak of war between Great Britain and Germany, Gandhi and the Congress Party had taken up a position which is summed up in the following statement: 'India cannot regard herself as involved in a war said to be for democratic freedoms, when she herself is deprived of freedom.' They stuck firmly to this position, even after Russia entered the war. They took advantage of the position of British imperialism to intensify the struggle for national independence. While the National bourgeoisie adopted this 'Leninist' tactic, the Indian Communist Party adopted a Social Democratic tactic: it declared in favour of support for British imperialism against its German rival. During the summer of 1942 the colonial authorities began a policy of brutal repression against the national movement. They arrested Gandhi and all the members of the executive of the Congress Party and banned all the party's activity. At the same time they legalized the Communist Party, which had operated illegally since 1934.[28]

In the same month of May 1942 there took place the interview between Molotov and de Gaulle which has already been mentioned.[29] In return for the General's support, as well as that of the British and Americans, for the Soviet demand for the opening of a second front, the Soviet minister offered Moscow's good offices to persuade the resistance and the French colonies to recognize the General's authority. This was followed shortly afterwards by the beginning of the French Communist Party's policy – examined above – of submission to de Gaulle and defence of the French Union.

Throughout this year the Soviet government supported the Yugoslav instruments of British imperialism, the royal government in exile in

London and Mihailović's Chetniks. It brought strong pressure to bear on Tito's partisan forces to make them abandon their revolutionary policy and take their stand, like the French and Italians, on 'national unity'.

In January 1943, when the victory at Stalingrad had produced a sharp improvement in the military situation, Stalin renewed his pressure on the question of the 1941 frontiers. In March the Americans and the British agreed to make concessions on Carelia, Bessarabia and Bukovina, but maintained the opposition with Eden. Roosevelt said that they might have to give way on everything, but in return for Russian concessions.[30] One of these was spelt out publicly by the North American Press and officials. Stalin was to give more specific and more reliable guarantees of having finally given up any idea of 'fomenting world revolution'.

The highly authoritative *New York Times* recognized on 20 November 1942 that the Soviet leader had already made noticeable progress in this direction: 'Stalin's slogans . . . are not Marxist slogans urging the proletarians of the world to unite, but slogans about patriotism, liberty and the fatherland.' This, however, was not enough, and stirring up fears of the reversal of alliances, the *New York Times* wrote that Hitler's Germany might be able to persuade a number of countries of the need to join it in a crusade against the USSR if there continued to exist a 'Communist International inspired by the Trotskyite ideology of world proletarian revolution'.

On 9 March 1943 Vice-President Wallace, rightly regarded as one of the strongest supporters of cooperation with the USSR, said, 'War would be inevitable if Russia again adopted the Trotskyist idea of fomenting world revolution.'[31]

As we have seen, these requests were heard, and there is no need to repeat the analysis of the dissolution of the Comintern presented in the first volume of this book. That dissolution symbolized the abandonment, not of the 'Trotskyist' idea of world revolution (this way of putting it was simply a piece of cunning on the part of the Americans to make things easier for the man to whom the message was addressed), but of any idea of bringing the terrible crisis through which the capitalist system was passing to a revolutionary conclusion. None of the necessary conditions for such a conclusion, however, was known in advance; they depended to a great extent, though not completely, on the direction taken by the advanced forces while the war was still going on. The direction indicated by the Comintern's last words meant a limitation in advance of the aims of the proletariat and the masses, their reduction to what was compatible with the 'permanent and vital interests' of the three great powers. The specific, practical definition of what was admissible exactly followed the course of the secret agreements between the 'Three', without giving the peoples the slightest chance of giving their opinion. To put it more precisely, the bourgeois classes of Great Britain and the United States (and through them those of a number of European countries occupied by the Nazis) possessed considerable opportunities of influencing the decisions of the two Western leaders, while the proletarian classes of Europe, and even more the colonial peoples, had no means of influencing the decisions of the one man who was the supreme representative of their interests. The only chance would have been for the Communist parties to adopt an independent revolutionary policy, but the leaders of these parties had long ago become unquestioning vassals of the Kremlin. The exception of Tito merely confirms the rule. As a result of this it was possible for the masses, including the Communist masses, to be ideologically and politically conditioned throughout the course of the war to the spirit of the 'grand alliance' and 'national unity', to class collaboration in the capitalist countries and to collaboration between the oppressed peoples of the colonies and the capitalist metropolitan states.

Writing in 1936 about the Franco–Soviet pact of 1935, and drawing on Lenin, Trotsky said,

However one may judge the advantages or disadvantages of the Franco–Soviet pact, still, no serious revolutionary statesman would deny the right of the Soviet state to seek supplementary supports for its inviolability in temporary agreements with this or that imperialism. It is only necessary clearly and openly to show the masses the place of these partial and tactical agreements in the general system of historical forces. In order to make use particularly of the antagonism between France and Germany, there is not the slightest need of idealizing the bourgeois ally, or that combination of imperialists which temporarily hides behind the screen of the League of Nations. Not only Soviet diplomacy, however, but in its steps the Communist International systematically paints up the episodical allies of Moscow as 'friends of peace', deceives the workers with slogans like 'collective security' and 'disarmament', and thus becomes in reality a political agent of the imperialists among the working classes.[32]

If he had not been assassinated, Trotsky could have seen that the 'idealization' of the thirties was no more than a timid venture, almost a childish lie, compared with the 'idealization' of the forties. The same scale could be applied to the deception of the masses. The 'grand alliance', the imperialist combination camouflaged as the 'United Nations', the alliance with the European bourgeoisies, became the panacea, capable not only of solving the great immediate problem of defeating the Axis powers, but also of establishing the new peace, democracy, national independence, social justice, concepts which – as befits idealizations – were flourished in their most abstract forms, empty of any class content.

The big American newspapers were quick to welcome the dissolution of the Comintern, seeing in this event 'a diplomatic victory of wider importance than the victories of Stalingrad and Cap Bon'. 'The world can breathe again,' said the leader writers. 'Trotsky's old folly has been abandoned. Marx's dream is over.' The *Chicago Tribune* wrote, 'Stalin has buried the dervishes of the Marxist creed. He has executed the Bolsheviks whose kingdom was of this world and who wanted universal revolution.' And the *New York Times,* acting as spokesman for the American government, called for this great decision to be followed by specific measures, the abandonment by Moscow of the Polish patriots, recognition by the Yugoslav partisans of the émigré government in London and participation of the French Communists in 'real unification'.[33] The first demand was wasted breath, because Stalin was not prepared for any substantial concession on the 'Polish question'. In the case of the Yugoslavs, the Western demands were satisfied only in appearance, although in this the fault was not Stalin's but Tito's. On the other hand, the participation of the French (and Italian) Communists in 'real unification' fulfilled the most secret desires of the great American paper and its advisers.

Once the train of history had lost its engine (as Marx had called revolution), it was open to the 'Three' to go on peacefully with the work of translating their 'permanent and vital interests' into specific decisions – at least in so far as such an ambitious operation was within the control of the 'great conductor'.

The first milestone on this new stretch was the conference of the Foreign Ministers of the USSR, Great Britain and the USA (with the representative of Chiang Kai-shek in a walk-on role), which was held in Moscow in October 1943. The communiqué issued at the end of this conference stressed that only maintaining the 'closest collaboration and cooperation' between the three great powers would make it possible, once hostilities had ceased, 'to preserve peace and stimulate to the full the political, economic and social wellbeing of the peoples'.

Among other measures, the conference prescribed the new political system which was to be established in Italy after the fall of Mussolini and the declaration of war on the Axis powers to be made by the Badoglio government. This was an excellent opportunity for the 'Big Three' to show how they understood the application of the principles set out in the Atlantic Charter and accepted by the USSR. They agreed to grant the people of Italy the right to 'the final choice of its own form of government', once the war was over. Until then real power, in all fields, and not just those concerned with the conduct of military operations, would remain with the allied military authorities. During this time – which the Allies expected to be long and which in fact lasted two years – the people of Italy would retain the right to the final choice of the government of its liking, while the allied authorities exercised the right to create political structures which would condition the Italian people to their liking, to avoid the possibility of surprises when that people was finally allowed to exercise its right.

The first specific measure designed to ensure this political development was the decision to keep Badoglio as leader of the government, against the wishes of the main anti-Fascist forces. We have already seen how the prestige and political skill of Togliatti contributed decisively to the subjection of the Italian Communists and the whole Italian left to the plan of the 'Big Three' and made them follow the path of 'real unification' urged by the *New York Times* (the *Times* only mentioned

the French Communists because its editorial was written on the eve of
Mussolini's fall.)

The Soviet position on the 'Italian question', together with its position on the 'French question' (support for de Gaulle and the subordination of the French Communist Party to his leadership) confirmed
Stalin's choice in the share-out of 'areas of influence', which was already
partly visible in his conversations with Eden and which can be summed
up as concessions (diplomatic and political) in the West to keep the East.
Indeed, in a strategy based on a 'share-out', there was no other choice,
because the instrument of the strategy was the movement of armies, not
the action of the masses of the people. If Stalin's strategy had included
the revolutionary struggle in Europe as a primary factor, the situation
created in Italy by the fall of Fascism would have provided it with an
excellent opportunity. The wave of strikes which had shaken northern
Italy in the spring of 1943, and the formidable mass movement of the
summer, showed clearly that the crisis of Italian society was ready to
turn into a revolutionary crisis, and this was confirmed in the following
months by the exceptionally rapid development of the partisan movement under the predominant influence of the Communists, Socialists
and members of the Action Party, and the impressive general strike by a
million workers in the occupied zone.[34]

The only point of real convergence between the Allies and the Italian
bourgeoisie on the one hand and the Italian workers on the other was the
struggle against Hitler's Germany, which could either help to strengthen
the revolutionary content of the crisis, as in Yugoslavia, or, on the contrary, to dilute it. This depended, basically, on the direction taken by the
advanced forces in Italian society, but the position of the Soviet Union
enabled it to exercise considerable influence. Even while keeping strictly
within the bounds of the United Nations declaration of principles, and by
invoking the need to develop to the full the war effort against Germany,
Stalin could have demanded, not only in secret negotiations, but publicly, immediate recognition of the full and unfettered sovereignty of a
people which had given such a magnificent example in the struggle
against the common enemy, the recognition of its right to choose immediately, in the liberated area and more generally as this area
expanded, democratically elected organs of government, chosen by the

unrestricted use of its democratic liberties. 'Only in this way,' Stalin might have said, 'only if the Italian people knows itself to be in control of its own future, will its morale in the fighting, the development of its energies and initiative, reach their highest level and make their maximum contribution to the operations of the allied armies. This approach to the Italian people will demonstrate to the other peoples of Europe the genuineness of the intentions proclaimed by the three great powers and encourage them to take the same course. We will be able to tell the German people that if they do with Hitler what the Italian people have done with Mussolini, the three great powers will immediately recognize the independence and sovereignty of the new democratic Germany.' Such a position would have won the Soviet Union the sympathy and support of the genuinely democratic and patriotic forces in Italy, and would have above all helped to demystify the policy of London and Washington. Such an attitude would have had the same effect on other European peoples. But in the 'Italian question' Stalin played the Allies' game and the PCI played Stalin's.

In this case, as in the case of his attitude towards de Gaulle, or that of his abolition of the Comintern, Stalin's principal justification, repeated with a number of variants by the official Soviet historians and taken up like an echo by the Western Communist leaders as a simultaneous justification of their own policy, was that in order to make sure of victory over Germany it was necessary at all costs to avoid a reversal of alliances. Since this justification concerns the whole of Stalin's policy up to the end of the war, we shall not analyse it until we have completed the catalogue of concessions made by Stalin to the reactionary and imperialist aims of his two big allies.

Once the foreign ministers had cleared the ground, the 'Big Three' could meet in person, in Teheran at the end of 1943. Part of the joint communiqué read:

With our diplomatic advisers we have surveyed the problems of the future. We shall seek the cooperation and the active participation of all nations, large and small, whose peoples in heart and mind are dedicated, as are our own peoples, to the elimination of tyranny and slavery, op-

pression and intolerance. We will welcome them as they may choose to
come into a world family of democratic nations.

Since this solemn promise, no less than the creation of a peaceful and
democratic world family from which tyranny and slavery, oppression and
intolerance would be finally banished, appeared over the signature of
Stalin, why should the workers of Europe and the world have any doubts
about the sincerity of Roosevelt and Churchill? The policy of 'national
unity' in the framework of the 'grand alliance' carried out by the Communists of France and Italy, received a solid foundation. Since, once
Germany was defeated, there would be a general democratic and peaceful solution, the main thing was to concentrate and unite the efforts of all
those who had an interest – of whatever sort – in winning the war. What
reason was there in Italy to oppose the carrying-out of this unification
and concentration under the supreme command of allied headquarters?
If, after the war, the people wanted socialism, all it would have to do
would be to vote accordingly, peacefully and democratically. The
interests which were opposed to it would give way before this popular
will. This, at least, was what the 'Big Three' promised, and what recalcitrant bourgeois could resist their all-powerful will?

At the same time as they were publicly reaffirming their generous
objects before the world, the 'Three' secretly continued, at the Teheran
Conference, the laborious task of giving them detailed practical form. In
a concession to Stalin, Churchill and Roosevelt accepted the Curzon
Line as the frontier between Poland and the USSR; in return Poland
would be given the German territories as far as the Oder. Stalin accepted, but indicated to his partners that he would be very glad to keep
Königsberg and its surroundings for himself. Churchill saw nothing
against this: the Poles would be very pleased to get the rich industrial
areas of Silesia in return for the Pripet marshes. Churchill and Roosevelt agreed that it was quite reasonable and natural for the Russians
to want access to warm waters, and Roosevelt in particular indicated
to Stalin that he would be able to recover Port Arthur and Dairen,
which had been taken from the Tsars by the Japanese during the
Russo-Japanese war and before that from China by the Tsars. On the
question of the Finnish territories occupied by the USSR, Stalin refused

to give them up. Churchill had the impertinence to remind him that in 1917 the Soviets had declared themselves in favour of a peace with 'no annexations and no indemnities'. Stalin's reply, made 'with a broad grin', was: 'I have told you I am becoming a Conservative.'[35] With regard to Germany, the 'Three' were agreed that the country should be split up. The discussion centred on the way this should be done. The main problem discussed at Teheran, however, was that of the second front. At first sight this appeared to be a purely military question, but in fact this was an essential aspect of the share-out of 'areas of influence'.

Differences over the opening of a second front had arisen between the Americans and the British. The Americans were in favour of opening it in France, since, according to the Soviet historian Deborin, they wanted to establish United States influence in Western Europe and weaken the British position. The British proposed the opening of the front in the Balkans because, again according to the same historian, they were trying to safeguard their interests in this area and to prevent a 'Soviet incursion'. Churchill insisted on his Balkan plan at the Teheran Conference, 'but the USSR delegation demonstrated that this plan had nothing to do with the task of defeating the Germans as quickly as possible, and had in reality other aims'.[36] In fact, as emerges from the more detailed account given by Deborin himself and is confirmed by the available records of the Teheran Conference, the Soviet delegation did not make the slightest reference to any 'other aims' of the British, but limited itself to discussing the problem merely from the point of view of military effectiveness. These were the terms in which it argued in favour of the opening of the second front in France, and gained the full support of the Americans. In both cases Stalin was acting on a fundamental political choice, which he hoped would enable him to achieve two aims at once, to win freedom of action in Eastern Europe and 'contribute' to deepening the contradiction which, he held, would create serious divisions between the imperialist powers after the defeat of Germany and Japan, the contradiction between the old European colonialist states, seriously weakened by the war, and the American super-power which aspired to replace them in exploiting the world.

Among the main concessions made by Stalin to his allies in the West in order to have his hands free in the East, a particularly sinister one concerns Spain. During the Second World War Churchill and Roosevelt consistently maintained the policy towards Spain which they had followed between 1936 and 1939. The letter Roosevelt wrote on 8 November 1942 to Franco, at the moment of the allied landings in North Africa, in which he described himself as 'your sincere friend' and 'assured him that he had nothing to fear from the United States', was not a simple tactical manoeuvre; it was the expression of a fixed policy. The same is true of Churchill's cynical statement to the Commons on 24 May 1944, according to which the internal affairs of Spain were a matter for Spaniards alone.

From the first day of the anti-Hitler coalition, Stalin acquiesced in the Spanish policy of Roosevelt and Churchill. The Soviet statement of 24 September 1941, approving the principles of the Atlantic Charter, has no mention of Spain, nor is there any such mention in any of the Soviet war documents or any of Stalin's public statements. The same silence will be found in the record of the negotiations between the 'Three', from the Stalin–Eden meeting at the end of 1941, when Stalin began his attempt to reform the map of Europe, through Teheran and the different Foreign Ministers' meetings, to Yalta: Franco's Fascist dictatorship remained untouchable.

And yet there were few European matters in which Stalin had such solid political motives for taking up a clear and firm position as the problem of Francoism. Not only because the Spanish people, in their three-year struggle, had been the first to resist the Axis powers; not only because Francoism was the product of the armed intervention of these powers; but for the simple reason that Franco was at war with the Soviet Union: the 'Blue Division' was part of the force which had invaded Soviet territory. Moreover, a declaration of war by the Soviet Union on Franco's Spain and an insistence that the Republican government-in-exile should be recognized as the only legal government, in the same way as the other governments-in-exile from countries occupied by the Nazis, were both actions which would have found support amongst the great majority of the public within the anti-Hitler coalition, including Great Britain and the United States.

But Stalin did not make the slightest effort to help the Spanish Republic during the war. He made not the slightest attempt to ensure that the victory over Fascism would also benefit one of the peoples which had shed the most blood for it. The maintenance in power of the Fascist dictatorship in Spain after the Second World War is one of the clearest results of Stalin's policy of sharing out 'areas of influence'. Nor is the derisory decision, made at Potsdam on a Soviet initiative, to exclude the Franco regime from the United Nations enough to absolve the Kremlin before history of its heavy responsibility for the fact that the regime was able to survive the disaster of the Axis.

But let us return to the question of the second front. Stalin had demanded its opening constantly since June 1941, presenting it as the essential condition for victory over Germany. So essential did he regard it that the practical, immediate object of the abolition of the Comintern, as was noted in the first volume (Chapter 1) was to smooth the path to agreement on the opening of this second front. And Stalin's concessions to allied policy in regard to Italy, France and Spain were also directed to this end, though the concessions also concealed, as we have seen, a plan with wider implications. In his 'order of the day' for 1 May 1944 Stalin reaffirmed strongly that the defeat of Germany was only possible if a second front were opened in Western Europe. After the Normandy landings he was constant in his praise for the 'precision' with which 'the decision of the Teheran Conference on joint actions against Germany' had been carried out. 'The brilliant realization of that decision,' said Stalin, is 'one of the striking indications of the consolidation of the front of the anti-Hitler coalition'.[37]

Following the Kremlin's lead, the Communist parties had carried on for three years a violent campaign for the opening of a second front, and it is therefore hardly surprising that at the moment of the landings the Communist press should have greeted the event as 'the fulfilment of what all mankind has daily been eagerly asking and hoping for'.[38] From 1947 on onwards, once the 'grand alliance' had collapsed and under the pressure of the demands of the new Soviet foreign policy and the evidence of the facts – which meanwhile had fully revealed the secret intentions behind the second front – the Kremlin found itself compelled to destroy this myth of its own creation. Soviet historians were given permission to reveal this facet of history, provided always, of course, that they ignored the awkward questions this critique could provoke about Moscow's policy during the period of the 'grand alliance'. The Soviet historians' version, which is still in circulation, can be summed up in the following three points:

1. The dominant idea of Anglo-American strategy in the military operations in Europe was to let Germany and the USSR weaken each other as much as possible and meanwhile to develop allied military power to the maximum in order to be able to intervene at the right moment with fresh forces and impose the sort of peace which was in the interests of imperialism. The military aid and food supplied to the USSR was what was strictly necessary to prevent a German victory and prolong the German–Soviet duel until this 'right moment' should come.

2. These calculations proved wrong in the course of 1943. After the victory at Stalingrad and the further heavy blows struck by the Soviet army at the enemy during the spring and summer of 1943, Germany's war-weariness became clear, while the military potential of the Soviet Union was increasing day by day, both as regards the manufacture of weapons and the mobilization of human resources and as regards the fighting spirit of its armies. At the same time the extent of the resistance movement in the occupied countries seriously alarmed the Anglo-American leaders. 'In these conditions, a further delay in the opening of a second front in Northern France would involve the risk of severely weakening the post-war position of the United States. The British and American leaders found themselves obliged to make a sharp change of policy, which they did in August 1943 at the Quebec Conference.'[39] At this meeting Churchill tried to assert the British interest in having the second front opened in the Balkans, but the Americans imposed the decision which corresponded with their interests. Once this decision had been taken, Roosevelt and Churchill left for Teheran, where the British Prime Minister again defended his Balkan plan, but Roosevelt and Stalin were in complete agreement in favouring a landing in France.

3. During the early months of 1944 'it became clear that the Soviet Union was capable of defeating Nazi Germany and liberating the European countries, including France, with no forces but its own'.[40] In addition, 'the French people's liberation struggle, which was tending to

turn into a general insurrection against the German invaders, had begun to worry world reaction.' This prospect seemed to overcome the last hesitations in London and Washington, and the allied landing on the Normandy beaches was carried out with the sole aim of 'frustrating the democratization of the countries of Western Europe and blocking the route to the west to the Soviet army'.[41]

This Soviet version of history rests on a solid analysis of Western documents and has been borne out by the policy practised by the American imperialists in Europe from the moment that their armies set foot on the continent. Soviet historians have been able to respect the truth on this specific question – if we ignore the inevitable simplifications and elements of propaganda of a version submitted to the 'judgement of the party' – because after 1947 Moscow had no need to continue to lie about this section of history. On the contrary, for the reasons already mentioned it had to reveal the truth about it. From this point Soviet historians could make use of such a reliable tool as the class interest which must inevitably have dominated military and political decisions in London and Washington. It would indeed have been absurd if Anglo-American strategy had been inspired by a wish to promote the strengthening of the Soviet Union and the coming to power of the European working-class parties.

Nor were the Soviets alone in holding the view that at the end of 1943 and the beginning of 1944 the USSR was capable of defeating Germany and liberating Europe with no forces but its own and those of the national resistance movements. In November 1943 Roosevelt thought that 'by next spring, the way things are going in Russia now, maybe a second front won't be necessary'.[42] And in May 1944 Admiral Leahy, Roosevelt's Chief of Staff, argued in a report on the relation of forces at that time that in the event of a break in the 'grand alliance' and war with the Soviet Union, the United States could at the most defend Great Britain, but not defeat the Soviet Union. 'In other words, we would find ourselves involved in a war which we could not win.'[43] It should also be remembered here that at this period the United States was in one of the hardest stages of the war against Japan, while the Soviet Union had secured its Far Eastern front by the Soviet–Japanese pact of 1941.

The second front therefore was an essential condition, not for the defeat of Germany, as Stalin claimed, but to forestall the danger of socialist revolution, which was emerging in Western Europe. This was simply one aspect, though of course one of the most important, in the sharing out of 'areas of influence' in Europe. The day on which Stalin approached the problem of the second front, from the moment the 'grand alliance' began to take shape, was inspired by this aim. Instead of explaining to the peoples of Europe that their liberation had to be in the first place the result of their own armed struggle and that this was the only way they could hope to control their own fate, instead of holding up as an example the formation in Yugoslavia of a national liberation army and the setting-up of popular power in the liberated areas, and inciting the resistance in France, Italy and other countries to follow this path, Stalin's arguments and Soviet propaganda for the second front – like their echoes in the propaganda and policies of the Communist parties – encouraged illusions about the liberating and democratic mission of the British and American armies, and encouraged the tendency to consider armed resistance movements as auxiliary and subordinate forces.

A feature of this attitude was that it became stronger as the military situation became more favourable to the Soviet armies. The firmest Soviet statements on the need for a second front date not from 1941 or 1942 when the situation of the Soviet armies was at its most difficult; they begin in spring 1943, coinciding with the dissolution of the Comintern, become firmer towards the end of the year, and the strongest statement of all is the one already mentioned included in the 'order of the day' of 1 May 1944. In this Stalin, after announcing that the Soviet army was preparing to throw the invader back across the frontiers of the fatherland, added that the task of liberating the peoples of Europe could not be undertaken without 'the joint efforts of the Soviet Union, Great Britain and the USA, by joint blows from the east dealt by our troops and from the west dealt by the troops of our allies'. Stalin insisted: 'There can be no doubt that only this combined blow can completely crush Hitlerite Germany.'[44]

This declaration amounted to a recommendation – and, coming from Stalin, an order – to the Communist parties of the West on the eve of the allied landing: any action by the forces of the resistance and all national political objectives should be subordinated to the actions and objectives of the Anglo–American forces. And this was the rule – strictly observed in practice, as we have already seen, by the Communist Parties of France and Italy – which led the Greek Communist Party to the Varkiza capitulation.

In parallel with the intensification of his insistence on a second front, as an absolute necessity for the military defeat of Germany and the liberation of the occupied countries, Stalin stressed the ideological justification for this subordination to the Allies which he demanded of the European left. He insisted that the unity of the 'grand alliance' was growing daily stronger, and the community of interests and aims among the 'Big Three' greater. As a result of this, the peoples could put their trust in them. In proportion as the contradictions increased within the coalition – as Zhdanov was to recall in 1947, as Soviet and Western historians were later to show, and as could not have been otherwise once the defeat of imperialist Germany was within sight, since the struggle against Germany was the only force of any strength which held the coalition together – in proportion as this inevitable process developed, Stalin increased the dose of mystification.

On 9 October 1944, when the Soviet armies began to cross the Soviet frontier and penetrate into Romania and Bulgaria, Stalin and Churchill agreed on their respective percentages of influence in the Balkans. In essence, Churchill resigned himself to letting Stalin do as he liked with Romania, Bulgaria and Hungary, provided that he left Churchill's hands free in Greece and allowed him a 50 per cent 'influence' in Yugoslavia, a deal which the 'Father of the Peoples' accepted with generosity.[45] On 6 November, in his speech on the anniversary of the October revolution, Stalin extolled the unity of the 'Big Three' and predicted a long life for it. It was in this speech that he gave the clearest expression to his view that the alliance between the USSR and the two great capitalist states was based, not on 'accidental and temporary' motives, but on 'vital and lasting interests'. Naturally, said Stalin, differences appear from time to time, but

the surprising thing is not that differences exist, but that they are so few, and that as a rule in practically every case they are resolved in a spirit of unity and coordination among the three great powers. What matters is not that there are differences, but that these do not transgress the bounds of what the interests of the unity of the three great powers allow, and that, in the long run, they are resolved in accord with the interests of that unity.

After mentioning, in support of these claims, the discussions on the second front, and the more recent ones on the structure of the future United Nations Organization, Stalin added:

A still more striking indication of the consolidation of the front of the United Nations are the recent talks in Moscow with Mr Churchill, the head of the British Government, and Mr Eden, the British Foreign Secretary, held in an atmosphere of friendship and a spirit of perfect unanimity.[46]

Thus the negotiations which had seen the secret completion, with consummate cynicism, of the share-out of 'areas of influence' in the Balkans, in which Stalin had left Churchill – as he put it in his telegram to Eden of 7 November –[47] the 'freedom' to launch the British navy and British tanks and aircraft against the Greek people, this typical example of secret diplomacy and disregard for a people's right to self-determination, was presented by Stalin – on an occasion as appropriate as the anniversary of the October revolution – as the most striking proof of the unity between the three great powers.

The armed British intervention against the Greek resistance aroused strong opposition among liberal opinion and working-class circles in Great Britain and the United States. Leading newspapers, including the London *Times*, expressed their disapproval. The operation was condemned by the trade unions, by almost all Labour MPs and by a section of the Liberals. The motion of confidence put down by Churchill obtained only 279 votes of the total of 615 members in the Commons. According to the evidence of his son, Roosevelt was scandalized by the British methods, and Secretary of State Stettinius made an official statement reaffirming that the United States supported the right of peoples to decide their own futures and were hostile to any intervention in the internal affairs of any country.[48]

All of which means that the political situation was extraordinarily

favourable for a Soviet gesture in support of Greek democracy. In this
final stage of the war against Fascism, actions as openly reactionary as
Churchill's could not but provoke the most widespread aversion, and the
USSR enjoyed immense prestige among the peoples of the West. Moreover, the military situation could not have been more favourable.
The Soviet armies had reached the frontiers of Greece, Yugoslavia and
Bulgaria in October, and the last of the German forces had had to
evacuate the Greek peninsula, leaving it completely under the control of
the resistance. The British troops which had been landed at Piraeus
controlled no more than the ground they stood on. If the secret agreement between Churchill and Stalin had not existed, nothing could have
prevented a few Soviet units from continuing south to Athens to 'link
up' with the British expeditionary force. This military presence, supported by a statement from Moscow similar to that of Stettinius, would
have shattered Churchill's plan. But Stalin not only made not a single
military or diplomatic move to defend the Greek resistance, not only
maintained a guilty silence during the thirty-odd days that British tanks
and aircraft machine-gunned the population of Athens; he even put
pressure on the Greek Communist leaders to agree to the Varkiza capitulation – which was far from being the inescapable outcome of the
relation of forces.[49]

While Churchill was devoting large numbers of tanks and aircraft to
his little war against the Greek resistance, von Rundstedt broke through
the allied front in the Ardennes and threatened the Anglo–American
armies with a new Dunkirk.[50] (The British offensive in Athens began on
5 December, the German offensive in Belgium on the 16th, and both
continued until mid-January.) On 6 January Churchill sent a message to
Stalin, urging him to bring forward the Soviet offensive planned for the
end of January so as to relieve the serious situation in which the allied
armies were placed on their principal front. Stalin could have asked why
the allied armies did not attack on the Apennine front, and why the
armoured divisions and aircraft engaged in Greece against the Greek
people were not sent to that front, on which an allied offensive could rely
on the powerful support of the partisan army active on the territory
occupied by the Germans. Instead of this, Stalin sent Churchill an immediate reply, and promised that, in spite of the bad weather on the

eastern front, which made it difficult to use aircraft and artillery, the Soviet army would bring forward its offensive. 'Rest assured,' said Stalin's telegram, 'that we shall do all in our power to support the valiant forces of our allies.'[51] Sure enough, five days later the Soviet army attacked on a 1,200-km. front, finally forcing Hitler to accept, according to General Guderian's memoirs, 'that the western front must go over to the defensive so that forces could be made available for transfer to the east'.[52]

As the Soviet official history explains, Stalin knew very well, and had known for some time – and it was confirmed by events in Greece – that the allied armies had landed on the continent to 'complete their imperialist plans for Germany, save from total annihilation the reactionary forces, prevent the democratization of the countries of Western Europe and close the route to the west to the Soviet army'.[53] Stalin knew that on 18 December, two days after the beginning of von Rundstedt's big offensive, the British had moved troops from Italy to Greece, instead of moving them in the opposite direction, from Greece to Italy for an attack in the Apennines to relieve the allied position in the Ardennes.[54] Stalin knew that the western front was no longer necessary for victory over Germany, and had not been since early 1944; he knew that the Soviet armies, with the help of the European resistance movements, were capable of imposing the final decision. But Stalin did not hesitate to accept a considerable increase in Soviet losses – the inevitable result of mounting an offensive in bad weather conditions, which made it difficult to use aircraft and artillery, and drawing to the eastern front part of the German troops stationed on the western front – in order to help 'the valiant forces of the allies'. He did not hesitate to take a decision which, in such a situation, would inevitably not hesitate to have the effect of facilitating the further advance of the British and American armies towards the heart of Germany and equally of facilitating operations against the Greek resistance fighters and giving the allied troops in France and Italy greater freedom of movement to meet any action by the resistance which threatened the bourgeois system in these countries.

The Soviet historians, who reproduce the official version, justify Stalin's decision of 7 November 1945 by saying that by acting in this way the Soviet government 'was fulfilling, disinterestedly, consistently

and honourably, the commitments it had undertaken and giving necessary help to its allies'.[55] If we ignore the 'disinterestedness' and the
'honour', the language of this apologetic justification gives a quite accurate description of the real content of Stalin's action. Stalin was indeed
'consistently fulfilling the commitments he had made' to his imperialist
allies, to precisely the same extent as he failed to fulfil his duty to the
European revolution.

However, apart from a few vague phrases, such as those just quoted,
the Soviet official history gives no explanation of the immediate reasons
which determined the decision Stalin made on 7 January 1945. While
there were general motives, which are perfectly intelligible in the light
of Stalin's overall policy – 'commitments undertaken' – it is certain that
considerations stemming from the particular moment at which the decision was taken also played a part. The Soviet historians do not reveal
these, but hint at them when they stress that the German offensive in the
Ardennes was planned with a specific object in view, to teach the Allies,
by dealing them a sudden blow, that their interest lay in a separate
peace.[56] By his 'generous' gesture, Stalin in all probability intended to
show his allies how much it was to their advantage to keep a *soiuznik* so
generously disposed to help with the carrying out of Anglo-American
plans on the continent. In other words, Stalin wanted to avoid the threat
of a separate peace. But, as we shall see, he had no fear of taking such
risks when questions affecting the agreed Soviet 'areas of influence' were
involved. To ward off the possibility of a separate peace he was prepared
to make concessions, provided that they affected only the interests of the
revolutionary movement in the 'areas of influence' assigned to the
British and Americans, and not in his own.

When the 'Big Three' met at Yalta at the beginning of February, the
sharing-out of Europe was already well under way. Apart from the
points already mentioned, a preliminary agreement had been reached in
the course of 1944 on the crucial problem of zones of occupation in
Germany. The agreement was ratified at Yalta without difficulty, no
doubt because each of the 'Three' regarded it as temporary and compatible with his longer-term plans for Germany. The line of the Elbe
amply satisfied the most ambitious security demands of the Soviet
state, as this was seen by Stalin and his generals. (Engels showed re-

markable foresight when he wrote, in 1853, that Russian expansionism, invoking the pan-Slavist myth, would not be satisfied until it had obtained its 'natural frontiers', which corresponded, more or less, to a line running from Danzig or less, to a line running from Danzig or Stettin to Trieste.)[57] On the other side, British and American capitalists were naturally satisfied at being able to get their hands on the most highly industrialized areas of Germany.

For the rest of Europe, even though the demarcation of 'areas of influence' was practically fixed, it remained to solve the problem of what might be called the 'shares of influence' of the Western allies in the zone under Soviet Russian control. Just as Stalin controlled certain 'shares of influence' in the area under Anglo-American control through the Communist parties and their participation in the governments of France, Italy and other countries, the recognition by Roosevelt and Churchill of Soviet control in Eastern Europe did not mean that they had given up all idea of having political and economic footholds in these countries. The secret Stalin–Churchill agreement, for example, provided for elements, 'areas' and 'shares'. Greece was to stay an area of absolute Anglo-American control, and Bulgaria, Romania and Hungary were in the area of Soviet control, but the Greek Communists had a right to a 10 per cent influence in the organs of the monarchical state, which was a vassal of Britain and the USA. If they had been satisfied with such a modest percentage, Churchill would not have felt obliged to persuade them with bombs. Once these arguments had proved their force –13,000 national liberation army dead in Athens alone – and the Greek Communists, in the Varkiza agreement, had agreed to the disarming of ELAS throughout the country, Churchill, honouring his agreement with Stalin, offered no opposition to the Greek Communist Party's legally taking the modest place alloted to it by the agreed compromise in the democratic order symbolized by George II and General Plastiras.

And with the same scrupulousness with which Churchill respected, in Greece, the percentages agreed with Stalin, Stalin was to do the same in the countries within the Soviet area of influence. The problem was tackled in practical terms at Yalta, in the cases of Yugoslavia and Poland. With regard to Yugoslavia, the 'big Three' limited themselves to making an explicit recommendation that the Tito–Šubašić agreement should be implemented rapidly.[58] The difficult problem at Yalta, as in the previous negotiations, was Poland.

Stalin saw Poland as the central link in the chain of defences which was to protect the security of the Soviet state, and this is why the new Polish state had to offer guarantees to the Kremlin in all areas. The genuinely pro-Soviet forces were, however, very weak in Poland. During the period of the German–Soviet pact Stalin had treated the Polish nation and people as enemies; his methods had been indescribable and had had the predictable effect of sharpening the traditional anti-Russian feelings of Polish nationalism, which were comparable only with Polish fears of Germany. Even the small Communist groups had not escaped Stalin's blows.[59] There is consequently nothing surprising in the fact that the main forces of the Polish resistance should have formed around the bourgeois and Social Democratic parties, which as early as 1939 had set up a government-in-exile based in London, which was recognized by the Western allies as the legal government of Poland.

Thus to secure the Polish state he needed, one which would be unconditionally pro-Soviet – a sure link in the defence system – Stalin could not afford the smallest concession to any democratic process, whether of bourgeois democracy or proletarian democracy. He could rely only on the setting-up, by authoritarian measures, of a state apparatus under the firm control, especially in army and police matters, of the Soviet security services. To obtain this it was necessary, among other measures, to destroy the organized armed forces of the resistance, which were very strong and under the control of bourgeois or Social Democratic leaders. The political shortsightedness of these leaders, which led them into the premature Warsaw rising of 1944, made Stalin's schemes easier. The German troops took on the task of doing to the Polish nationalist resistance what British troops were a little later to do to the Greek revolutionary resistance.[60] At any rate the basic problem of the hostility of the great majority of the Polish people to Poland's entry into the Russian defence system still remained unsolved. Roosevelt and Churchill were prepared to make large concessions to the motives of 'security' pleaded by Stalin, but insisted on a 'share of influence' in the new Poland and in addition pressed for the appearances of democracy to be preserved; both were under heavy pressure from public opinion, which had been aroused to sympathy with the cause of Poland from the beginning of the war. They finally succeeded at Yalta in persuading Stalin to 'widen' the provisional government put together in the Kremlin and installed in Warsaw by the Soviet army, by adding a number of figures who had the support of the government-in-exile. The final administration was to be produced by general elections which the new provisional government would organize as soon as possible.

The Western 'Big Two' had hardly arrived back in their capitals when they learned that their colleague in the East had not the slightest intention of carrying out his undertaking. Stalin was insisting that discussions on the new Polish government should be limited to 'people who have demonstrated by deeds their friendly attitude to the Soviet Union, who are willing honestly and sincerely to cooperate with the Soviet state'.[61] And who better than Stalin himself to determine the degree of friendship honesty and sincerity towards the Soviet Union in the minds of the candidates for the Polish government? Stalin rightly insisted that his qualifications in the matter should be recognized, a step which threatened to make the Western 'share' much smaller than the Soviet 'share of influence' in Greece. The two Western leaders reacted vigorously. In one of his last messages to Stalin, Roosevelt gave a barely disguised warning that any solution 'which would result in a thinly disguised continuance of the present Warsaw regime' could lead to the break-up of the 'grand alliance'.[62] Churchill sent a similar message to the Soviet leader at the same time.

Stalin would not move, even though this threat of a break was given additional plausibility by its coincidence with a very significant event, the first occasion on which the possibility of a separate peace between the Nazis and the Western allies acquired any substance. Around the middle of March representatives of the allied High Command had had secret conversations in Switzerland with representatives of the German High Command. They had already started when the Western powers, no doubt fearing that the Soviets would be informed by the other side, notified Moscow, justifying the talks by the pretext of a possible capitulation by the German army occupying northern Italy. The Soviet government asked to take part in the talks, but the British and Americans refused, which could only increase Moscow's suspicions. In a message to Roosevelt dated 3 April (Roosevelt's message to Stalin about Poland was dated 1 April), the Soviet leader claimed that it was certain that the talks in Switzerland had led to 'an agreement with the Germans, whereby the German Commander on the Western front, Marshal Kesselring, is to open the front to the Anglo-American troops and let them move east, while the British and Americans have promised, in exchange, to ease the armistice terms for the Germans'. Thus, continued Stalin, 'what we have at the moment is that the Germans on the Western front have in fact ceased the war against Britain and America. At the same time they continue the war against Russia, the ally of Britain and the USA.'[63]

These alarming signs were made worse a few days later by the death of Roosevelt and the succession as president of Truman, who had told the *New York Times* in 1941 that in his view, out of Germany and Russia, the United States should support whichever seemed to be winning.[64] But Stalin still made no concession over Poland. In a message to Truman and Churchill dated 24 April he set out with unparalleled cynicism his view that each of the 'Big Three' should decide, without interference from the others, the form of government to be established in countries they considered vital to their national security:

Another circumstance that should be borne in mind is that Poland borders on the Soviet Union, which cannot be said about Great Britain or the USA.

... You evidently do not agree that the Soviet Union is entitled to seek in Poland a government that would be friendly to it, that the Soviet Union cannot agree to the existence in Poland of a government hostile to it ... I do not know whether a genuinely representative government has been established in Greece, or whether the Belgian government is a genuinely democratic one. The Soviet Union was not consulted when those governments were formed, nor did it claim the right to interfere in those matters, because it realizes how important Belgium and Greece are to the security of Great Britain. I cannot understand why in discussing Poland no attempt is made to consider the interests of the Soviet Union in terms of security as well.[65]

At the same time as he was fighting on the diplomatic front to obtain the same 'freedom' in Poland as Churchill had in Greece, Stalin ordered the Soviet army and security services to begin the methodical elimination of the activities of the non-Communist resistance. He did not refrain from using methods such as the following. The principal military and political leaders of the resistance were invited to friendly conversations by the Soviet military authorities; they were given safe-conducts and guarantees of safety. Once they reached the place proposed for the meeting they were all arrested and taken secretly to prisons in Moscow. Several months later they appeared before a Soviet military tribunal and were sentenced to ten years' imprisonment on charges of attempted sabotage against the Soviet army. Many local resistance leaders were similarly arrested and executed without trial.[66]

It will be seen that Stalin had no hesitation in risking the 'grand alliance' if the stake was Moscow's control over the countries which history had designated as part of the Soviet defence system. At the same time, however, and at Stalin's orders, Thorez was disarming the resistance and putting the Communist Party under the leadership of de Gaulle, arguing from the danger of a reversal of alliances. This was also the pretext under which the magnificent resistance movement of northern Italy surrendered its arms to the Allies and the Greek Communists accepted the disarmament of ELAS. Stalin considered it legitimate to run the risk of a conflict with the Western allies for the sake of his sovereignty over the Soviet defence system, and at the same time insisted that Communists in the Anglo-American 'area of influence' should regard as a crime any revolutionary action which might unleash a similar conflict. If any such action provoked armed intervention by the British or Americans, there could be no reliance on Soviet military assistance (as long as the Western intervention did not affect the Soviet defences): Greece was a warning.

The problem of 'areas' or 'shares' of influence in Europe was not discussed in detail at Yalta except in the cases of Germany, Poland and Yugoslavia. (In regard to Germany it is important to note that not only were the boundaries of the occupation zones fixed, but agreement was also reached on their dismemberment, and a committee of the 'three' set up to study it.)[67] In the case of the other European countries, the three powers agreed on the norms to be followed for joint intervention 'where in their judgement conditions require'. In fact, all the previous compromises in connection with the share-out of Europe were renewed.

Yalta, however, did more than study European questions. A secret protocol provided that the Soviet Union should enter the war against Japan shortly after the end of hostilities in Europe, and that once the Japanese were defeated 'the former rights of Russia, violated by the treacherous attack of Japan in 1904', would be restored. The Soviet Union would recover Sakalin and all the neighbouring islands; China would lease Port Arthur to her and Dairen would be internationalized; the East China and South Manchuria railways would be operated by a joint Sino–Soviet company. In short, the Soviet Union would take over the bases and concessions obtained by Tsarism in the Far East at the time of the division of 'areas of influence' in China among the Western powers. There would even be an extra, the Kurile islands, which belonged to Japan. There were also talks between the three Foreign Ministers at Yalta about Iran, at that time divided into British and Soviet 'areas of influence', and Moscow's hope of a share in control over the Dardanelles.

Yalta was thus an essential stage in the carving-out of 'areas of influence' throughout the world, and not just in Europe. At the same time it was the high point of the great mystification which concealed this carve-up and presented the 'Big Three' as the guardian archangels of peace, democracy and the national independence of the peoples. Hundreds of millions of human beings, and among them millions of Communists, firmly believed in the solemn declaration signed by Churchill, Roosevelt and Stalin:

Our meeting here in the Crimea has reaffirmed our common determination to maintain and strengthen in the peace to come that unity of purpose and of action which has made victory possible and certain for the United Nations in this war. We believe that this is a sacred obligation which our governments owe to our peoples and to all the peoples of the world.

Only with continuing and growing cooperation and understanding among our three countries and among all the peace-loving nations can the highest aspiration of humanity be realized – a secure and lasting peace which will, in the words of the Atlantic Charter, 'afford assurance that all the men in all the lands may live out their lives in freedom from fear and want'.

The Undoing of Stalin's Opportunism

As has already been noted, the behaviour of the 'Big Three' in the weeks which followed Yalta is an eloquent illustration of their 'common determination' to maintain 'unity of purpose and of action' and 'continuing and growing cooperation and understanding' in order to establish a 'secure and lasting peace'. The Western powers accused Stalin of not respecting the agreement about Poland. Stalin accused the Western powers of negotiating separately with Germany. Every day brought new causes of tension. Churchill showed himself particularly aggressive. He tried to convince the American leaders that Soviet Russia, exalted until that moment by Churchill himself as a heroic and loyal ally, in fact represented 'a mortal danger to the free world'. Four days after the German surrender he wrote to Truman: 'An iron curtain is drawn down upon their front. We do not know what is going on behind.' He suggested to Roosevelt's successor that he should not evacuate the American armies before forcing new concessions out of Stalin, the German territories east of the Elbe, which, under the Yalta agreements, were to be included in the Soviet occupation zone.[68] (The Americans had occupied these territories, getting there before the Russians because the Germans had left the way clear.)

Churchill's nervous aggressiveness at this moment reflected the weakness of the British position. 'A mortal danger' was indeed threatening the interests of British imperialism in the Baltic and in Eastern Europe, in the Balkans and the Dardanelles and in the Middle East. It threatened the constant premise of British foreign policy, the maintenance of a European balance of power which would prevent the domination of the continent by any one power. Great Britain came out of the war seriously weakened. Financially she was at the mercy of the United States. Militarily she could not match, by a long way, the other two 'great powers'. Without American protection, the British 'shares of influence' within the area under Soviet control were in danger of evaporating. Churchill also feared that the two 'super-powers' might reach a

425

world-wide arrangement without taking account of imperial interests, or even at their expense. As well as contradictions between the Soviets and the Americans, there were contradictions between the Americans and the British, and Stalin was relying on these. This is why Churchill's diplomacy used the slightest opportunity to poison relations between the Soviet Union and the United States.

While Great Britain's chief ambition, like France's, was to preserve her colonial empire, the aim of the powerful American capitalist system was to destroy all barriers which hindered its world expansion. The practical significance of Roosevelt's idealism was nothing but this. Addressing the two houses of Congress, meeting in joint session a few months before Yalta, Roosevelt's Secretary of State, Cordell Hull, had solemnly proclaimed: 'There will no longer be need for spheres of influence, for alliances, for balance of power, or any other of the special arrangements through which, in the unhappy past, the nations strove to safeguard their security or promote their interests.'[69] This open world, which in addition was exhausted by war, was the ideal world for American super-capitalism: the market of its dreams for its huge industrial apparatus whose production had doubled during the war, and a sphere of investment equal to the vast volume of capital it had accumulated. Instead of a world divided into areas of influence there would be one world-wide area of influence, the American area. Roosevelt and his colleagues included in this vision collaboration with the Soviet Union; in their view American industry's contribution to the reconstruction of the USSR would have advantages for both countries and would be reflected in the political education of the Soviet regime. As a result of this beneficial support, 'socialism in one country' would become able to fit smoothly into the Roosevelt world.

The proofs of good will which Stalin had given during the course of the war, the dissolution of the Comintern, the policy of 'national unity' followed by the Communist parties, the abandonment by the Latin American Communist parties of the struggle against Yankee imperialism, etc., encouraged Roosevelt and his colleagues to believe in the viability of the *pax Americana*. Other facets of Stalin's *Realpolitik*, however, conflicted with Roosevelt's view. This was true above all of the doctrine set out by Stalin in his document of 24 April, which was quoted above, on the Polish question and applied in practice from 1939 in the Baltic states, Bessarabia and the rest, the doctrine according to which each of the 'Big Three' could do as he wished with the countries as he considered vital to his security. Roosevelt's idealism admitted exceptions here, in the case of countries such as Cuba, Puerto Rico, the Philippines, Mexico, etc., when the security of the 'great American democracy' was involved, but it could not admit them when the aim involved was to guarantee the security of 'communist totalitarianism' or 'British imperialism'.

Nevertheless the American leaders did not think that this disagreeable aspect of Stalin's *Realpolitik* was, for the time being, sufficient motive for a breach, or even for giving up the attempt to achieve a fundamental compromise with the Soviet government. They kept in mind other essential factors. First, it had been clear to the North American leaders since 1943 that they were going to be faced with another super-power, one, indeed, which was behind the United States in economic development, but which had a clear military superiority on the continent of Europe. At the time of the Yalta Conference the American generals knew that in the event of a conflict with the USSR the Soviet armies would reach the shores of the Atlantic.[70] They also knew that in addition to its military superiority the USSR could rely on another weighty advantage: while the defeat of Germany left the bulk of Soviet military strength free, a large part of American military strength was still engaged in the war in the Pacific. At the beginning of 1945 it was thought in Washington that it would be necessary to move part of the forces engaged in Europe to the Pacific, that the war with Japan could continue for a considerable time and that the Soviet Union's entry into that war was very desirable, if not essential. (The American leaders feared that, when the time came, the Japanese army fighting in China would fall back on Japan, making the final assault more difficult and more costly.)

And there was yet another important problem which drove the American government to look for an understanding with Moscow in the Far East; this was China. One of the main aims of Washington in the Pacific war was to consolidate the Chiang Kai-shek regime, thanks to which American capitalism could be assured of economic penetration and political control in China. Success in this enterprise would be made considerably easier if the Chinese Communists continued their collaboration with the Kuomintang bourgeoisie in the same spirit of loyalty and moderation which had been shown by the Italian and French Communists in collaborating with their own bourgeoisies. To achieve this purpose Washington needed the good offices of Stalin. There were therefore pressing reasons, in the first half of 1945, before the explosion of the atomic bomb and the surrender of Japan, for the American government to seek agreement with Moscow in spite of the tensions stemming from the Polish situation and other Eastern European problems.

The same factors which forced Washington into a policy of conciliation towards Moscow, in spite of the instinctive anti-Communism of Truman and his team, make it even clearer to what extent the overall relation of forces in Europe in the spring and summer of 1945 was swinging in favour of a bold revolutionary policy in the countries where internal conditions were also favourable. In the event of an Anglo-American military intervention against the revolutionary movement, the Soviet Union was in an exceptionally favourable military and strategic position to give decisive military help. But from the point of view of Stalin's policy, these two factors – the strategic and military advantage and the revolutionary possibilities in the areas recognized by Moscow as Anglo-American 'areas of influence' – were to be exploited to secure Washington's recognition of the European defence barrier and the other Soviet demands (bases in the Dardanelles, an area of influence in northern Iran, interests in Turkey, etc.). The first factor meant that the European buffer zone was an established fact, militarily invulnerable. Stalin's aim, however, was to have this fact recognized, and to make it part of a general, world-wide agreement with the United States. Under the terms of this agreement American credits and industry would contribute to the reconstruction of the USSR, so far following the plans of the Roosevelt team, but in conditions which would avoid political dependence and would tend to ensure bipartite control of the world, and not the political supremacy of the United States.

The decision not to take advantage of the revolutionary possibilities existing in western and southern Europe, or of those in China, a decision which, at the time of the abolition of the Comintern, could have been interpreted as a mere manoeuvre, now acquired substance. It now appeared as a practical, real concession – all the more valuable to the Americans in that the danger of revolution was real – quite adequate as compensation for recognition of the European defences and the other Soviet demands. To achieve a real division of the world with American imperialism – the real meaning of the references in the Yalta declaration to 'a secure and lasting peace' – Stalin used all these cards and one more, which could not be absent from the grand strategist's hand, inter-imperialist contradictions. Stalin calculated that, once Japan and Germany were out of action, the contradictions could only grow between American capitalism's need for world expansion and the desire possessing Great Britain, France, Belgium and the Netherlands to retain their colonial empires.

The Potsdam Conference, which opened on 17 July, still fell within the strategic and military context favourable to the Soviet Union, and its results seemed a step in the direction planned by Stalin. The Americans gave way in the main on the Polish question – accepting insignificant concessions from Stalin – and did no more than make timid protests about the course of events in other countries in the Soviet orbit.

However, an event took place on the eve of the Conference which substantially altered the objective premises of Stalin's model and the whole course of world politics. On 16 July the American atomic bomb had been successfully tested in the Alamogordo desert. Suddenly the United States no longer needed Soviet help to settle Japan, as Hiroshima (6 August) and Nagasaki (9 August) were to show. Tokio surrendered on the 14th. Under the secret Yalta agreement the USSR was to have declared war on Japan no later than three months after the fall of Germany, on 8 August at the latest. By this date the USSR had still not fulfilled its obligations in this matter, but Moscow had an excellent excuse. The Yalta agreement provided that the 'restitution' to the USSR of the bases and concessions taken over by Japan in 1905 should be ratified by the National Chinese government of Chiang Kai-Shek. The Chinese refused, and had not given their consent by 8 August. This suited Stalin perfectly, since it allowed him to retain, in negotiation with the United States, a card as important as the Soviet attitude in the

Pacific war. But Hiroshima proved the effectiveness of the new weapon. Stalin waited no longer for Chiang Kai-Shek to ratify the Yalta agreement. At 5 p.m. on 8 August the Soviet Union declared war on Japan. On 14 August not only the territories envisaged at Yalta, but in addition the whole of Manchuria and Korea as far as the 38th parallel, passed into Soviet hands.

Monopoly of the atomic bomb became a privileged factor in Washington's policy. Truman did not lose a second in proclaiming that the United States had become 'the most powerful nation in the world – the most powerful nation, perhaps, in all history'.[71] American imperialism firmly turned the corner towards world dominion. This, however, did not exclude a certain prudence, since the American generals were very well aware that while the atomic bomb could reduce a number of Soviet centres to the state of new Hiroshimas, it would still be difficult to prevent the Soviet army from advancing from the Elbe to the Channel. In his reply to Churchill's Fulton speech, Stalin warned that 'a new military campaign against Eastern Europe' would have unhappy results for the interventionists: 'We can say with certainty that they would be defeated, as they were defeated twenty-six years ago.'[72] In Washington the warning was taken seriously, and Truman did not follow the advice of those who urged him to brandish the bomb to force the USSR to fall back to its frontiers. Kennan's so-called 'containment' policy was chosen.

Stalin nevertheless took the view that the objective basis for an understanding with the United States continued to exist. 'I do not believe in the real danger of a new war,' he said in September 1946. 'I do not consider that the atomic bomb represents the imposing force that some political leaders would have us believe. Atomic bombs are designed to frighten the "weak", but they would not be enough to decide the outcome of a war.' Besides, 'the monopoly cannot last long ... I am convinced that international collaboration, far from decreasing, can only increase.' In other words the bomb made no fundamental change to the relation of forces and was at the most a temporary advantage; the solution still, therefore, lay in understanding.

A month later he replied with a firm 'no' to the question whether tension between the United States and the USSR had increased. In

December 1946, in reply to Roosevelt's son, who asked him whether
collaboration between the USSR and the United States was possible,
Stalin said, 'Yes, of course. It's not only possible; it is the only wise
course, and completely within the realm of possibility.' The Soviet
Union, according to Stalin, was ready to make a long-term economic
agreement with the United States, involving a substantial development
of trade and American loans. As the main element of the Soviet contribution, Stalin offered explicitly 'to pursue a common policy with the
United States on Far Eastern questions'.[73]

China was in fact one of the most important cards Stalin thought he
still held. After the surrender of Japan he had pressed the Chinese Communists to come to an arrangement with Chiang Kai-shek,[74] and at the
'Big Three' Foreign Ministers' conference held in December 1945 there
was agreement 'on the need for a united and democratic China under the
control of a national government, based on wide participation by the
democratic forces in the organs of the national government and the end
of civil disorders'. (The expression 'democratic elements' referred to the
Communists, 'organs of the national government' to the Kuomintang
and its army, in which the Communist armed forces were to be incor-
porated, and 'civil disorders' to the struggle between the Communists
and the Kuomintang.) Fundamentally this was a solution of the 'national
unity' type, as in France and Italy, which would ensure the leadership of
the Chinese bourgeoisie and the development of the country into a bourgeois democracy.

But the Chinese Communists would not adapt to this solution, in spite
of Stalin's pressure, and in 1946 Chiang Kai-shek, with the help of
American planes, technicians and money, launched a large-scale
offensive against the people's army. At the end of 1946 things were
going badly for Chiang Kai-shek and his protectors, and the offer Stalin
made in his conversation with Roosevelt's son 'to follow a common
policy with the United States in Far Eastern questions' took on a very
precise meaning: to put pressure on the Chinese Communists in order to
reach a solution to the civil war which would be satisfactory to common
(Russian and American) interests. In Washington, however, Stalin was
thought to be playing a double game: who could believe that the Chinese
Communists were pursuing an independent course? This, nevertheless,

was true. In an internal document of April 1946 addressed to the restricted group of the CCP leadership, Mao analysed the international situation and regarded it as possible that a compromise would be established between the USSR and the United States. This compromise, however, he said, 'does not require that the peoples of the different countries of the capitalist world should therefore make compromises in their own countries'. The aim of the reactionary forces, he added, 'is resolutely to destroy all the democratic forces they can destroy and prepare to destroy later those they are unable to destroy at present'. Faced with this situation, 'the popular democratic forces must apply the same principle to the reactionary forces'. According to a note in the Chinese edition, in this document Mao was criticizing 'certain comrades' who hesitated to meet the offensive launched by the United States–Kuomintang bloc with a revolutionary war.[75] We may take it that the 'comrades' referred to supported Stalin's line as it emerged from the agreement between the three powers in December 1945.

During the two years between Potsdam and the announcement of the Marshall Plan the policy of 'containment' under the protection of the atomic 'umbrella' and by not sparing the dollars began to produce its first results. In Greece terrorist repression forced the Communists once more to take the path of armed struggle. In France and Italy the reconstruction of the military and civil structures of the capitalist state went ahead rapidly, and the working-class movement – as we have seen – lost ground. Moscow was forced to withdraw its troops from northern Iran and was unable to obtain the military base it had demanded on the Turkish coast near the Dardanelles. In the Far East the Soviets were completely excluded from intervention in Japan, which became an American protectorate. It was in Germany, however, that the Western allies dealt the severest blow to Soviet plans. Moscow failed to secure four-power control of the Ruhr, which would have enabled it to restrict considerably the real power of the Western allies in their occupation zones and to prepare the way for a further extension of Soviet 'influence' over the whole of Germany. (For this, Stalin was relying heavily on the military weakness of Great Britain and France and on the evacuation within a short period of the American troops, which Roosevelt had implied at Yalta. However, under the protection of the atomic 'umbrella'

Truman did his best to make West Germany the main stronghold of American imperialism in Europe.)

The 'Truman doctrine' was proclaimed in March 1947, and gave the Americans a justification for establishing themselves in Greece and Turkey and dominating the Middle East and the eastern Mediterranean, taking over as policeman from the English in these important strategic areas. With the Marshall Plan Washington laid the foundation for a rapid reconstruction of German economic strength and completed the subordination of the European bourgeois governments, as well as opening up a huge market to North American industry. In Paris, Rome and Brussels the orders of the great benefactor were rapidly obeyed. The Communist ministers were dismissed and the 'advance towards socialism in democratic and parliamentary legality' was unceremoniously stopped. Nor was the possibility ruled out in Washington that the lure of dollars would attract some of the People's Democracies. The favourable reception given at first to Marshall's offer by the governments in Warsaw and Prague showed that this hope was not without foundation. But to imagine that Stalin could give way on this was a serious misapprehension.

During the summer of 1947 Stalin found himself trapped in a situation which the Soviet state had always tried – with success – to avoid since the time of Lenin, the formation of an anti-Soviet bloc made up of all the capitalist states. The situation in 1947 had the additional feature that the bloc was taking shape under the leadership of the most powerful state in history. There could be no doubt that this was disaster for the 'peace' Stalin had sought, the 'peace' which was to ratify the division of the world into 'areas of influence' on the basis of a world-wide Soviet–American agreement. It was the collapse of 'peace' based on the abandonment of revolutionary struggle and the practice of class cooperation on a world scale, in order to make it possible for the two 'super-powers' to collaborate and to ensure the 'peaceful building of Communism' in one country. (In September 1946 Stalin first stated his view that 'Communism in one country is perfectly conceivable, especially in a country like the Soviet Union.')[76]

With his usual pragmatism, Stalin had projected on to the new situation which emerged from the war the role played by imperialist contradictions between the world wars and during the second war. The cornerstone of Stalin's strategy throughout these periods had been, as we have noted, the exploitation of these contradictions and the total subordination of revolutionary possibilities to this exploitation, both within the capitalist states and in the colonies. From the point of view of the interests of the Soviet state, seen from a nationalist point of view, this strategy proved extremely effective. Nevertheless, the second great world crisis of the capitalist system, the defeat of Fascism and the crushing of German and Japanese imperialism, was followed, inevitably, by a new surge of revolutionary struggle in both the capitalist metropolitan countries and the colonies. Even under the restraint of Stalin's policy, which most of the Communist parties followed – the policy summed up in the 'testament' of the Comintern – this new movement was enough to alarm the bourgeoisies everywhere, democratic and anti-Fascist as they were, and to drive them to unite across national and colonial contradictions in order to bar the way to the revolutionary threat.

The result was the falsification of Stalin's prediction that once Germany and Japan were beaten the struggle between the United States and the European colonialist countries would dominate world affairs. The check imposed by Stalin's policy on the revolutionary movement proved insufficient to prevent the spirit of the working class and democratic forces from alarming the bourgeoisie on both sides of the Atlantic, but it was enough to dampen this spirit to such an extent that even in the countries where it reached its greatest strength within developed capitalism (France and Italy) it proved powerless, not only to force radical political change, but even to prevent these states from becoming part of the anti-Soviet bloc led by the United States. In other words, the subordination of the Communist parties to Stalin's strategy had in the end the opposite results to those which had originally been predicted to justify it; it became a threat to the security of the Soviet state.

QUESTIONS AND CONJECTURES

The judgements of certain Western historians and politicians who are champions of the 'free world' and enjoy pointing out the 'tricks' by means of which Stalin obtained his satellites and the other aims of his world strategy, while idealizing the policy of Roosevelt, show not only a lack of objectivity but also ingratitude. If the 'free world' did not lose some of its finest flowers in the crisis, there can be no doubt that it owes this to Stalin. It is true that no hypothesis on the course that history might have taken, rather than the one it did take, can be proved. It would be idle to argue that if the Soviet leader – who was also the supreme commander of the world Communist army – had placed the European revolution among the priorities of his strategy, then that revolution would inevitably have triumphed. On the other hand, it can certainly be argued that Stalin, with the help of Western Communist leaders who faithfully applied his policies, made an invaluable contribution to solving the difficult problem which faced the leaders of Anglo-American capitalism from 1939 onwards – how to defeat their dangerous German rivals while still avoiding the danger of revolution in the vital centres of European capitalism.

As we saw in the first part of this study, Trotsky took an excessively optimistic view of the revolutionary situation which would be created in Europe as the result of a Second World War. This optimism derived from his view of the state of Capitalism, the exhaustion of its historic capacity to develop the forces of production, etc. However, his prophecy that the Second World War could result in revolution on a European scale was not an extremist fantasy. It expressed a real possibility, and one which the bougeoisie realized from the first day of the war. This possibility arose not out of the fact that the capitalist system had reached the limiting stage postulated by Trotsky – who was here repeating the mistake of Lenin's analysis during the First World War – but not of the method it was forced to adopt in order to carry out a 'readjustment' of its structures and pass on to a new stage of development.

The Second World War was the most serious crisis which the capitalist and imperialist system had experienced in its whole history. Yet, at the same time, it revealed spectacularly, even while the war was on, but even more afterwards, the vitality which the system considered as a whole still possessed, the enormous potential of its industrial, technical and scientific structures, its ability to manipulate the masses and keep them in subjection to the values, ideologies and political attitudes necessary for the survival of the system. It demonstrated the political intelligence of the old ruling classes, and their skill in manoeuvre, the fruit of centuries of experience. Like the war of 1914–18 and the economic crisis of 1929, the Second World War showed – on a much larger scale – that the 'death-throes' of dying capitalism would last a good while longer. (The prolongation of the agony gave official Marxism the time and opportunity to fit it into a learned scheme of periodization. It was first claimed that the 'general crisis' of capitalism had begun with the 1914–18 war and the Russian Revolution. After the Second World War, since the patient was still alive, it was decided that the inter-war period was only the 'first stage' of the 'general crisis'. This first stage was followed by a second, which began with the war of 1939–45. In 1960 it was ruled that the second stage was over and the 'third' beginning. How many more 'stages' will we see?)

The global vitality of capitalism, however, included ossified structures which came into sharp conflict with the movement of the system, which was based on three power-centres, Germany, Japan and, above all, the United States. The control exercised by old Anglo-French capitalism over vast colonial territories and over the backward areas of southern and eastern Europe was a serious obstacle to the expansive potential of these centres. Anglo-French capitalism, threatened in its most precious interests, was not prepared to yield without a struggle. For American capitalism, which had a large field for expansion at hand in Latin America and could more easily advance into the Anglo-French colonial territories, the problem did not present itself as one involving war. For German and Japanese capitalism, however, the only way open was the traditional one of war.

From the point of view of the five main capitalist powers, the Second World War, like the first, was a war for markets, colonies and raw materials, and at the same time it meant the transition of the system as a whole to a new phase, that of state monopoly capitalism. The three powers which were in the lead in this new phase had designs not only in Anglo-French territory (in addition to the colonial territories of Holland and Belgium), but also on Soviet territory. The fact that the United States tried to achieve this objective by alliance with its future victims, while its dangerous rivals tried to do it by military conquest, gave great political and military advantages to the former, but made no essential difference to the nature of the aims of one side or the other.

After the experience of the years 1917–20 the bourgeoisie in all countries was fully aware of the dangers involved in the terrible operation which the horrifying logic of the system now again made necessary. The danger appeared all the greater in view of the existence of the Soviet state with its army and the Communist International. It is true that by the outbreak of war the European revolutionary movements had been defeated and forced underground in almost all the countries of the European continent, but how would the masses react to the effects of this new slaughter? Would not the Communist cells which still existed be able to take advantage of the situation? After all in 1917 the Bolsheviks had only been a handful of revolutionaries.

Each bourgeoisie looked at these unknown factors differently, in the light of the internal situation of its own country. German capitalism was sure of itself, once the labour movement and the Communist Party had been crushed in its country. It thought that military victory would allow it to destroy by similar means any seeds of revolution in the rest of Europe. Japanese capitalism took a very similar view, since it too had reduced its labour movement to impotence. On a quite different basis – a reformist integration of the proletariat unequalled in the capitalist world – the United States was in a more favourable position than any other power to face the test of war. The British bourgeoisie could not feel the same confidence, as the great strike of 1926 had emphasized, but the Labour Party at least offered a fairly solid guarantee. This situation looked very different in France. It was clear that in the system of industrial capitalism France was the weakest link. Added to the obsolescence of its political and economic structures was the radicalization of the proletariat, shown by the social explosion of 1936, the hegemonic position acquired by the Communist Party within the labour movement and the spread of Communist influence among large groups of intellectuals and other social sectors. The French Communist Party's exemplary moderation during the period of the popular front was not enough to dispel the fears of the bourgeoisie: was it a temporary tactic or a basic change in the party? Italy, which had undergone considerable capitalist development under Fascism, was an unknown from the point of view of the solidity of the bourgeoisie. It seemed clear that its situation could not offer the security of Germany, but, equally visibly, it did not contain any element as disturbing as French Communism.

Outside the industrial capitalist zone, situations capable of turning into revolutionary crises under the impact of the world war were numerous: the Asian colonies, the republics of Latin America, the backward states of eastern and southern Europe. The most serious and most obvious threat from the point of view of world capitalism, however, apart from the entry of the USSR into the war, lay in the possible coincidence of Fascist defeat (and Soviet victory) and a proletarian revolution in France, which would mark the beginning of a process which could end in revolution over the whole continent of Europe. The British and American bourgeoisie were fully aware of this danger, and their whole policy, all their strategic plans and military operations throughout the war, were profoundly influenced by it, particularly in the last stages of the conflict, when the presence of the Soviet Union, now the first military power in Europe, poised for victory, made itself felt everywhere. At this period the French resistance appeared a considerable force, led largely by the Communists, the possibility of revolution could be clearly seen in Italy and it became a fact in Yugoslavia and Greece.

The Americans and the British were in agreement on two fundamental aims, the need to defeat their rivals and save capitalist and industrialist Europe from proletarian revolution. They were also naturally in agreement about the need to forestall or crush, as the case might be, any threat of revolution in other parts of the world, and especially in China. They might differ over the means to achieve these ends, but on the ends themselves their views were identical. Contradictory interests came into play above all in connection with the colonial problem, but that was a question for the future rather than an immediate problem. The community of interests in the most important aims, together with the crumbling British empire's heavy dependence on the United States, was a solid bond for the Anglo-American alliance. The difficult problem lay in the contradiction between their two principal aims, since the defeat of Nazi Germany was a necessary condition for a revolution in Europe and the internal logic of the anti-Fascist war

pointed the peoples of the European continent in the direction of revolution. A similar problem faced the Anglo-American alliance in the
Pacific war, especially in connection with China. In the minds of the
leaders in Washington and London, however, the Far Eastern problem
was less dramatic than the problem in Europe. At that time they underestimated the chances of the Chinese Communists and the other revolutionary movements in Asia.

The necessity to forestall revolution in Europe logically forced the
governments of Great Britain and the United States to seek a compromise with Germany, and, as is well known, they devoted all their efforts
to this right up to the outbreak of war. But the logic of German imperialism was quite different: for it, military victory on the European continent and in the British Isles would enable it to achieve simultaneously
two aims, to remove for an indefinite period any threat of revolution in
Europe and also to secure an economic and political basis for future
expansion. This programme of German imperialism's represented for
the British and Americans no less a threat, and above all a much more
immediate and precise one, than the possibility of revolution in Europe.
Faced with the unavoidable necessity of defeating Germany in order to
protect its vital interests, the Anglo-American alliance was obliged to
explore another course which might combine the defeat of Germany
with the preservation of capitalism in France: a wide-ranging agreement
with the Soviet state and the Communist movement. This possibility
showed itself first at the time of the Popular Front, but its first important demonstration, which showed how far the Soviets could go in this
direction, was the German–Soviet pact, in support of which the Kremlin
did not hesitate to force the Communist parties to abandon their anti-
Fascist strategy. Nevertheless, this action was not entirely conclusive,
because the Soviet Union had signed the pact with Germany in a position of weakness, and it was not therefore a sufficient basis to predict
Soviet behaviour in a position of strength, such as they would enjoy if
the Nazis were defeated. But the British and Americans had no alternative to this course, though they combined it with the elementary precaution of acting in such a way that the USSR would be weakened to
the maximum in its duel with Germany.

Experience was to show, as we have seen, that the compromise desired by Washington and London was perfectly possible. It enabled them to overcome the underlying contradiction between their main European aims, the defeat of Germany and the prevention of continental revolution. They were less successful in Asia, but the responsibility for that was not Stalin's.

From 1943 onwards, the possibility of a revolutionary outcome to the anti-Fascist war in Europe was clearly visible in four countries, France, Italy, Yugoslavia and Greece. The defeat of Germany came into sight at the same time, together with the important part to be played in that defeat by the Soviet armies, whose general offensive developed rapidly on all fronts during the summer of that year. It was the year when most of the British and American press shouted its warnings, and when the leaders of the Anglo-American coalition demanded the dissolution of the Comintern and the clear acceptance by the Communist parties of a political line excluding any prospect of revolution. It was the year in which Stalin willingly accepted these demands, since they did not affect his strategic and political aims, and indeed could be useful to him as bargaining counters in the great negotiation with the Allies. The Yugoslav Communists resisted Moscow's instructions; the Greek Communists hesitated, and during 1944 made concessions to Moscow which were to prove fatal to them. Thorez and Togliatti accepted Stalin's line unconditionally, since anyway it coincided with the neo-reformist turn in these leaders' political views which had begun at the time of the Popular Front. The leading groups in these two parties, which had been formed in these views, offered no resistance. From this point the possibility of revolutionary development in France and Italy was seriously threatened; the position was as it would have been in Russia in the course of 1917, if Lenin's 'April Theses' had been rejected by the Bolshevik party. The bourgeois revolution would have consolidated itself, one way or another, but the proletarian revolution would not have taken place, and historians and revolutionaries, would still be arguing whether the possibility had really existed and whether or not Lenin was a leftist adventurer, as they are twenty-five years later about France and Italy.[77]

The simple fact that the argument continues without any sign of being settled is sufficient proof that historical scholarship has found the

Revolution and Spheres of Influence

famous possibility solid enough. It was not fantasies which aroused the fear of the French and Italian bourgeoisie and their American protectors in those years. The bourgeois Italy which had emerged from the Risorgimento had known no more serious national crisis than the one which began in 1943, and the same can be said of France since the Paris Commune. The national disaster of 1940 had spotlighted the weakness of French capitalism. The state collapsed and was replaced by a caricature state in the service of the occupier; the calamities of war were increased by the humiliation of a shameful defeat and the German occupation.

The causes of all this were clear: out-of-date social and economic structures, rotten and impotent parliamentarism, colonial parasitism and technical backwardness. The ruling classes and their political groupings were discredited. It was they who bore the full responsibility for the disaster. But the most serious aspect of the situation from the point of view of the French bourgeoisie was the clear shift to the left which took place in the proletariat and other sectors of society, reflecting a realization of the causes of the crisis and the location of responsibility. The reason why the masses quickly turned to the Communist Party, in spite of its absurd policies during the period 1939–41, and why the party acquired leading positions in the resistance, was that the most active and advanced sectors, expressing the still confused movement among the masses, were looking for a radical solution to the crisis of the bourgeois system.

The same phenomenon unfolded in Italy. The responsibility of the Fascist regime for the national crisis was inextricably bound up with that of the big industrialists and landowners, who had shown themselves incapable, in fifteen years of dictatorship, of overcoming the chief weakness of Italian capitalism, the underdevelopment of the south, and had led the country into colonial adventures and imperialist wars. The Fascist dictatorship itself, however, was also the result and the proof of the impotence of the Italian bourgeois democracy which emerged from the Risorgimento. The ruling classes of the peninsula had failed with both these forms of government, and the formidable mass movement which followed the fall of Mussolini, with its clear inclination to the left, and the striking advance of the Communist Party, were a reflection, even

441

sharper than in France, of the tendency towards a revolutionary solution of the national crisis.

Never before in the history of either of these countries had the real movement so strongly or so objectively challenged the bourgeois order. Never before had the mass of the workers, the intellectuals, the whole society, lived through such an exemplary demonstration of the need for a new economy, a new state, for the rule of a new social class. Could the Communist Party fail to consider the socialist alternative without losing its *raison d'être*? Could it let such an opportunity as this go by without carrying the critique written into events by the real movement over on to the level of political theory and action?

Two aspects of the problem must be distinguished here. One is the exploration to the full of the objective situation, of common experience to raise the political consciousness of the masses and create an informed desire for revolutionary change, the working-out of tactics and a strategy which could organize and prepare the forces capable of imposing such a change, with the principal aim of a seizure of power, *not by the Communist Party, but by a combination of all the social and political forces willing to support a socialist alternative.* This was the inescapable duty of any Marxist revolutionary party in a situation of radical national crisis, such as existed in France and Italy in 1940–45.

This was independent of the other aspect of the problem, the question whether such a course would result in victory for the revolution. This question could not be answered except in the course of the action itself; only the action, in combination with other factors, could create the favourable situation, the relation of forces which would make possible the decisive step, the seizure of power. (In April 1917 no one could guarantee, nor did Lenin ever claim, that conditions favourable to a seizure of power by the Bolsheviks would inevitably come into being. The April policy was not the only factor which determined the emergence of these conditions in October, but without that policy those conditions would not have existed.) The leaders of the Communist Parties of France and Italy, who controlled the general line of their parties during the Second World War from Moscow, under Stalin's direct control, 'solved' the problem on the very first day, immediately, that is, the United States and Great Britain became the allies of the USSR. In France and Italy there could be no socialist outcome; the aim was to be the restoration of bourgeois democracy.

Such an abdication, such a denial in practice of what Communists thought they were and continued to proclaim that they were, required theoretical and practical justifications of comparable weight. As long as the war lasted, the principal justification, which absorbed all the others put forward from time to time, could be reduced to the following schema: (*a*) The victory of Hitler's Germany would mean the destruction of the Soviet Union and the crushing for an indefinite period of the working-class movement in Europe; (*b*) therefore, the principal aim must be victory over Germany; (*c*) to ensure the defeat of Germany, the essential condition was to ensure the solidarity of the anti-Hitler coalition; (*d*) raising the problem of a socialist perspective, making the aim the seizure of power by the proletariat, would inevitably lead to a confrontation with the Western allies which would threaten the chances of victory; (*e*) therefore, it was impossible, at the present stage, to consider the socialist alternative.

This reasoning presented itself as indisputable, the product of simple common sense. Only hardened leftists, Trotskyites and other irresponsible elements – 'Hitlero-Trotskyites' in Thorez's language – could question such basic truths. The motives which led the majority of active Communists, notably those of France and Italy, to accept this common-sense logic have already been mentioned. The initial propositions (*a*) and (*b*) were, of course, indisputable. On the other hand, proposition (*c*), from which (*d*) and (*e*) derived, contained a thesis which was much less indisputable. This maintained that the cohesion of the anti-Hitler coalition – understood as the alliance of the United States and Great Britain with the Soviet Union and the alliance of Germany's European bourgeois rivals with the working-class and anti-Fascist movement – was an indispensible condition of victory. This view excluded the possibility that there could develop in the course of the war a new relation of forces based on an alliance of the Soviet Union with the liberation movements of the European peoples which would be capable of ensuring the defeat of Germany and upsetting the plans of the Anglo-American imperialists. The exclusion of this possibility *a priori* was reflected in the refusal to adopt a policy which could help to create it. As the official

443

Soviet history recognizes, this possibility took tangible form towards the end of 1943 and the beginning of 1944, when the allied landing on the continent was no longer necessary to ensure the defeat of Germany. Its essential aim was to save Western Europe from revolution. Would this aim have been achieved if the policies of the French and Italian Communist Parties had been different, if they had been like that of the Yugoslav Communists?

The possibility of carrying on the struggle on two fronts was given a practical demonstration in Yugoslavia from 1941 onwards. The main enemy was the Fascist occupier and his Quislings, and the secondary target was the allied enemy, which was trying, while the war was still being fought, to establish the foundations for a restoration of the regime of the bourgeoisie and large landowners and of the country's dependence on Anglo-American imperialism. This strategy also proved itself just as effective in the war against Hitler as the strategy which attempts had been made to justify in the name of simple common sense: the scale of operations carried out by the Yugoslav liberation army against the occupier far surpassed that of the operations of the French and Italian resistance. Paradoxically, the strategy inspired by simple common sense recoiled against its main apparent justification, to obtain the greatest efficiency in the fight against the occupier. The practical effect of the refusal of the French and Italian Communist Parties to give a revolutionary content to the war of national liberation in order to avoid a conflict with the policy of the Western allies and the national bourgeoisie was not only to make it easier for the allies and the bourgeoisie to restore the bourgeois order, but also to lead to a failure to mobilize against the invader energies and forces among the people which could only have been brought into action by revolutionary fervour, an awareness of struggling for social emancipation, for the power of the workers. We have seen in detail in the previous pages how common-sense logic led the Communist Parties of France and Italy to subordinate themselves, the proletariat and all the forces of the left to the leadership of the Western allies and the bourgeois wing of the resistance, whose policy was to reduce to the minimum the participation of the working-class and popular forces. The 'national unity', urged as more powerful because it was broader, proved in practice both narrower and weaker than the revolutionary national unity created in the struggle in Yugoslavia.

It is hardly necessary to explain that the type of confrontation, and the way it was linked to common action, would vary with the development of the war in Europe and other sectors, and in each country. The first necessity was for the struggle to be political, avoiding armed conflict as much as possible, especially in conditions unfavourable for the revolutionary forces. The Yugoslavs provided a model of political intelligence in the way in which they understood the dialectic of confrontation and common action, combining the open political struggle with united actions when possible, armed confrontations with the Chetniks and negotiations with the royal government and the Allies. At the same time as they were creating their own power and building a revolutionary army, they allowed the old English fox to think that he could obtain by negotiation what he could not take by force. They even managed to get weapons delivered to them by the Western allies before receiving Soviet supplies.

The problem for the Italian and French Communists – assuming that they were interested in a revolutionary policy – was not, of course, to imitate the Yugoslav strategy, but to work out their own strategy of confrontation and common action. Nevertheless the Yugoslav example indicated some of the essential conditions for tactics of this sort. The first of these was the formation of the working-class and left-wing anti-Fascist forces into an independent movement, with its own programme and its own completely autonomous armed forces; the second, the creation of a new popular power in the course of the war against Hitler by encouraging, as far as circumstances allowed, the direct participation of the masses in the new power. Other equally important aspects could be mentioned, but this has already been done in the section on the struggle in Yugoslavia. Was it really true that the situation in France and Italy made a similar course impossible?

It is significant that in the face of the Yugoslav criticisms at the founding meeting of the Cominform the French and Italian Communist leaders did not even try to assert the impossibility of this. They evaded the core of the problem by claiming that if they had tried to take power the British and American armies would have intervened to prevent them. This was evading the core of the problem, because they were being criticized, not for not trying to take power, but for following, from as early as 1941, a policy which implied the abandonment in advance of any such aim, a policy, indeed, which adopted the opposite aim, the restoration of bourgeois democracy, a policy of subordination to the bourgeois allies. The danger of intervention by the British and American armies did not arise in France until the summer of 1944. What stopped the French Communist Party from having a policy in the previous three years designed to prepare the working class, ideologically, politically and organizationally, for a struggle to give a socialist ending to the unprecedented crisis of bourgeois France? Why, instead of helping to tie the resistance to Gaullist leadership and the old system of the bourgeois parties, did it not support and lead the opposing tendencies which appeared in the resistance? Why, when faced with the restoration of the old power which Gaullism represented, did it not fight, right from the start, for the creation of a new power arising out of the resistance and based ultimately on the mass of the workers? Many signs showed the depth of the revolutionary current (at a time when the masses believed that the Communist Party was the party of revolution). In spite of the ultra-opportunist policy of the PCF during those three years, the liberation meant, that in many areas, as non-Communist historians admit, the working-class and popular forces had power within their reach; the masses flocked to the Communist Party and supported the left-wing movements in the Socialist Party, the unions and other organizations. These signs also made it starkly clear, in retrospect, that if a different policy had been followed in the previous period the level of consciousness of the movement, its fighting spirit and its desire to enforce a radical change would have been much stronger. But, even starting from the level reached by the movement in the months after the liberation, was there not a possibility of directing it towards revolutionary goals? This is a question which the leaders of the PCF have always avoided. To left-wing criticisms they have always replied, and continue to reply, that the combination of conditions favourable to a takeover of power did not exist.[78] That, however, was not the question. The question lies in the fact that the party followed a policy designed to eliminate any possibility of the emergence of conditions favourable to a takeover of power, not only by the party, but also by the whole of the revolutionary wing of the resistance. Their policy was that of a fire brigade at the outbreak of a fire. In the period between the liberation of Paris and the capitulation of Germany (almost a year), no one except the Communist Party and the unions it controlled could have prevented the gathering development of the mass movement. In reply to the Gaullist policy of abolishing the committees of liberation and the patriotic militias, the embryo of the dual power created by the resistance, the PCF could have organized strikes, factory occupations, mass demonstrations and other forms of action. It could have encouraged the transformation of the liberation committees into direct organs of the masses, supported by the organs of workers' power in industry. The party had the power to promote movements of this type and to encourage the unity of the left around a programme of socialist democracy. The problem of power could be considered realistically only in the context of a policy intended to strengthen the mass movement, dissipate illusions about Gaullism and the Allies (illusions created by the party itself during the preceding period), etc.

But, as we have seen, the policy of the PCF was quite different. It co-operated with de Gaulle in the elimination of the resistance, it told the working class that it would have to tighten its belt in order to restore the capitalist economy; it held back – which was perhaps worse – the liberation movement in the French colonies; it disseminated illusions about the peaceful, parliamentary road; it continued to idealize the Allies. This was a new version of the traditional reformist, nationalist policy of the right wing of French Social Democracy.

In Italy the possibility of carrying out a policy which dialectically combined the war against Hitler with the struggle for a socialist outcome became actual with the fall of Mussolini, when, in Togliatti's words,[79] the old foundations of the bourgeois state collapsed, including its military organization, and there began the largest popular insurrection in the whole history of Italy, which was led principally by Communists, Socialists and progressive intellectuals. When Togliatti landed at Naples in 1944, the need to choose between two policies, confusedly reflected in the conflict between anti-Fascism and the King, Badoglio and the Allies, began to appear. One policy attempted to associate the

447

working-class parties and the petty bourgeois left against the monarchy, the traditional right and the Allies; the other tried instead to weaken the contradictions, to form a closer association of left and right, working class and bourgeoisie, under the sole command of the allied military authorities and behind the slogan 'First win the war'. The first political line might have led to the formation of the new 'historical bloc' discussed by Gramsci. The second, the policy of 'national unity', in the event eased the task of the old ruling classes and led finally to the restoration and modernization of Italian capitalism.

It was not 'national unity', but 'national differentiation', which could have upset the game of the old ruling classes, which had been plain since the fall of Mussolini. It could have revealed to the masses the forces which were genuinely struggling for the social and political renewal of Italy, its national independence, and those which were working for the return of the big industrialists and the landowners, with the aim of placing Italy in subjection to a new imperialism. 'National unity' did not, in spite of Togliatti's claims, give the working class the leading role; it merely gave it the illusion of that role. Real control was in other hands. In order to make themselves a real hegemonic class, the working class would have had to combine *in action* the problem of national liberation with that of agrarian revolution in the south and the islands, with the struggle for *socialist* democracy. Togliatti's strategy – a reproduction of that adopted by the Comintern in the Spanish revolutionary war – dissociated these aims at the very time that the real movement, the serious crisis of social and political structures, the awakening of the masses, was tending to join them in a single revolutionary process. During the two years between the allied landings and the rising in the north the PCI did nothing to organize the struggle of the peasant masses for the land, and opposed the tendencies in favour of fighting for a socialist solution which began to emerge within the great proletarian movement in the north. The policy of 'national unity' consisted in practice of holding back the mass movement in order to avoid the break-up of the coalition government and any confrontation with the Anglo-American military authorities.

The movement of the masses, asserting itself at every level as an autonomous power, with its own programme, was the only force ultimately capable of preventing the restoration of traditional power which gradually took place. The military presence of the Allies would have required, of course, different methods from those used by the Yugoslavs, an essentially political type of confrontation. But the presence and attitude of the Anglo-American military authorities was, on the other hand, a living lesson which the working-class and anti-Fascist left could have used to increase the national consciousness awakened by the war of liberation, by demanding full and unrestricted recognition of Italian sovereignty, the right of the people to free choice of their organs of government and a promise by the Anglo-American military authorities not to interfere in Italian internal affairs.

The essential obstacle to the development of a strategy to push ahead with the fight for the land and for other revolutionary changes did not lie in the Italian situation. It lay in the PCI leadership's submission to the line laid down by Moscow. Such a strategy could have extended the foundations of dual power and increased the political isolation of the Allies and the right. It could have created a powerful independent movement of the working-class parties and the left-wing anti-Fascist forces, and made it possible to connect the great proletarian rising in the north with the revolutionary movement in the south. If the Yugoslav Communists had followed Stalin's instructions as contained in Dimitrov's message of March 1942, similar 'obstacles' would have arisen in Yugoslavia.

Togliatti and Thorez more than once referred to the example of Greece to justify their policies. The catastrophe of the Greek resistance could, however, have been avoided, in spite of Stalin's unbelievable treachery, if the Greek Communist leaders had resisted Soviet pressure and not capitulated at a moment when they were in control of almost the whole country and were backed by a seasoned popular army. Eighteen months later, in much less favourable conditions, they took up the struggle again and were able to hold out for three years, with foreign aid which bore no relation to the size of the American intervention and effectively ended in 1948. If the Greek Communist leaders had not given way to Stalin in December 1944 and January 1945, the British expeditionary force would have found itself in an unenviable situation.

In the early months of 1945 Germany was nearly defeated. The Soviet armies, with the addition of sizable detachments from Bulgaria, Romania and Poland – and of course the Yugoslav liberation army – possessed a decisive military superiority over the forces of the Western allies in Europe. The United States was tied up, for how long it was impossible to say, in the war in the Pacific. It was the moment when the democratic and reforming ideals of the resistance enjoyed the maximum of popular enthusiasm. What would have happened if in this situation the working-class movements of France and Italy had gone over to the offensive in support of the power of the workers and the whole left, with a programme of democratic and socialist changes (not 'Communist' power or a 'Soviet' programme)? Would the West have intervened? Could Roosevelt or Truman have faced the political consequences of taking over Hitler's role as chief enemy of the European left? From a military point of view, could they even have made the attempt? (The danger could not be ignored, just as in 1917 it was impossible to ignore the danger of an intervention by the German armies, which did take place and almost crushed the Russian Revolution. It is hard to think of any revolution secure against all danger. There was, however, one notable difference in the situation of 1944–5, which was that the real danger came not so much from a possible intervention by the capitalist armies as from the very likely failure to intervene of the armies which were regarded as the standard-bearers of the October revolution. This is what happened in Greece. On the other hand, it should be admitted that the case of Greece itself shows how difficult such operations were in the situation of that time.)

But conjectures and questions about what might or might not have happened in the past must stop. History was decided at Yalta, when the 'areas of influence' were shared out. Stalin laid down the law to the Communist parties without meeting any resistance, except from some future heretics in the underdeveloped countries. In the centres of capitalism Communist neo-reformism fell in step with the 'grand alliance'.

When we began our analysis of Stalin's strategy during the Second World War, we referred to one of the factors which affected it the most, to which we must now briefly return. The foreign policy of the Soviet bureaucracy could not do other than reflect, in some form, its domestic policy. After wiping out the best representatives of the October revolution, after destroying proletarian democracy and depriving the people for many years of all political life, after discrediting the socialist ideal in the eyes of the Soviet workers by proclaiming that this regime of poverty and police dictatorship was finished, socialism, in short, after polluting the sources which could have kept alive the revolutionary spirit and formed an internationalist class-consciousness, the Soviet leaders were incapable of giving the war against Hitler's Germany a revolutionary or socialist character. This fact was independent of all the other reasons we have analysed (strategic considerations, interest in maintaining the 'grand alliance', etc.), which were anyway strongly conditioned by the internal situation. Continuing therefore in the same direction, and starting from the type of social consciousness which their ideological mystifications and political opportunism had formed, the Stalinist leaders gave the war the only character they could give it, that of a patriotic war. Hitlerism was first and foremost the new face of the traditional enemy, the 'Teuton', who dared to attack *Belikaia Rossiia* – as the new national anthem called it – and not the grave-digger of the German working-class movement and the Spanish revolution. 'They are not fighting for us,' said Stalin in a moment of sincerity during an interview with Ambassador Harriman, 'they are fighting for Mother Rus.'[80]

In the minds of millions of muzhiks and worker-muzhiks the Stalin myth was closely mingled with that of the great Tsars, combined with traditional patriotism, the glories of the past, a revived religion. Stalin and the party skilfully used every means to build these springs of patriotism into the new state, and Lenin was ritually invoked on every occasion to increase the prestige of the new Lenin. From the point of view of the international aims of the war, the Soviet leaders did not add a comma to the aims proclaimed by the allied capitalist powers, national liberation for the peoples of Europe and democracy.

More accurately, they added one element, which was not exactly revolutionary or even progressive, pan-Slavism, the call for the unity of the Slav peoples. The transparent intention of this call, apart from its immediate effect as a rallying-cry against the traditional enemy of pan-Germanism, was to prepare ideologically for the future construction of the protective barrier. Europe was going through its second disastrous war twenty years after the end of the first. It was clear proof that national frontiers had become an anachronism hindering the development of the productive forces, making a lasting peace impossible and constituting a permanent source of rivalries and conflict. Had not the moment come to call on the European proletariat to fight for the socialist United States of Europe, the idea of which had been launched by the Bolshevik party at the beginning of the 1914–18 war and taken up by the Comintern in 1923?[81] But the Slav idea replaced the European socialist idea. The Slavs must unite; the other peoples of Europe could stay in their national shells.

We shall not dwell on these aspects of Stalin's policy, which other authors – in particular Isaac Deutscher – have examined in detail.[82] Deutscher has raised another problem of considerable interest. The victory of a socialist revolution throughout Europe would have meant the end of the isolation of the Russian revolution, but Stalin feared the effects of the interpenetration of the Soviet system and socialism in the areas of industrial capitalism. He thought, not without justification, that this would endanger the political and ideological basis of the bureaucratic and totalitarian system built on the basis of isolation. From being an objective influence on the system, isolation had become a necessary condition for its survival and for the privileges of its ruling class. Subsequent developments have confirmed Deutscher's view. Stalin and his successors have made every effort to maintain the isolation of Soviet society, not only from the West, but also from the other countries of the 'socialist camp'. 'Genuine contact between Russia and the "people's democracies" – free travel and free exchange of ideas – could easily have become another source of ferment inside Russia. Stalin had therefore to keep in being two "iron curtains", one separating Russia from her own zone of influence, the other separating that zone from the West.'[83]

As we have seen, the ill-starred European proletarian revolution had to overcome many obstacles to make its way through the great crisis of the 1940s. Victory at the end of the second decade of the century was denied it by the absence of a socialist party independent of the bourgeoisie. Victory at the beginning of the fifth decade would have required a party independent both of the bourgeoisie and of the 'fatherland of socialism'.

The main justification for the policy of 'national unity' disappeared with the capitulation of Germany in the spring of 1945, but the collaboration of the Communist parties in the bourgeois governments of France and Italy (and of a number of other European capitalist states) continued and, as we have shown, contributed to the restoration of the capitalist economy and its political superstructures. A new justification now became necessary, and this time it could not be merely, or essentially, tactical.

To fill this need use was made of the doctrine of 'new democracy' or 'people's democracy', created to meet another urgent necessity, that of defining the regimes which began to establish themselves in the countries liberated by the Soviet armies. The paradox was that while revolution had been avoided with skill and delicacy in France and Italy – where 'the working class and its allies were better organized than the forces of reaction and had a clear superiority over the ruling groups of monopoly capitalism and its political agents'[84] (the quotation is from Soviet historians) – in the Eastern European countries it had been encouraged by the same *raison d'état* which had blocked it in the West. It was obvious that the defensive barrier could not be built on capitalist structures. The following chapter will deal with this revolution, with the doctrine to which it gave rise and the use of that doctrine as a justification for the neo-reformism of the Communist parties of Western Europe.

The historic defeat of Fascism, the Yugoslav revolution, the revolutionary process begun in other East European countries as a result of their liberation by the Soviet army and the formation of the satellite system, the emergence of the USSR as a world power, the increased strength of the Western Communist parties: all this hid from Communists – who at that period lived in the euphoric dream described at the beginning of this chapter – and not only from them, the serious implications for the further struggle for socialism of the frustration of the revolution in Europe. Shortly afterwards, the Chinese revolution and, later, the collapse of the old colonial system had a similar effect. But if we see events in a historical perspective, it can be seen very clearly that this victory of the international bourgeoisie, this abdication of European Communism at the moment of its greatest influence – at the most favourable conjuncture in the half-century since the October revolution – has had an unhappy influence on the subsequent course of world events. It was the last, and most serious, effect of the ideological decay of the Communist International, and is one of the main objective causes of the present crisis of the Communist movement.

6

THE COMINFORM

THE SATELLITE REVOLUTIONS

The five Eastern European countries which were to become part of the Soviet defensive barrier differed greatly from each other at the moment of their liberation by the Soviet army. Czechoslovakia's industrial development contrasted with the predominantly agricultural character of the other four, which also differed among themselves in their balance between industry and agriculture. Poland, Czechoslovakia and Bulgaria were all Slav lands, but, while fear of Russia dominated the people of Poland, the Czechs and Bulgarians were strongly pro-Russian. Romania and Hungary had few cultural or ethnic links with Russia. Sympathy for the Soviet Union was accompanied in Czechoslovakia by the presence of a traditionally influential Communist Party, which during the resistance had succeeded in becoming the country's main political party. On a smaller scale, the Bulgarian Communists had strong traditions; they had organized a partisan movement of some importance and at the liberation were the most active and best-organized political force. The Communist Parties of Poland, Romania and Hungary, on the other hand, were still small organizations without much influence among the masses. Czechoslovakia had experienced twenty years of parliamentary democracy whereas the other countries had spent all or part of that interregnum under reactionary regimes of semi-Fascist dictatorships. Poland and Czechoslovakia had been on the winning side; Hungary, Romania and Bulgaria on the losing. A long list could be given of further important differences in every area.

The very fact that the Communist parties won power in these five countries at almost the same time (1947–8) and adopted a socio-political system of the same type shows that the determining factors in these developments were not internal ones. In Czechoslovakia the working class could have taken power at the moment of the liberation of the country and begun the socialist revolution on a fundamentally democratic basis. As H. Ripka neatly put it, what was artificial in Czechoslovakia was not the revolution but its postponement.[1] An analogous situation existed in Bulgaria, although there the different context would have required the revolution to take different forms.

In Poland, however, given the wide spread of existing political forces, the existing conditions only provided a basis for a bourgeois democracy, within which Communism and socialism could have worked to win the support of the masses. This was also the situation in Hungary and Romania. The Soviet Union could have protected those who fought for socialism in these three countries against any intervention by the imperialist powers and made it easier for them to act, for only their action was capable of bringing about a revolutionary change which was the fruit and the expression of the popular will.

In these three cases, however, the Soviet army substituted itself for the will of the masses. The army took over power and put the strategic positions (command of the army and the police, the means of communication, etc.) into the hands of the Communists, masking the real power at first under 'democratic and parliamentary' forms. As Rakosi admitted later, right from the liberation the party 'took absolute control of the political police, the AVO ... It was the only institution of which we kept total control for ourselves and firmly refused to share it with the other parties in the coalition in proportion to their respective strengths.'[2] The problem of the army was solved, again according to Rakosi, by reducing its strength to the absolute minimum (12,000 men instead of the 70,000 to which Hungary was entitled even under the terms of the armistice) and distributing it throughout the country. 'The presence of the Red Army,' said Rakosi, 'reduced the importance of the struggle we had to wage to bring the majority of the army under Communist influence ... The strengthening of the Hungarian army did not begin until 1948, after the Communist Party had taken over the Ministry of Defence.'[3] But Rakosi has never explained how exactly the party was able to get sole control of the political police and in effect abolish the army while it did not control the Ministry of Defence and was in a very small minority, as was shown by the elections of 1945 (in which the Communist Party won 15 per cent of the votes, against the 85 per cent of the other parties in the coalition, including 57 per cent for the Small-holders' Party).[4] In Romania and Poland the Communist Party took control of the army in the first few months.

'The export of revolution is nonsense. Every country will make its own revolution if it wants to, and if it does not want to there will be no revolution,' was the answer Stalin gave in 1936 to an American journal-ist's question.[5] Just over two years later this 'madness' was tried in the Baltic countries, the eastern areas of Poland, Bessarabia and Bukovina, but then it could be presented in a different light. From 1945 onwards, Poland, Hungary and Romania became classical examples of the 'ex-ported revolution', carried out from above by a power deriving from a liberator-occupier. This did not prevent this power from carrying out a good many progressive – and in some respects revolutionary – tasks of social transformation (agrarian reform, nationalization of industries, re-construction, etc.), which for a time won it the support of the mass of the workers and of large numbers among intellectuals and other social groups. 'The reforms achieved in the countries of Eastern Europe during the years 1945-7 can be regarded as a national achievement, ac-complished with the more or less active, more or less sincere support of all the democratic parties,' says Ferenc Fejtő in his *Histoire des démocraties populaires*.[6] The growth of Communist influence and organization, says the same author – who cannot be suspected of par-tiality towards the Communists – cannot be explained simply by the presence of the Soviet army, but was due also to the fact that the Com-munists were the most determined and dynamic agents in the ac-complishment of this work, its main instigators. But these merits were overshadowed by a fact which became increasingly obvious to the people, that the Communist Party depended on a foreign power; it was in thrall to Moscow. The main decisions, and often less important ones too, were taken there, and not in Warsaw, Budapest, Bucharest or Sofia, or even in Prague, which had greater autonomy.

The fight against Hitlerism had been waged mainly under the banner of nationalism, and the liberation raised patriotic feelings to new heights. But the slogans of Slav unity were understood in Prague and

Sofia to mean a union of free and sovereign peoples. Even those who were most sympathetic to the liberators could not easily resign themselves to seeing a new domination, even with a 'socialist' label, replace the old. In the period 1945–7 the weight of this new independence was felt particularly in Poland, for reasons which have been mentioned, and in Hungary and Romania, which had been on the side of the losers. Although Bulgaria was also in this category, the pro-Russian attitude of the population and the size of its Communist Party earned it special treatment from Moscow. Romania and Hungary, however, as well as living under military and police rule, were crushed by economic tribute exacted as reparations, for the support of the Soviet troops based in the two countries, and under various other heads. German property, which included the main businesses and bank deposits in the country, passed into the hands of the Soviet state.[7]

Since they were unable to compete in patriotism with other political groups once Soviet interests became involved, the local Communists strove to show themselves true patriots in disputes with the other People's Democracies. Obliged to justify the loss of the eastern territories, the Polish Communists not only became the champions of anti-German feeling but also drove the hardest line with the Czechs in the dispute about the Teschen (Cieszyn) area. The Czech Communists, having been forced to give up Ruthenia to the USSR, showed themselves just as intransigent as the Poles in this dispute, and uncompromising towards Hungary over the problem of the Hungarian minorities in Slovakia. (It was necessary in the end to 'interchange' a half-million Hungarians living in Slovakia for a smaller, but still considerable, number of Slovaks living in Hungary.) The Romanian Communists, who were obliged to defend the USSR's annexation of Bessarabia and Bukovina (carried out under the protection of the German–Soviet pact), showed their patriotism against the Hungarians (who came off worst in all these territorial readjustments) over Transylvania. The Bulgarian Communists had a chance to show theirs against the Romanians over Dobrudja and the Serbs (after Tito's excommunication) in the Macedonian problem. Moscow acted as arbiter in all these quarrels, in which one virtue notable by its absence was socialist inter-nationalism.[8]

The great 'regulator' of the transformation of Eastern Europe was, of course, Stalin's policy, with its aim of forming all the countries of this region into a political and military system to defend the western frontiers of the USSR and increase the economic area available for what Moscow regarded as the building of socialism. This implied the establishment of regimes which would give the Kremlin adequate political guarantees.

During the stage with which we are concerned Stalin tried to reconcile the construction of these regimes with an attempt to reach a permanent global agreement with the United States. Real power was to remain in hands which the Soviet Union could regard as safe, but it suited Stalin at the same time to observe as ostentatiously as possible the principles of formal democracy laid down in the Yalta declaration and other documents such as the United Nations Charter and the Potsdam agreements. Measures against capitalists and landowners were essential not only to destroy the bases of classes hostile by nature to a preferential alliance with the Soviet Union and still more to integration in its economic orbit, but also to create the social basis required for the maintenance in power of pro-Soviet groups; yet it was in Stalin's interest that these measures should not appear as an attack on the capitalist system, or private enterprise, in general.

To these considerations stemming from the policy of the 'grand alliance' must be added another, of major importance, which derived from the characteristics acquired by the Soviet regime. This could not allow the revolutionary process begun in the neighbouring countries to produce socialist democracy, with organs of political and economic control which genuinely derived from the working people and were under their control. Only a process of this sort could quickly stir up and harness the energies and ideas of the masses, educate them and remove them from the ideological influences of the old ruling classes, build a solid barrier against the policies of imperialism and so provide the USSR with its strongest defence. However, neither the Soviet bureaucracy nor the leading groups in the Communist parties, which had been formed in the Stalinist period, were compatible with such a process. The exception of the Yugoslav way – which to some extent was a step in this direction – confirms the rule, and what it reflected was nothing other than the formation, during the national revolutionary war, of a leading group with new characteristics.[9]

The considerations which we have just been examining, taken as a whole, in large measure determined the economic and political structures of these People's Democracies. They determined the 'postponement' of socialist revolution in Czechoslovakia and its replacement by what Gottwald defined as 'democratic national revolution'. They determined the fact that in Bulgaria, though Dimitrov headed the government and power was more or less in the hands of the Communists and other left-wing groups, the party decided that the task was not the building of socialism but 'the consolidation of the democratic parliamentary system'.[10] In response to these considerations, the 'democratic national revolution' was exported to Poland, Romania and Hungary, where the actual control of power by the Communists, who lacked the political base which would have allowed them to exercise it, was concealed behind a façade of sham parliamentarianism. The Communists were forced to become election fixers, as the reactionary parties had been before, but even this method was not enough to channel parties like the Smallholders' Party in Hungary and Petrov's Agrarian Party in Bulgaria, in which the main bourgeois forces had taken refuge, into the mainstream of 'new democracy'. With the expert help of the Soviet secret service, plots had to be fabricated to justify repression against these parties. The parliamentary system was very soon to turn into farce, even in Czechoslovakia, the only one of the five countries in which it had possessed some authenticity.

The path taken in the countries of Eastern Europe after their liberation by the Soviet army was completely new to the Communist parties. The closest experience – and one which was to be presented as the first example of a 'People's Democracy' – was that of the Spanish Republic of 1936–9, but, apart from the fact that this experience had taken place in the exceptional circumstances of civil war and foreign intervention, it had lacked what was the determining factor in the People's Democracies of Eastern Europe, the presence of the Soviet army. The explanations of the nature and development of 'People's Democracies' in terms of 'Marxist–Leninist' doctrine which were provided during these years were vitiated at the root because the crucial role of this factor could not be considered and analysed without prejudicing Soviet diplomacy or 'giving' arguments to the propaganda and strategy of the capitalist powers.

Reduced to essentials, the theory of 'People's Democracy' was based on the following argument: Once the political power of the financial and landed oligarchy had been destroyed by the liberation, which cut it off from its economic basis by expropriation and nationalization, long-term cooperation became possible between the working class, small peasant proprietors and the middle bourgeoisie, industrial, commercial and agricultural, as part of a gradual transition to socialism. The nationalized sector would continue to grow and the capitalist sector to decline, and small peasants would gradually and voluntarily go over to cooperative forms of production, until the whole economy rested on a socialist basis. The class struggle would go on, but would take peaceful and evolutionary forms within the democratic parliamentary system.

This type of development was claimed to be guaranteed from the moment when the working class (that is, the Communist Party) took control within the governing coalition, and the new world-wide relation of forces produced by the war allowed the Soviet Union to protect countries which set out on this path from any intervention by imperialism. This – said the Soviet theorists and the Communist leaders of the People's Democracies – was a road to socialism different from the Soviet one and one which had been opened as a result of the 'new historical conditions' created by the definitive building of socialism in the USSR and the victory of the Soviet state in the Second World War.

Dimitrov went further than anyone when he claimed that while, 'for the transition to socialism, the dictatorship of the proletariat was essential [in 1919]', now 'in many countries the problem of the achievement of socialism presents itself as a problem of collaboration between the working class and the peasants, artisans, intellectuals and other progressive sectors of the people.'[11] (The 'other progressive sectors of the people' were of course the industrial, commercial and agricultural bourgeoisie, whose political representatives formed part of the 'national front' and the 'popular democratic government', or 'people's government', as it was usually called.) This was the dominant view in the years

1945 and 1946, as long as hope lasted of a global agreement between the USSR and the United States.

With the beginning of the 'cold war' and the collapse of illusions, both in the 'grand alliance' and in the 'little alliances', old Dimitrov had to make his self-criticism, announce that the dictatorship of the proletariat continued to be as necessary in the forties as it had been in the twenties, and admit that, while different from the Soviet system, 'People's Democracy' also fulfilled the functions of the dictatorship of the proletariat.[12] It hardly needs saying that the 'functions of the dictatorship of the proletariat' were understood in their Soviet sense as meaning the abolition of any pretence of proletarian democracy, the dictatorship of the Communist party or, more precisely, of its leading group. The only remaining difference between 'People's Democracy' and the Soviet system was the retention in the former of a parody of political 'pluralism' as part of a caricature of a parliamentary system.

This view – in its initial form, before the switch of 1947 – was adopted by the Communist Parties of France and Italy as a doctrinal justification for their entry into bourgeois governments, after the defeat of Germany had robbed them of their previous tactical grounds. Governments of 'national unity' were to be regarded as a first step towards 'People's Democracy'; nationalization as a first blow against monopoly capitalism. Once the Communist Party and its allies had gained control of the state through universal suffrage, the nationalized sector would begin to acquire a socialist character, and would be gradually widened. The state would no longer be at the service of the capitalist oligarchy, but would turn into that state of People's Democracy. This model was naturally associated with the idea of the new world balance of power, thanks to which collaboration between the USSR and the USA in the spirit of Yalta would finally prevail. If the people voted by a majority for the Communist Party and its allies, the capitalist powers would be forced to respect the popular will.

In this way the model of development which seemed to be establishing itself in the East was transferred to the West by a process of abstraction from the factors which had made it possible. There was a pretence that the Communist parties had won, or were in the process of winning, control of the state by exclusively democratic and parliamentary means and that they retained power by the same means.

An example can be seen in Thorez's report to the assembly of the Seine federation of the PCF on 8 June 1947, which deals at length with the 'new democracy'. Referring specifically to Poland and Hungary, in other words to the two countries in which the Communists would not have been able to keep themselves in power for a day if genuinely free elections had been held, Thorez claimed that 'the people's government' in those countries maintained 'the people's power' on the basis of 'democratic elections, with a parliament democratically elected by procedures more or less similar to those with which we are familiar'.[13]

It is hard to say whether the Western Communist leaders were merely deceiving the mass of the militants, or whether they were also deceiving themselves. Whichever it was, they did not deceive the other political groups called to accompany them on the new road to socialism. The impotence of Communist neo-reformism came in the first place from the dialectic of the class struggle, nationally and internationally, which refused to fit into the new doctrinal schema, but it was further aggravated by the reaction provoked by the events in Eastern Europe in the other reformist groups in the working-class movement, quite apart from that of the 'democratic bourgeoisie'.

We shall not attempt a theoretical critique of these ideas at this point. The 'cold war' performed the function of practical criticism, and they did not reappear until after the Twentieth Congress of the Soviet Communist Party, when they were developed with much greater theoretical elaboration. We shall come back to the subject when we examine this period. For the moment it is enough to note that the doctrine of 'People's Democracy', in its Western version, was not based on any analysis of capitalist society capable of producing new conclusions about the dynamic of its structures and the behaviour of its classes. The doctrine arose in the most pragmatic manner imaginable, with no basis in any other objective datum than the new world relation of forces, the assessment of which by the official theologians was very soon proved wrong by the actual course of events. The powerful Communist Parties of France and Italy were unceremoniously removed, without resistance on their part, from the governments of their countries, and instead of moving towards 'People's Democracy' Western Europe moved towards a new development of capitalism. American capitalism established a firm base in Western Europe.

In the East the class struggle sharpened. The bourgeois classes, encouraged by the American super-power, used every means to intensify their opposition to any reforms which reduced their economic base and to the increasing political monopoly of the Communist parties. American imperialism's economic offensive, with the mirage of the Marshall Plan, confirmed the futility of the idyllic course dreamed of during the period of Yalta and the liberation. In the face of world capitalism the economic fragility of the People's Democracies became clear. The economies of these countries depended heavily on trade with the West, and this dependence began to be felt heavily when a start was made on reconstruction.

In Czechoslovakia, for example, between the third quarter of 1946 and the first quarter of 1947 imports from the USSR fell by half and exports to the USSR by a third. In the same period imports from the United States tripled and exports to the United States increased by half. In the first quarter of 1947 the USSR was in sixth place in Czechoslovakia's foreign trade, in both imports and exports. This tendency, as we have seen, continued to grow.[14] In view of these facts, and on the basis of the illusions which still existed about national and international developments, it is easy to see why the Czech government decided, on 4 July 1947, to take part in the Paris Conference summoned to discuss the Marshall Plan.

Similar tendencies appeared in other People's Democracies. In 1945 the USSR took 93 per cent of Polish exports and provided 91 per cent of its imports. In 1946 the percentages were 50 per cent and 70 per cent.[15] The Polish Communists also declared themselves in favour of discussing the American aid proposals. Such tendencies were, of course, incompatible with the construction of a satellite system, at least in the form conceived by Stalin. On 8 July 1947, while the Polish government was deliberating with the intention of taking part in the Paris Conference, Moscow Radio announced that Poland had refused to take part. On the same day a Czech delegation left for Moscow, where Stalin put the problem to it in a way that had at least the merit of clarity: since the intention of the Marshall Plan was to isolate the USSR, there was no point in talking about it.

Other tendencies which threatened the cohesion of the satellite system appeared at the same time. In spite of their subordination to the USSR, and probably without any intention of questioning it, a number of the People's Democracies made plans for bilateral links and treaties of alliance. Yugoslavia especially emerged as a pole of attraction. The Yugoslav plan for a Balkan Federation, for the formation of a state running from the Black Sea to the Adriatic and ruled by Tito, who had already given proof of his independence, was more than enough to awaken Stalin's morbid suspicion.[16]

In this way, during the summer of 1947, the development of the situation both within the satellites and in Western Europe and the new, frankly anti-Soviet line adopted by Washington called for a drastic revision by the Kremlin of its previous policy, both in Soviet foreign policy and in that of the Communist parties of East and West. It became necessary to 'tighten the screws'. The setting up of the Cominform was a result of this necessity.

THE COMINFORM AND THE NEW TACTICS

Stalin reacted to the new world situation with his own logic. Now at the height of his glory, sure of his infallibility and used to the autocratic methods he had imposed for twenty years both on the Soviet state and party and on the international Communist movement, he could not for an instant consider subjecting the policy followed so far and the new problems created to critical analysis by the movement. Looking down at events from his Olympian height, he did not even feel bound to go through the formality of holding a world conference or congress to give the appearance of collective sanction to decisions taken in advance, as had been done with the last congresses of the Comintern. All he need do now was summon representatives of the parties he considered useful for the specific ends he had in view. Adding to the Soviet party the parties of the People's Democracies and the two main parties of the capitalist world gave him, he thought, a sufficiently representative body to take over the role played until its dissolution by the executive of the

Comintern, that of imposing on the Communist movement as a whole the line decided by the Soviet leadership. In addition, the composition of the Cominform was determined by very exact considerations. The main line of Stalin's reply to the American offensive was to form the satellite countries into a monolithic bloc under Soviet control. For this reason the parties of these countries were invited to the secret meeting in Poland. Secondly, Stalin's main battleground in the situation of that time was Europe, and here he had two closely linked aims: to ensure the invulnerability of the satellites and to prevent the success of the American plan to combine all the Western European countries, including West Germany, into a single bloc led by Washington. This explains the presence at the Polish meeting of the two most important parties of this area.

These two parties, as we have seen, were to be cast as scapegoats for the failures produced by their fidelity to the Kremlin's policy, and to give them an opportunity of redeeming their opportunist errors they were given a special task, the upsetting of American plans in Western Europe. On the other hand, no Communist party from the colonial world, not even the Chinese Communist Party, was invited to the founding conference of the Cominform. Nor was the Greek Communist Party, which was at that very moment engaged in armed struggle against American intervention.

There is a simple reason for these absences. Stalin's aim, contrary to the opinion held at the time by the politicians of the 'free world', was not to unleash a world-wide revolutionary struggle against American imperialism. His strategic objective was still the same; only his tactics had changed. Stalin intended, by taking a 'hard' line, to force Washington to recognize the division into 'zones of influence' within the framework of a world-wide compromise guaranteeing bipartite control of the world by the two super-powers. The concessions Stalin was ready to make to reach this agreement related to the colonial world and in particular the Far East. As for Greece, he had already abandoned it to Churchill and if it was handed over to the Americans he was not going to make a fuss.

All these nuances are reflected in the report made by Zhdanov in Stalin's name to the conference of the nine parties. This report has a special importance for the course followed by the Communist movement until the death of Stalin. Just as the tactical and strategic line of the Communist parties between the dissolution of the Comintern and the formation of the Cominform was defined in the 1943 resolution, so it was defined for the next five years by Zhdanov's report and the statement of the nine parties, which did no more than sum up the main ideas of the report. After 1953 the Cominform in practice ceased to exist (though its official disbandment did not take place until April 1956), and a change could be seen in the general line of the Communist movement in response to the new turn in Soviet foreign policy.

Without showing the slightest concern to explain why Stalin's predictions about the world which would emerge from the war – a world united and controlled by the confident collaboration of the 'Big Two' – had proved false, the main part of Zhdanov's report argued that after the war the world had divided into two 'camps', 'the imperialist and anti-democratic camp on the one hand and the anti-imperialist, democratic camp on the other'.[17] In the imperialist camp 'the fundamental leading force is the United States', and Great Britain and France were members 'as satellites of the United States'. Then comes a list of states who play a 'supporting' role: 'The imperialist camp is supported by colonial states such as Belgium and the Netherlands, countries with reactionary and anti-democratic regimes such as Turkey and Greece, and countries which are politically and economically dependent on the United States, such as, for example, those of the Middle East and South America, and China.' Lastly, the imperialist camp also 'draws support from the reactionary and anti-democratic forces in every country' and from the 'military opponents of yesterday' (Germany and Japan).

In the anti-imperialist camp 'the *base* consists of the USSR and the countries of the new democracy'; 'adherents' of this camp are Indonesia and Vietnam, and 'sympathizers' include India, Egypt and Syria. 'The anti-imperialist camp *draws support* from the working-class and democratic movement in all countries, from the fraternal Communist parties, from the national liberation movements in all colonial and dependent countries and from the help of all the democratic and progressive forces which exist in each country.' In this camp *the leading role is taken by the Soviet Union and its foreign policy*.

It will be seen that the term 'camp' in the first place denotes a bloc of states. Social and political forces not organized into states play only a subordinate, make-weight role. Each camp is built up around its 'leading' state; it has a base, made up of this guiding state plus the states directly under the control of the leader, and can rely on the 'support' of other political and social forces. The Communist parties outside the 'base' of the anti-imperialist camp act as a make-weight. And indeed, the function they in fact performed in applying the line laid down by the Kremlin followed this definition very closely.

The strategic objectives of the two camps, in Zhdanov's formulations, were as follows. The aims of the imperialist camp are 'the strengthening of imperialism, preparation for a new imperialist war and the struggle against socialism and democracy'; the aims of the anti-imperialist camp, on the other hand, are to fight 'against the expansion of imperialism and the threat of new wars, the strengthening of democracy and the elimination of the traces of Fascism'. The 'fundamental task' of the anti-imperialist camp is described as 'to ensure a lasting democratic peace'.

Neither in Zhdanov's report nor in the declaration of the nine parties was there any mention of the struggle for socialism in the capitalist countries, even as a long-term prospect, linked to more immediate aims. This omission cannot be regarded as accidental when we remember that this was the first definition of the world strategy of the Communist movement after the dissolution of the Comintern, and it appears even less accidental when related to other important and significant omissions. The two revolutionary actions of any scale in progress when the Cominform was created, those which embodied the most immediate hope of leading into the socialist revolution – the Chinese civil war and the Greek rising – were passed over in complete silence. There was no analysis of their deep implications; they were not presented as examples to other peoples; the Communist parties and democratic forces of the world were not asked to show solidarity with the fighters in China and Greece.

This silence is all the more eloquent given the fact that the Americans were directly engaged in both conflicts. Zhdanov devoted a mere four lines in his long report to American intervention in China and Greece, without any mention of the revolutionary response of the Communist parties concerned. In contrast, he devoted a large part of his report to a denunciation of the Marshall Plan, the main aims of which he described as follows:

First, to give help, not to the impoverished victorious countries, but to the German capitalists ... to restore the power of imperialism in the countries of the new democracy and force them to abandon their close economic and military collaboration with the Soviet Union ... to form a bloc of states linked to the United States by agreements and to grant North American credits as the price of the surrender by the European states first of their economic and then of their political independence.

In short, the Marshall Plan, according to Zhdanov, meant a refusal by Washington to grant the USSR the large-scale economic aid she had sought since Yalta. It meant that American policy was a threat to the cohesion of the satellite bloc and that the United States intended to erect barriers against an extension of Russian influence in Europe, particularly in Germany. As a result, the true motives underlying Stalin's mobilization of international Communism and its allies against 'the plan for the enslavement of Europe' appear in full clarity. This is why Zhdanov's report ended by stressing the 'special task' which fell to the French and Italian Communist Parties: 'They must take up the banner of the defence of the national independence and sovereignty of their countries.' If these parties were capable 'of placing themselves at the head of all the forces willing to defend the cause of national honour and independence, no plan for the enslavement of Europe will be able to succeed'.

With the exception of the 1944 resolution which dissolved the Comintern and marked the abandonment of the struggle to find a socialist solution to the European catastrophe, there are few documents in the history of the Communist movement which so clearly reflect the subordination of the world revolutionary struggle to the demands of Soviet foreign policy as this report of Zhdanov's. This is expressed not only in the definition of aims, of priority 'fronts'; it also comes out in the problem of forms of struggle, in the attitude to armed struggle as a form of revolutionary action. The silence about the civil wars in Greece and China (the Vietnamese war of liberation got only two lines) is due not merely to Stalin's willingness to make concessions in this part of the world. It also follows from the definition of the 'fundamental task of the post-war period', the preservation of peace. According to Zhdanov, the USSR 'is interested in creating the most favourable conditions for the creation of Communist society', and 'one of these conditions is peace abroad'. But the Soviet government believed, in Vishinsky's words to the United Nations a few days before Zhdanov's report to the Cominform, that 'in the present situation any new war turns *without fail* into a world war'.[18] Local wars were therefore a serious danger to the 'fundamental task', which was the 'building of Communism in the USSR'. Revolutionary wars, such as those in Greece and China, were therefore not the recommended forms of struggle against imperialism. They embodied the risk of involving the Soviet Union in another conflict. That is why they were not mentioned in Zhdanov's report, and why the Greek fighters received no worthwhile aid from the Soviet Union and were finally crushed. And if the Chinese one day surprised the Communist movement by their victory, it was a victory won by their own strength, and by ignoring Stalin's advice, which would have pushed them into a compromise with Chiang Kai-Shek and the Americans.

That peace should be preserved was without any doubt a strong desire of the peoples after six years of war, but hard reality very soon showed that, while the USSR might need *its* peace to 'build Communism', the peoples of very many parts of the world needed *their* wars to free them from colonial slavery; they had no other way. That was their 'fundamental task', in spite of the sacrifices it implied. Moreover, the improvised dogma that any local war would without fail turn into a world war had no scientific basis, and events were to show its weakness. Neither super-power felt the slightest desire to unleash a new world conflagration; they brandished the risk of one for localized political or strategic ends, but no more. Nevertheless the dogma was useful as a justification for a few capitulations and a good many acts of opportunism.

The two other panels of the triptych which Stalin unveiled before the Communist movement were 'national independence' and 'democracy'. It was the duty of Communists to unite 'all the forces willing to defend the cause of national honour and independence'. At the same time as he berated the European bourgeois liberals and social democrats who, ignoring 'national honour', put themselves at the service of the Americans, Zhdanov made efforts to explain to the bourgeoisies of Europe the threat to their interests represented by American plans. Under the pretext of defending you against a totally imaginary threat from Communism, he told them, the American capitalists are in fact trying to take over European markets and force you out of the colonies. This meant that there was a possibility – which the Communist parties should make fullest use of – that one part of the bourgeoisie, the one which could understand the close connection between its pecuniary interests and the noble ideals of national honour and independence, might make common cause with the Communists against the rapacious plans of the Americans. This is the essence of Zhdanov's analysis. But, for this possibility to become a reality, it was necessary for the third panel of the triptych, democracy, not to go beyond pale pink. Pushing it towards red, openly proposing a socialist alternative to capitalism, would be to confirm the 'Communist menace' which was the complete justification of American policy. This is why, here again, the prospect of a socialist revolution is notably absent from Stalin's new line, just as in the previous period it had been eliminated in order not to upset the 'grand alliance'.

It can easily be seen that Stalin was still remaining faithful to what had been the cornerstone of his strategy since his establishment in power. The political line he laid down for the Communist movement in 1947 continued to give priority to the exploitation of inter-imperialist and inter-capitalist contradictions rather than that between bourgeoisie and proletariat. Since the former had been momentarily buried under the European bourgeoisie's fear of revolution and the prospect of dollars, the primary task of the Communist parties was to resurrect them. More vigorous methods would have to be used to defeat the centrist and Social-Democratic politicians who fell in with American plans, and it could prove useful for this purpose to encourage class struggle in the economic field, contrary to the practice of the previous period.

The strategic objective, however, was to re-establish national unity with the section of the bourgeoisie threatened by American expansion, to create a 'vast front' for peace and national independence. This line, of course, did not concern the Communist parties of the satellite countries. There, as will be seen in the next chapter, the march towards 'socialism' was to be speeded up, even by forcing the process by administrative and repressive measures and putting in power Communist leaderships totally subservient to Moscow, in order to give the 'base' of the 'anti-imperialist camp' a monolithic structure.

This strategy was meant to counter the American offensive and give the USSR time to catch up in atomic weapons, and its final aim was a new world balance of power which would force the United States to accept the great compromise sought by Stalin. Nor was the possibility ignored that the announcement of the counter-offensive could itself make the Americans think and induce them to make a swift change of policy. Zhdanov's report was skilfully nuanced to allow Washington to see the outstretched hand under the clenched fist.

It is certainly clear that the aim was not to attack the bases of the great capitalist stronghold, but the more modest one of containing its *expansion*, and this is spelt out in the report. (This is the reason for the absence of any discussion of the problems of the colonial revolutions, of socialist revolutions in industrialized regions, or of the class struggle in the United States.) Zhdanov subsequently indicated, clearly enough to be intelligible to experts, the area in which this expansion was intolerable to Soviet interests – its European satellites – and that in which it would like an agreement recognizing the primacy of those interests, that is, Germany. As to others, Stalin's spokesman confines himself to noting the areas dominated by the North Americans (Japan and Latin America) and the areas they wish to dominate (the British, French and German colonies, China, Greece, Turkey, etc.), without the slightest reference to any Soviet claims there and showing no interest in the revolutionary struggles going on there. With regard to Latin America, for example, the underlying meaning of Zhdanov's report was fully revealed by a statement of Molotov's a few months later. In reply to an American accusation that international tension was provoked by the Soviet Union's policy in Eastern Europe, Molotov said; 'It is known that the United States of America is also pursuing a policy to strengthen its relations with neighbouring countries – for instance Canada, Mexico, and also other countries of America – which is fully understandable.'[19] In other words, 'Let each of us respect the other's zones of influence, and everything can be sorted out.'

Zhdanov's silence about the revolutionary war in Greece and China was equivalent to a diplomatic emphasis on the Soviets' favourable attitude to American interests in both the Middle and Far East. It implied, in particular, that the offer 'of a common policy with the United States of Far Eastern problems', made by Stalin in December 1946,[20] was still open. There was, of course, one condition: that the United States should abandon its claims to domination in Europe. Zhdanov insisted on the 'possibility of collaboration between the USSR and countries with different systems, on condition that the principle of reciprocity is observed and agreements made are kept'. 'Everyone knows,' he added, 'that the USSR has always been faithful, and continues to be faithful, to obligations it has undertaken. The Soviet Union has shown its willingness and desire for collaboration.' In other words, collaboration between the USSR and the United States remained possible on the basis of Yalta, Potsdam and the other agreements. Zhdanov added an important clarification: 'The Soviet government has never been opposed to the use of foreign credits, and in particular North American credits, as a means of speeding up economic reconstruction.' The only condition the Soviet government made was that such credits 'should not be a burden and should not lead to the economic and political enslavement of the debtor state by the creditor state'. In other words, the door was still open to a revised and corrected Marshall Plan which did not tend to create blocs hostile to the USSR or undermine the unity of the satellite system.

The liberal circles in the United States at the time, which gathered around Henry Wallace, who had been Vice-President with Roosevelt, fully understood the coded message contained in Zhdanov's report. They tried to convince public opinion that Stalin's offer of co-operation should be taken up, but failed lamentably.[21] The American ruling classes felt themselves strong enough to impose a *pax Americana* on the world, or, which comes to the same thing, to alter to their advantage the division of zones of influence produced by the war.

GENERAL RETREAT OF THE COMMUNIST MOVEMENT IN THE WEST

Zhdanov's report and the setting-up of the Cominform – the latter at first sight the resuscitation of the 'Red Lazarus' buried in 1943 – were received in bourgeois circles as a threat to the 'free peoples', whose defence as the 'Truman doctrine' proclaimed, the United States had altruistically undertaken. These events were seen in such circles as the proclamation of a world-wide revolutionary offensive. Once they had rejected general negotiation on the bases proposed by Stalin, it was completely in the interest of the imperialist leaders to have this version believed. The bogey of the 'red peril' provided an excellent ideological excuse for uniting the conservative forces of the world under American control.

In fact, Stalin's new policy was essentially defensive in character. Its main aim was to strengthen the position it had won in Central and Eastern Europe and in the Far East, while trying at the same time to prevent the consolidation of anti-Soviet blocs. The task of the Communist parties of the capitalist world, in carrying out their role of 'support' for the 'base' of the anti-imperialist camp, was 'to take the lead in *resistance* to imperialist plans for aggression and expansion', as Zhdanov's report put it. This new 'resistance' was to have no other strategic aim than the very utopian one of creating a bourgeois democracy jealous of its national honour and independence in the face of Washington's 'hegemonic' pretensions. This gave a special 'offensive' tone to the new policy, a verbal violence in the denunciation of American policy and its Social Democrat 'lackeys' which usually concealed a lack of ideas. (In this aspect of verbal violence the new policy recalled the good old days of the 'third period' of the Comintern, the days of 'social Fascism'.) In addition forms of struggle began to be used which had almost been forgotten during the years of collaboration in government – strikes, demonstrations and even confrontation with the authorities. But the offensive or defensive content of a policy is not determined simply by the tactics used, and verbal violence can serve – or more often do disservice to – any policy.

The growing movement of strikes in Western Europe, which began in the autumn of 1947 and continued until the end of 1949 (there was a a marked fall after this, except in Italy, where the peak was in 1950–55), was an expression of the defensive action of the working class in the face of the offensive of employers and state. It was an attempt to defend their fundamental interests against the rationalization measures which helped to prepare for the 'take-off' of the European capitalist economy which took place at the beginning of the 1950s.[22] Finding themselves back in opposition, and in an attempt to mobilize the masses against the 'third force' governments which had gone over to the service of American policy, the Communist parties tried to take over the leadership of the labour struggles instead of trying to restrain them as they had in the period 1945–47. They made efforts, with very little success, to link these struggles with campaigns for 'the defence of peace and national independence', opposition to the Marshall Plan and the banning of the atomic bomb.

In autumn 1947 a wave of strikes swept over France, involving more than two million workers. Since the movement took place when the Cominform resolutions had just become public, the government thought it was faced with a 'Communist plot' and put the country in a state of siege. It called up 8,000 reservists, disbanded units of the security forces regarded as unreliable and adopted a series of measures against the working class. In various towns clashes broke out between workers and the forces of repression, resulting in four deaths, hundreds of wounded and thousands of arrests of workers.

There was, of course, no Communist plot; there was nothing but the fear of the bourgeoisie, which still imagined itself to have been on the brink of revolution three years before, and the fact that the French Communist Party was smarting from the criticism made of its sins of opportunism at the Cominform meeting. The party wanted to use the opportunity to show Moscow that it too could take the hard line when Soviet policy required it, even if the French situation was not favourable. It tried to give the strikes a political character, and forced the CGT leadership – against the wishes of its socialist group – to include among the movement's aims the struggle 'against the plan for economic domination embodied in the Marshall Plan' and 'against the new fomenters of war who have found accomplices in our country'.[23] These slogans drew little response from the mass of the strikers, and still less from the rest of the population. Who could believe that people whom the PCF itself had so recently described as great allies of France, champions, with the USSR, of peace and the independence of the peoples, could have become, from one day to the next, sinister fomenters of war who were out to reduce France to slavery? Why could not the great ally's dollars help to restore the ailing French economy? Was it not the same French Communist Party which until only the other day had presented the economic restoration of French capitalism as the Number One task of the working class?

The PCF did not succeed in politicizing the strike, but it did provide Léon Blum with magnificent arguments to prove the automatic subordination of the Communist Party to Soviet policy and call for a split in the trade-union movement.[24] A few months later Force Ouvrière set itself up as a socialist trade-union congress, taking with it half a million CGT members. On 9 December the CGT ordered a return to work without having obtained any of its main economic demands. A year later the miners went on strike again, and the government's reply was the same: occupation of the coalfields with troops, mass arrests, etc. As in the autumn of 1947, the government, this time in the person of its Minister of the Interior, the Socialist Jules Moch, accused the Communist Party of obeying the orders of the Cominform and preparing for a takeover of power.[25] Though effective as propaganda, the part of the accusation about a seizure of power was absurd. The aim of the leadership under Thorez was to create the maximum difficulty for the government and worry the Americans at a time when the Soviet blockade of Berlin was at its height and no one knew what the outcome would be. The miners' strike, which had economic grounds, gave them an excellent opportunity, and this is why they tried to prolong and even stiffen it, when a considerable number of strikers was beginning to support a return to work.[26] In 1944–5 the advanced groups of the working class had been followed by the great mass of the working population with great political turbulence; then the proletariat had been in a position of strength. Thorez had called on the miners and other groups of workers not to use their strength, not to strike, but to collaborate with the bourgeoisie in economic reconstruction. In 1948, when the masses had fallen back into political passivity as a result of disappointment in their hopes for social renewal, Thorez addressed the miners in the words Zhdanov had used at the Cominform meeting: 'The main danger facing the working class now is to underestimate its own forces and overestimate those of the enemy.'[27] Zhdanov had made this statement in 1947, when the political situation in Europe had already changed completely. Thorez repeated it in 1948, when the political regression had become much stronger, as was shown by the isolation in which the miners' strike took place. Between 1947 and 1951 the proportion of the profits of the big capitalist companies in French national income rose from 36 per cent to 48 per cent, while the proportion of earnings fell from 47 per cent to 33 per cent. The offensive of the employers and the state succeeded in all its aims, and the ultimate cause was not that the working class underestimated its strength in this period, but that the Communist Party, in its unconditional application of Stalin's policy, underestimated it in 1944–5.

The Italian Communist Party also submitted to Stalin's new policy as defined by Zhdanov, but less mechanically than the French party. It made efforts to promote the struggle among workers and peasants, but without trying to force things, without losing sight of the fact that the political trend was going in favour of the right, as was shown by the 1948 legislative elections, in which the Christian Democrats won 48.5 per cent of the votes and an absolute majority of seats. Moreover, unlike the French party, the Italian Communists could rely on the solidarity of the majority of the Socialist Party, although the minority hostile to the Communists was gaining ground.

The attempt on the life of Togliatti in July 1948 provoked an immediate and massive reply: eight million workers declared an impressive general strike which paralysed the country for two days. Some groups in the party suggested giving the strike an insurrectionary character, but the leadership – following the advice given by Togliatti himself before he lost consciousness – ruled that given the situation that would be adventurism. They may have been right, but the July explosion showed in retrospect how strong had been the revolutionary potential which the leadership of the PCI had refused to exploit in the unique situation of 1943–5.

Like the PCF, the Italian party devoted all the attention demanded by the Cominform to campaigns for peace and the banning of the atomic bomb, against the Marshall Plan and the Atlantic Pact; it was nevertheless able to view the specific problems of Italian society with a certain rigour, even while retaining the reformist outlook of the previous period. In the early stages – before Tito's condemnation – it was even possible to get the impression that Togliatti wanted to keep his distance from the Cominform. The report he presented to the Sixth Congress of the party in January 1948 made hardly any mention of the new body which had just been set up and, when it did, stressed that the Cominform was not the Comintern and that 'the paths of development of the democratic movement in the different countries of Europe cannot be the same.' Togliatti also said, 'Our voluntary and fraternal collaboration [in the Cominform] has for the moment a consultative character.'

The two big parties of Western Communism were able in one way or another to stand up to the risks of the 'cold war' and to the unfavourable effects of their subordination to Soviet policy, but other, weaker, parties, went through serious crises. The relative success enjoyed after the liberation by the Communist parties of the Scandinavian countries, Belgium and the Netherlands, Austria, Switzerland, etc., was very soon over. The Spanish Communist Party was heavily hit by the Franco dictatorship, which, with the open protection of the United States, brutally intensified repression against the whole working-class and democratic opposition. Without any international help, and in particular with no help from the Soviet Union – while the Americans lavished support on the royalist government – the Greek Communists were obliged to give up the armed struggle in August 1949. The damage done to the Communist parties of Latin America and some Asian countries was also severe.

A later chapter will return to the general retreat of the Communist movement in the capitalist world during the years of the 'cold war'. However, before giving a general assessment of this period – which, in addition to the set-backs just mentioned includes the great victory of the Chinese revolution and the prelude to the victory of the

Vietnamese – we shall analyse in turn three situations which contain events, tendencies and phenomena which are of great importance for an understanding of the course taken by the Communist movement during these years and afterwards. The first of these is the Soviet-Yugoslav split, its repercussions on other Communist parties and the evolution of the satellites. The second is the victory of the Chinese revolution. The last is the famous 'struggle for peace' which became the central task of the Communist movement during the period of the 'cold war'.

7

THE YUGOSLAV BREACH

Since all those outside the obedience and service of our Holy Mother the Catholic Church, fixed in their errors and heresies, strive to estrange pious and faithful Christians from our Holy Faith, we have decided that the true remedy is to avoid all contact with heretics and suspect persons and to extirpate their errors in order to avoid the danger of so great an offence to the Holy Faith and the Catholic Religion in this part of the world.

The General Apostolic Inquisitor of our realms and possessions, with the agreement of the members of the General Council of the Inquisition and after consulting Us, has decided to set up the Holy Office of the Inquisition in these new provinces.

PHILIP II, 25 JANUARY 1569

THE SETTING-UP OF THE BUREAUCRATIC POLICE DICTATORSHIP IN THE SATELLITES

Stalin had given the Communist parties of the People's Democracies the task of completing the conquest of power, eliminating from the political scene all the groups hostile to integration into the Soviet orbit, whether connected with the Western powers or hesitating between the two 'camps'. This task was pushed ahead rapidly in the last months of 1947 and in the course of 1948. The problem in fact presented no great difficulties, since the controls of the state were already in the hands of the party and the Soviet army was on the spot or near. In Poland, Hungary, Rumania and Bulgaria, and in Slovakia, the big agrarian parties were put out of action during 1947. These parties, which had enjoyed a very broad social base among the peasants and the urban petty bourgeoisie, had traditionally been the main political instruments of the liberal bourgeoisie, but after 1945 they had begun to act as a refuge for the remains of the old dispossessed oligarchies. They had connections with the Western powers. It was not possible to eliminate them by the use of democratic parliamentary tactics, and since the Communist parties were unwilling to try a new type of direct revolutionary democracy they had to fall back on that of 'plots'. Control of the Ministry of the Interior and the efficient help of the Soviet secret services made it easy to take advantage of the contracts which the leaders of these agrarian parties maintained with representatives of the Western powers in order to accuse them of conspiracy against the regime. It was in this way that the main political figures in these parties were arrested and given heavy prison sentences or executed. Others managed to go into exile in time.[1]

In the rapid progress towards a monopoly of power which the Communist parties of the People's Democracies began after the setting up of the Cominform, the most spectacular event was what has become known as the 'Prague *coup*'. In Czechoslovakia, where the Communist Party had the support of the immense majority of the working class, which, as a result of the country's high level of industrialization, formed the main social force, the bourgeois parties had, paradoxically, maintained their identity and cohesion much more solidly than in the other People's Democracies. The reasons for this paradox have already been mentioned. In the other countries of the Soviet buffer zone it proved impossible to reconcile Communist – and through it Soviet – leadership with genuine operation of a system of parliamentary democracy, but this was possible in Czechoslovakia, precisely because of the existence of strong Communist influence and a numerous working class – as long as there was no break between the USSR and the United States and the internal revolution was artificially contained within limits acceptable to the liberal bourgeoisie. Once the first condition disappeared, and with it the second, a crisis in the system was inevitable. The bourgeois parties believed they could turn it to their advantage at the parliamentary elections fixed for May 1948. Surveys carried out by the Communists themselves indicated that they would in fact lose votes.[2] But the Czech

Communist Party took steps to avoid such a risk. It intensified political action among the masses and strengthened its control of the national police system. (As in the other People's Democracies, the party had controlled the Ministry of the Interior since 1945.)

On 20 February the twelve ministers belonging to the National Socialist (Beneš), Czech Populist and Slovak Democratic Parties submitted their resignations in protest against the appointment of eight Communist police superintendents in Prague. They hoped that the Social Democrat ministers would follow them and that President Beneš would be able to use the ministerial crisis to force the Communists to give way over the police appointments. However, under pressure from the workers, mobilized by the Communist Party and the trade unions, the centrist leadership of the Socialist Party adopted the position of its left wing and kept its representatives in the government. The Communist Party replied to the bourgeois parties' manoeuvre with an appeal to the masses. It called on them to organize, set up action committees in workplaces, neighbourhoods and villages, and form workers' militias which were then immediately armed by the police. It organized meetings and demonstrations everywhere to urge President Beneš to form a Gottwald government 'without reactionaries'. Throughout the country it arrested the best-known anti-Communists and opponents of the USSR. It widened the National Front by bringing in the trade unions, youth organizations and cooperatives and other mass and professional organizations under its control.

With this 'widening' – which the bourgeois parties and the Socialist Party had always vigorously opposed – the Communist Party made sure of absolute control on the Executive Committee of the National Front, which now adopted a political programme calling for a purge of the political parties and the strengthening of ties with the USSR. The army, whose main leaders were Communists (the Minister of Defence, Svoboda, was a Communist sympathizer), observed the course of events sympathetically. The Social Democratic leadership – whose headquarters were occupied by left-wing Socialists, supported by the Communists – took the further step of agreeing to cooperate in the solution proposed by the Communists. On 25 February Beneš gave way and asked Gottwald to form the new government, in which the representatives of the bourgeois parties were now no more than decoration.

The inner working of events can be clearly seen. It was not the free play of parliamentary democracy which enabled the Communists to win complete control of power, but their full use of their extra-parliamentary strength, the masses, the police, the army. The smooth progress of the operation was also protected on the northern, eastern and southern borders. (To leave no doubt about the Soviet 'presence', the deputy Soviet Foreign Minister arrived in Prague on the eve of the crisis.) But instead of saying what had in fact happened, instead of simply arguing from the right of the workers to carry out the revolution 'postponed' in 1945 – basing himself on the official view that the Communist Party was the conscious representative of the working class – instead of that, in presenting his new ministry to parliament, Gottwald claimed that 'the readjustment and reconstitution of the government have been carried out in a strictly constitutional, democratic and parliamentary manner'.[3]

The fiction was confirmed by the elections. These took place as planned on 30 May, with only one 'slight' modification: there was only one list of candidates, that of the National Front, which had of course been prepared by the executive, on which, as we have seen, the Communist Party had secured an absolute majority. The single list received 88.92 per cent of the votes. Beneš resigned on 6 June and on the 14th Gottwald was raised to the Presidency of the Republic.

Later, after the Twentieth Congress of the Soviet Communist Party, the Czech fiction was to be used as an example of the possibility of a socialist revolution by peaceful and parliamentary methods. 'The Communists,' said Mikoyan, 'came to power by making an alliance not only with the other workers' parties, which were close to them, but also with the bourgeois parties which supported the single National Front. The people of Czechoslovakia won their victory by the method of the peaceful extension of the revolution.'[4]

This final success of the Communist Parties' takeover of power meant, again according to the official line, that the regimes of the People's Democracies now began to carry out the functions of the dictatorship of the proletariat. The dogmatic conception of the dictatorship of the proletariat current in the Stalinist period, however, required it to be led by a single working-class party, the Marxist-Leninist party. The 'creative development' of Marxism in the Cominform period went no further than to admit the presence of petty bourgeois and agrarian parties in national fronts, suitably purged and submissive and with no real power, which were supposed to ease the spread of the Communist Party's influence among the petty bourgeoisie. (Experience showed that this Machiavellianism deceived no one except its own authors, and not always them.) Dogma did not allow a similar method to be used with the Social Democratic parties, or even with their left wings. The solution for them was to force them to merge with the Communist Party, though only, of course, after a suitable purge of their membership.

Shortly before the Cominform meeting Gomulka wrote an article on Socialist–Communist unification, in which he declared himself against any mechanical or bureaucratic solution of the problem:

> No mechanical unity can replace ideological unity. Mechanical unity would mean that the PSP and POP would merge without paying any attention to the differences which exist between them, without analysing the social causes of these differences, without defining their aims and the methods to be used to achieve them ... We know perfectly well that the creation of a single working-class party is a long-term ideological process.[5]

At that time Dimitrov and other Communist leaders held the same views. Nor did the internal situation of the Socialist parties in the People's Democracies give any reason to expect that the 'ideological process' which could lead to unification might be a short one. At the end of 1947, the position of the left wings had been weakened, as was shown at the congresses of the Socialist Parties of Czechoslovakia and Hungary, and even the left wings still had serious differences with the Communist parties on fundamental questions about methods of building socialism, internal party discipline and other matters. In particular, they did not accept subjection to the Soviet party.

From January 1948, however, as though touched with a magic wand, all the Socialist parties of the People's Democracies expressed a wish to merge with the Communist Party: in January the Romanians, in April the Czechs, in June the Hungarians, in December the Poles and the Bulgarians. Curious events occurred. The Twenty-fifth Congress of the Hungarian Socialist Party rejected unification with the Communists by a comfortable majority at the end of 1947; six months later the Twenty-Sixth Congress unanimously agreed to unification. At the Cominform meeting held in November 1949 Togliatti made a report on the problems of 'working-class unity'. The resolution adopted on the basis of his report noted that

In the People's Democracies historic achievements in working-class unity have been registered: united working-class parties, united trade unions, united cooperative, youth, women's and other organizations have been established.

These 'achievements', Togliatti explained, could not have been realized without

an open and determined struggle against the right-wing Social Democrats, only by exposing and isolating them, removing them from leading posts and expelling them from the ranks of the Socialist parties. This task was accomplished, although sometimes slowly and irresolutely, by the left-wing Socialists with the effective aid of the Communists.[6]

Togliatti gave no further details, and Communist documents of the period contain no circumstantial account of this 'determined' struggle or of the methods used to remove the 'right-wing Social Democrats' from leading positions and even to exclude them from the Socialist parties. If an open clash of ideas had really taken place, if decisions had really been taken freely by Socialist militants themselves, convinced of the need for unification, it is obvious that Togliatti would not have foregone the opportunity of analysing such an important experiment in detail.

But the history of the 'effective help' with which the Communists stiffened the slowness and indecisiveness of the left-wing Socialists remains to be written. The sources will be found in the police archives of the various countries, since – does it need saying? – the magic wand was nothing other than the removal from the Socialist parties of all opponents of unification. This purge was carried out by repression and intimidation, details of which are only known in the cases of well-known

Socialist figures imprisoned or forced into exile.[7] Of the leaders of the Social Democratic left who took part in this operation, some adapted to Stalinism, but others soon experienced imprisonment or political ostracism.

The elimination of the political forces of the bourgeoisie and the announcement that 'building of socialism' had begun won support in the early stages by arousing the hopes of the proletarian masses, or at least of broad groups of these, and of fairly large numbers of intellectuals. But illusions rapidly disappeared, giving way to concealed discontent, fear and above all political apathy. In its 'popular democratic' form, the dictatorship of the proletariat proved just as undemocratic and even less popular than in its 'Soviet' form. It was less popular, among other reasons, because in the People's Democracies it embodied dependence on foreign power. The system of bureaucracy and police control which called itself the representative of the proletariat while depriving the proletariat of any real participation in the politics of its country was in its turn controlled by a more hidden system whose job it was to guard the monolithic unity of the Soviet defence barrier.

Once the unbelievers had been rendered harmless, the main danger in these new provinces of the empire was heresy. Beria, the Grand Inquisitor of the period, went into action, with all the consequences that involved. The purgers began to be purged.

THE HERETICAL REVOLUTION

On 28 June 1948 the Cominform resolution condemning the leadership of the Yugoslav Communist Party was published in the People's Democracies. The news, as *Le Monde* said next day, had an effect everywhere 'nothing short of a bomb'. In the previous months the Western press had echoed rumours of difficulties between Moscow and Belgrade. (In February, *Le Figaro*, for example, had reported that the Romanian Communist Party had given orders for Tito's picture to be removed from all windows in which it had been displayed alongside those of Stalin, Dimitrov and Groza.)[8] No one, however, had suspected that the dispute could reach such proportions, least of all those most involved. In the eyes of Communists these rumours were obviously mere slanders on the parts of the bourgeois press. The only people Stalin told about the dispute – or rather about his version of it – were the senior leaders of the other seven parties which, with the Soviet and Yugoslav parties, made up the Cominform. The rest of the world Communist movement read the news in the papers like anyone else.

Before analysing the Cominform resolution we shall quickly note the main antecedents of the crisis, drawing on the information at present available. This information is still incomplete, because the Soviet archives are still closed to historians, a handicap which affects the study of all these problems.[9] As we have seen,[10] the conflict which arose during the war between the policy of the Yugoslav Communists and Stalin's strategy was followed by a *rapprochement* between the two countries, particularly after 1946, when the deterioration in relations between Moscow and Washington was particularly sharp. Nevertheless the serious differences of the war period should be regarded as the first effects of the crisis of 1948, if only because they revealed the existence in the Yugoslav leadership of a desire for autonomy hard to reconcile with the view held in Moscow and in the Communist movement as a whole of the relations which should hold between the 'leading party' and the led. If an internationalist attitude had prevailed in Moscow, the nationalist aspect which naturally went with the Yugoslav desire for autonomy would have faded away. Instead, the clash with Great-Russian nationalism made it all the keener. Between the liberation of Yugoslavia and the beginning of the crisis which led to the 1948 break, the latent conflict between the two nationalisms showed itself in a series of significant incidents and problems, most of which were known only to members of the leading groups and were not publicly disclosed until the acute phase of the crisis or after the break.

At the end of 1944, after the liberation of Belgrade, there were many incidents of violence and ill-treatment of the civilian population by Soviet soldiers. Reactionaries naturally used these incidents in their struggle against the new regime. The revolutionary masses, including the Communists, couldn't understand it, and found it even harder to understand why the culprits were not punished with the utmost severity. The matter became an important political problem, which Tito himself and the Yugoslav leaders had to raise with General Korneyev, head of the Soviet military mission.

The General's immediate reaction was to describe this step as an insult to the Red Army. During the discussion one of the Yugoslav leaders explained that the affair was acquiring an even greater political significance from the fact that the members of the British military mission did not commit such excesses and the people were beginning to remark on the contrast. This brought General Korneyev to boiling point; for him such a remark meant comparing the Red Army with the armies of capitalist countries, which he regarded as an intolerable insult.[11]

In the years that followed Stalin mentioned this episode several times in the presence of the Yugoslav leaders, and in 1948 it became one of the 'proofs' of their anti-Soviet attitude.[12] Similar cases of misbehaviour by some Soviet troops – contrasting with the correct behaviour of the majority – had taken place in other countries, notably Hungary, and of course Germany, where the 'right of conquest' was applied widely. In none of these countries, however, did Communist leaders dare to raise the matter with the Soviet military authorities.

Another significant incident, this time in foreign affairs, took place in 1945 In April Yugoslavia had signed a mutual aid pact with the USSR. Shortly after, Anglo-American troops entered Trieste, where Yugoslav partisans were already stationed. Washington and London presented Tito with an ultimatum ordering him to evacuate Trieste. In vain the Yugoslav leader applied for the help of the Soviet army. At the end of May he made a speech in Ljubljana, the capital of Slovenia. Referring to reports in the Western press that Yugoslavia was claiming Trieste in order to hand it over to the USSR, Tito insisted: 'We have no wish to be dependent on anyone, whatever may be said or published ... We do not want to be small change; we do not want to be involved in any policy of spheres of influence.' On instructions from the Kremlin, the Soviet Ambassador in Belgrade hastily informed the Yugoslav leaders that his government regarded this speech as 'an act of hostility towards the Soviet Union', and that any future similar act would be publicly denounced by Moscow.[13]

After 1945 the dispute between Moscow and Belgrade spread to economic problems. Two tendencies emerged within the Yugoslav party leadership. The minority, represented by the Minister of Finance and the Minister for Industry (Zhujović and Hebrang, who was also president of the planning commission), reflected the Soviet view. The majority was led by Tito, Kardelj and others. The first group favoured slow economic development, in view of the country's lack of credits, skilled workers and technicians, and also in view of the 'higher interests of the USSR'. The second called for a crash programme of industrialization by mobilizing the enthusiasm of the workers, obtaining credits and Soviet technical assistance.[14]

At the same time however, the Yugoslavs were opposed to some of the forms of 'economic aid' proposed by Moscow, and especially the 'joint companies'. In appearance, Stalin gave way on this last point and admitted in conversation with the Yugoslav leaders that 'joint companies were a form of collaboration with dependent countries and not with independent friendly countries'. But tension persisted on other questions, such as the terms of the Soviet loans and fixed prices for trade between the two countries, which the Yugoslav leaders regarded as harmful to their national economic development.[15]

Another problem which played a large part in the Soviet-Yugoslav crisis was that of the Balkan and Danubian federation. As early as 1944 Tito and Dimitrov, in a break with the nationalist attitudes mentioned in a previous chapter, had begun to draft a constitution for a Balkan federation. Differences appeared over the structure of the federation, and in addition the British and Americans made known their opposition. Stalin, who had agreed in principle to the idea – although in fact, as appeared later, he was far from happy about it – took advantage of this opposition to ask the Yugoslavs and Bulgarians to suspend all negotiations. They were resumed in 1947. The Bled Conference, held at the end of July, in which leaders of the two countries took part, produced a series of agreements – among others one for a customs union – which amounted in practice to the basis of the federation.[16] There were still differences, however, on one essential point: should the federation be composed of eight equal republics (the seven which made up the federal state of Yugoslavia plus the Bulgarian republic), as the Yugoslavs wanted, or should it be made up of two states (the Yugoslav and the

Bulgarian), as the Bulgarians wanted, which would have the effect of placing the republics which made up the Yugoslav federation in an inferior position to the Bulgarian republic? In January 1948, in a sensational statement, Dimitrov outlined a much more ambitious project, the creation of a Balkan and Danubian federation or confederation including all the People's Democracies plus Greece. (In December 1947 the revolutionary government of Markos had been formed in the mountains of northern Greece, and the entry of Greece into Dimitrov's plan was clearly based on the assumption that the uprising would succeed.) Dimitrov explained that this question 'had not yet been discussed in our conferences'.

When it matures, and it must inevitably mature, then our peoples, the People's Democracies, Romania, Bulgaria, Yugoslavia, Albania, Czechoslovakia, Poland, Hungary, and Greece – yes, Greece – will settle it. It is they who will decide what it shall be – a federation or a confederation – and when and how it will be formed. What I can say is that our peoples have already begun to work out a solution for this problem.[17]

This statement appeared in *Pravda* in Moscow, but a few days later (29 January) the paper published a semi-official note indicating the Soviet leadership's complete opposition:

It was impossible for *Pravda* not to publish Comrade Dimitrov's statement, which was published by the newspapers of other countries, but this does not mean that the editors of *Pravda* agree with Comrade Dimitrov on the question of a federation or customs union between the countries mentioned. On the contrary, the editors of *Pravda* believe that these countries have no need of any sort of more or less dubious or artificial federation, confederation or customs union.

At the same time as publishing this public reprimand to the most distinguished figure in the world Communist movement after himself, Stalin urgently summoned the Bulgarian and Yugoslav leaders. The meeting took place on 10 February. Dimitrov and Kardelj tried to defend their positions. Stalin would allow no discussion; he gave orders. He ridiculed Dimitrov: 'Whatever you do, you bandy words like a woman of the streets. You want to astonish the world as though you were still Secretary of the Comintern.' Faced with the plan for a Balkan and Danubian federation, he insisted on the immediate formation of the Bulgarian–Yugoslav federation according to the original Bulgarian plan. He ordered that once this plan was carried out the new federation should annex Albania. The next day Molotov summoned Kardelj and gave him a document to sign committing Yugoslavia to consult the Soviet government before making any step in foreign policy.[18] This meeting marked the beginning of the attack on the Yugoslavs, secret at first, whose first open sign was revealed by *Le Figaro* – the sudden disappearance of Tito s portrait from the shop-windows of Bucharest.

Stalin's opposition to the Dimitrov–Tito plan needs no explanation. The idea of an independent association of People's Democracies went directly counter to all Stalin's plans, and the interesting question the plan raises is how it could have been worked out and, still more, outlined in public by Dimitrov. There is not yet enough information available for a definite answer, but at least it seems clear that the old Communist leader's position, like those of Tito and Gomulka – who, it seems was also in favour of the idea of some sort of federation of People's Democracies[19] – shows that a movement for autonomy against the great protector was trying to emerge in the leading circles of the East European countries. The idea of a federation was undoubtedly connected with the idea that it was necessary to follow new roads, different from the Soviet one, in the march towards socialism. This idea had already been formulated in the previous period, and its principal theoretician – in so far as one can talk of theoretical development here – was Dimitrov himself.

At the tripartite meeting in Moscow (between the Soviets, Bulgarians and Yugoslavs), the problem of the Balkan and Danubian federation appeared as linked with the Greek question. The Yugoslavs and Albanians were firmly supporting, as far as they were able, the armed struggle of the Greek Communists. Shortly before the Moscow meeting the Albanian government had asked the Yugoslav government to send two divisions to the Greco–Albanian border. Belgrade gave a sympathetic reply, but Molotov informed the Yugoslavs that the Soviet government was completely opposed to this, and threatened that Moscow would make its attitude public if the governments in Belgrade and

Tirana did not cancel their planned actions. At the meeting on 10 February Stalin announced without any attempt at evasion that the armed struggle in Greece had no future and that the Yugoslavs should break off their help to the Greek Communists. It was obvious, in view of the military resources committed in Greece by American imperialism, that the revolutionary forces could not win without Soviet military help, and Stalin refused to get involved in this area. (Zhdanov's report at the Cominform meeting is clear enough about this.) The inclusion of Greece in the plan for a Balkan and Danubian federation, however, amounted to a public proclamation that the Communist movement was prepared to increase its help to the Greek fighters. This was a challenge to Washington which was incompatible with Stalin's strategy.

Throughout this period, from the liberation to the 1948 break, another concealed, but most serious, conflict existed between Moscow and Belgrade. It remained more clandestine and secret than the others – as suited its nature – but in it was acted out the fundamental question in the dispute: was Yugoslavia to be an independent country or a 'socialist' colony? This conflict was the underground war in which the Soviet and Yugoslav secret services engaged in from 1945.

The Soviets organized their network by recruiting agents in every quarter, and above all in the leading circles of the Yugoslav Communist Party and government, in the army and the police, in the economic organizations and the diplomatic corps. The Yugoslavs tried to prevent this recruitment, and tried to discover and keep watch on the Soviet network. It was an old story, but it took place now for the first time between two states which claimed to be Socialist and two parties which claimed to be Communist.

A first step on the Soviet side was to overcome the scruples of the Yugoslav Communist contacts, torn between loyalty to their people and party, to which they were attached not just by ideology and national sentiment but also by the four years of blood and sacrifice of the war of liberation, and loyalty to the Soviet Union, which every Communist regarded as the highest expression of the revolutionary cause. The Soviet agents used arguments like this: 'The enemy can be found among the most important leaders [here they mentioned the cases of Trotsky, Bukharin and others]; we can never be completely sure, and in this case it is preferable to rely on a higher and more experienced organization like the Soviet Union.' Beria's men generally spoke well of Tito, but let it be understood that his entourage contained 'suspect elements' who needed to be watched.[20]

The same sort of things went on in the other People's Democracies, with the difference that there the Communist parties offered no resistance. The resistance of the Yugoslav leaders to this secret system responsible for maintaining the monolithic unity of the satellite system around the ideology and policies of Moscow was without doubt one of the main causes of the break between the Kremlin and the Yugoslav party.

All these events make it clear that from as early as the end of the war Stalin had been constantly preoccupied with finding a way to bring the Yugoslavs to heel. He tried various methods, according to the political situation, mixing warnings and abrupt demands with compromises and concessions. In 1946 Stalin tried to flatter Tito's vanity – real or supposed – by praising his merits in private while disparaging Dimitrov, Thorez, Togliatti and La Pasionaria.[21] Zhdanov used the prestige the Yugoslav Communists had won as a revolutionary party to correct the opportunism of the French and Italians and make them toe the new anti-American line. At the time of the setting-up of the Cominform the Yugoslav party seemed to be the closest to the switch of policy ordered by Stalin, but it was in fact this switch which brought the hitherto secret conflict into the open. Stalin's anti-American strategy envisaged halting Washington's offensive in the areas and on the issues he regarded as vital to Soviet interests, while at the same time keeping open the possibility of a general arrangement recognizing the predominance of American interests in other areas and on other issues. One of these areas was the southern Balkans. Stalin was not interested in challenging the *status quo* established in the peninsula, which implied American control in Greece and the rejection of Yugoslav claims to Trieste and Slovenian Carinthia, as well as of Macedonian aspiration to national unity. Yugoslav foreign policy, on the other hand, was centred on opposition to this *status quo*, and so embodied the danger of a major dispute with Washington which would involve the Soviet Union. Yugoslav 'adventurism' was becoming a more serious danger to Stalin's new strategy than the government-and-parliament-centred opportunism of the French and Italian Communists.

Nevertheless, this problem does not seem to have been the main cause of the break. To judge from the available information, the Yugoslavs seem in the end to have accepted the demands of Soviet foreign policy. The breaking point came rather over the satellites; Yugoslavia's independent attitude was incompatible with Stalin's plans for integration. It had become a threat to the success of the plan as a whole, and not just in Yugoslavia. After the Cominform meeting, however, the Yugoslav leaders had not changed their attitude to this question in any way.[22] The bomb thrown by Dimitrov in the shape of the plan for the Balkan and Danubian federation showed how serious was the danger of infection among the other People's Democracies.[23]

Events had got to the point at which Stalin's patience was exhausted and his morbid suspicion exploded. It would soon be necessary to kill the virus to prevent its spreading further. Stalin's determination was also doubtless influenced by his belief in his infallibility and absolute power. As Khrushchev revealed in his 'secret speech' to the Twentieth Congress, Stalin was convinced that he had only to lift his little finger to destroy Tito. He was sure that if they were called on to choose between the Soviet Union and Yugoslavia, between Stalin and Tito, the Yugoslav Communists would not hesitate for a second. No doubt his secret service, by giving him the information he wanted to hear, reinforced this belief.

The first movement of Stalin's little finger was a message to the Yugoslavs at the end of February not to send to Moscow the trade delegation which had been due to go there in April to renew the trade agreement between the two countries. In practice this meant breaking off trade relations and placed Yugoslavia in a very difficult situation, since all its trade was with the Soviet Union and the People's Democracies. The USSR took 50 per cent of Yugoslav exports and sent Yugoslavia vital raw materials such as oil.

The Central Committee of the Yugoslav Communist Party met on 1 March. Tito and Kardelj, who had just returned from their meeting with Stalin in Moscow, explained the implications of the new situation. The Central Committee decided to resist Soviet pressure in all areas. It was revealed later that some members of the Central Committee were agents recruited by the Soviet secret service, which they immediately informed of the decisions taken.

From this point the little finger became more threatening. On 18 March the Soviet embassy in Belgrade informed Tito that Moscow had decided to withdraw the military advisers and instructors sent to help with the modernization of the Yugoslav army. The following day it announced the departure of the civilian group (engineers, technicians, economists, etc.). Moscow justified the first action by claiming that the military advisers and instructors had been subjected to unfriendly treatment, and the second on the ground that the civilian specialists had not been allowed to obtain the 'economic information' they wanted from any Yugoslav citizen, because an instruction had been issued that to obtain such information the Soviet experts should apply to the leadership of the Yugoslav Communist Party or the appropriate ministry.[24] Tito immediately wrote to Molotov expressing amazement at the reasons given by Moscow. The behaviour of the Yugoslavs towards the Soviet advisers, he wrote, had been 'not only correct but most hospitable and brotherly'. The decision about economic information had been taken

because every official in our ministerial offices had been giving information, needed or not needed, to everybody ... various people handed out official economic secrets which could come, and actually did come in some cases, to the knowledge of our common enemies.

We are not aware of any special understanding, such as is alleged in [your] message, [requiring] our officials [not] to give varied information of an economic character ... without the approval of our government or the Central Committee ...

The letter ended:

From all this it must be deduced that the above-mentioned reasons have not led the Soviet government to proceed with these steps. And it would be our desire that the government of the USSR should frankly state what the matter really is; that they tell us what, in their view, is not in accord with friendly relations between our two countries ...

In so far as the government of the USSR obtains information from various other persons, we are of the opinion that such information should be handled with reserve, since it is not always given in an objective, correct or well-meaning spirit.

This letter began the escalation of correspondence which led to the Cominform meeting (in the second half of June) and the publication (on 28 June) of the Cominform resolution condemning the Yugoslav heresy.

Stalin replied to Tito on 27 March. He began by describing Tito's explanations as 'untrue' and 'utterly unsatisfactory'. He insisted on the right of Soviet experts to obtain 'information' on any subjects they wished, and issued a list of fresh charges against the Yugoslavs. The first point which scandalized the Soviet leader, the head of a state famous for the freedom with which it allowed foreign Communists to move freely and without surveillance, and obtain any information they wanted, was that 'Soviet representatives . . . are being put under the control and supervision of Yugoslav security officers . . . Such a practice is encountered by Soviet representatives only in bourgeois countries, and then not in all of them.' Another charge was that 'anti-Soviet statements' were circulating 'among the leading comrades in Yugoslavia, such as "the CPSU (B) is decadent", . . . "great-power chauvinism is rampant in the USSR", . . . "the USSR is trying to dominate Yugoslavia economically", "the Cominform is a means of conquest of other parties by the CPSU (B)", . . . "socialism in the USSR has ceased to be revolutionary".' Such travesties of the truth scandalized Stalin, but above all because they were being made secretly when there was nothing to prevent criticism from being frank and open. Stalin had never restricted the right of other parties to criticize:

We recognize unconditionally the right enjoyed by every Communist Party, thus also by the Yugoslav Communist Party, to criticize the CPSU (B), as the CPSU (B) has the right to criticize any other Communist party. But Marxism demands that any criticism be open-minded and honest, and not behind the scenes and slanderous; when the criticized is deprived of any possibility of answering the critics . . . [it is] a slander and an attempt to discredit the CPSU (B). This is an attempt to overthrow the Soviet system.

But the 'Soviet system' could hit back:

> One should not disdain to recall that Trotsky, when he intended to declare war on the CPSU (B), also began by accusing the CPSU (B) of decadence, of narrow nationalism, of great-power chauvinism. Of course, he covered all this with left-wing phrases about the world revolution. Nevertheless, as is known, Trotsky himself was a degenerate, and afterwards, once he had been proved for what he was, he openly joined the camp of the sworn enemies of the CPSU (B) and the Soviet Union.
>
> We imagine that the political career of Trotsky is sufficiently instructive.

Having given the Yugoslavs such bracing encouragement to exercise their right of criticism, Stalin went on to make use of the Bolshevik party's right to criticize the Yugoslav party on questions of its internal affairs and its policies. He showed great anxiety at the lack of internal democracy within the party. Its central committee had not been elected, but 'co-opted'. There was no criticism or self criticism and, worst of all, the party cadres were under the supervision of Ranković, the Minister of the Interior. Nothing like this had ever happened in the Bolshevik party, and therefore, explained Stalin, 'it is understandable that we could not consider such an organization of a Communist party to be Marxist–Leninist and Bolshevist'.

As regards the policy of the Yugoslav party, Stalin's anxiety was aroused mainly by two points, first that the Yugoslav party did not fight vigorously enough against the kulaks, and so fell into Bukharinism, and second that, instead of exercising its leading role openly, it did it through the Popular Front. (The Popular Front in Yugoslavia, unlike the Popular Fronts of other countries, was not a coalition of parties, but a mass movement with a revolutionary programme which had been created during the war of liberation.)

Stalin's attack in his letter was concentrated on Djilas, Vukmanović, Kidric and Ranković, whom he named and described as 'dubious Marxists'. These men controlled, respectively the ministries of press and propaganda, the army, the economy and the interior, those, in other words which the NKVD was most anxious to infiltrate. If Tito removed these 'dubious Marxists' who 'slandered the Soviet Union', matters could be patched up. The ministers mentioned offered their resignations to Tito, but he had sufficient experience of the Comintern to know where such concessions would lead.

On 12 April the Central Committee of the Yugoslav party met to examine Stalin's letter. With the exception of two members, who, as was learnt later, were agents of the NKVD, the Central Committee approved a firm answer, which, among other things, contained the following passage: 'However much affection any of us may cherish towards the country of socialism, the USSR, in no way can he have less affection for his own country, in which socialism is being built as well ... for the sake of which hundreds of thousands of its most progressive sons have given their lives.' On the problem of the Soviet experts, military and civilian, the letter recalled that in 1946 the Yugoslav government had informed Moscow of the difficulties it was meeting in paying the experts the extremely high salaries (in relation to those of the Yugoslavs) demanded by the Soviet government; a Soviet specialist with the rank of colonel or lieutenant-colonel, for example, received four times the income of a Yugoslav General commanding an army corps and three times that of a federal government minister. The Central Committee's comments on this point ended: '... we felt [that this was not only] a financial burden [but also] politically incorrect, since it was hard to explain to our people.' The Yugoslav Central Committee's firmer opposition concerned the activities of the NKVD:

We consider it incorrect that officers of the Soviet intelligence service should enlist our citizens in our country whilst we proceed towards socialism, and enlist them for purposes of an intelligence service. We are unable to give it [any other] interpretation than ... as being directed against our country's interests. This is being done despite the fact that our leadership and our officers of state security have protested ... and have let it be known that we are not willing to tolerate this any longer ...

We possess evidence showing that some officers of the Soviet intelligence service ... besmirch our leaders with suspicions, belittle their prestige and show them as incapable of their tasks and as suspicious characters... [This cannot be justified as] a struggle against some capitalist country ... we cannot avoid coming to the conclusion that this activity serves the purpose of ruining our unity at home; that it is meant to destroy all confidence in the leadership ... demoralize the people and ... compro-

mise their respect for the state leadership . . . This sort of activity [cannot]
be regarded as loyal towards our country, which is entering upon socialism
and is the truest of allies of the USSR.

We are unable to [accept that] the Soviet intelligence service should
[develop] its network inside Yugoslavia. We have organized a state security service and have our own intelligence service . . . to fight against . . .
foreign capitalist enemies and the class enemy within our own country. If
. . . Soviet intelligence officers should require any information or assistance in this respect, they could obtain it any time they wanted.[25]

The meeting of the Yugoslav Central Committee on 12 April 1948
was Stalin's first historic defeat. It was the first time that an overwhelming majority of the Central Committee of one of the main Communist
parties had defied his threats and orders. It was the first time that not
only a Communist party but also a revolution and a revolutionary
state led by Communists resisted his *Diktat* and dared to stand up to the
formidable NKVD. Words were now followed by actions as Ranković's officers began to arrest party and state officials who were known
to be Soviet agents. At the same time the party leadership secretly
informed the most trusted militants of what was happening. The story of
Trotsky had been more instructive to the veteran Yugoslav Communists
than Stalin could have imagined. But the battle was only beginning.

Stalin set the Cominform mechanism in motion. This, mainly, was
what he had created it for. He sent the member parties a copy of his
letter of 27 March to the Yugoslavs and, without enclosing the Yugoslavs' letters, called on them to make statements. There was no need for
them to know the Yugoslavs' arguments; it was enough to know what
Stalin thought of them. Moscow warned them that the documents in
which they declared their positions should not be sent to the Yugoslavs,
but only to Stalin. The text of the replies has not been published, but
according to Yugoslav sources they were all similar, all supported Stalin
unreservedly and called on the Yugoslav party to retract. Rakosi's reply
in particular angered the Yugoslavs, who still remembered the horrors
committed by the Hungarian Fascist troops during the war. Rakosi had
also complained a number of times in confidence to the Yugoslav Communist leaders about the behaviour of the Russian army in Hungary,
accusing it of plundering the country and displaying anti-semitic

tendencies. The Bulgarian reply was little different, although Dimitrov urged the Yugoslavs – according to their account – to stand firm.[26] The weight of his ideological formation, and also perhaps tactical considerations, made the old Lion of Leipzig draw back submissively each time a dispute with Stalin brought him to the edge of a conflict.

Stalin's next letter – a reply to the Yugoslavs' letter of 13 April — was dated 4 May, and marked a new stage in the escalation. It claimed that 'the ambassador of the USA in Belgrade is behaving as if he were a master in his own house', and that government and party posts were full of 'the friends and relatives of the hangman of the Yugoslav peoples, Nedić (the Yugoslav Quisling)'. But the letter deeply offended the Yugoslavs, above all by attempting to minimize the role of the Communists and the Yugoslav revolutionary army in the liberation of the country and the victory of the revolution, and attributing the decisive blow to the Soviet armies. Referring to May 1944, after the German attack on Tito's headquarters, Stalin's letter said:

... when the national liberation movement in Yugoslavia was passing through a severe crisis, the Soviet armies rushed ... to the assistance of the Yugoslav people, broke down the resistance of the German occupying army, freed Belgrade and thus created the conditions [which brought] the Communist Party power.

With his customary skill in manipulating history, Stalin this time distorted it – thereby contradicting the version of the events of summer 1944 in Yugoslavia which the Soviets themselves had given four years before[27] – in order to denigrate the Yugoslav party and turn the other parties of the Cominform against it. The passage quoted ends: 'The merits and successes ... of the Communist parties of Poland, Czechoslovakia, Hungary, Romania, Bulgaria, Albania, are not in anything smaller than the merits and successes of the Yugoslav Communist Party.' The fact that the French and Italian parties were having 'less success' than the Yugoslav party was to be explained by the Soviet army's inability to give them the same help as it gave the Yugoslavs in 1944. The main difference was that 'the leaderships of these Communist parties behave modestly and do not shout about their successes', while the Yugoslav leaders 'have pierced the ears of all with their exaggerated self-glorification'. Stalin then summarized his previous charges, added some new ones, such as that the Yugoslav deputy foreign minister, the ambassador in London and a number of other officials were British agents – all without the slightest evidence – and ended:

The Yugoslav comrades ... should also take into account that by remaining in such a position they deprive themselves of the right to claim material and other assistance from the Soviet Union, since the Soviet Union can only give assistance to its friends.

In this letter Stalin rejected the suggestion made by the Yugoslavs in their last letter, in which they had invited a delegation from the Soviet party to go to Yugoslavia and see on the spot that the situation was not as Moscow described it. Stalin proposed, instead, that the matter should be brought before the Cominform. The Yugoslav Central Committee met on 9 May and rejected this suggestion in the following terms:

We do not try to avoid criticism on any question of principle. But we feel in this case [that we have been] deprived of a right to equality and therefore are not able to accede to your suggestion that the matter be decided by the Cominform Buro. Nine parties have received your first letter and we have not been informed of this before. These parties have taken a stand in resolutions.

The Central Committee meeting examined the cases of two party leaders and members of the government, Zhujović and Hebrang. It had been discovered that they were Stalin's agents and a decision had been made to try them. A threatening telegram arrived from Moscow, and the NKVD prepared a plan to kidnap Zhujović and take him to the Soviet Union by air. When the Soviet agents wanted to go into action, however, it was too late; Zhujović was already in prison. On 19 May a messenger from the Kremlin arrived in Belgrade and repeated the invitation to a Cominform meeting. The Central Committee discussed the matter again and confirmed its earlier refusal.

According to later Yugoslav disclosures, in addition to the reasons mentioned above, it was felt that there was no guarantee that the delegation would be able to return safely to Yugoslavia. The spectre of 1937 was in everyone's mind; many Yugoslav Communists had been executed in that year in the Soviet Union. Nor had Tito forgotten what had happened at the same time to the Politburo of the Ukrainian Communist Party, which had taken a critical attitude to Stalin's policy of Great-Russian nationalism. To make them see reason Stalin sent Molotov to Kiev. Having failed to make the members of the Politburo change their minds, Molotov called a meeting of the plenum of the Ukrainian Central Committee, but this supported by a majority the position taken by its Politburo. Stalin then summoned the Politburo to Moscow to discuss the matter. Hardly had the members of the Politburo reached Moscow than they were arrested by the NKVD and shot shortly afterwards. In a sense, Tito was a survivor of the terrible Stalinist purges of the thirties, which goes far to explain his farsighted reactions of 1948.[28]

Stalin now used further forms of pressure in an attempt to bring the Yugoslav Party before the bar of the Cominform. In his last letter (22 May), he accused the Yugoslavs of 'breaching the united socialist front of the People's Democracies and the Soviet Union', and spoke for the first time of 'treason'. The Yugoslav leadership stuck firmly to its positions. On 25 May it publicly announced its decision to call a party congress to give all the militants an opportunity to pronounce on the dispute after hearing the facts. General assemblies of the local organizations were held almost everywhere, and the correspondence between Stalin and Tito was read. Congress delegates were democratically elected in the proportion of one delegate per two hundred members. The Tass correspondent was invited to the meeting of the Belgrade organization. Once there was no more hope of the Yugoslavs' attending the meeting, the Cominform met in their absence and adopted the resolution proposed by the USSR, which combined in summary form the critical points from Stalin's letter.[29] According to Yugoslav reports, the Soviet delegation, led by Zhdanov, Malenkov and Suslov, met some resistance from a number of delegations, who found the text of the condemnation too sharp. To remove these hesitations, Zhdanov announced: 'We possess information that Tito is an imperialist spy.'[30]

This categorical accusation was not for the moment added to the Cominform resolution; the ground had first to be prepared in the Communist movement, and 'proof' provided. This was the function of the campaign of ideological terrorism launched on the basis of the Cominform resolution, and Rajk's trial, a year later, was to provide the 'proof' in the same way that the Moscow trials of 1937–8 had provided the 'proof' that Trotsky had been a spy for the world bourgeoisie from his tenderest years.

At the head of the resolution stood the true reason for the condemnation, the resistance of the Yugoslav leaders to Soviet control. The offence was, of course, presented in such a way that it could not fail to arouse the indignation of any good Communist: 'Slander of Soviet military experts and attacks on the reputation of the Red Army'; persecution of Soviet civilian experts, who were forced to 'follow a special routine to allow them to be watched by the Yugoslav state security organizations and followed by their agents'; 'slanderous propaganda about the "degeneracy" of the Communist Party of the USSR (Bolsheviks)' drawn from 'the arsenal of counter-revolutionary Trotskyism', etc.

The remainder of the resolution was devoted mainly to a criticism of the supposed political errors of the Yugoslav party (its anti-Soviet attitude was of course more than an error; it was a crime), in an attempt to prove that 'anti-Sovietism' was indissolubly linked with serious political and theoretical deviations from Marxism–Leninism. At the founding meeting of the Cominform the Yugoslav leaders, like the representatives of the other parties which made up the organization, had given a detailed account of all aspects of their policies. Neither the Soviet delegates nor any of the others had then made the slightest criticism; on the contrary, the Yugoslav party had been regarded as the model of a revolutionary party and it was in this capacity that it acted as prosecutor in the discussion of the French and Italian parties' opportunism. In other words, the Cominform in 1947 judged the policy of the Yugoslav party to be perfectly Marxist–Leninist, while in June 1948 it decided that the very same policy was no longer anything of the sort, but had become nationalist, Bukharinist, Menshevik, Trotskyist and anti-Soviet.

The Yugoslav party was the only member of the Cominform to have successfully combined the war against Fascism with a revolution against capitalism, and it now found itself accused of 'abandoning the Marxist theory of classes and the class struggle' by those who themselves had followed the path of class collaboration on a national and international scale. The Cominform resolution included as part of Marxist theory the Stalinist dogma that the class struggle inevitably sharpened in the stage of the transition from capitalism to socialism and condemned the Yugoslavs for not taking account of this. According to the Cominform, the Yugoslav party was not carrying out a thorough struggle against the kulaks. This accusation had already appeared in Stalin's letter of 27 March, and the Yugoslav leaders, no doubt impressed by this criticism from the guardian of orthodoxy, made the mistake of immediately announcing the rapid elimination, not only of kulaks, but also of small private trade and industry, only to find themselves accused in the Cominform resolution of irresponsible adventurism.

Secondly, the Cominform denounced the Yugoslav leadership as revisionist on the Marxist–Leninist doctrine of the leading role of the party. The Yugoslav party had been the only one in Europe, apart from the Greek, to conceive of the unity of the resistance, not as a coalition from above with the bourgeois parties, but as a revolutionary mass movement with socialist aims. The Popular Front, the organized political expression of this movement, grew in prestige and influence, and in a number of cases the Communist leaders thought it opportune for the Popular Front and not the Communist Party to present to the country proposals and policies which had in fact been worked out by the party leadership. In practice, the Communists controlled the whole government of the country, not only through the decisive influence they had acquired during the revolutionary struggle, but also because they controlled all the key positions, in the first place in the army and the police. There was not the slightest danger of the leadership of the party slipping out of their hands, but Stalin used these facts to accuse Tito and his colleagues of tendencies to 'liquidate' the Yugoslav Communist Party.

Thirdly, the Cominform accused the Yugoslav leaders of setting up a 'bureaucratic system' within the party, with the result that the party was left without 'inner party democracy ... elections ... criticism and self-criticism'. This internal organization was common to all the Communist parties – election of the controlling bodies, for example, where it took place, was limited to the 'election' of candidates chosen in advance by the existing leadership, but the Cominform tried to make the Yugoslav party take exclusive responsibility for it and described it as 'disgraceful, purely Turkish' (*sic*) and 'terrorist'. This meant that the Yugoslav party was credited with having the system which Stalin had long ago set up in the Soviet party, as the Twentieth Congress was to reveal some years later. In one of his letters Stalin had accused the Yugoslavs of not having called the party congress since the end of the war. This charge no longer appeared in the Cominform resolution, perhaps because the Yugoslavs had decided to call the party congress immediately, but no doubt also because someone had discreetly reminded Stalin that the Soviet party had now gone ten years without holding a congress and none was in preparation. (The Nineteenth Congress of the CPSU was not held until the end of 1952, fourteeen years after the Eighteenth Congress.)

The Yugoslav Communist Party was no model of democracy – far from it – but in this situation the leaders were saved, as was the revolution, by their realization that they could stand up to Stalin's attacks only by winning the support of the party base and the mass of the workers. They were able to do this as a result of the radical nature and authenticity of the Yugoslav revolution. It is well known that in contrast to the other countries of Eastern Europe, where the decisive factor was the Soviet army, in Yugoslavia it was the armed struggle of the people, organized and led by the Communist Party. The most important Communist leaders of the other People's Democracies arrived in their countries behind the Soviet army, and those who, like Gomulka, Rajk and a few others, had fought in their own country were immediately surrounded at the liberation by those who had come from Moscow, when they were not relegated to subordinate positions. Tito and his comrades, however, had shared the dangers and privations of the resistance fighters, and this had created bonds of mutual trust. War and revolution had reshaped leaders and led, moulding them in the same national revolutionary spirit. The mass of Yugoslav Communists was certainly as alienated as the Communists of other countries; their consciousness was dimmed by the fetishism of ideological commodities which carried the famous label of the October revolution. This was Stalin's principal asset. The Yugoslav party leadership realized that the only cure for the alienation of the bulk of the party was the truth. All the elements of the problem had to be put before it: Stalin's letters, the Cominform resolutions, the Yugoslav replies, the activities of the secret service, the unilateral breaking-off of trade relations and the rest. Everyone must have the opportunity to compare actions and words.

The Cominform resolution ended with an appeal to the Communists and people of Yugoslavia to overthrow the Titoist leadership. Stalin and his allies were sure that Tito's first step would be to conceal this document from the country and prevent its distribution. The document also contained the allegation that the Yugoslav party leaders had taken 'the path of outrightly deceiving their party and people by concealing from the Yugoslav Communist Party the criticism of the Central Committee's incorrect policy'. When this passage was written it was already some weeks since Stalin's letter had been read at local assemblies of the Yugoslav party. Scarcely had the Cominform resolution been issued when *Borba*, the central organ of the Yugoslav party, published half a million copies of the full text and the Yugoslav reply. That issue of Borba was published on 30 June. On 5 July Duclos wrote in *L'Humanité*: 'The fact that the Yugoslav leaders have not published the information bureau's resolution shows that they are unsure of their arguments and afraid to let their people know the facts.' The Yugoslav ambassador in Paris called in vain on the editor of *L'Humanité* to publish a correction. None of the member parties of the Cominform, who had just accused the Yugoslav party of a lack of 'internal democracy', published the reply of the Central Committee of the Yugoslav Communist Party to the Cominform resolution. Nor did they include it in their internal bulletins.

Many Yugoslav Communists believed that Stalin had been misinformed. For men who professed the Stalinist religion it was not easy, even with all the sources of information available at the time, suddenly to shift to secular Marxism, and all the harder when the pope of the Kremlin was at the height of his glory. A meeting of Communists in Belgrade decided to send him a telegram reading: 'We believe sincerely in you. We believe that you will do all in your power to silence this unjust accusation against our party and Central Committee.'[31]

For a time the leaders of the Yugoslav party did not attack this trend. They realized that the Stalin myth could be eradicated only by the practical experience of each militant, and on the other hand they still had hopes that the Soviet leaders would give way before the firm and almost unanimous reaction of the Yugoslav party and people and allow agreement to be reached. The Fifth Congress of the Yugoslav Communist Party, which opened on 21 July, was held under the sway of this illusion. While strongly reaffirming the party's position and rejecting the Cominform accusations, Tito said: 'We hope that the comrade leaders of the CPSU (B) will give us an opportunity to show them here, on the spot, everything that is inaccurate in the resolution.'[32] The resolution adopted by the Congress, while firmly rejecting the Cominform's indictment, authorized the Yugoslav Communist Party to rejoin the organization once the dispute with the Soviet party was settled. After its election by secret ballot – the first time a Communist party had used the method – the Congress ended its sessions with cheers for Stalin, the USSR and Tito.

Stalin's immediate reply was to organize a *coup d'état* against Tito. The NKVD could rely on three Yugoslav generals, including the Chief of the General Staff, who enjoyed great prestige as a result of his role during the war of liberation. But the three generals failed to persuade other officers to join them, and tried, unsuccessfully, to escape to the Soviet Union. The Chief of Staff was killed by a Yugoslav border guard, and the two others arrested shortly after. This incident showed that, in spite of the support of a large majority of the party and people for Tito's policy, Stalin could find supporters among the Yugoslav Communists: some because they had compromised themselves with the Soviet secret service, others because their Stalinist formation predominated over any other considerations.

Faced with this danger, the Yugoslav party fell back on the same methods that Stalin used, the secret service, the police, all the organs of coercion controlled by the state. Already, at the Congress, Tito had called for firm resistance to 'all attempts to break up the unity of our party and the unity of our people', and the resolutions passed by the Congress included calls for increased vigilance and a purge of the party.

However, the party leadership at the same time gave the people the chance to compare words and actions. Soviet broadcasts, which mounted a violent campaign of denigration against the Yugoslav leaders, were not jammed. Stalin's letters were published on a vast scale. In the press the 'arguments' of the other side were openly refuted. The Stalin myth gradually faded from the minds of the Yugoslav Communists, and they began to remember the Tsars of the past, who had disguised their plans for expansion in the Balkans behind the slogan of the liberation of the South Slavs from the Turkish yoke. Soviet propaganda's clumsy references to the undying friendship between Russia and Serbia helped to emphasize the historical continuity of Moscow's policy. The repeated incidents on the borders with Hungary, Romania and Bulgaria also contributed, as did the disturbing movements of the Soviet troops stationed in those countries. The Yugoslav Communists and people gradually became convinced that the avalanche of ideological accusations in fact concealed a threat to their dearly bought national independence.

The precise considerations which kept Stalin from using force remain unknown. We may suppose that the international tension existing at the time was an important factor. The possibility could not be excluded that a Soviet intervention in Yugoslavia would be followed by further intervention, this time from America, and extension, as it were, of her existing intervention in Greece, with all the risks that involved of a general conflict. In addition, the Yugoslav people's army and its experience of guerrilla fighting could not be ignored. Stalin's caution no doubt made it easier for the Yugoslavs to resist. It is equally possible that, in spite of the initial failure of his attempts at ideological intimidation and the *coup d'état*, Stalin believed that the heretical state, whose position could hardly be more desperate, would soon collapse.

Stalin's offensive also coincided with a whole series of provocations by the Western powers. During the first three months of 1948 American planes violated Yugoslav air space twenty-one times. During the election campaign in Italy the reactionary forces linked with the Americans made allegations that Yugoslavia had built launching sites for V1 and V2 rockets near the Italian frontier and was concentrating troops to attack Trieste. The United States, Great Britain and France took advantage of the situation to revise a number of clauses in the peace treaty with Italy and award her Trieste.

Most dramatic of all, however, was the economic situation. The breaking-off of trade relations with the Soviet Union and the rapid deterioration of those with the other People's Democracies, the stopping of Soviet technical aid and the other measures placed Yugoslavia in the position of having either to seek an accommodation with the Western powers or to perish. In his report to the Fifth Congress Kardelj had proclaimed the decision of the Yugoslav party to hold fast to the line of a united front with the Soviet Union and the People's Democracies while at the same time forcing them into the open by asking, 'Are you going to abandon our country to the pressure of imperialism?' At the international conference on the Danube, held shortly after the publication of the Cominform resolution, the Yugoslav delegates supported the Soviet representatives against the Western diplomats. But matters rapidly became clear: either Yugoslavia submitted, or Stalin in practice abandoned it to imperialism. At the same time the fierce anti-Yugoslav campaign orchestrated by the Kremlin announced that Tito was preparing to do a deal with the imperialists. It was a neat trap: either the Yugoslav regime collapsed or it provided the 'proof' that Stalin was right and Tito was indeed an agent of imperialism.

Already in the early months of 1949 the People's Democracies, following the Soviet example, had practically ended all trade with Yugoslavia. The Yugoslav revolution now found itself forced to do what the October revolution had done before it when it was left similarly isolated and surrounded by the capitalist world, to open trade with the capitalist countries and seek credits and technical assistance. To explain that this political course did not mean the abandonment of socialism, Tito used arguments very similar to those used in the past by the Bolsheviks. In a speech on 10 July 1949 at Pula, he said, 'When we sell our copper to buy machines, we are not selling our consciences, but only our copper ... With the machines we receive from the West we shall continue the building of socialism.'

The capitalist states were naturally quick to give sympathetic answers to the Yugoslavian appeals. They did not need to make this small and backward country abandon its claim to be building socialism; what mattered to American imperialism and its servants was that Yugoslavia should be able to assert its independence in the face of Russian imperialism. At the height of the 'cold war', Stalin made them a present of an 'objective' ally. Some Western commentators and politicians expressed fears that 'Titoism' might give the ideals of Communism a new attractiveness by demonstrating the possibility of an 'anti-Stalinist' Communism, but the most intelligent elements of capitalism realized that any attempt to restore the old regime would not only meet the firm opposition of the Communists and the revolutionary majority of the Yugoslav people, but would also be playing into Stalin's hands. The anti-Tito campaign demonstrated this daily. Each trade agreement Yugoslavia made with Western countries, each credit she obtained, was received by Moscow and the Communist parties of the Cominform as a new proof that Tito was selling himself to capitalism. Had not the Cominform resolution announced that Tito's 'anti-Soviet' policies were inevitably leading Yugoslavia towards the loss of its independence and its transformation into a colony of the imperialist countries?

Six years later, during his journey of repentance to Belgrade, Khrushchev announced, 'We have visited many parts of the country. We have talked to workers and have been able to see that, in spite of the difficulties Yugoslavia experienced as a result of the deterioration in relations with us, Yugoslavia has not abdicated her sovereignty and has maintained complete independence in the face of the imperialist camp.'[33]

During the summer and autumn of 1949 the 'deterioration' in Soviet–Yugoslav relations reached a critical point, and the threat of Soviet military intervention became increasingly urgent. A pretext was available in the case of White Russians living in Yugoslavia who had been recruited by the Soviet secret service. After the October revolution thousands of White Russians settled in Yugoslavia. When the new regime was established many of them immediately announced their support for the USSR, and the Moscow government granted Soviet citizenship to about 6,000 of them, among whom Beria's organization recruited many agents. In 1949 Ranković's police arrested some of these. Moscow came to their defence, and sent threatening notes to Belgrade. The last, date 18 August, appealed to the right of 'Soviet citizens' living in Yugoslavia to the free expression of their 'democratic views' and described the regime's attempts to prevent them as Fascist:

In no country except one with a Fascist system is the expression of democratic views regarded as a crime. In the present state of Yugoslavia it is the ground for the illegal arrest and cruel punishment of people who criticize the Fascist regime which exists in Yugoslavia ... There are only two governments in Europe, the Greek and the Spanish, which regard the resolution of the Communist parties' information bureau as a criminal document. These two governments are Fascist. From that it can be deduced that the Yugoslav government is the third government to regard the resolution of the information bureau as a criminal document, regarding its distribution and the very fact of knowing about it to be a sufficient basis for imprisoning thousands of people.

(As we have seen, the Yugoslav Communist Party had produced and distributed half a million copies of the resolution, which could be found – with Stalin's letters – in any Belgrade bookshop, but this fact did not exist for the Soviet government.) The note denied that the Cominform resolution recommended the overthrow of the Titoist leadership, and claimed that it merely called for the convening of a congress of Yugoslav Communists at which the party leadership would be changed, which was perfectly proper since, the document explained, 'the congresses of Marxist parties do not meet to glorify their leaders, but to analyse from a critical standpoint the existing leadership and, if necessary, renew it or replace it by another leadership. In all Marxist parties in which internal democracy existed this method of changing the leadership was natural and perfectly normal.' There was no need to look any further than the Communist Party of the USSR!

With regard to the 'ill-treatment' inflicted on the 'Soviet citizens' arrested, the note described three cases (presumably the most extreme). In the first the prisoner was 'beaten for several days, forced to stand upright without moving for several hours and kept without sleep, food and water for two days'. In the second the prisoner 'received no food for six days', and 'during interrogations was struck on the legs with a rod'. In the third case the prisoner 'was subjected to interrogation at night for twenty-two consecutive days. He was required to answer questions about his views on the Cominform resolution. He was maltreated several times in the course of these interrogations, and several times placed in a cell in which he could only stand upright.' Such unspeakable methods, unknown in the USSR, could not but move Stalin's humanitarian conscience to anger: 'Can a regime which practises such horrors and uses such brutal methods be called a People's Democracy?' demanded the Soviet government note. 'Would it not be more correct to say that a regime under which people are ill-treated in this way is a Fascist, Gestapo regime?' The note ended with the remark that if the Yugoslav government did not comply with the Soviet demands, the Soviet government 'would be obliged to have recourse to other, more effective means of defending the rights and interests of the Soviet citizens in Yugoslavia and to restrain the agents of the Fascist violence which has been let loose'.[34] What were these 'other, more effective means' to which the Soviet government referred? At this period the economic blockade of Yugoslavia by the USSR and the People's Democracies was complete. The campaign of defamation seemed to have reached its limits. Apparently, nothing was left but military intervention. The Western press was filled with alarming reports of the movement of Soviet troops in the People's Democracies bordering on Yugoslavia and semi-official statements by the United States and the European countries announcing their readiness to intervene if needed. Tito again announced Yugoslavia's readiness to face any eventuality. Then, instead of Soviet military intervention, there was the Rajk trial and the second Cominform resolution against Yugoslavia. Before this, however, a new 'proof' of Tito's 'treachery' was put into circulation.

We have already seen that at the beginning of 1948 Stalin ordered the Yugoslav Communists to stop helping the armed struggle of the Greek Communists. The Yugoslav party did not comply, but the Cominform's condemnation made it extremely difficult for it – as may be imagined after the events described above – to go on helping the Greek fighters on the scale they needed. From the time of the Cominform resolution Yugoslavia had to keep its forces practically in a state of alert, ready to go into action, should Stalin decide on military intervention. The Cominform resolution also had catastrophic effects within the Greek party and the partisan army. Many activists, including General Markos, the head of the revolutionary government established in the northern mountains, did not accept the condemnation of the Yugoslav party and were subjected to a vast purge organized by Zachariades, the General Secretary of the Greek party. At the end of 1948 Zachariades added the post of chief of the armed forces to that of General Secretary of the party. As the Greek press admitted later, the situation of the government troops in the autumn of 1948, in spite of American technicians and arms, was becoming alarming. In the course of the year the revolutionary army had achieved a number of remarkable successes. From the end of 1948, after the removal of Markos and the anti-Yugoslav purge, the course of the civil war swung sharply in favour of the government forces, a change attributed by the Greek press to the military skill of General Papagos.

It remains unclear even now whether the new direction taken by the civil war, which was to lead to the final defeat of the revolutionary forces in August 1949, was mainly the result of the intensification of American military intervention[35] (while Soviet aid continued to be notably absent), or whether the decisive factor was the internal breakdown of the revolutionary forces as a result of the developments mentioned. It is even possible that Zachariades, carrying out specific instructions from Stalin, deliberately worked for the collapse of the armed struggle. It is likely that everything – except perhaps the 'skill' of Papagos – combined to bring the Greek revolution to its tragic end.

What is certain, on the other hand, is that the leadership of the Greek Communist Party under Zachariades, as if it did not have enough to do in fighting the Greek monarchy and the Americans, embarked on a secret war and open propaganda against the Yugoslav party. It was presumably obeying Cominform instructions, since it was in the Cominform's interest to use the prestige of the Greek Communists within the Communist movement to reinforce its slander campaign against Yugoslavia.[36]

During the summer of 1949, when the defeat of the people's army was almost complete, the royalist troops reached the borders of Albania and Yugoslavia. About the middle of July the Belgrade government announced its intention to close the frontier, justifying its decision on the grounds of the repeated incursions of Greek royalist troops into Yugoslav territory. Immediately, 'Radio Free Greece', controlled by Zachariades, accused Tito of assisting the government offensive in the border area. The anti-Tito campaign had a field day: Tito had sold himself to the Americans and the Greek monarcho-Fascists; he had stabbed the democratic army in the back! On 28 August Moscow radio broadcast a communiqué from the Albanian Ministry of Defence also announcing the closing of the border and warning that in order 'to preserve peace all armed persons coming from Greece, whether monarcho-Fascists or democrats, will be disarmed'. This action, however, coming from a government controlled by Moscow, was not a 'stab in the back', but only a measure 'to preserve peace'. Until the death of Stalin the Communist movement's official version can be summed up in this comment from a French Communist journal: 'The Truman government would have lost in Greece as it lost in China, if Tito's treachery had not allowed the Anglo-Saxon imperialists to win a military victory at the last minute.'[37] After Stalin's death Tito's 'treachery' disappeared as if by magic from the official explanations of the Greek defeat, the causes of which were reduced to two, American intervention and the errors of the Greek Communist Party under Zachariades' leadership. The responsibilities of Stalin and the Cominform remain to be determined.

It seems very likely that the closing of the border was not prompted solely by the consideration officially announced in Belgrade. The action also fulfilled two other functions, that of preventing an incursion into Yugoslav territory of armed forces under the orders of the Cominform (just as in Albania's case it was intended to prevent the entry of pro-Yugoslav elements)[38] and of making a gesture to smooth relations with Washington at a time when the threat of Soviet military intervention seemed to be coming alarmingly close. In this case, as in others (such as the Balkan pact with Greece and Turkey), if Tito did not sell his soul with his copper, he was at least forced to make it extremely flexible.

But did Stalin leave him an alternative? From one point of view the situation of the Yugoslav revolution was even more dramatic than that of the October revolution. The October revolution could at least rely on the solidarity of the international revolutionary proletariat in the face of capitalist encirclement. But in the face of encirclement by Russian imperialism, camouflaged under the label 'socialist', and by the Communist movement, still totally alienated by Soviet 'myths', the only defensive move abroad still open to the Yugoslav revolution was to take advantage of the 'cold war' between capitalist imperialism and the new imperialism which was beginning to appear. The heart of the problem was whether the tacit alliance with the United States and its vassals, and with the reformist wing of the working-class movement, was compatible with the development of the socialist revolution inside the country. To explore this tortuous path or sacrifice itself to Stalin's colonialism, this was the inexorable dilemma which faced the Yugoslav revolution.

THE TRIALS

In terms of Cominform propaganda, which started with the 1948 resolution and was enriched in the course of time by the new 'evidence' with which events provided it, the Yugoslav heresy had taken the following course up to the summer of 1949. In the first stage Tito & Co. went from Marxism–Leninism to nationalism; once on the nationalist slope, they slipped in a new stage into anti-Sovietism, clashing with the Soviet Union and the Bolshevik party (which amounted to a complete abandonment of internationalism, since, as is well known, the touchstone of internationalism is a party's attitude to the USSR), and finally rolled into the imperialist camp and even began to turn into Fascists. The original sin was clearly nationalism. On the other hand, this scheme had the disadvantage of presenting the Yugoslav leaders, from one point of view, as patriots, heroes of national independence. It fulfilled its defamatory function satisfactorily with 'mature' Communists, but could have unfortunate effects on the non-Communist population of the People's Democracies, whose national feelings rebelled against Russian domination, or on some of the ordinary Communists who had just joined the parties of these countries.

The Rajk trial was intended to provide the 'irrefutable' proof that Tito and his associates not only had never been Marxists or Communists, but had not even been patriots; ever since the war against Hitlerism they had been no more than contemptible agents of the Hitlerite or Anglo-American secret service, to whom they had sold the sovereignty and national independence of Yugoslavia. True patriotism, both in Yugoslavia and in the other People's Democracies, was indissolubly linked with loyalty to the USSR, the ultimate guarantee for these countries of their national independence. This was 'proved' by the Rajk trial. (It has not been generally noticed that the 'proof' given by the Moscow trials that Trosky, Bukharin and the rest were agents of Germany and Japan was also designed to discredit them in the eyes of most Russians, whose patriotism was reaching a peak at that period in the face of the danger of German and Japanese aggression.)

Laszlo Rajk had been a member of the Hungarian Communist Party since the 1930s, when he was a university student. He had fought with the international brigades in Spain. After the defeat of the Spanish Republic he was interned in French camps. He led the underground Hungarian Communist Party during the resistance. He was Minister of the Interior of the Hungarian People's Democracy from its formation until about the time of the publication of the Cominform resolution against Tito, when he became Foreign Minister.

On 15 June 1949 the Hungarian Communist Party (more correctly, the Hungarian Workers' Party) announced in a communiqué that Rajk and Szonyi – another Communist leader – had been expelled from the party as 'spies for the imperialist powers and Trotskyite agents'. On 10 September the Hungarian government published the indictment against Rajk and other party and government leaders. On the 17th the trial opened in a large hall in Budapest. The hearings were public and, since space was limited, invitations were issued. Sixty foreign journalists attended. *Pravda* sent the novelist Boris Polevoi. Diplomatic representatives were also able to attend the trial. The elaborate spectacle, an exact reproduction of the Moscow trials, unfolded without a hitch. All the accused admitted the crimes with which they were charged and a number of others as well. Rajk was sentenced to death and hanged with three of his fellow defendants. Out of respect for the uniform two military leaders were granted the concession of a firing squad. The other defendants were sentenced to heavy terms of imprisonment.

In 1956, after the Twentieth Congress, the Hungarian authorities admitted that it had all been a farce. Rajk was 'rehabilitated'. 300,000 workers, students and intellectuals marched through the streets of Budapest in a national tribute and demanded the removal of a system which allowed the staging of such criminal farces by the very people who called themselves the representatives of the proletariat and of socialism. Soon after, Russian tanks went into action to save the crumbling system. The

fact that the reactionary forces in Hungary and the real agents of imperialism tried, as might have been expected, to exploit the rising of the
workers and the people, gave them an alibi. But one of the main reasons
for the Soviet armed intervention in Hungary, as of that which took
place twelve years later in Czechoslovakia – where, since the same alibi
was not available, they had to invent one from scratch – was to prevent
the uncovering of political crimes in the People's Democracies. This
explains why essential aspects of the internal staging of these trials,
especially as regards the intervention of the main organizers, the Soviet
leaders and their secret services, are still inadequately understood, in
spite of the revelations of a few victims who survived.[39] Their meaning
and their political motivation, however, are quite clear. In the case of the
Rajk trial the prosecutor himself described it exactly:

> This trial is not, strictly speaking, the trial of Laszlo Rajk and his
> accomplices. It is Tito and his henchmen who are in the dock ... It is
> clear that in condemning Laszlo Rajk and his band of conspirators the
> Hungarian People's Tribunal also morally and politically condemns those
> traitors of Yugoslavia, the criminal band of Tito, Ranković, Kardelj and
> Djilas. It is in this that the international importance of this trial lies.

As Ferenc Fejtö accurately observes in his *Historie des
démocraties populaires*, 'the Rajk trial was no more than a substitute
for the Belgrade trial which could not take place. Rather than defendant,
Rajk was a witness, the star witness in the case against Tito.'[40] Rajk
began his 'confessions' with a self-portrait. He depicted himself as a
miserable, worthless creature, in the pay of Horthy's police as early as
1931 – when he had just entered the party. When he went to Spain
(where he was wounded three times), it was not to fight Fascism but to
work for the Gestapo. He worked as a Gestapo agent in the French
concentration camps in which the international brigade members were
interned, and in the Hungarian resistance as leader of the underground
Communist Party. The other defendants painted equally black pictures
of themselves.

Once their reputation as spies and police informers was established –
which seemed to make their evidence thoroughly credible to the Stalinist court – the defendants began to accuse the Yugoslav leaders,

describing how on such and such dates, in such and such circumstances, they had all been recruited by the Gestapo, the French Deuxième Bureau or the British and American espionage services. In these descriptions the international brigades turned into a nursery of police agents and spies, who were sent direct from the French concentration camps into the countries of Eastern Europe. There, placed at the head of the underground Communist parties, they continued to recruit police agents or spies among the Communists. The Yugoslav revolutionary war, in particular, had, in these stories, been organized and led by Gestapo agents. The Hungarian resistance was similar. The agents were men of parts, working at the same time for the Anglo-American and for other police forces. Once the Germans were defeated, this band of spies was naturally taken over by Allen Dulles, head of American espionage in Europe. The Budapest trial provided no details about the other People's Democracies; it was merely implied that the 'monstrous imperialist plot' must have had ramifications in them. A few hints were thrown out of obvious places to look: members of the international brigades, Communists who went into exile in the West before the war, militants in the internal resistance etc. Above all suspect were those who had kept up contacts with the Yugoslav Communists, whose name was now synonymous with espionage. What Communist leader in the People's Democracies had not at one time or another, had contact with the Yugoslavs?

All this applied just as much to the Western Communist leaders. If the method of the Rajk trial had been followed through, it would have led to the conclusion that the leading organs of the Communist Parties of France, Italy, Spain and the rest were probably just as rotten with police agents as those of the People's Democracies. And what about the higher circles of the Soviet Communist Party, which, after all, had had the widest contacts with the exposed or potential spies of all the other Communist parties, beginning with the Yugoslav?

Starting from this hypothesis and going back into the past of a series of Western and Eastern Communists as was done with Rajk, Tito and others – it would have been easy to reach the conclusion that the Communist International had been created by the German espionage service – there was that suspicious journey of Lenin's in a sealed train through the Kaiser's Germany! – which would have made it possible to explain a point of Stalinist history which still remains obscure: why the Comintern had been led in its early years by expert agents of the Gestapo such as Zinoviev, Trotsky, Bukharin, etc. Later, in the period of the Popular Fronts, it could have been shown that the Comintern had gone over to the service of Anglo-Franco-American intelligence. Naturally, similar conclusions could be obtained about the Soviet state. Happily, however, the method used at the Budapest trial concealed another, much more rigorous and scientific one: the lists of spies or trainee spies were drawn up in advance in Beria's offices on instructions from the Infallible. In this way there was no danger that purely formal logic might lead to dangerous conclusions. Only when the spies had been selected was 'evidence' of their activity collected: contacts, meetings, periods in prison (that is, contact with the police), dealings with liberals or social democrats (frequent in the periods of anti-Fascist alliances and clear proof of connections with the bourgeoisie), contacts with the military or diplomatic missions of Britain or the United States (and what Communist leader in certain positions did not have such contacts, directly or indirectly, in the period of the 'grand alliance'?), the ultimate proof of connections with imperialism and its intelligence services, and so on. Once the Infallible, with the help of his intelligence, decided that a particular Communist was a spy, the collection of evidence – 'irrefutable proof', as the indictment in the Budapest trial called it – was a simple matter.

The only problem was selection. This was where the intelligence services sometimes made mistakes through the bureaucratic routine which dominated their actions in this field as in others. So, for example, some of the international brigade volunteers whom Rajk described as having been sent by the Gestapo from French concentration camps to Yugoslavia had never been in these camps, and one of them, Vukmanović, had never even been in Spain. Apart from these minor bureaucratic errors, however, the method used, the selection of spies or trainee spies in advance, made it possible to set limits in space and time to the process of logic and so to confine the epidemic accurately to the area and period desired, according to the political and ideological problems to be solved. For this period, the Infallible decided that the epidemic of spies in the

Communist movement should be limited to the satellites, and in particular to those who had refused the honour of membership.

Two and a half months after Hungary came the turn of Bulgaria. On 30 November the public prosecutor published the indictment against 'the group of conspirators and criminals led by Traicho Kostov'. Kostov was known in the Communist movement as an old revolutionary, co-founder with Dimitrov of the Bulgarian Communist Party and for a period a leading official of the Comintern. He had been formed by thirty years of underground activity mass struggle, armed insurrection and, finally, a position of leadership in the People's Democracy. According to the indictment, however, Kostov was something else. In the first place, he had – like Rajk and almost all those who had become spies – a Trotskyite post. 'The principal features of his career,' said the indictment, 'are duplicity, treason and criminal conspiracy against the most sacred interests of the Bulgarian working class and people.'[41] It was revealed that Kostov had recommended the Comintern leadership, to employ Tito in leading positions in the Yugoslav party. (This was the only genuine fact in the indictment and also of course one of the most serious charges.)

Kostov was not as precocious an agent as Rajk, and did not sell himself until 1942. Shortly after he went over to the service of British intelligence, who recommended him to get in touch with Tito. Kostov made an agreement with Tito to overthrow popular power in Bulgaria with the support of Yugoslav military forces. (Rajk had also revealed his plot with Tito to overthrow popular power in Hungary, with the help of Yugoslav forces which were to intervene disguised as Hungarians, with the cooperation of units of Horthy's old army and police which were concentrated in the areas of Austria occupied by the British and Americans.) The plan of the conspiracy provided for the arrest and assassination of Dimitrov. These, and other equally serious ones, were the 'facts' mentioned by the Attorney General.

The solemn rite of inquisition opened to the public in Sofia on 7 November – the anniversary of the October revolution – in the hall of the central headquarters of the People's Army. The spectators included foreign journalists, diplomats and the inevitable 'workers delegations'; it was an exact repetition of the performance presented in Budapest. Suddenly, however, to general surprise, the unexpected happened. Kostov went back on the confessions he had made during the preliminary 'examination', and formally denied all the charges brought against him. Disconcerted, the president of the court ordered an immediate recess, to allow the defendent to re-read his statement, as though it were a lapse of memory. When the court resumed, however, Kostov firmly maintained his retraction. The Bulgarian press made no mention of such an intolerable departure from the ritual. Tass mentioned it in a dispatch which described Kostov's behaviour as 'insolent'.[42] The old revolutionary, who, unlike the Budapest defendants, had found the strength to recover his will after all the physical and moral tortures inflicted on him, maintained this 'insolent' attitude to the end. When the time came for him to make his final statement, he strongly confirmed his retraction. This time, however, the directors of the performance were warned, and Kostov had hardly begun to speak when a storm of shouts and whistles from the public gallery drowned his voice. The system of simultaneous translation into four languages, provided for the use of foreign journalists, mysteriously broke down. In spite of his protests of innocence, Kostov was sentenced to death and executed, leaving doubt hanging over the justice of the Bulgarian People's Democracy. Several days later the doubt was removed; the press published a letter written by Kostov before his death in which he retracted his retraction and admitted his guilt in full. When Kostov was rehabilitated in 1956, it was revealed that the letter was a forgery, as had been all the charges and confessions presented at the trial.

The hunt for heretics and their punishment began in the People's Democracies at the very same time as Stalin launched his offensive against the Yugoslav revolution. In Albania Dodje, the Secretary of the party organization and Minister of the Interior, who was very close to the Yugoslavs, was removed from these positions before the publication of the Cominform resolution. He was tried and sentenced in the strictest secrecy along with other well-known leaders of the party, and executed in June 1949. In Romania, Patrascanu, who had been General Secretary of the party until 1945 and had later held the highest offices in the party in addition to becoming Minister of Justice, was arrested in the summer of 1948 with other well-known militants. That same summer Gomulka lost his post of General Secretary of the Polish party and was accused of, among other crimes, nationalism, resistance to rapid collectivization of agriculture, lack of vigilance, toleration of intellectuals and, above all, failure to understand the leading role of the Communist Party of the USSR [Bolsheviks]'.[43] In January 1949 Gomulka, General Spychalski and other leaders were expelled from the party. In Czechoslovakia the purge of 'Titoists' and other 'right-wing deviationists' began immediately after the 'Prague coup' – which coincided with the beginning of Stalin's attack on the Yugoslavs – and continued for months under the leadership of Slansky, the General Secretary of the party.

Thus in the year between the Cominform resolution against Tito and the Rajk trial the purge in the Communist parties and state institutions of the People's Democracies took on considerable proportions; the cases mentioned above, which involved the leading circles, were the only ones to be made public, because of the importance of the accused. No public reports, and no doubt no internal ones, were ever made of the thousands of middle-rank or grass-roots militants who lost their positions or were expelled from the party. Only the party members directly connected with each case were in the know. The big purge began with the Rajk trial. This put the final touches to a political and ideological platform which was to be the basis of the operation in all the People's Democracies and, at the same time, of the intensification of the campaign against Yugoslavia. The two aspects were closely connected.

In the second half of November 1949 there took place the third – and last – meeting of the Cominform. There were three items on its agenda, 'the defence of peace and the fight against the warmongers', 'working-class unity and the tasks of the Communist and workers' parties' and 'the Yugoslav Communist Party in the power of assassins and spies'.[44] Suslov and Togliatti introduced the first two items, which will be discussed in a later chapter, and Gheorghiu-Dej, the General Secretary of the Rumanian Communist Party, introduced the third. He began by declaring that the events which had taken place since the Cominform resolution, and in particular the Budapest trial, had 'fully confirmed the correctness of the resolution and the exceptional theoretical and practical value of this document for the world revolutionary movement'. Its 'masterly prevision' and 'scientific insight' made it 'a historical turning point in the orientation and activity of the entire world revolutionary movement'. It had helped the Communist parties to 'become still more deeply imbued with the realization that fidelity to the homeland of socialism, the Soviet Union, is the touchstone and criterion of internationalism'. Gheorghiu-Dej added: 'Comrade Stalín has rendered immense assistance to the international Communist movement. With his genius and insight, he warned us against a number of ideological deviations and misconceptions and helped us to combat them successfully. This assistance of Comrade Stalin was the salvation of many Marxist parties.'

The theoretical value of the resolution of June 1948, its scientific quality and the historic turning point in the attitudes and activity of the world revolutionary movement were thus confirmed by the confessions of a group of alleged spies and police agents. On the basis of these confessions – and of them alone – Gheorghiu-Dej made the most grotesque accusations against the Yugoslav Communist leaders, claiming that during the war they had been simultaneously agents of the Gestapo and of Anglo-American intelligence. The fact such crude assertions were blindly accepted by millions of Communists indicates the level to which official 'Marxism' had fallen at this period. 'Gheorghiu-Dej's report went on:

When the Information Bureau published its resolution, the Belgrade Fascist fiends began to complain that they were the victims of injustice. But their sole idea was to conceal their shady past and their connections with Anglo-American imperialism as long as possible. The Budapest trial came as a thunderbolt to the Tito clique.

The facts proved that it was not a case of blunders, but of a deliberate counter-revolutionary, anti-Soviet, anti-Communist policy, conducted by a gang of spies, professional informers and agents provocateurs with a long record of collaboration with the police and bourgeois secret services. A large number of the present Yugoslav leaders were sent into Yugoslavia from the concentration camps in France as long ago as 1941.

Churchill sent his son Randolph with a special mission to Tito. Later, the old reactionary and mortal foe of the USSR met Tito personally. Already then, the imperialists showed great interest and trust in Tito and his clique.

On the other hand, the exposures of the Yugoslav General Popivoda have revealed in its true light the compromising attitude of Tito, Ranković and others towards the Nazi invaders and the Gestapo, and also their dastardly betrayal of the Yugoslav partisans at the most serious moments of the war.

The facts revealed at the Budapest trial, in the Bulgarian People's Republic, in the Romanian People's Republic and in other People's Democracies have completely demonstrated that Tito, Ranković, Kardelj, Djilas, Pijade, Gosnjak, Maslarić, Bebler, Mrazovic, Vukmanović, Koca Popović, Kidrić, Nesković, Zlatić, Velebit and others, Rajk, Brankov, Traicho Kostov, Patrascanu and their confederates are agents of the British and American imperialist secret services. Already at the time of the Second World War, these contemptible spies and traitors were helping the British and American imperialists to prepare support bases for the accomplishment of their plan of world domination. This gang of spies and traitors were introduced like a Trojan horse into the ranks of the Communist and workers' parties. In obedience to the orders of their masters, they made it their criminal aim to seize the direction of the party and state in the countries where the working class had come to power, to crush the revolutionary movement and to bring about the restoration of the rule of the bourgeoisie.

Stalin, who had divided Yugoslavia with Churchill in deepest secrecy, was now accusing Tito of secret agreements with 'the old reactionary and mortal foe of the USSR'. He could not forgive the Yugoslav Communists for not obeying his instructions during the war, for successfully carrying out a revolutionary policy instead of submitting, as Stalin had ordered, to the bourgeois forces.

The report pronounced it as certain that the regime in Yugoslavia had become Fascist, the headquarters of American intelligence in south-eastern Europe, an advance detachment of the forces being prepared for a war on the USSR and the People's Democracies, etc. It ended as follows:

Let us raise still higher the victorious banner of proletarian internationalism, by fostering devotion to the Soviet Union – the first socialist country, the foundation of the world revolutionary movement and the main bulwark of the struggle for the peace and liberty of peoples – to the

great Bolshevik party, the leading force in the world revolutionary movement, and to the genius who is the teacher of labouring humanity and the
leader of the struggle of the peoples for peace and socialism, Comrade
Stalin.

In this way the sinister spy stories put together by the Kremlin's
intelligence services and recited at the Budapest trial – learnt by heart
with the help of the well-tried pedagogical method of torture – became
Marxist–Leninist educational material, 'to raise the political and ideological level of its cadres'. This, said Gheorghiu-Dej, quoting the
Cominform journal, was essential if 'the party of the working class' was
to 'get to grips with and beat the enemy always and everywhere, no
matter what mask he dons'. The inspired educator had already provided similar material twelve years before when he organized similar
trials, but the new material was a considerable enrichment of Marxism.
The Trotskyite and Bukharinist spies of the thirties had managed to
create no more than a few splinter groups which were soon discovered
and destroyed; history had still to show what could be achieved by the
underground work of imperialism and its intelligence services. In the
cases of Yugoslavia and the People's Democracies, these services revealed
the full extent of their hellish resources. They had proved capable of
nothing less than the organization and leadership of the anti-Fascist war
and proletarian revolution in one country, and had then established a
People's Democracy in order to be able to use it later, when the time
came, to overthrow the other People's Democracies – the real ones, set
up by the Red Army – and so prepare the conditions for a war against
the USSR and the establishment of imperialism's world domination.
The enemy's genius bore comparison only with that of the Guide of the
Peoples.

The new resolution adopted by this meeting of the Cominform on the
basis of Gheorghiu-Dej's report laid down two essential tasks for the
Communist parties:

The Information Bureau of the Communist and workers' parties therefore considers that the fight against the Tito clique of hired spies and
assassins is the international duty of all the Communist and workers'
parties.

... The Information Bureau considers it one of the most important tasks of the Communist and workers' parties to enhance revolutionary vigilance in their ranks to the utmost, to expose and eject bourgeois-nationalist elements and agents of imperialism, under whatever flag they may disguise themselves.

Gheorghiu-Dej also had a list of suggestions for 'enhancing revolutionary vigilance'. First,

we must put our own party house in Bolshevik order ... The principal means for this is the verification of party members. It has been carried out in the parties of a number of the People's Democracies and has yielded good results.

Always look for the good Bolshevik housekeeping seal of approval. Remember that the enemy

will endeavour to use people like Rajk, as well as every weakness and fissure in the ranks of the party and the government service, and malcontents, nationalist elements and people with dubious pasts.

Good Communists could never relax their 'ideological vigilance'.

They must display genuine Bolshevik irreconcilability to all deviations from proletarian internationalism ... In science, literature, painting, music and the cinema there must be keen vigilance, and an irreconcilable attitude towards all trends alien to the working class, and towards the propaganda of cosmopolitanism.

After the Cominform meeting, and in accordance with the attitudes and methods recommended there, the great purge spread through all the Communist parties of the People's Democracies, sucking in hundreds of well-known leaders and a huge mass of ordinary militants and cadres. Our knowledge of this vast operation is still very fragmentary, but the facts which have emerged are revealing. The extent of the purge is in itself remarkable.[45] The Czech Communist Party, which had had 1,300,000 members at the time of the 'Prague coup', had more than two million by the end of 1948. In 1954 it had no more than 1,400,000. The Polish party had 1,400,000 members in 1948 and 1,110,000 in 1952. In Romania the party went from a million members in 1940 to 700,000 in

1951, in Hungary from 1,200,000 in June 1948 to 850,000 in February 1951. The Bulgarian party had 500,000 members in December 1948 and in 1951 had fewer than 300,000. These figures are not an exact reflection of the extent of the purge, since recruitment continued during the period. According to Ferenc Fejtő, the total number of people purged in all these parties between 1948 and 1952 was around two and a half million. Of these between 125,000 and 250,000 were imprisoned. The number of those executed is unknown.

Among the victims were many leaders and senior officials: three general secretaries (Kostov, Gomulka, Slansky), one president (Szakasits, in Hungary), several deputy premiers (of Albania, Bulgaria, Poland and Romania), tens of ministers and members of the senior party leadership, a hundred or so generals, etc.[46] In Hungary those arrested in the two years which followed the Rajk trial included Janos Kadar (the present General Secretary of the party), who succeeded Rajk at the Ministry of the Interior, Gyula Kallai, Rajk's successor at the Foreign Ministry, Losonczy, Secretary of State in the Prime Minister's office after the liberation, and other well-known activists. Sandor Zold, who replaced Kadar at the Ministry of the Interior after his arrest, committed suicide in 1951 to avoid detention. (The Ministry of the Interior was the most dangerous place at such moments, and one could be fairly sure of being both judge and judged.) The old Romanian Communist leaders Vassili Luca (Finance Minister) and Teohari Gheorghescu (Minister of the Interior) were arrested in 1952. Luca was sentenced to death and then reprieved. In the same year Ana Pauker, the Foreign Minister and a very well-known figure in the Communist movement since the time of the International, was removed from the government and party leadership, though not arrested.

In Poland, Gomulka, who, as has been mentioned, was removed from the General Secretaryship of the party in 1948, was expelled from the government in January 1949. In November of the same year he was expelled from the party at the same time as Kliszko, another old Communist leader, General Spychalski, and several others. In 1951 the trial took place of a large group of generals and army officers on charges of spying and high treason. According to the 'revelations' of the accused, Gomulka and Spychalski had planned to establish a Titoist regime in

Poland and restore the western territories to Germany. Gomulka was not charged, however, though this did not prevent him from staying in prison from the end of 1950 until 1956. In 1948 the Czech Communist Party underwent a first wave of purges, organized by the general secretary of the party, Slansky. After the Cominform meeting a new wave began. 'This time it will be much more severe than in 1948,' Slansky announced. So indeed it was. It began by removing the leading group in the Slovak party (Clementis, the Foreign Minister in the central government, Husak, the purger of today, then President of the Council of Slovak Commissioners, Novomeski, Commissioner for Education, and others) and ended by sweeping away Slansky himself and other leaders of the Czech party, who were charged with high treason, espionage, sabotage and complicity with Zionism. Their trial took place in 1952. Slansky and ten other accused, all veteran Communists, were hanged.[47]

In his violent pamphlet on the degeneration of Marxism and its transformation into an ideology of cynical justifications – with religious aspects – Costas Papaioannou quotes the confession of a demon exorcised by means of relics of Saints Marcellus and Peter: 'I am a satellite and disciple of Satan. For a long time I was the porter at the gate of hell, but several years ago, with eleven of my companions, I began to lay waste the kingdom of the Franks. As we were ordered, we destroyed the corn, the wine and all the other fruits produced by the earth for the use of man.' Papaioannou comments: 'Who can fail to recognize the confession of a "Trotskyite monster" or a "Judaeo-Titoist". Everything is there, the obscure origin (the gates of hell, the sump of reaction), the sudden promotion to the rank of qualified saboteur, the abject submission to the orders of a Satanic, Trotskyite, Titoist or other centre, and even the moralizing intentions.'[48]

The confessions recited by the possessed Communists before mounting the scaffold or going down into the hell of prison indeed bear a strange resemblance to the exorcisms of the Middle Ages, with their double function of explaining and conjuring away natural calamities and social evils. All the difficulties which emerged in the new attempts to 'build socialism', all the evils which weakened the satellites, were now explained and justified by the secret activity of the diabolical bands of

Rajks, Kostovs, Gomulkas, Patrascanus, Slanskys and the rest, the servants of Judas Tito, who was himself a servant of Satan Truman. In the same way the economic difficulties and political tensions of Soviet society in 1936–8 were explained by the no less diabolical activity of the Trotskyite and Bukharinist gangs. In the words of the prosecutor at the Slansky trail:

> Citizen judges:
> ... The moral face [of these criminals] has been shown to us in all its horror. We are aware of the peril we have been in. The crimes that have been revealed have made us realize the real causes of the serious defects in numerous sections of our party, our state and our economy. Like octopi with a thousand tentacles they clutched at the body of our Republic to suck its blood and marrow.
> ... For a certain time they managed to distort the just policy of our party, falsify reports, figures, cadre files, deceive the leadership of the party under Klement Gottwald and even insolently deceive the President himself.[49]

After laying bare, with the help of the imaginary crimes of imaginary criminals, the true causes of all failures, past and present, after demanding exemplary punishment for the 'monsters with human faces', the prosecutors' final speeches and often even the very confessions of the 'monsters' themselves – endowed not only with human faces but also with 'Marxist–Leninist' language – ended with appeals to strengthen monolithic unity round the Stalinist leadership. They called for a struggle to preserve the purity of Marxism–Leninism and an increase of revolutionary vigilance, for the practice of self-criticism and above all for the fulfilment and surpassing of production norms. The prosecutor quoted above ended his speech as follows:

> The conspirators have caused losses to our country amounting to millions, and yet we are victoriously accomplishing the aims of the Five-Year Plan and constructing a new life, a marvellous life, for ourselves and the generations to follow us. The tireless efforts of millions of workers have thwarted a handful of conspirators. In these last days thousands of indignant letters have arrived in court expressing the firm decision of our workers to repair as soon as possible all the damage done by these

imperialist mercenaries . . . Ever more vigilant, ever firmer and closer to its leaders and Klement Gottwald, our Communist Party is leading the people to a marvellous future.[50]

With the evil spirits driven out and the possessed burned, the road to the promised land lies open before the docile flock of the Master.

'Why may we not see [in these trials],' writes Papaioannou, 'a sort of indirect, "magic self-criticism" on the part of the regime itself, history's revenge on the ideology which has so stubbornly denied its own nature?'[51] Why not indeed? When, in the 1930s, the real movement of Soviet society, its contradictions and conflicts – reflected in the economic bottlenecks, the social tensions, the silent opposition inside and outside the party – reached a point where they could no longer be hidden or even justified by ordinary failures in the execution of the party's always correct policy, the regime had to use 'magical' explanations. It could not use the Marxist – Marx's – method because that presupposes unhindered criticism, completely free discussion and research without taboos, and the regime was the negation of such conditions. For self-analysis on Marxist principles it would have had to begin by abolishing itself. Nor could it fall back on its ideology, official 'Marxism', since the function of this ideology was to conceal contradictions, not to reveal them, to produce arguments for the system, not criticisms of it, to mystify the real movement, not to reflect it and explain it rationally. The ills of the system, those which it was impossible to ignore, had to be presented as alien to its nature, structures and superstructures, as imported by agents alien to Soviet society.

Ten years later a similar situation occurred in the People's Democracies. Neither the 'Soviet' regime nor the 'People's Democracies' could stand a Marxist analysis of the dispute with Yugoslavia, of the relations between Moscow and the satellites, of the true nature of the political systems established in the latter, or of the economic, social and other effects of these factors. Nor could they use official 'Marxism', the function of which, even more perhaps than in the thirties, was still purely apologetic and justificatory. 'Magical' explanations had once more to be revived. History, the real movement, took vengeance once more on the bureaucrats and their cynical ideology. Some years later, with a 'secret report' and other events, this revenge was to take on Homeric dimensions.

The power of suggestion of Stalin's 'magic', like that of the old magic, depended on the concealment of its methods and manipulations. Once these were, even partly, revealed, the spell was broken and gave way to revulsion and a crisis of conscience among those who had taken the world of lies and police control as the best of all possible Marxist worlds. Nevertheless there were still many who clung desperately to the meagre remains of their old faith, and new credulous believers came to fill the gaps left by those who decided to try and rediscover Marxism or by those who finally gave up hope. This story, however, will be discussed later. Here we shall only discuss the internal mechanisms of Stalin's 'magic'.

Arthur London's *On Trial* here provides us with exceptionally interesting material, even if London does not always draw all the conclusions which follow in sound logic. As well as confirming and illustr.ting what is already known and has been partly – only partly – confessed by the appropriate official authorities (that is, that there were neither crimes nor criminals and that only the trials were criminal), London's evidence shows that the trials in fact had the aim ascribed to them in the account above. Even more important, however, in this writer's opinion, is the fact that *On Trial* takes the mechanism of the trials to pieces and reveals how they were planned and carried out.

The starting-point was a general schema reflecting the political aims it was desired to achieve, rather like the draft of a film script. There was then a discussion to discover which actors possessed the necessary combinations of characteristics for the main roles. For example, in the Budapest trial it was important that the main actor should have had many contacts with the Yugoslav Communist leaders, that he should have been active in the underground, have been arrested, be of petty bourgeois origin, and so on. Since the departments responsible for the work had access to the party archives, which contained detailed biographies of active members, the selection presented no major problems. Once suitable people had been chosen, a start was made on teaching them their parts, combining for the purpose the well-tried technique of physical and mental torture and use of the subjects' party experience and formation. During this stage it could be seen whether the candidate in fact combined all the required characteristics, and whether he learnt his part well or put up unexpected resistance to the instructors' convincing arguments. So the choice of actors was gradually settled, and the script finished, being filled out with new details not contained in the draft, as those who were called on, 'for the good of the party', to play the parts of spies, stoolpigeons, degenerate petty bourgeois, Zionist Jews, and so on, once caught in the machinery, became active collaborators in the farce. The work became collective. The executioner-instructor-Communists and the criminal-Communists vied with each other in reaching perfection in the weaving of a web of history and formulating confessions. This was done with care to avoid leaving confused phrases: 'on such and such a date I had a meeting with the Yugoslav So and So' was rejected in favour of the more precise 'on such and such a date I had a meeting with the Titoist spy So and So'. Once the confession had been edited, with the content, phraseology and details 'the party needed', all that was left was to learn it by heart, without the slightest possibility of error, without forgetting the places where the president of the tribunal would interrupt to ask a prearranged question (which the accused also – as well as the president of the tribunal – had to learn by heart) and, of course, the desired answer. The final result was a production of the play – the trial itself – in which everything was minutely planned, organized and timed. Disagreeable surprises, such as those produced by Kostov at the Sofia trial or by Krestinski at the Moscow trials, were rare. London's book contains the details of the process, of which we have given only a very schematic account. A feature which is very important in his account is the part played by what is known in Marxist–Leninist terminology as 'party training'.

At this point in our story, long explanations of the characteristic features of this 'training' are not necessary. In every Communist, the conviction of being a Marxist revolutionary overlapped with views and attitudes totally alien to Marxism. If Marx's motto, as reflected in his work, was *de omnibus dubitandum*,[52] that of his successors a century later could be summed up in the phrase, 'The party is always right'. And if it occasionally made mistakes, 'Better wrong with the party than right against it'. Stalin was infallible, the Soviet Union sacred. Loyalty to

Stalin and the Bolshevik party – which was identified with Stalin – and to the Soviet Union – which was identified with the Bolshevik party and Stalin – was regarded as the essential characteristic of the good militant. For more than twenty years, successive generations of Communists had been trained in the sheep-like Marxism, with all its Marxian demons exorcised. Combined with blind faith in Stalin and everything that came from the USSR, the internal life of the Communist parties, the habit acquired of never discussing instructions from above in a critical spirit, the invariable norm requiring unanimous, monolithic agreement, had to such an extent conditioned the minds of Communists and produced in them such conditioned reflexes that they became an easy prey for any mystification wrapped up in 'Marxist-Leninist' phrases and carrying the Soviet label.

With regard to the technique of the trials, another particularly important ingredient should be noted, which also formed part of 'party training' – the method of 'self-criticism'. Just as criticism and discussion had been emptied of their original content to become no more than tediously approving glosses on the instructions of the leadership, so 'self-criticism' as commonly practised in Communist parties no longer had much connection with the commonly understood meaning of the practice. The militant or body concerned generally accused himself of collective faults, and especially of those of the leaderhip. He played the role of the scapegoat. After the catastrophe of 1933 the leadership of the German Communist Party was the scapegoat for the errors of Stalin and the Comintern executive. In 1947, at the founding meeting of the Cominform, the French and Italian Communist leaders were in their turn scapegoats for the opportunism of Stalin's policies during the 'grand alliance'. A close connection existed between the confessions at the trials and these acts of 'self-criticism' to which militants and parties had become accustomed. In both cases individuals or particular bodies took on collective responsibility, while real problems were disguised or distorted and the status of higher authorities was magnified. The difference lay in the nature of the 'offences' and in the fact that to produce the 'self-criticism' in the trials torture was used. 'Party training' was a necessary, but not a sufficient, condition to make Communists agree to play the role of spies, stoolpigeons, etc., in the 'higher interest' of the party. Torture was the midwife of these supreme sacrifices, which would have been worthy of the Aztec gods. 'Party training' had prepared Communists not only to act the parts of spies, but also to believe these spies' confessions when their language, structure and style bore such a striking resemblance to those of the usual acts of 'self-criticism'. It was completely a matter of fate whether they were called on to play one part rather than the other. London's book is a terrifying illustration of this close connection between 'party training', the manufacture of 'confessions' and the credulity with which Communists accepted them.

On Trial, like other documents which appeared during the brief Czech 'spring', confirmed what had seemed clear since the Twentieth Congress, in spite of the absence of documentary proof, that the trials in the People's Democracies were directly organized by Soviet experts. In some cases, indeed, senior figures from the Kremlin intervened on the spot.[53] The monstrous police organization controlled by Stalin and Beria, which had complete power over the Soviet state and party, as Khrushchev admitted in his 'secret report', also controlled all the satellites, with the help of local police forces. We saw that this was where the breaking point with Yugoslavia came, in the resistance of Tito and his collegues to the setting-up of this organization in their country. One of the aims of the trials in the People's Democracies was to break down all resistance to their implantation in these countries on an even wider scale. The silence of the 'secret report' on this point is indicative of the scale of this implantation. To reveal it would have been to strike a fatal blow against the continuance of Soviet control over the satellites.

In July 1953, when the fantastic spy hunt, which had lasted for five years, was not yet over in the People's Democracies and the No. 1 specialist had just died, the Central Committee of the Soviet Communist Party announced that the No. 2 specialist had been unmasked as an agent of imperialist intelligence. According to the confidential reports sent by the Soviet leaders to the leaders of the Cominform parties, the decisive proof that Beria was also a spy was a letter found on him at the time of his arrest which was addressed to Ranković and asked him to put Beria in touch with Tito.[54]

The Great Purge of 'spies' and of their direct or indirect helpers, directed by the 'spy' Beria under the control of the Great Observer, was one of the essential elements – at once effect and cause – of the political course which dried up the revolutionary vigour of the Communist parties of the People's Democracies. The energy which these regimes had possessed in previous years was atrophied into the Stalinist model, carrying bureaucracy to extremes, abolishing all forms of freedom, making lying a law and law a farce. This held back technological and scientific development, falsified economic – and all other – analyses, imprisoned culture in the inanities of 'Zhdanovism', fostered the nationalism it claimed to be fighting, fed the anti-Russian feeling it claimed to be eradicating, and discredited socialist ideals. It transferred the dramas of the Soviet regime to the People's Democracies, with the addition of all that that involved in the loss of national independence. The brutal campaign of slander against Yugoslavia and the imposition of arbitrary Soviet orders on the People's Democracies cast doubts on the Marxist hypothesis that the proletarian revolution would create brotherly relations among nations on a basis of equality and freedom.

This political course was very largely conditioned by that followed in the USSR in the years between the victory over Hitler and Stalin's death. During this period the serious contradictions of the Stalinist system worsened, and the ruling bureaucracy tried to overcome them by the now traditional methods of ideological and police repression, while the Stalin personality cult grew to the proportions which are now familiar. Under pressure from the GSE internal contradictions, the struggle for power among the Kremlin cliques at the disappearance of this sinister old man intensified. These developments, and the crisis which began with Stalin's death, will be treated in a further volume of this book, together with the crisis in the People's Democracies so conscientiously prepared by the Great Sorcerer's apprentices. These crises showed that the 'system' still worked in the Soviet Union, where it had a solid base in a population anaesthetized by thirty years of myths and political 'guidance' and paralysed by the ubiquitous network of the secret police, a population which wanted more than anything, after so many years of hardship and sacrifices, a little material comfort. In the People's Democracies, on the other hand, the base of the system looked very fragile. The crisis here set large social groups in motion, in particular among intellectuals, students and the working class. It revealed the political weakness of the ruling bureaucracies, which had not been formed by a long organic process, as in the USSR, and who were faced by the threefold contradictory pressure of internal progressive forces, the remains of the old ruling classes and peremptory Soviet demands.

THE CAMPAIGN AGAINST TITOISM IN THE WESTERN COMMUNIST PARTIES

The Communist parties of the capitalist world unanimously adopted the great ideological, political and repressive operation organized by the Kremlin. Immediately the Cominform resolution against the Yugoslav Communist Party was published, the Central Committee of the Italian party published a short statement which said, 'After hearing the report of Comrades Togliatti and Secchia on the recent meeting of the Communist Parties' Information Office, the Central Committee has approved, without the slightest reservation, the decisions taken by the information office.' The Politburo of the French party simultaneously made a similar statement. Following traditional practice, the controlling bodies took this serious decision without the slightest consultation with ordinary militants or intermediate officials. But at least they could pretend to be basing their judgement on fact, since they had obtained their information from their representatives at the Cominform meeting. On the other hand, the controlling bodies of the other parties of the capitalist world had taken no part in the affair, any more than they had in the setting-up of the Cominform or in the 'discussion' of the policy adopted by that body. They learnt of the condemnation of the Yugoslavs from the press, but all of them immediately adopted appropriate resolutions – without asking for further explanations or waiting for them to be given – similarly approving, 'without any reservation', the condemnation of those who, such a short time before had been presented as model revolutionaries. They all reacted in the same way to the second Cominform resolution, which claimed that the Yugoslav party was in the hands of 'spies' and 'assassins', and that the Yugoslav revolution had become Fascist. All the Communist parties of the capitalist world also approved unconditionally the great purge in the People's Democracies, the verdicts in the successive trials, the execution, imprisonment and political

elimination of hundreds of Communists known for their long revolutionary activity. They accepted as the most natural thing in the world the
transformation of these men into 'spies', 'watchdogs' of imperialism and
'Fascist monsters'.

For over five years the public and internal campaign against the
Yugoslav heresy and the hunt for heretics in the People's Democracies
reached such proportions in the Communist parties of the capitalist
countries as to make the campaign against Trotskyism in the thirties
seem trivial by comparison. We leaders of the Spanish Communist Party
had a particularly shameful role to play. The prestige which the PCE
had won in the international Communist movement by its struggle in the
years 1936–9 now helped to give credence to the slanderous accusations
against those who had risked their lives on Spanish soil, fighting side by
side with Spanish Communists and anti-Fascists. 'Pretending to be
friends, and camouflaging themselves among the fighters who came
from all countries to defend the cause of freedom in Spain,' announced
the official spokesman of the PCE, 'the Titoist spies helped the ex-
ecutioner Franco and stabbed the Spanish people in the back. Later the
Titoist spies, continuing their work of provocation in the French concentration camps, caused the deaths of thousands of Spanish Republicans. The Hitlerites were able to trace and assassinate many of the
most heroic Spanish fighters by using the miserable Titoist
spies.'[55]

Each Communist party made its 'own' contribution to the Kremlin's
operation. Even the Chinese Communist leaders, whose own past experience placed them in a better position than anyone to understand the
real issues in the Soviet–Yugoslav dispute fell into line. As we saw in
the first part of this book, Mao's resistance to the Soviet leadership
preceded Tito's by several years. Just like the Yugoslav revolution, the
Chinese revolution was able to succeed thanks to the insubordination of
its leaders to Stalin, who tried to impose on them, as on the Yugoslavs, a
policy of national unity subordinated to the bourgeois forces and to the
requirements of the lasting compromise which Stalin was trying to reach
with American imperialism. In 1949, however, the same leaders described the Yugoslavs as 'traitors' and 'renegades'; they declared that if
they had followed the Titoist road 'it would never have been possible to

achieve national liberation in China', which would have become 'a colony of imperialism like Yugoslavia'.[56]

Nevertheless, the attitude of the Chinese Communist Party on this occasion was more moderate and discreet than that of other parties, particularly the European ones. Differences also appeared among these, however. The honours of the anti-Tito campaign outside the 'socialist camp' were undoubtedly won by the French Communist Party. Summarizing activity in this field and calling for its intensification, a leader of the PCF wrote in June 1950:

> Hardly a day passes without the appearance in our press of reports and articles on the situation in Yugoslavia. However, this work is often very formal in character, hasty and insufficiently methodical ... The quality of the texts published, and not merely their number, must rise considerably. Our press must regard reinforcing the campaign against Tito as an aim of first importance.[57]

The press campaign was supplemented by the publication on a vast scale of tracts and pamphlets like the one entitled *La Yugoslavie sous la terreur de Tito*. The PCF did not limit itself to propaganda. It organized a 'mass struggle' against the sending of 'military' supplies to Tito:

> The action of Figeac against the manufacture of propellers for Tito, and at Nice in connection with the V2 launching ramp believed to be intended for Tito, is only a beginning ... It must be extended to the whole country and in particular to areas such as Grenoble, where large orders of electrical supplies for Tito are being manufactured.[58]

The PCF also organized a campaign against tourism in Yugoslavia, with the slogan: 'Not a single self-respecting young worker, not a single sincerely progressive student, not a single young democratic Frenchman must go to Yugoslavia for his holidays!' And against Yugoslav artistic exhibitions in France:

> Not only the Exhibition of Medieval Yugoslav Art in Paris, but also showings of Yugoslav films should have been occasions for Communists and supporters of peace to demonstrate in appropriate ways the sort of policy concealed behind this artistic propaganda, in appearance neutral

and disinterested, which is directed at petty bourgeois intellectual circles and plays upon their wavering, unstable and credulous attitudes.

(The PCF called on the 'supporters of peace' to take a stand against the warmonger Tito.) With the authority of a man who, as a good Marxist, accepts only scientifically demonstrated facts and judicially proven offences – such as the transformation of Yugoslav socialism into Fascism and the crimes of the spies Rajk, Kostov and the rest – the author of this text was appalled at the credulity and naïvety of French intellectuals who were unable to see the evil, anti-Soviet, imperialist intentions behind the Exhibition of Yugoslav Medieval Art: 'One blushes for the naïvety of some French intellectuals who have tolerated and supported these grotesque frauds, no doubt on the pretext that this was pure art.'[59] Even Yugoslav sport was a dangerous propaganda weapon of the Titoist heresy, but fortunately the Communist press had proved its doctrinal firmness on the sports field and the party leadership presented this as the line to follow in cultural matters: 'The firm attitude of our party press on the occasion of Yugoslav sporting events should be a model of what ought to be done in the cultural field.'[60]

In June 1951, in the PCF political journal, Étienne Fajon summarized the development of Yugoslavia since the 1948 break and the lessons to be drawn from the trials in the People's Democracies. The article was called 'The Farsightedness of the Bolshevik Party and the Crimes of the Fascist Tito Clique', and contained passages such as the following:

As regards the internal situation, the Titoist clique has completed the abolition of the system of People's Democracy . . . In order to facilitate the complete restoration of capitalism, the government last year 'decentralized' the state sector of the economy (which in any case had ceased to be the property of the people since power was in the hands of the enemies of the people). The management of enterprises was entrusted to so-called 'workers' councils', which largely rely on private capital because of the catastrophic situation of the Yugoslav economy . . . The exploitation of the working class in Yugoslavia is terrible . . . In some concerns 70 per cent of the workers have tuberculosis . . . Bloody repression is practised everywhere, especially against Communists faithful to proletarian internationalism and the independence of their country. Tens of thousands of them are in prison or have been tortured to death or murdered in cowardly ways ... The Belgrade government has completely eliminated the independence of the Yugoslav Republic, which is now reduced to the role of a colony and a base in the service of the American multimillionaires ... As early as 1949, the trials of Rajk in Hungary and Kostov in Bulgaria made it possible to penetrate the real past of the Yugoslav ruling clique; it provided proof that they were cheap spies, with connections from many years back with the information services of Washington and London. One of the main tasks assigned to these wretches, as part of the preparations for a third world war, was to organize plots against the new system in the People's Democracies, to prepare in them, with the help of local traitors, the counter-revolutionary *coups d'état* essential to turn these countries into bases for attacks on the USSR. The scope of this plan, which the resolution of the information bureau did much to stifle at birth, has recently been illustrated by the discovery of the criminal activity of Clementis and his associates in Czechoslovakia.[61]

This small sample of the action of the French Communist Party against the 'Fascist Tito clique' and in support of the trials gives an idea of the similar activity carried out by the other Western Communist parties. As we have already mentioned, however, this did not have the same virulence everywhere. The Italian Communist Party's campaign against Titoism, for example, was much less intense than that of the PCF, and its tone remained less aggressive. Looked at in retrospect, the Italian Communists' action against Titoism could be said to have lacked the zeal and unconditional support for the Soviet Union so marked in the French Communists. The report of the Seventh Congress of the PCI, held in 1951, makes only the odd reference to the problem. The most explicit is by Togliatti, but in almost all the other contributions there was little sign of the problem of Titoism.[62] This can confidently be regarded as a reflection of some of the typical features of the Italian Communist Party which distinguish it from the other big Western Communist party – and which have since developed further – and of the importance of domestic political considerations, and in particular the concern to maintain solidarity with the Socialists. The PCF had nothing to lose in this respect, since its isolation could not become more complete. This was the position of most Communist parties, especially in Europe and America. By acting as totally subservient instruments of Kremlin policy in its most obscurantist and repressive aspects, the Western Communist parties increased their isolation. In the years of the 'cold war' and McCarthyism their complicity in 'Stalinist McCarthyism' deprived them of moral and political authority in the eyes of large groups of democratic and progressive workers. Even the struggle against the threat of war was falsified from the moment that Yugoslavia was included among the principal bases of American imperialism as a mystification to disguise the explosive situation created by Stalin's policies on Yugoslavia's frontiers with the 'socialist camp'.

Even within the parties, in spite of their monolithic appearance and the credulity of their members for the 'treason' of Tito, Rajk, Kostov, Gomulka and the others, in spite of the characteristics of party formation examined above, doubt began to worm its way into the minds of many Communists. In an indirect and distorted way, this began to be reflected in the speeches of the leaders. 'Militants and party organizations are a long way from always opposing an insuperable barrier to these attempts at police penetration,' Thorez announced in his report to the Thirteenth Congress of the PCF.

The workers, in their natural straightforwardness, cannot imagine the mean methods of prying and provocation to which their class enemies resort. Many comrades show a credulity and naïvety which the informers exploit to carry out their vile task. In spite of this the trials of the traitors Rajk and Kostov have shown that these spies and their leader Tito have long been in the pay of the Anglo-American information services . . . Can we believe that the present governments and their American bosses are not trying to slip their agents into the working-class and democrative movement? Do we not see the use they make of their Titoist subsidiary and the Trotskyite splinter groups?[63]

Starting from these reflections by the General Secretary, Étienne Fajon explained the action which should be taken:

We must strike without hesitation, in public, with a large-scale campaign of political explanation, each time a Titoist agent or any other police spy is found in the party. We must beware of paying attention to possible recantations; these are merely following the rules of the double game, which has always been taught to the enemy's agents.[64]

The examples of Tito, Rajk, Kostov, Gomulka and the others were to be the models for detecting police penetration within the party. The struggle which was necessary against this threat – which any revolutionary militant could understand – was used to crush any signs of doubt or dissent, and in particular any doubts about Stalin's policies. As the PCF intellectual journal put it, what had happened to Tito and other 'spies' showed 'how treason inevitably begins at the moment a Communist questions his unconditional loyalty to the USSR'.[65]

In this atmosphere of ideological terrorism, 'spy fever' and police provocation, Communists who had doubts about what was happening in the 'socialist camp' generally chose to keep quiet rather than fall into the category of spies and *agents provocateurs*. Even internal arguments which were now beginning, or had begun in the previous period, and had no connection with the Tito question were now described as part of the 'great plot' of imperialist intelligence which had been discovered through the farsighted vigilance of Stalin. In the Spanish Communist Party, for example, a series of cases took place between the defeat of the Republic and 1949:

The case of the Fascist Tito gang in Yugoslavia, the trial of Rajk and his accomplices in Hungary and now the accusation against Kostov in Bulgaria show that the Anglo-American information services made enormous efforts during our war to infiltrate their agents into the Communist parties; they show that these services inherited agents recruited by the Gestapo from the cowards and renegades, the traitors to the party, who fell into their hands. Something similar happened in Spain. The party is familiar with the experiences of Monzon, Trilla and some others, who became enemy agents. The enemy took advantage of the exceptional circumstances in which they acted for a time to give them the aura of 'resistance fighters' and 'heroes'. They urged them to penetrate the Central Committee and political bureau of the party. Indeed, for a time they succeeded in raising themselves to the leadership of party organizations in France, North Africa and even in Spain. If the party and its leadership had been weak in dealing with these traitors, if they had not taken vigorous measures to remove them, how far might things not have gone? They would have been Spanish Titos, Rajks, Kostovs ... This is precisely what happened before, with the group of agents around Hernandez and Castro, and, earlier still, in the PSU in Catalonia, with del Barrio, Serra Pamies, Victor Colomer, Ferrer and Co. The party and its leadership did not hesitate to sweep away this refuse, in the knowledge that purges strengthen the party. If they had allowed such degenerate and corrupt elements to remain in the party, if they had compromised with them ... how would we be led today, by our Marxist-Leninist-Stalinist revolutionary principles, our identification with the front of the Communist and workers' parties, with the Bolshevik party and the great Stalin, or by the gangsters and adventures of the Franco and Anglo-Saxon intelligence services? ... The answer is obvious: by purging itself of the imitators of Rajk and Kostov, of the enemy agents, the party has become stronger and solider. Lastly, the expulsion of the traitor Comorera from the ranks of the PSUC is another step in this direction. By acting in this way, our party is being faithful to the teaching and example of the Bolshevik party.[66]

In all this list of 'cases' none involved treason, as had to be admitted later, though it was never said in public. Only one of those mentioned, Enrique Castro, went over, many years later, to support Franco. There were political differences, internal struggles for the leadership or problems of personal corruption, but neither spying nor police plants – at least no evidence for them has been produced. The reputation of some of these men as resistance fighters – for example, Monzon and others not mentioned, such as Quinones – was not manufactured by the enemy, but came from the part they in fact played, with their successes and their mistakes.

There were few Communist parties which failed to discover in their ranks Titoist, anti-Soviet or nationalist agents and police spies, and even if they could not compete with the parties in power in organizing trials they went as far as the particular conditions of capitalism allowed. The most spectacular case was that of André Marty and Charles Tillon, an event which shook the French party towards the end of 1952. Both were members of the party's political bureau, and both had won prestige by their part in the insurrection of French sailors in the Black Sea in support of the new Soviet republic and by their part in the Spanish civil war. Tillon was one of the principal organizers of the armed forces of the French resistance. Both were accused of 'serious offences', which were summed up in the following charges: that they 'had questioned the Stalinist political leadership of the General Secretary of the party, Comrade Maurice Thorez', and had organized a Factional conspiracy against the leader who was the guarantee of, among the other virtues of the party, its 'unconditional and unfailing adherence to the Soviet Union'.[67] Both men – according to their accusers – had shown alarming signs of anti-Soviet nationalism, which naturally made them slip down the same slope as Tito: 'Their views are closely similar to those of Tito.' Among the symptoms of 'Marty's inadmissible suspicion' of the Soviet Union, it was mentioned that on a visit to Moscow in 1949 he had 'shown suspicion, to say no more, of the security organs of the socialist state'.[68] Since old Marty refused to 'confess', the political bureau decided that he was a police spy, and as such he was expelled from the party. Tillon was reduced to ordinary membership and condemned to political ostracism.

As well as these spectacular cases, the PCF had others of less importance, such as that of Professor Marcel Prenant, who was accused of anti-Sovietism for casting doubt on the biological theories of Lysenko. The *Histoire du PCF*, written by a group of militants (including Marcel Prenant and other well-known resistance fighters) who at this period began to come into conflict with Stalinist methods, gives the following description of the situation within the party:

Fear of slanderous accusations reduced militants to silence. The depositions, trials and arbitrary expulsions aroused doubts among many comrades. For anyone who had doubts it was the beginning of a long moral martyrdom. He was accused on all sides and ruined whatever he did. If he agreed to the thoroughgoing self-criticism demanded of him, he supplied the material for his condemnation. If he refused to accuse himself of errors and crimes which he had not committed, his 'resistance of self-criticism' was taken as proof of his position as a conscious agent of anti-Communism. While the 'commissions of inquiry' in the People's Democracies and the USSR carried the 'investigation' of charges as far as torture and death, [in France] the central control commission of the party drummed up 'evidence' and framed the accused militant to the point of dishonourable expulsion.[69]

In France, as in other countries, many militants silently left the party, while others remained by suppressing their doubts, which were soon to be given dramatic confirmation. In general, however, only a few intellectuals took the step of expressing public disapproval and resigning from the party.[70]

Among non-Communist left-wing intellectuals disapproval of the course taken by the Communist parties and the USSR was practically universal. During the war and the first few years after it the European Communist parties had considerably increased their influence in intellectual circles. The reappearance of the Stalinist inquisition provoked an abrupt reaction. On top of Zhdanovism, the trials and the campaign of lies against Yugoslavia came the first report of concentration camps in the USSR. The combination was more than enough to make any independent thinker, not protected by party blinkers, wonder about the nature of the regime and the political party which could produce and include such phenomena. A symptomatic feature was the fact that the French edition of Koestler's *Le Zéro et l'Infini* sold more than 400,000 copies.[71]

To add a final touch to the resemblance which is apparent at this period between the Communist movement and the medieval Church, the Stalin cult, which had begun in the thirties and been intensified during the war and the post-war period, began, after 1948, to take on a tone of mystical love. The end of Gheorghiu-Dej's report on 'The Yugoslav Communist Party in the Power of Assassins and Spies' is a particularly good example of this. The Cominform meeting at which this report was presented took place just before Stalin's seventieth birthday (December 1949). The transports of anathemas launched against the Enemy were matched by the violence with which the Saviour was extolled. (We have already quoted the passage in the report which said, 'The genius and insight [of] Comrade Stalin was the salvation of many Marxist parties.') From all the corners of the planet, caravans of offerings arrived at the Kremlin. Molotov's and Malenkov's articles on such a solemn occasion, after describing the earthly journey of the Guide and his immortal deeds and writings, ended as follows:

This is why the trust of the workers of our country in the wise leadership of Comrade Stalin is so unlimited, why their faith in the inspiration of Stalin is so strong, why the love of the Soviet people and the workers of the whole world for Comrade Stalin is so immense ... The peoples of the Soviet Union, and hundreds of millions from all the peoples of the world turn their eyes in gratitude towards Comrade Stalin. Progressive mankind sees in Comrade Stalin its guide and beloved master and has confidence because it knows that the cause of Lenin and Stalin is invincible.[72]

'Would that man be a Communist whose heart did not overflow with affection for Stalin, the leader and friend whose seventieth birthday we have celebrated with joy,' exclaimed Thorez to a storm of applause at the Twelfth Congress of the PCF.[73] Among the innumerable panegyrics of these years, none sums up better the bigotry which dominated the party than the painful criticism of Picasso's portrait of Stalin which appeared in *Les Lettres Françaises*:

Where does this picture express the goodness and love of men which can be found in any photograph of Comrade Stalin? .. [It] totally fails to reflect the intelligence and brotherhood which adorn Stalin's character ... [It] expresses nothing of what we feel about our beloved friend, the father of us all, the man we love above all, whose death we cannot bring ourselves to believe in ... The nobility and kindness which distinguish the immortal face of Stalin in the highest degree are more than absent ... Where are the glow, the smile, the intelligence, in a word, the humanity, so clear in portraits of our dear Stalin? ... Picasso is in danger of spreading misunderstanding and confusion among Communists and the friends of our party.[74]

This was the essence of the complaint: until then, everything had been perfectly simple for good Communists, and it was a great pity that the great artist's irreverent genius should spread confusion in this way.

A few days later a report which no good Communist would normally have believed turned attention away from the uninspired face produced by Picasso's pencil. A statement dated 4 April from the Ministry of the Interior of the USSR announced the rehabilitation and release of the leading medical specialists arrested some months earlier on charges of plotting against the Soviet regime. The case had been reported on 13 January. According to *Pravda*, these leading representatives of Soviet medicine, who had been several times decorated with the Order of Lenin, had confessed that, instead of doing all they could to care for Zhdanov and other party leaders, they had made a deliberate attempt to murder them by means of their medical treatment, and later they had begun preparations to murder Stalin and some military leaders. Mostly Jews, they confessed to working on behalf of Zionism, and American intelligence.[75] Now this was all a lie, and the confessions were said in the 4 April statement to have been extorted by torture, 'in violation of legality'. With a few exceptions, particularly among Communist doctors, who found it hard to believe in the picture of doctors committing murder in the course of their work, most Communists had once more believed in the existence of the plot. *Pravda* had said it; truth had spoken. Soviet justice – justice itself – declared it. Moreover, after five years of unbroken conspiracies it had become a habit. If so many eminent Communists with brilliant revolutionary pasts had been no more than 'monsters with human faces', why should there not be 'monsters with human faces and stethoscopes'? What Communists could not believe was the statement of 4 April; this was much more likely to spread confusion than Picasso's portrait. For the first time in the history of the Soviet regime it was officially admitted that a plot, identical with so many others, had been nothing but a farce. For the first time the use of torture was admitted. For the first time it was admitted that important chiefs of Soviet security manufactured fake plots and extorted confessions by the use of torture. Suddenly everything began to seem confused.

In order to re-establish clarity, particularly in view of the many conspiracies and trials it might prove necessary to 'cancel', the heirs of the deceased needed to invent a highly placed scapegoat. No one fitted the bill better, to start with, than the supreme head of the secret police. With the new Azev unmasked,[76] everything became plain once more, as the political bureau of the guiding party of Western Communism announced:

The political bureau of the French Communist Party is in complete solidarity with the Central Committee of the Communist Party of the Soviet Union, which, in unmasking the agent of international imperialism, Beria, has performed another very great service for the cause of the international workers' movement. The French Communist Party approves and congratulates the Central Committee of the Communist Party of the Soviet Union:

(*a*) for foiling the plans of Beria to take over the leadership of party and state with the ultimate aim of restoring capitalism;

(*b*) for preventing this criminal from sabotaging the consolidation and development of Soviet agriculture and weakening the kolkhozes in an attempt to create difficulties for the food supplies of the Soviet Union;

(*c*) for making it impossible for this agent of the imperialists to damage the friendship of the peoples of the USSR, the fundamental base of the multi-national socialist state. The hopes placed by the imperialists in their agent Beria have proved vain, and nothing can prevent the glorious Communist Party of the Soviet Union, model for all Communist and workers' parties, more united and stronger than ever, from leading the Soviet Union in its onward march on the road to the building of Communism.[77]

Nevertheless Marx's motto, *de omnibus dubitandum,* had sunk its first roots in the consciousness of thousands of Communists. The breach made in the Stalinist monolith by the Yugoslav revolution began to widen.

8

THE EAST TAKES OVER

For the Chinese Communists, who are part of the great Chinese
nation, flesh of its flesh and blood of its blood, any talk of Marxism in isolation from China's characteristics is merely Marxism
in the abstract, Marxism in a vacuum. Hence to apply Marxism
concretely in China ... becomes a problem which it is urgent for
the whole party to understand and solve. Foreign stereotypes
must be abolished ... dogmatism must be laid to rest and be
replaced with the ... Chinese style and spirit ... To separate
internationalist content from national form is the practice of
those who do not understand the first thing about internationalism.

MAO TSE-TUNG, 1938

In December 1947, when in the two Europes the Communist parties
were entering the dismal period of the Cominform and capitalism was
discovering a new energy throughout the West, Mao Tse-tung made the
following announcement to the Central Committee of the Chinese Communist Party:

The Chinese people's revolutionary war has now reached a turning
point. That is, the Chinese People's Liberation Army has beaten back the
offensive of several million reactionary troops of Chiang Kai-shek, the
running dog of the United States of America, and gone over to the
offensive ... This is a turning point in history ... It is a turning point
from growth to extinction for imperialist rule in China, now over a hundred years old. This is a momentous event. It is momentous because it is
occurring in a country with a population of 475 million and, having
occurred, it will certainly culminate in victory throughout the country.
Furthermore, it is momentous because it is occurring in the East, where

over 1,000 million people – half of mankind – suffer under imperialist oppression.[1]

It was indeed true that the turning point in the Chinese civil war in the second half of 1947 was a historic event. From that point the revolutionary army's offensive swept on without interruption until the revolution was victorious throughout the country. On 1 October 1949 the People's Republic of China came officially into existence. While the working-class movement in the West, after letting slip the exceptional opportunity offered by the second great crisis of the capitalist system, was floundering on the path of reformism, an army of peasants, with Communist leaders drawn mainly from the intelligentsia, was submerging Peking and Shanghai, Nanking and Canton. The bridgeheads of European and American capitalism on the eastern edge of Asia were falling into the hands of the biggest agrarian and anti-imperialist revolution in history. And it was the intention of this revolution – or, to be precise, the aim of the party which, with it, had seized power in October 1949 – to develop into a socialist revolution.

Until 1917, all Marxists, including Lenin, thought that the Asiatic societies would inevitably have to go through the stage of capitalist development. At the Second Congress of the Communist International Lenin modified his view on the matter and suggested that 'with the help of the proletariat of the advanced countries' the Asian revolutions could miss out the capitalist stage.

The Communist Party of China now made its preparations to put this view to its first test.[2] It could certainly have no illusions about the help to be expected from the proletariat of the advanced countries, which had not only failed to take power in any of those countries but had also made not the slightest effort to prevent American intervention in support of Chiang Kai-shek. On the other hand, there was the Soviet Union and the People's Democracies. The Soviet Union's victory over Nazi Germany had been one of the decisive factors in creating the international situation in which the victory of the Chinese revolution was possible. Not merely by its role in the defeat of Japan, but by its very existence, the military power of the Soviet Union had been a considerable check on American intervention in China.[3]

Nevertheless, the possibility of obtaining help from the Soviet Union in the period now beginning must have seemed fraught with difficulties in the eyes of the Chinese party leaders. The 'cold war' which Stalin launched against the revolution which had dared to keep its autonomy and originality, in addition to the methods which he used to control and reduce to uniformity the other People's Democracies, were a sharp illustration for the new China of the two roles between which the Kremlin could force it to choose: vassal or enemy?

Were Mao and his close collaborators aware of this alternative? There is not enough information to give a definite answer. Mao's group did, however, have experience of dealings with Moscow (similar to that of Tito and his colleagues in the war of liberation, and wider than that of the Yugoslavs in some respects) which must have helped them to understand the Soviet–Yugoslav dispute. There were also certain features of the ideological formation and political activity of the leading group of the Chinese party which tended in the same direction. These features arose out of the objective characteristics of the Chinese revolution and were deliberately cultivated from the time Mao took over the leadership of the party. What has already been said in Part One on the first stage of the Chinese revolution need not be repeated here, but we shall consider very schematically some moments in the later period which are directly relevant to this problem.

THE CHINESE REVOLUTION AND THE 'GRAND ALLIANCE'

At the end of Part One (p. 293) we reproduced Mao's statement of 1943 according to which, after its Seventh Congress, the Communist International made no further interventions in the internal problems of the Chinese party. We suggested that this fact could be explained by the coincidence which existed from 1935 onwards between the Chinese Communist Party's policy of a united anti-Japanese front, the Comintern's popular front policy and the Soviet foreign policy of the period. But this coincidence did not exclude important divergences. While the Comintern's popular front policy very closely followed the requirements of Soviet foreign policy, this was not true of the Chinese party's policy of the united anti-Japanese front. For the Maoist leadership this tactic presupposed permanent struggle to ensure the predominance of the revolutionary forces within the temporary alliance with the Kuomintang. Moscow's attitude was different. In 1937 the Soviet government had signed a pact with the Kuomintang government, which provided for aid in the form of military material and specialists,[4] and its main desire was that Chiang Kai-shek should devote his army to the war against Japan, instead of using a large part of it to attack Communist bases. But for Chiang the Communists were the main enemy. As he put it on one occasion, 'The Japanese are a disease of the skin, the Communists are a disease of the heart.'[5] The undeclared civil war between the Chinese Communist Party and the Kuomintang could only be ended if Mao made fundamental concessions, if he submitted to the leadership of the Kuomintang and disbanded his forces within Chiang's army. This was the course the Kremlin was urging him to take by making use of old party militants like Wang Ming, who unreservedly supported Stalin's policies.[6] This pressure became more direct after Germany's invasion of the Soviet Union.

In April 1941 Moscow, abandoning its previous policy of alliance with official China, made the non-aggression pact with Japan which has already been mentioned. The Chinese party kept an eloquent silence in the face of this action, which placed it in a similar position to that of the European Communist parties after the German–Soviet pact. The April pact made it easier for the Japanese to consolidate and extend the positions they had won in China and, in particular, removed pressure from the Japanese forces occupying the north of the country, which could now be launched against the main Communist bases.[7] It hardly needs saying that Stalin did not consult the Chinese Communist leaders when he decided on the pact with Japan, and from the information at present available it seems that he gave them no military aid in the preceding period (1937–40), while he did supply aid to the Kuomintang.[8] But when Germany attacked the USSR and it looked likely that Japan, in spite of the pact, would do the same, Stalin remembered the existence of the Chinese Communists. He now asked them to use all their military forces against the much stronger Japanese forces. He asked them to make efforts – which in fact meant concessions – to strengthen unity with the Kuomintang (so that they too could concentrate their forces against the occupiers). This was revealed recently by *Kommunist*, the official journal of the Soviet party:

Mao and his sectarians openly sabotaged our party's proposals, which were that the Japanese forces should be paralysed by joint [CPC–Kuomintang] action and prevented from attacking the USSR at a moment when the Hitlerite army was achieving short-lived successes on the German–Soviet front ... Mao's passivity in the war against Japan, when the interests of the international proletariat required the maximum acceleration of anti-Fascist operations, is shown by numerous facts. It is enough to recall that from 1941 to 1942 the strength of the units of the People's Army used against the Japanese decreased steadily. In January 1943 the Soviet correspondent in Yenan reported that all the troops had received orders not to engage in operations against Japan, and to fall back if contact were, by chance, made. Their duty was, as far as possible, to reach a truce with the enemy.[9]

In a distorted, and indeed slanderous, form the *Kommunist* version reveals the real conflict which grew up between Mao's strategy and Stalin's.

Realizing the overwhelming superiority of the Japanese in weapons and normal military organization, Mao systematically avoided making the People's Army fight conventional battles. He applied on a large scale the tactic of guerrilla warfare which had been tried out and developed into a theory as early as the Kiangsi period. According to one of the best Western observers,

Military operations by Communist troops were extremely fragmented, partly because their political aims led them to spread over as large an area as possible in order to establish contact with the population, and partly because their arms and equipment were infinitely inferior to those of the Japanese. Their guerrilla warfare was even further removed from regular war than were the Kiangsi campaigns; they worked in small units, never larger than a regiment.[10]

This method of fighting was very closely connected with the implantation of the new revolutionary power in the large rural areas in the provinces occupied by the Japanese. In short, Mao was applying the theory of 'protracted war' which he had developed in 1938. He did not exclude a transition to mobile warfare at a later stage:

> Since the war is protracted and ruthless, it is possible for the guerrilla units to undergo the necessary steeling and gradually to transform themselves into regular forces, so that their mode of operation is gradually regularized and guerrilla warfare develops into mobile warfare.[11]

The sudden collapse of Japan after Hiroshima meant that this phase did not occur in the war against Japan, but Mao's strategy had not been devised merely with this war in mind. Its long-term perspective was the inevitable continuation of the armed struggle against the reactionary forces of the Kuomintang (a struggle which hardly ever stopped during the war against the Japanese). Its plan was to accumulate forces for an eventual civil war, not to sacrifice them prematurely. In other words, the ultimate goal of Mao's strategy was not the limited one of national liberation; it included social revolution. It is well known that the close connection between these two aspects was the secret of the Communist victory in China.

Mao's politico-military strategy was opposed to Stalin's at different levels. As long as there was a danger of a Japanese attack on the Soviet Far East, that is, until about 1943, the dispute appeared mainly as one of military tactics, as *Kommunist* now recognized. While Mao was keeping forces in reserve and preparing them for the coming Chinese revolution, Stalin wanted both Mao and Chiang to throw all their military contingents against the Japanese. The Americans had an equal interest in this as a means of bringing some relief to their war effort in the Pacific.

On his side, Chiang was keeping the Kuomintang army in reserve for the inevitable settlement of accounts with the Communists. At the beginning of the war Chiang had thought that the Japanese might help him to destroy the Communists. Taking advantage of the fact that the People's Army was at that time under the formal authority of the national government, he sent it to attack the main body of the invading forces.[12] Mao did not fall into the trap. He disobeyed Chiang as he was later to disobey Stalin. If he had given way to Stalin's insistence in

1941–3 the revolutionary army would have largely worn itself out, and when Japan capitulated the Chinese Communists would have found themselves at the mercy of the Kuomintang and the Americans. It should be borne in mind as a fundamental element in the situation that throughout the period of the war against Japan the Chinese Communists received no military aid from the Soviets. Stalin called on the Chinese Communists to intensify their military operations against the Nippon army, but he did nothing to lessen their tragic inferiority in weapons.[13]

On a more general political level, Mao's strategy conflicted with the Kremlin's longer-term aims. The Chinese party's revolutionary ambition – the victory of Communism in China – could hardly be reconciled with Stalin's great hope of reaching an agreement with the United States, in Asia as well as in Europe, on the basis of a division of 'spheres of interest'. Even on the most optimistic view, such a division was only possible in Asia if a regime took root in China in which the Communists were under the control of the national bourgeoisie led by Chiang Kai-shek. This is why Stalin never ceased his pressure on the CPC leadership to reach a compromise of this kind with the Kuomintang. At the same time he supported the American policy which sought to make Chiang Kai-shek abandon his ingrained anti-Communism and make certain concessions to the Chinese party in order to ease its integration into a Kuomintang regime.

In the autumn of 1944 Roosevelt sent General Hurley as ambassador to Chiang. On his way Hurley stopped in Moscow and examined the situation in China with Molotov. Relying on this interview, he managed to 'convince' the Chinese dictator of the following points: '(1) Russia is not supporting the Communist Party in China, (2) Russia does not want dissensions or civil war in China, and (3) Russia desires more harmonious relations with China.'[14] In conversations with Hurley (15 April 1945) and Hopkins (28 May 1945), Stalin declared that the Soviet aim was the reunification of China under the control of Chiang Kai-shek. Hopkins informed Truman that Stalin had promised that 'he would do everything he could to promote the unification of China under Chiang Kai-shek', and had said that 'no Communist leader was strong enough to unify China'.[15] (In June 1944 Stalin had said to Harriman,

'Communists, the Chinese Communists? They are to Communism what margarine is to butter.')[16]

These statements, which are attributed to Stalin and his assistants by American politicians, might be taken as diplomatic cunning were they not supported by other facts and by the whole orientation of Stalin's 'grand alliance' policy. On 14 August 1945 Moscow signed a 'Sino–Soviet treaty of friendship and alliance' with Chiang Kai-shek, under the terms of which, and in accordance with the secret agreement made at Yalta, the USSR recovered the bases and concessions which Tsarist Russia had stolen from China and lost in the Russo–Japanese war of 1905. Chiang's government fiercely resisted these Russian claims – this was the moment when, one after another, the Western powers were renouncing their former concessions in China and when China was being given the status of a great power and a permanent member of the UN Security Council – and gave way only after Stalin promised not to support the Chinese Communists.

This, at least, is the version of some historians.[17] It is supported up to a certain point by the events which followed the capitulation of Japan, but only up to a certain point. The Soviet army which liberated Manchuria, for example, did not give the Chinese Communists the vital help it could have given them. Instead of handing over to them the industrial installations of the region – which were the largest in China – the army dismantled them and sent them to Russia as war booty. Instead of allowing them to take power in Mukden (Shenyang), the main railway junction and industrial centre of Manchuria, and other cities, the Soviet authorities made an agreement with Chiang to hand them over to his troops. When they were in a position to transport units of the People's Army to Peking and other cities of North China in advance of the nationalists, they did not do so, with the result that the nationalists, ferried by American ships and aircraft, were able to establish themselves there.

On the other hand, the Soviet military authorities did not prevent the People's Army and Chinese Communist organizations from extending their organization into the agricultural areas of Manchuria, or even from taking over towns such as Changchun and Harbin. Most important of all – this was Stalin's great gift to the Chinese Communists – the Soviet command handed over to Mao's troops a share of the weapons of the Japanese army in Manchuria.[18] (It is of course true that to act otherwise, that is, to refuse to hand over part of the Japanese weapons to the Communists when the largest part went to the Kuomintang, would have been too scandalous behaviour on the part of the leader of international Communism.)

In other words, Stalin was holding out one hand to Mao and the other to Chiang, and at the same time pushing them to come to terms. He ratified the recognition of Chiang as head of the Chinese state and gave him some help in establishing his authority in the North, but insisted that Chiang should take the Communists into his government. (Shortly after the signing of the Sino–Soviet treaty and under the combined pressure of Moscow and Washington, Chiang Kai-shek invited Mao Tse-tung to discuss the Chinese Communist Party's entry into the government.) Stalin enabled Mao to lessen a little his inferiority in weapons, but in return he pressed him to make concessions to the Kuomintang.

REVOLUTIONARY WAR OR 'NATIONAL UNITY'

For information about Stalin's pressure on Mao there is a first-class source whose version, to the best of our knowledge, has never been denied by Moscow. This was mentioned in a previous chapter and will now be reproduced with more detail. According to Kardelj in February 1948, Stalin gave him and Dimitrov the following account:

... after the war we invited the Chinese comrades to come to Moscow and we discussed the situation in China. We told them bluntly that we considered the development of the uprising in China had no prospects, that the Chinese comrades should seek a *modus vivendi* with Chiang Kai-shek, and that they should join the Chiang Kai-shek government and dissolve their army. The Chinese comrades agreed here in Moscow with the views of the Soviet comrades, but went back to China and acted quite otherwise. They mustered their forces, organized their armies and now, as we see, they are beating Chiang Kai-shek's army. Now in the case of China we admit we were wrong.[19]

The negotiations between Mao and Chiang, which began in September 1945, produced no practical result. While the negotiations were going on, Chiang ordered his troops to attack the areas held by the Communists, and Mao ordered his to resist and to crush the attackers.[20] By the autumn of 1945 the civil war was an undeniable fact. Soviet and American pressure, the aim of which was to impose a 'national unity' solution on the two armed forces confronting each other in China, increased. At the Foreign Ministers' conference in December 1945, the 'Big Three' agreed on the need for 'a united and democratic China led by a government of national unity and based on a broad integration of democratic elements into all the organs of the national government and on an end to civil disorders'.[21] The negotiations between the Kuomintang and the Chinese Communist Party began again with increased urgency. In January 1946 a Consultative Political Conference was held, which decided on a truce in military operations. The conference adopted a long series of resolutions which seemed to meet the provisions of the 'Big Three' agreement, but were in fact only a cover for Chiang's preparations to resume the offensive against the revolutionary forces and those of the Communists to put up effective resistance to the counter-revolutionary forces. Meanwhile, in Washington, advocates of increased aid to the Chinese dictator – to enable him to establish himself by military force – gained strength. By the summer of 1946 the civil war had spread to the whole country and, in spite of occasional new efforts at negotiation, grew steadily in intensity until the total collapse of the Kuomintang.

Chiang Kai-shek returned to the attack in July 1946. At that moment his army enjoyed a heavy superiority in numbers of regular units and in weapons; it had 500 aircraft, mostly piloted by Americans, whereas the People's Army had no planes until the victory. It had the help of thousands of American officers and advisers and was very generously supported financially by Washington. For a year, up to the summer of 1947, the nationalists seemed to be going from victory to victory. In reality, they were occupying towns which the People's Army, following a well-tried strategy, was not defending. They were lengthening their lines of communication and dispersing their forces in areas which were hostile and riddled with revolutionary agitation. The People's Army fought only where it had a clear superiority. It extended and consolidated the new power in ever vaster rural areas, where the agrarian revolution automatically became a tangible reality. It encircled towns, cut lines of communication and isolated the nationalist divisions. At the same time the Communists intensified their underground activity in the urban centres held by the enemy, winning over doubters and taking advantage of the dissensions inside the Kuomintang's corrupt political and military apparatus.

The relation of forces very soon turned in favour of the Communists. Between the summer of 1947 and that of 1948 the People's Army went steadily over to the attack, in Manchuria, in North China and in Central China. The stage predicted by Mao in his theory of 'prolonged war' was beginning, the transition from a guerrilla war to a mobile war. A whole series of spectacular victories followed during the autumn of 1948. The People's Army liberated Manchuria, took hundreds of thousands of prisoners and seized large quantities of war material. Superiority in weapons (in spite of the lack of aircraft) and regular troops swung to the side of the revolutionary forces. In January 1949 the People's Army entered Peking. In the spring it crossed the Yangtse and entered Nanking and Shanghai. It reached Canton in the autumn. By the end of the year the whole of continental China, apart from a few outlying regions which were liberated shortly afterwards, was under the control of the new revolutionary power.

The turn of the civil war which took place in the summer of 1947, the rapid and victorious offensive of the revolutionary army, which took it in a year from Manchuria to Canton, cannot be explained simply by the skill acquired by the Communists in political and military tactics as a result of twenty-five years' experience of revolutionary war. Nor can it be explained merely by the Communists' revolutionary fighting spirit, discipline, self-sacrifice and operational efficiency. Without all these factors the victory would not have been possible, but they alone are not a complete explanation, and in particular do not explain the speed of the counter-offensive.

Among the main causes of the collapse of the Kuomintang, all those who have studied the period of the Chinese revolution point to its own internal decay, its incompetence and its corruption. Apart from the

Chinese Communist leaders, one of the first to realize this was Marshall. His mission to China, before he took over the State Department in February 1947, enabled him to get to know Chiang's regime from the inside. In 1947, at an inter-ministerial meeting, he forecast its collapse. In February 1948 he told the National Security Council that 'under present conditions of disorder, of corruption, inefficiency and impotence of central government', Chinese problems were 'practically insoluble'.[22]

But the impotence and the breakdown of Chiang's regime were only the reflection of a deeper reality, the advanced stage of 'revolution-arization' of Chinese society. The revolution organized, programmed and embodied by the People's Army and the Communist Party of China made contact in its advance with a diffused, spontaneous and ubiquitous revolution. After thirty years of civil wars, peasants' and workers' up-risings, revolutionary guerrilla warfare, the Japanese invasion and the war of national liberation, this had established itself in people's minds and had severely disrupted traditional structures.

The Japanese invasion was the crucial test for all the political forces which claimed to be able to solve the problems of this changing China. After revealing itself in 1925–7 as the enemy of the agrarian revolution, the Kuomintang had shown itself incapable, in 1937–45, of organizing national resistance. It compromised itself by directly or indirectly collaborating with the enemy on many occasions. On the other hand, the Chinese Communist Party, which during the first and second civil wars had become known as the party of revolution, during the war against Japan also became known as the party of national independence. Political and social groups which swung between it and the Kuomintang went over to its side, or asked for a genuine alliance with it. When Japan capitulated, Chiang Kai-shek's government would not have been able to set up its power over the greater part of the territory without the existence of a set of factors unrelated to the underlying reality of the country. These included the US–Japanese agreement that the Japanese forces should surrender only to Chiang's troops and the transport of Chiang's troops (which were isolated in the south-west of the country) by American ships and aircraft to Central and North China, the international status of Chiang's government (which had been recognized by the 'Big Three' as the only legal government of China), the Sino-Soviet treaty of August 1945 which strengthened the nationalist government in its struggle with the revolutionary forces, and the behaviour of the Soviet army in the north and Manchuria in implementing this treaty, and finally the active aid of all sorts with which the American government immediately supplied Chiang's.

The Kuomintang regime was really restored artificially, imposed on a country which was demanding just what the regime intended to prevent, civil peace, radical social changes and real national independence. From the moment of liberation from the Japanese yoke the Kuomintang showed itself to be the party of civil war, the enemy of all social change and the instrument of a new foreign domination, that of the United States. There were only two possibilities which would enable it to consolidate its power for any length of time: either that it would crush the Communists by military force or that they would capitulate politically, allow themseves to be 'integrated' into the regime, disband their military forces, submit to Chiang Kai-shek's leadership and for all practical purposes abandon their revolutionary programme. From the point of view of the Kuomintang, the previously mentioned negotiations were a tactical manoeuvre to gain time and prepare their military forces to bring about the first solution, while at the same time exploring the possibility of the second. If the leadership of the Chinese party had given way to Stalin's demands, the second possibility might have come about. The Communists would have found themselves once more the prisoners of the Kuomintang, as in 1925-7, and the tragedy of that period might have been repeated at any moment. If, in Western Europe, 'national unity' led to the exclusion of Communist ministers and the isolation of the parties, in Chinese conditions a similar type of 'national unity' would very probably have resulted in a new massacre of Communists.

One of the historic virtues of Mao and his colleagues is their complete clarity on this question, which appears in documents of the period. Both in the period immediately before the capitulation of Japan and in that which followed it, Mao entertained no illusions; he considered civil war unavoidable, and prepared the party to face it. In his report to the Seventh Congress of the party, two months before the capitulation of Japan, he said:

To this day the chief ruling clique in the Kuomintang is persisting in its reactionary policy of dictatorship and civil war. There are many signs that it has long been making, and is now stepping up, preparations to unleash civil war as soon as the forces of a certain allied country have cleared a considerable part of the mainland of the Japanese aggressors. It also hopes that the generals of certain allied countries will do the same job in China as the British General Scobie has been doing in Greece.[23]

Later in his report, he referred to the experience of 1927:

In 1944 the Kuomintang government presented a so-called memorandum demanding that the Communist Party should 'disband, within a definite time limit', four-fifths of the armed forces of the Liberated Areas. In 1945, during the most recent negotiations, it has further demanded the handing over of all the armed forces of the Liberated Areas by the Communist Party, after which it will grant the Communist Party 'legal status'.

These people tell the Communists, 'Hand over your troops and we will grant you freedom.' According to their theory, a political party that does not have any army should enjoy freedom. Yet whatever freedom the Chinese Communist Party enjoyed during 1924–7, when it had only a small armed force, vanished with the Kuomintang government's policies of 'party purge' and massacre.[24]

Mao ended his final speech to the Congress with these words:

At this moment two congresses are being held in China, the Sixth National Congress of the Kuomintang and the Seventh National Congress of the Communist Party. They have completely different aims: the aim of the one is to liquidate the Communist Party and all the other democratic forces in China, and thus to plunge China into darkness; the aim of the other is to overthrow Japanese imperialism and its lackeys, the Chinese feudal forces, and build a new democratic China and thus lead China to light.[25]

Immediately after the September negotiations Mao told a meeting of party activists, 'The Kuomintang and the Communist Party are sure to fail in their negotiations, sure to start fighting and sure to break with each other.' But the negotiations were necessary. By agreeing to them the Communists had 'exploded the rumour spread by the Kuomintang that the Communist Party did not want peace and unity'.[26]

THE BOGEY OF CHINESE 'TITOISM'

The Maoists have not yet revealed the history of the struggle inside the party during these years. From documents available at present, such as the document of April 1946 already quoted,[27] it appears that some influential leaders of the CPC supported the solution for which Stalin was pressing, that a *modus vivendi* with Chiang Kai-shek should be reached at all costs. In their eyes the revolutionary war was doomed to failure from the moment the Kremlin began to look for a compromise with the United States. It is likely that Stalin's pressure on the leadership of the Chinese party persisted until at least the end of 1946 or the beginning of 1947. In December 1946 Stalin told Roosevelt's son that the Soviet government was prepared 'to follow a *common* policy with the United States on Far Eastern questions'.[28] During the years 1945 and 1946 the Soviet and Western European Communist press published almost no news about the Chinese People's Army, the revolutionary changes in the liberated areas and the rest. They limited themselves in general to denouncing the support from 'reactionary circles' in the United States for 'reactionary circles' in the Kuomintang, making this support appear the main obstacle to a policy of 'national unity'. And, as we have already seen, Zhdanov's report to the founding meeting of the Cominform mentioned China only in relation to this intervention. The revolutionary content of the civil war was not mentioned, and the problem of the solidarity of the international proletariat with the Chinese revolutionaries was not raised. The Chinese Communist Party was not invited to become a member of the Cominform. It was clear that Mao's policies, like Tito's during the war of liberation, were no longer on the same wavelength as Stalin's. The spectacular triumph of Mao's line in 1949 could not but arouse Stalin's anxiety. Tito was a worrying memory.

Stalin's anxiety must have been all the sharper in view of the fact that what had happened was more than that Mao's strategy had been proved right by events. For the first time a Communist party had reached power in a big country whose mentality, ideological formation and internal development differed considerably from those of the Soviet party. It was a party aware of its originality and world importance. The leadership of the party had systematically cultivated these differences for over ten years, in latent conflict with Moscow orthodoxy, in spite of the ritual invocations of Stalin and his ideas which accompanied the 'Sinification' of Marxism. The *Kommunist* article mentioned above shows that this was the point of view from which Moscow saw the 'movement for the rectification of style' organized in Yenan in a number of stages between 1941 and 1945. This 'movement' consisted in study and discussion of a series of ideological, political and organizational problems with the aim of teaching the party to use the Marxist method and to reject dogmatic views, subjectivism and formalism, in other words, to unite Marxist theory and the practice of the Chinese revolution. 'Just as it was revolutionary and necessary to fight the old stereotyped writing and the old dogmatism during the period of the 4 May Movement,' said Mao, 'so it is revolutionary and necessary today for us to use Marxism to criticise the new stereotyped writing and the new dogmatism.'[29] Thousands of activists passed through this school, which was a means of spreading Maoist ideas in the party and giving cohesion to its ranks under the command of Mao. Mao's theories on revolutionary war, 'the new democracy', the way to reconcile contradictions in the party, etc., were canonized as the truth of Marxism for China. The terms 'Chinese Marxism' or 'the sinification of Marxism' began to be heard. *Kommunist* now reveals that Wang Ming and others were criticized for their 'dogmatic attitude to Russian Marxism'.

This ideological movement – which, in spite of its anti-dogmatic intensions, may be considered as the beginning of the Mao cult – reached a climax at the Seventh Congress of the Chinese party. Liu Shao-chi's report 'on the Party' includes the following passage:

The General Programme of the Party Constitution stipulates that the Thought of Mao Tse-tung shall guide all the work of our Party. The Constitution itself provides that it is the duty of every Party member to endeavour to understand the fundamentals of Marxism–Leninism and the Thought of Mao Tse-tung. This is a most important historical characteristic of our amendment of the Constitution at the present time.[30]

(So 'characteristic', indeed, that such language would have been un-thinkable in the statutes of any other Communist party.) The report goes on:

For over a century, the Chinese nation and people, who have known profound misfortunes, have accumulated immeasurably rich historical ex-perience in the course of their bloody struggles for their own emanci-pation. Their practical struggles and the experience thus gained inevitably culminated in the creation of great theories of their own, thus showing that the Chinese nation is not only a nation capable of fighting, but also a nation which has a modern scientific revolutionary theory . . .

. . . This theory is none other than the Thought of Mao-Tse-tung – Comrade Mao Tse-tung's theory and policy regarding Chinese history, Chinese society and the Chinese revolution.

The Thought of Mao Tse-tung is the thought that unites Mar-xist–Leninist theory with the practice of the Chinese revolution. It is Chinese Communism, Chinese Marxism.

The strengths and originality of this new departure are heavily em-phasized:

. . . Because of various conditions, such as the very great peculiarities in China's social and historical development and her backwardness in science, etc., it is a unique and difficult task to carry out the systematic Sinification of Marxism from its European form to a Chinese form – in other words to use the Marxist standpoint and method to resolve the various problems of the contemporary Chinese revolution. Many of the problems encountered in the process have never been raised or solved before by the world's Marxists . . . This can never be accomplished, as some people seem to think, by simply reading Marxist works over and over, reciting them by heart and quoting from them. It is none other than our Comrade Mao Tse-tung who has so remarkably and successfully car-ried out the unique and difficult task of the Sinification of Marxism. This constitutes one of the greatest achievements in the history of the world Marxist movement.

In these texts awareness of an undeniable fact – that the Chinese revo-lution, like all great revolutions, was in the process of producing its own theory – is combined with the beginnings of a cult which was to lead to a dogmatization of various new ideas, as had happened with Leninism. But we shall not analyse these texts here; what interests us now is the fact that Stalin could hardly be expected to accept the axioms of the Seventh Congress of the Chinese party or Mao's politico-military strategy. The Chinese revolution was the first important theoretical challenge to Stalinist orthodoxy, just as its practical course was a challenge to the policy of the 'grand alliance'. This was a challenge on a world scale, since, as Liu Shao-chi's report said, the new theory meant 'a further development of Marxism in the national-democratic revolution in the colonial, semi-colonial and semi-feudal countries' which would 'make great and useful contributions to the cause of the emancipation of the peoples of all countries, and of the peoples of the East in particular'. From 1945 onwards, the Chinese Communist Party began to assert the status of its ideas and experiences as a model for revolution in backward countries. It began to present itself as the successor to the Soviet party.

As the victory of 1949 became clearer, and particularly in the course of that year, a series of articles appeared in Soviet doctrinal publications which discreetly dotted the *i*'s. Passages from Mao's works were quoted in which he paid homage to the role and the example of the Soviet Union, Lenin and Stalin, with no mention of the 'Sinification' of Marxism and with an implied criticism of the Maoist theses of the original development of revolution in colonial and semi-colonial countries. According to one of these articles:

The general laws of social development are identical for Eastern and Western countries alike. One can speak only of differences in the pace or in the particular forms of this development. In this sense, people's democracy in the East does not differ in its basic outlines from people's democracy in the West . . .

The whole course of the national-colonial struggle, the immense victories won by the democratic forces in East Asia, startlingly confirm the truth of Lenin's and Stalin's teaching on the national-Colonial question and demonstrate the triumph of all-conquering ideas of Marx, Engels, Lenin and Stalin.[31]

For this Soviet theoretician, Mao's ideas simply did not exist. And according to another article:

> The works of Comrade Stalin, and in particular his works on the Chinese question, have been of enormous significance for the party in its formulating a correct Marxist-Leninist policy. Basing himself in these works on a profound theoretical analysis of the situation in China, Comrade Stalin defined the characteristics of the Chinese revolution, brilliantly predicting its course and indicating the conditions in which it could succeed.[32]

In November 1949, shortly after the proclamation of the People's Republic of China, the World Federation of Trade Unions held a meeting in Peking. One of the Chinese speakers, Liu Shao-chi, firmly defended the Maoist position:

> The way taken by the Chinese people in defeating imperialism and its lackeys and in founding the People's Republic of China is the way that should be taken by the peoples of many colonial and semi-colonial countries in their fight for national independence and people's democracy ... This way is the way of Mao Tse-tung.[33]

Statements in which some Asian Communists expressed their desire to follow the Chinese example were omitted from the summary of this meeting published by the journal of the World Federation of Trade Unions.

It was clear that the revolution in the enormous area of China, like revolution in little Yugoslavia, contained the dangers of heresy. The proclamation of the Chinese People's Republic on 1 October 1949 – just before the Cominform's announcement that the People's Republic of Yugoslavia was in the hands of 'spies and assassins' – was not only the hardest blow received by the imperialist system since the October revolution; it also meant that the Kremlin was faced with the nightmare of an Asian Titoism, incomparably more dangerous than Titoism in the Balkans. Some Western observers noted the possibility, without regarding it as immediate, that the nightmare might become reality.[34] The parties of the Cominform also thought it necessary to put a stop to such 'speculations'. The French Communist Party journal, for example, wrote in March 1950: 'Proletarian internationalism is deeply rooted in the Communist Party of China, and we may be confident that the hopes of a "Chinese Titoism" cherished by the imperialists are doomed to a bitter disappointment.'[35]

THE SINO-SOVIET ALLIANCE

And, for several years, the nightmare was banished. The international situation exerted strong pressure on both Mao and Stalin to keep on good terms. The 'cold war' was reaching its climax. Mao could not know how far the United States would go in its support of the defeated Chiang Kai-shek, now a refugee on Taiwan, and in any case American imperialism was the main threat to the new China. On his side, Stalin needed to strengthen his international forces. In April 1949 the Atlantic pact had been signed. In May the Soviet government had had to abandon the blockade of West Berlin. Japan was becoming an American military base facing the Soviet Far East. Moreover, in spite of the explosion in July of the same year of the first Soviet atom bomb, the American advantage in this field was as clear as that of the Soviets in conventional military forces. The negotiations between Mao and Stalin, begun in Moscow in December 1949, ended in February 1950 with the signing of a thirty-year Sino-Soviet treaty 'of friendship, alliance and mutual aid'. In June 1950 the Korean war broke out, and this was for three years to be a strong bond on the new alliance.

In addition to these international conditions, other factors must have played a part. The relations between the two parties had not yet been put to the test on the level of relations between states. (Similarly in the case of Yugoslavia, the divergences which arose during the war did not themselves lead to a break; relations became hostile when the new Yugoslav state came into existence and the incompatibility between its sovereignty and the policies and methods of the Comintern was revealed in practice.) Mao may have thought that with a country like China, with 500 million people and an army of several million troops who had just proved their fighting qualities, Stalin would be more careful about acting as he had in the case of the little countries of Eastern Europe.

In addition, the economic situation of China, after twenty-five years of almost uninterrupted war, was completely catastrophic. The Chinese Communists thought that the USSR would give them the help they urgently needed. They faced immense economic and technical problems for which they were not prepared. The Maoist theory of the 'new democracy' put forward a general attitude to the relations and roles of the different classes, the character of the new regime, but to build it something more was needed. The Chinese Communist Party thought it had found the solution in the model and the experience of the building of the Soviet state. On the eve of victory, Mao discussed the problem in the following terms:

> The serious task of economic construction lies before us. We shall soon put aside some of the things we know well and be compelled to do things we don't know well. This means difficulties. The imperialists reckon that we will not be able to manage our economy ... At first some of the Soviet Communists also were not very good at handling economic matters and the imperialists awaited their failure too. But the Communist Party of the Soviet Union emerged victorious and, under the leadership of Lenin and Stalin, it learned not only how to make the revolution but also how to carry on contruction. It has built a great and splendid socialist state. The Communist Party of the Soviet Union is our best teacher and we must learn from it.[36]

Was this a sincere belief or a diplomatic statement made with an eye to the new stage? Mao had always manoeuvred with great skill to avoid direct conflicts with Moscow. At the same time as he opposed the men and tendencies which, within the Chinese party, stood for unconditional acceptance of Moscow's orders and views on the Chinese revolution, he recognized and proclaimed the leading role of the USSR and Stalin in the international Communist movement.[37] There is no indication that he ever made the slightest critical comment on the internal problems of the USSR or on Stalin's policies in the Western Communist movement. (From the information available about his life, it seems that Mao was as ill-informed about these problems as other Communist leaders were about Chinese problems.)

Between Mao's Chinese adaptation of Marxism as it presented itself around 1949 and Stalin's Russian version there was a much wider area of common ground than is now admitted by eager defenders of Maoist originality. The main areas of divergence were the problems of revolutionary war, strategy and the forms and methods of the Chinese revolution in its destructive stage, and these naturally declined in importance when the problems of the constructive stage had to be tackled. On the other hand, these divergences acquired international importance as the liberation struggle developed in the third world.

For a time, however, the Korean war and internal Chinese problems meant that the differences between Stalinist orthodoxy and Maoist theories on the paths of revolution in the countries oppressed by imperialism took second place. For the work of internal construction the Chinese Communists, following Mao's advice, set themselves to learn from the Soviet party. They stopped when experience – as had happened in revolutionary tactics between 1925 and 1927 – taught the pupils that their teacher was equally inadequate to help them in the building of the new regime.

If, in 1949, the factors mentioned drove Mao to reach the closest possible understanding with Stalin, Stalin too had to bear in mind, in addition to the threat from America, the dispute with Yugoslavia. There are reasons for assuming that Stalin had every reason not to involve himself in a similar problem with the Chinese party, whose great victory gave it immense prestige in the international Communist movement and among all oppressed peoples. His interest, in fact, was to take advantage of this prestige. All the propaganda of the Cominform and the Communist parties presented the triumph of the Chinese revolution as the fruit of Stalin's inspired leadership, and of his views and strategy, advice and directions. Here is a sample: 'At every stage of the Chinese revolution and struggle for national liberation, Stalin was there to point out the problems, to help in correcting mistakes, to point out the dangers to be avoided and the right path to follow, on the basis of the domination of the proletariat.' (In 1949 the industrial proletariat in China was under 1 per cent of the population and, after the terrible repression of 1927, it was hardly capable of taking any part in the revolutionary struggle. The proportion of workers in the CPC, again in 1949, was under 3 per cent and the overwelming majority of the leading activists were drawn from the intelligentsia.[38] According to the Cominform version, the proletariat had been the hegemonic force of the Chinese revolution. Stalin had worked miracles.) The article continues:

Stalin's analysis of the special features of the Chinese situation is what gave the CPC the basis on which to build its programme, its strategy and fighting tactics ... Stalin scientifically forecast the Kuomintang's betrayal (in 1927) ... Stalin developed with regard to China the Leninist–Stalinist theory of colonial and semi-colonial countries ... The strengthening of the influence of the Chinese party in the working class is also due to Stalin's advice ... Stalin protected the Chinese revolution from Trotskyism ... Only the study and assimilation of Stalin's theoretical views enabled the Chinese Communist Party to see its way clearly, correct its mistakes and lead the revolution and the revolutionary war to victory.[39]

The effect produced by such statements on the Chinese leaders may be imagined, but for the moment they seemed not to let it upset them. They had to swallow many cruder insults in this period, and did so with the same impassiveness. Without going into details of Sino-Soviet relations up to the death of Stalin, we may mention that under the agreements annexed to the treaty of 1950 the restoration to the Chinese government of the Manchurian railway was postponed to 1952, unless the peace treaty between the USSR and Japan were to be signed in the interval. The withdrawal of Soviet troops from the naval base at Port Arthur was also put off to the same dates, and the problem of Dairen was held over to be studied afresh after the conclusion of the peace treaty. The Chinese government had to recognize the 'independence' of Outer Mongolia, that is, its continuance under Soviet control.[40] In Sinkiang the Chinese had to accept the establishment of two mixed companies of the type rejected by the Yugoslavs. In 1954 Mao called for the complete and immediate transfer to China of the Soviet holding in these companies.[41]

As regards economic credits, the Chinese leaders had calculated their needs at between $2,000m. and $3,000m. They obtained from Moscow a credit of $6om. a year for five years. This total of $300m. was less than the Soviet government had lent Poland shortly before.[42] As to the Soviet experts sent to China, the same problem arose as we saw in Yugoslavia: their salaries were much larger than those of their Chinese colleagues. Given the economic level of the people and the habits of austerity in which the Chinese Communists had been brought up, it is easy to imagine the psychological and political effects such a situation inevitably produced. And there were no doubt many other things which contradicted the official clichés about 'Sino-Soviet friendship'. Nevertheless until after the events of autumn 1956 in Hungary and Poland nothing the Chinese said cast any doubt on this idyllic picture. In December 1956 Mao said:

> In his solution of a number of particular problems Stalin showed a tendency to great-power chauvinism, and did not pay enough attention to equality of rights. He did not educate cadres in a spirit of modesty, and sometimes interfered unjustly in the affairs of fraternal countries and parties. This had many serious consequences.[43]

But the Maoists did not, then or later, make an objective and documented historical analysis of the intervention of Stalin (and the ruling Soviet bureaucracy) in the different phases of the Chinese revolution, and in particular in that of 1949–53. There may be a reason for this in that any such analysis would imply a critical study of certain aspects of Mao's own activity, which is a difficult task while the cult of his thought and personality persists. But it remains true that until this work is done the Chinese Communists will be unable to give a convincing explanation of the present dispute with the Soviet party.[44]

Unifying the country politically and creating a planned economy would, in Chinese conditions inevitably have led to a process of bureaucratization on an even larger scale than in Russia in 1917, but there can be no doubt that the effect of importing Soviet models could only be to stimulate and hasten this process in every sphere: party and state, economy and ideology. The extreme complexity of Chinese problems and the attempt to achieve socialism in such a country objectively required the starting of a permanent discussion and development of research free from censorship with the broad participation of the masses and intellectual activists and including criticism of Soviet attempts. Instead of that the Soviet model was dogmatically adopted as the only possible one.

Another result of the Chinese party's subordination to Stalin in this period was that the considerable experience which the Chinese revolution had accumulated during its struggle for power and its theoretical and practical lessons could not become the property of the international Communist movement, and in particular of Communists in colonial and semi-colonial countries. There were exceptions, such as the Vietnamese Communists and some Communist groups in South-East Asia which had traditional links with the Chinese, but in general the Chinese revolution was made known to the rest of the world in a Soviet version. The broad interpretation put forward by this version is illustrated by the article previously quoted: Stalin was the originator, and the Chinese Communists had done no more than apply his ideas and instructions. Everything was contained in the works of Stalin, the Marxist analysis of Chinese reality, the course of the revolution, the strategy and tactics which had brought it to victory, etc. During these years the Chinese experience, rather than enriching the Marxist theory of revolution, tended to reinforce Stalinist dogmatism and glorify its creator. The victory of the Chinese Communist Party also acted as a consolation for the Western Communist movement and obscured for a time the consequences of the failure of the European revolution, and the congenital impotence of American Communism. In addition the display of 'Sino-Soviet friendship' and the glorification of the aid given by the Soviet Union to China were invaluable as support for the Cominform's version of the Soviet-Yugoslav dispute. There was naturally no problem with Mao, it was implied, because he was an internationalist, unshakeably loyal to the USSR, the touchstone of internationalism. Not like the Judas Tito. This proved that the fault in the dispute was not Stalin's. Communists could have clear consciences.

In spite of all this, the Chinese party's subjection to Moscow during the Cominform period was much less absolute then that of the Communist parties of the European People's Democracies. Stalin acted with a degree of prudence, and Mao had behind him a force which the Communist leaders put in power by the Red Army did not have. A year after the proclamation of the People's Republic of China, the intervention of Chinese 'volunteers' in the Korean war showed spectacularly, as much to the Kremlin as to Western governments, that Chinese Communism was among the leading world powers.

Immediately after the death of Stalin his heirs realized the need to make some concessions to a fact as undeniable as the power and prestige of the Chinese revolution, at the same time as they tried to use it to reinforce their positions – both internal and international – in the delicate situation created by the death of the great autocrat. They considerably increased economic and technical aid to China and raised the status of the Chinese party in the world Communist movement, and for the first time granted Mao the title 'great theorist of Marxism and Leninism'.[45]

But events soon showed that Moscow was unwilling to acknowledge Peking as more than a brilliant second in world Communism, and then only on condition that Peking faithfully echoed Moscow and cast no doubt on Soviet orthodoxy in any sphere. The disciples to some extent repeated the manoeuvre which the master had tried with Tito between 1945 and 1947, and the results were similar, but on a Chinese scale. The persistence of Great-Russian nationalism inflamed Chinese nationalism as it had previously inflamed nationalism in Yugoslavia. The nightmare of 'Chinese Titoism' became a reality of colossal dimensions. But this problem will be discussed later.

The Chinese revolution was the second great act of the world revolutionary process which began in 1917. It was the first major defeat of imperialism – and, importantly, of American imperialism – after the Second World War. It gave the struggle of the colonial and semi-colonial peoples for national and social liberation their present impetus. Inspired by the Chinese revolution, this struggle, for a period which is not yet finished, took over from the proletariat of the advanced capitalist world the leading role in revolutionary action. But the claim that after the Chinese revolution the course of world revolution will consist of the encirclement of the 'world of the city' (the area of advanced capitalism) by the 'world of the country' (the underdeveloped continents) is no more than an illegitimate generalization from the actual course of the Chinese revolution and a futuristic projection of the equally real and visible fact just mentioned, that in revolutionary action 'the West' has been replaced in the leading role by 'the East'. There are no grounds for predicting that this will be the last change of roles. On the contrary, some faint signs, on the levels of theory and of action, seem to indicate that the Western proletariat – a type of manual and intellectual proletariat very different from the one familiar to Marx and Lenin – may again play the leading role on the stage of history. Nor should it be forgotten that the (equally 'new') proletariat of the so-called 'socialist' countries will also have to have its say. The course of the world revolution still has many surprises and many changes of personnel in store.

9

THE NEW WORLD BALANCE

THE 'PEACE FIGHTERS'

As was made clear in the analysis of Zhdanov's report in Chapter 6, the new 'general line' imposed by Stalin in 1947 on the Western Communist parties was not a correction of his previous opportunism, but a continuation of it in different form. It was the adaptation of these parties' policies to the response the Kremlin wanted to make to Washington's expansionism. Once more socialist aims were indefinitely postponed. Before, they had been pushed on one side for the benefit of the grand coalition against Hitler; they now suffered a similar fate for the benefit of the great anti-American front which the Kremlin was attempting to form in an effort to impose on the White House a world-wide arrangement on the basis of an allocation of 'spheres of influence' which would satisfy Soviet interests.

The basic tactical idea of the new line was to make the maximum use of the contradictions between American expansionism and the national bourgeoisies of Europe or other areas, to unite, as Zhdanov put it, 'all the forces which are prepared to defend the cause of national honour and independence' and mobilize all 'supporters of peace' against the danger of a third world war. The main aim was to mobilize all possible forces to bring the American leaders to their senses and force them to return to the policies of Yalta. This would enable the Communist parties of the West to return to the policy of national unity followed until 1947, the peaceful, parliamentary road to socialism.

For reasons which have already been explained, the attempt to exploit inter-imperialist contradictions had little success, at least until the death of Stalin. Calls to 'defend the cause of national honour and independence' aroused little response outside the Communist parties and a narrow range of intellectuals. The only aspect of the new line which took on any reality at all, though even then only as propaganda, was the 'peace struggle'. The Berlin crisis (June 1948–May 1949) was the first of a succession of landmarks in the 'cold war' which increased international tension and gave apparent substance to the danger of a third world war. In April 1949 the NATO treaty was signed, followed in September by the US Congress's acceptance of a proposal to supply members of the alliance with arms to the value of $1,500m.

On 25 September a Tass communiqué confirmed the explosion of a Soviet atomic bomb – first announced by Truman a few days earlier – and revealed that the USSR had possessed the bomb since 1947. In June 1950 the Korean war began. At the meeting of the Cominform held in November 1949 the 'peace struggle' in the face of the danger of 'direct aggression' on the part of imperialism against the USSR was defined as the central task of the Communist movement, taking precedence over all others.

Next to the 'peace struggle' in the order of priorities came the 'cold war' against Yugoslavia. The two tasks were closely connected since, as we have seen, Titoism was regarded by the 'socialist camp' and the Communist parties as one of the main bases of American imperialism in its preparations for aggression against the Soviet Union.

The organization of the 'peace movement' began in 1948. In August of that year in Poland the World Congress of Intellectuals for Peace met in November the national congress of the French 'Fighters for Peace', and in the following months various meetings of the same type took place in a number of European countries. From 20 to 25 April 1949 there was held, in Paris and Prague,[1] the first World Congress of the 'Fighters for Peace', at which seventy-two countries were represented. According to the documents of the congress, there were already by this date 600 million *organized* 'peace fighters'. It should be explained, however, that this impressive figure included all the 'peace fighters' of the USSR, China and the other People's Democracies, where mere membership of the human race was sufficient qualification for membership of the shining new pacifist army. In the rest of the world, with some variation, the 'fighters for peace' were reduced to the members of the Communist parties and of the mass organizations it controlled (trade unions, women's, youth and cultural organizations).

The participation of a number of non-Communist public figures from the worlds of science and art, together with the inflation for publicity purposes of figures which it was impossible to check, might give the unaware the impression that the movement went beyond the normal political and social sphere influenced by the Communists. In reality it did nothing of the sort, as the leading circles of the Communist parties were quite well aware. The 'Peace Committees' set up in towns, districts, factories, etc. were made up – with a few exceptions – of Communists and their sympathizers.

The main activity of the 'peace fighters' consisted in collecting signatures to innumerable documents addressed to public opinion and to such bodies as governments, parliaments, the United Nations, etc. These called for the banning of the atomic bomb and for general disarmament, and protested against the Atlantic alliance and German rearmament, supporting the successive initiatives of Soviet diplomacy (the synchronization in this respect removed any doubt about the identity of the conductor of this orchestra). Signatures were the peace fighter's main weapon. In March 1950 the permanent committee of the World Congress, meeting in Stockholm, decided to launch an appeal for the banning of the atomic bomb and to organize the collection of signatures for this purpose. 500 million signatures were collected in seventy-nine countries. Among them were those of 'the whole adult population of the USSR, the whole adult population of the People's Democracies and of 223 million Chinese'.[2] In other words, 400 million signatures in the eleven countries in which citizens signed with the same impressive efficiency and unanimity with which they voted for the single lists at elections. The sixty-nine remaining countries produced 100 million signatures, including a total of 31 million for France and Italy (14 and 17 million respectively). In the other capitalist states the figures dropped disappointingly: two million in the USA, two million in Western Germany, a million in the United Kingdom, etc.[3] Even if the authenticity of all these signatures is admitted – a very naïve assumption – the result was hardly impressive. It should be noted that the official number of signatures was 100 million lower than the number of 'peace fighters' who, according to the first World Congress, not only existed but were also organized. Nevertheless the operation was described by its promoters as an 'authentic universal referendum of the peoples'.[4]

While the 'peace fighters' were laboriously collecting signatures to the Stockholm appeal, the Korean war broke out. In November 1950 the second World Peace Congress, meeting in Warsaw, adopted a new appeal to the peoples. To the usual slogans about the banning of the atomic-bomb, general disarmament, and so on, was added an appeal for an end to the war in Korea. As is well known, American intervention in Korea, from the very beginning of the fighting, took place under the flag of the United Nations – which was at that time under the absolute control of the United States – and was supported by troops from the other member states. Nevertheless, the second World Congress of 'peace fighters' saw nothing odd in addressing an appeal to the UN to 'take up its high responsibilities by ensuring a solid and lasting peace in accordance with the vital interests of all the peoples'.[5] At that moment the Chinese 'volunteers' had gone over to the offensive and towards the end of December the American troops and the other units of the expeditionary force were on the brink of disaster. But in the face of atomic blackmail Stalin's aim – accepted on this occasion by the Chinese and the Koreans – was not revolutionary victory in Korea, but the ending of hostilities on the basis of the *status quo*, that is, the division of the country. The Communist movement, through the peace movement or directly, limited itself to exerting pressure for this solution. The purpose of the armistice in Korea was to bring nearer the world agreement sought by Stalin. This aim guided the action of the World Peace Council (set up at the second World Peace Congress) in February 1951, when it launched an appeal for the signature of a 'peace pact' between the 'big five' and organized the required campaign for signatures to support the suggestion (which was taken up a little later by the Soviet government). Thanks to an increase in the 'adult population' of the USSR, China and the People's Democracies, the total of signatures this time reached 600 million.

For five years (1948–52) the national and world peace congresses and conferences, the assemblies, meetings, festivals, appeals, petitions and resolutions for peace, the hundreds of millions of signatures (always the same!) followed each other without a break under the fighting slogan approved by the second World Congress, 'Peace will not wait, peace must be won!' It was to be won by signatures. The great world army of signature collectors went from victory to victory, guided by the infallible Helmsman of Peace, whose historic role in the crusade was immortalized by the painter Bielopolski: against a background of dense crowds there stood out the massive figure of Stalin, holding in one hand the Pen and in the other the Stockholm appeal, so showing humanity the way to be followed to achieve a solid and lasting peace, the way of signature.[6]

Stalin described the aims of the 'peace movement' as follows:

The current peace movement has the aim of drawing the popular masses into the struggle to preserve peace and avert a new world war. It does not therefore seek to overthrow capitalism and establish socialism; it limits itself to democratic aims in the struggle to preserve peace. In this respect, the present movement to preserve peace differs from the one which existed during the First World War, which, in trying to transform the imperialist war into a civil war, went further and had socialist aims.[7]

Accepting the Stalinist line in order to give unquestioning support to Soviet diplomacy, the Communist parties had in fact committed themselves to a typically pacifist campaign, which excluded not only socialist aims, but even anti-imperialist ones. The leaders of the main Communist parties of Latin America, for example, opposed the explicit discussion of the problem of national independence within the peace movement.[8] In this they were putting into practice the rule laid down by Suslov (who had been made responsible within the Soviet Communist Party's political bureau, after Zhdanov's death, for organizing the international Communist movement) at the meeting of the Cominform which took place in November 1949: 'The Communist and Workers' Parties must use every means in the struggle to ensure stable and prolonged peace; they must subordinate all their activities to this paramount task of the day.'[9]

In the French party, for example, this subordination was reflected in the 'programme for national safety' adopted at the Twelfth Congress of the party in April 1950. Not only was there no mention of the socialist alternative, even as a distant prospect, but the programme of nationalizations and other democratic reforms which had been so prominent up to 1947 was also abandoned. The PCF called for the creation of a 'united peace front' to include 'patriots of all political views'.[10]

At the Seventh Congress of the Italian Communist Party Togliatti declared that 'the problem of peace ... has become the most important of all, and on it depends the solution of all the others'. For that reason, he said,

the Communist Party, the strongest party in the opposition to the present government of the Italian bourgeoisie, *is prepared to renounce its opposition, both in parliament and in the streets,* on the formation of another government which would radically change Italy's foreign policy by withdrawing the country from commitments which are leading it inevitably towards war.

Togliatti stressed the beneficial results such a solution would have within the country, by leading to 'an easing of tension between the different political and social groups' and making possible the resumption of the policy of 'national unity'. 'The basic elements of the policy which we put to the country at the end of the war,' said the leader of the PCI, 'still apply, even if the political conditions have changed.' In contrast to Thorez, Togliatti did not avoid reference to the socialist perspective, but mentioned it only to insist that the path to which he was proposing to return 'would lead gradually to a profound transformation of the economic structure', which was why the PCI's socialist aims 'are not incompatible with its offer to abandon opposition to a government which followed a policy of peace'. Togliatti went on:

To be more precise and more specific, I maintain that there already exists a political platform for a movement to defend peace and transform social and economic structures such as we envisage and on which we believe the welfare of Italy depends. That programme is the constitution of the Italian Republic.[11]

In other words, the only policy the 'Big Two' of European Communism had to offer the working-class movement was a return to the course followed between 1944 and 1945, which had led to the recovery of

European capitalism and its subjection to American monopolies, and the isolation of the Communist parties.

This pacifist and reformist strategy adopted by the European Communist parties was, moreover, remarkably unrealistic. Given the extent to which the various national bourgeoisies depended, economically, politically and militarily, on their American protectors, it was an illusion to expect even a fraction of these groups to pay any attention to the blandishments of Thorez and Togliatti. And in the event these were voices in the wilderness. The source of this lack of realism can be traced to Stalin's incorrect assessment of the state of inter-imperialist and inter-capitalist contradictions in this period. In fact, any possibility of the development of European capitalism – and so of a reformist policy – inevitably involved dependence on the United States. And any effective struggle against American control would have had to be anti-capitalist, revolutionary and anti-pacifist – it could not, objectively, have been anything else. The idea of an anti-American national capitalism in Europe at this period was completely utopian (as the failure of Gaullism showed). But since Soviet diplomacy was faced with the necessity of fomenting opposition to American policy everywhere, and since the aim of this diplomacy, reciprocal recognition of spheres of influence, turned out to be incompatible with the development of revolutionary policies in American spheres of influence, the only possible policy for the European Communist parties was the one they in fact followed. Its lack of realism was reflected in the combination of right-wing opportunism in content with sectarian and occasionally adventurist opportunism in forms and methods.

The peace movement, as has already been said, was reduced to a chameleon disguise for the Communist movement and its offshoots. Other forces could have taken no real part in it for the simple reason that the peace movement had to be strictly subservient to every twist of Soviet foreign policy. Within the movement it was impossible to put forward socialist aims – as though the socialist alternative was not the only genuine basis for a 'stable and prolonged' peace – because these were in contradiction with the aims adopted at that period by Soviet diplomacy. On the other hand, the status of a 'fighter for peace' was incompatible with sympathy or neutrality towards Titoism.

Among the main pieces of 'evidence' offered as proof of the existence of an imperialist plot against the USSR were the trials in the People's Democracies. The genuine 'peace fighter' had to believe in these like any Communist. Social democracy was 'unmasked' – for its collaboration with American policy, not for its collaboration with the national bourgeoisie – in language which recalled the days of 'social Fascism'.

Attempts were made to politicize economic strikes, not as part of a general socialist strategy based on national conditions, but around the slogans of the campaign for general disarmament, the banning of the atomic bomb, and so on.

The ineffectiveness of the signature campaign, and the void into which the pacifist policy fell, led the Communist parties on occasion to the opposite extreme of attempting violent action in the streets when the basic political conditions for this did not exist. An example of this is the the demonstration organized by the PCF against the presence in Paris of the American General Ridgway, the only result of which was to illustrate the isolation of the party and the absence of any response among the workers to its abstract anti-American campaign.[12] On the other hand, the PCF made no attempt to organize mass action on any scale against the French government's colonialist war in Vietnam.

The main justification offered by the Soviet leaders for the policy which they were imposing on the Communist movement was the existence of a serious threat of aggression against the Soviet Union. (It was this that gave rise to the threat of a third world war, which was only conceivable if the two super-powers clashed directly.) In his report to the November 1949 meeting of the Cominform Suslov said just this: 'The North-Atlantic bloc envisages *outright aggression* against the democratic states of Eastern Europe and, first and foremost, against the Soviet Union.'[13] The general tone of his speech implied that the danger was immediate. The governments of Washington and London, according to Suslov, were 'carrying on their preparations for war at top speed'. In the months that followed, the propaganda of the Communist parties reinforced this alarmist tone. 'Peace hangs by a thread,' Thorez told the Twelfth Congress of the PCF in April 1950.

But the analysis of the balance of forces which Suslov made in the same speech did not exactly justify such dramatic predictions. If Suslov were to be believed, the situation of the 'imperialist camp' could not be more disastrous. 'Both in America and Europe,' he claimed, 'an economic crisis is inexorably maturing.' Everyone, 'even the most ardent admirers and eulogists of the Marshall Plan', was forced to admit that the Marshall Plan had failed. The economies 'of the European Marshallized countries' were 'in a state of complete derangement'. The official announcement that the USSR had possessed the atomic bomb since 1947 had 'caused consternation and dismay in the camp of the imperialist and warmongers' and had 'diminished its strength'. The 'antagonisms between capitalist countries, and in the first place between the USA and Great Britain', were becoming more acute. 'The reckless foreign policy of the Wall Street and City imperialists' was suffering 'defeat after defeat'. 'The collapse of "atomic diplomacy", the failure of the Marshall Plan, the collapse of the imperialists' subversive schemes in south-eastern and central Europe, the bankruptcy of America's policy in China', all these were only a few of the failures suffered by 'the foreign policy of the imperialists'. In sharp contrast, 'the camp of peace, democracy and socialism' was forging ahead. 'The economy of the Soviet Union is steadily progressing from year to year, and from month to month', and its agriculture was 'making steady headway'. The People's Democracies were achieving 'big successes' in their economic and political development, and were 'strengthening' their relations with the USSR. The 'national liberation movement in the colonies and dependencies' was achieving 'immense successes'. (Suslov's reference here to the importance of the Chinese victory is one of the rare objective facts in his report.) 'A major victory for the camp of peace and democracy and one more defeat for the imperialist camp' was the establishment of the German Democratic Republic. Another 'eloquent' testimony to the strengthening of the camp of Good and the weakening of the camp of Evil was 'the progress everywhere to be observed of the democratic, and especially the working-class, movement, headed by the Communist parties, the growing influence of the Communist parties among the masses' and finally the existence of '600 million organized fighters for peace'. Conclusion: 'The relation of forces in the international arena has fundamentally changed and is continuing to change, in favour of the camp of peace, democracy and socialism.'

Suslov made no mention at all of another element in the relation of forces which, however, had much more immediate weight and more reality than some of those he did mention. This was the well-known military superiority of the Soviet Union in Europe. It did not take a specialist in military matters to realize that in the event of war Stalin's soldiers would meet no obstacles in their path to the West. To remove all doubts on the matter, in February 1949 (a few weeks before the signature of the Atlantic Pact) Thorez took it on himself to answer a timely question from a 'comrade': 'What would the party do if the Soviet army occupied Paris!' Thorez's answer, more or less, was that the French workers would welcome them with open arms. A few days later Togliatti was asked a similar question about Italy, and gave the same answer.[14]

The interest of this curious episode, of course, lies less in the answers than in the certainty, already implicit in the questions, about what would happen if war came. (In 1951–2 the Western press published details of the NATO command's plans in the event of 'an attack from the USSR'. All the plans envisaged the rapid loss of France.[15] In 1955 Khrushchev revealed to American journalists that in 1950 the USSR had possessed superiority over the West.)[16]

Suslov kept silent on this fundamental aspect of the situation, but even so his analysis of the relation of forces could not help arousing many doubts about the possibility of 'direct aggression' by the United States and its allies against the USSR and its allies. To dispel these, Suslov put forward the following argument:

From the fact that the anti-democratic imperialist camp is growing weaker, the conclusion must not be drawn that the danger of war is diminishing. Such a conclusion would be profoundly erroneous and harmful.

The experience of history teaches that the more hopeless the position of imperialist reaction, the more frantic it becomes and the greater is the danger of its launching into military ventures.

The changing relation of forces in the world arena in favour of the camp of peace and democracy drives the imperialist and warmongering camp into fresh outbursts of frenzied fury.[17]

'The experience of history' may have a broad back, but here it is being given too heavy a load. The two cases of direct aggression in which the USSR was the victim do not support Suslov's argument – quite the reverse. In 1918 the imperialists of the Entente were not exactly in a desperate situation, and the Nazi imperialists attacked in 1941 when they had conquered the whole of Europe and thought themselves invincible. The leaders of world capitalism have inherited sufficient 'experience' of history for 'frenzied fury' not to be the deciding factor in their strategy. But some way had to be found to prove the existence of a serious threat of 'direct aggression' against the USSR by the imperialist camp, which, according to Kremlin theorists, was caught in an insoluble economic crisis and whose policies were going from defeat to defeat. On top of that, they had also lost the atomic monopoly – an undeniable fact – and were notoriously inferior in conventional forces. There was also public opinion in the various countries, which, to say the least, was far from keen to be dragged into another world massacre when the last one was still so close.

STALEMATE IN THE 'COLD WAR'

American imperialism's real plan at this period was not to launch into an adventure against the impressive military power of the Soviet Union, but to extend its control to the whole of the 'free world'. It was to consolidate capitalism in Western Europe, and especially in Germany, while at the same time making it economically, politically and militarily dependent on itself. It envisaged a similar operation in the Mediterranean basin, intensification of its exploitation of Latin America, penetration of the colonial spheres of its allies, a checking of the revolutionary movement outside the frontiers of the Soviet Union. It intended, in other words, to take on the role of world policeman and exploiter.

Specifically, the main aim of American policy was to consolidate what Zhdanov called 'the imperialist camp', while, of course, neglecting no possibility of weakening the opposite 'camp'. (In this connection it must be recognized that the best ally of the CIA was Stalin's policies in the satellites.) But Washington's global strategy, like Moscow's, also included the search for a compromise between the two super-powers.

In the last resort the problem was that no compromise was possible as long as the two parties had not reached a realistic, and therefore similar, appraisal of the relation of forces. In the first years after the war this was far from easy, in view not only of the revolution brought about in military techniques and doctrines by the appearance of the atomic bomb, but also of the extreme political instability which had arisen in many parts of the world. The 'cold war' was a sort of exploration or sounding carried out to gain a more exact knowledge of the forces and dispositions of the enemy. In the United States there were plenty of adventurist generals and politicians willing to call for the bomb to be dropped on Soviet nerve centres, but this was not official policy. In the view of those who worked out and applied the official policy, who were aware of the enormous military power represented by the Soviet Union, China and the European People's Democracies, the bomb was an instrument of 'deterrence'. Not only, and not so much, to deter the Soviet leaders from a direct initiative against Western positions (a more than unlikely event for anyone with only a moderate awareness of the basis, doctrine and practice of Soviet foreign policy), but to dissuade them from turning the Communist movement – and they were its real controllers – in a revolutionary direction, and to dissuade them from encouraging and giving practical help to revolutionary struggles where they occurred. Greece was the clearest, the most scandalous, but not the only example of the effectiveness of atomic 'deterrence'.

On a more general level, the whole policy of the 'peace struggle', of subordinating all the activities of the Communist parties to the central task of preserving peace, was dominated by atomic blackmail. In the same way the whole of American policy was dominated by the need to avoid at all costs a direct armed confrontation with the military power of the Soviet bloc.

The two most serious 'soundings' carried out during the 'cold war', those which gave the world the impression of being on the brink of a major conflict, were the Berlin crisis and the Korean war. In fact, both cases showed the firm determination of the two super-powers to maintain the positions they had won during the Second World War and to

make no attempt to modify them by war against each other. To the
American moves to integrate Western German into the politico-military
bloc of the Atlantic Pact Stalin replied with a blockade of the Western
zone of Berlin. General Clay suggested forcing a passage with an armed
convoy, but Washington decided to avoid any measure which might
provoke a new war, and the United States limited itself to supplying
Berlin with food by means of the famous airlift. The Soviet authorities
did nothing to prevent this. At the beginning they thought that the food
supply to the Western Zone could not be maintained by this means.
When, after some months, they could see the success of the operation,
they preferred to negotiate. The blockade was ended in May 1949.[18]
The 'sounding' of the relation of forces on the 'European front' ended in
a stalemate.

The second – and most serious – major conflict of the 'cold war' was
the Korean war. It is still impossible to say for certain who began hostilities.[19] Soviet and American military forces had been out of the
country for more than a year, leaving behind only teams of advisers and
instructors, but it is clear that Washington controlled the reactionary
regime of Syngman Rhee, south of the 38th parallel, while Moscow had
the final say in the decisions of the revolutionary regime established in
the north. If it is true that the northerners began the fighting – which
seems the most likely from the evidence available – the decision was
completely justified from the national and revolutionary points of view.
The lightning advance of the People's Army to the southern tip of the
peninsula also revealed the weakness of the government supported by
the Americans. Even supposing that the first 'provocation' on the demarcation line came from the southerners, the northerners' rapid and massive reply, and the development of their offensive, made it clear that the
decision to liberate the south by armed force had been taken well in
advance and that the operation had been carefully prepared. This would
not have been possible without the agreement and collaboration of
Moscow. In the absence of definite evidence to the contrary, the most
likely hypothesis seems to be that Stalin decided to probe the forces and
intentions of the United States in the Far East, making use for the
purpose of the Korean revolutionary forces' legitimate demands for the
unification of the country. It is possible that he wanted to test the official

American statements that South Korea was not part of the 'defensive perimeter' of the United States.[20]

But as soon as Washington decided to intervene and also brought in the United Nations on the side of the South, the Kremlin adopted a very cautious position. The Soviets did not even give air support to the northern forces, which were defeated thanks mainly to American ships and aircraft. Almost certainly in consultation with Moscow, Mao's government announced that it would not intervene unless MacArthur's troops crossed the 38th parallel, which amounted to a proposal to solve the conflict by a return to the *status quo*. But now Washington in its turn decided to prove Soviet strength and intentions, and forced the UN to vote for continuing the offensive towards the frontier with China. The intervention of the Chinese 'volunteers' again brought operations south of the 38th parallel, bringing the swashbuckling MacArthur's army to the brink of disaster. MacArthur proposed that atomic bombs should be dropped on Manchuria, and Moscow announced that Soviet troops would intervene if the bombing took place. Washington dismissed MacArthur, in spite of his prestige in American public opinion as the hero of the Pacific war, and Moscow did not even give the Chinese infantry the air support which would have enabled them to drive the imperialist troops into the sea. They were able to reform and again reach the 38th parallel.

Armistice negotiations began on 10 July 1951. Years passed before an armistice was signed, and during that time the strange war continued without any intention on the part of any of the participants to win it. In short, the sounding on the relation of forces between the two blocs on the 'Asian front', as on the 'European front', ended in a stalemate. Its price rose to almost two million dead and wounded, made up of about a million Koreans and a million Chinese.

In the second half of 1951 and throughout 1952, the two super-powers began to get a clear idea of each other's strength and intentions and of the new balance which had been established in the world. There was first a military balance. The Americans saw their 'deterrent' power increased by the development of the hydrogen bomb, but they no longer had the atomic monopoly and it was clear that the Soviets would also soon have the hydrogen bomb. Moreover, the entry on the scene of the People's

Republic of China considerably increased the Soviet bloc's superiority in conventional military forces. There was also a political balance. The 'spheres of influence' regarded as vital by the two super-powers were politically safe. Two Europes, two Germanies, no immediate danger of revolution threatening European capitalism, which was enjoying a new period of expansion as a result of the 'failure' of the Marshall Plan. All opposition to Soviet control in the satellite countries seemed to have been crushed. The 'cold war' against Yugoslavia had failed, and Moscow could do nothing but accept the *fait accompli*. There remained the colonial world, in vigorous ferment, but here the interests of the two super-powers were not as yet in direct opposition.

The moment for negotiation had arrived. In 1952 Stalin announced that the danger of war had diminished and that a meeting between the leaders of the great powers could be useful.[21] In September he said that the contradictions between the capitalist countries were 'practically' stronger than those between the camp of socialism and the camp of capitalism, and that wars between capitalist countries were therefore a more likely prospect than a war between capitalism and socialism.[22] In December he showed interest in the idea of talks with the new American administration (Eisenhower had just been elected President).[23] The 'cold war' was in the process of giving way to 'peaceful coexistence'. The death of Stalin and the change of presidents in the United States hastened the process, but the real cause lay elsewhere. Nevertheless it is undeniable that the serious problems which Stalin's death presented to the Soviet leaders had a considerable influence on the turn taken by Soviet foreign policy after 1953, a turn which, following tradition, brought about a similar turn in the general line of the Communist movement.

ASSESSMENT OF THE COMINFORM PERIOD

After the Twentieth Congress the activity of the Cominform began to be criticized in the Communist movement. Following traditional practice, there was no active discussion of the problem, but in party documents, the statements of leaders and historical essays, critical assessments appeared which can be summed up by the following quotation from an authoritative Soviet source:

Negative tendencies very soon appeared in the activity of the Cominform. Under the influence of Stalin's dogmatic views on the problems of peace, war and revolution, on relations between Communists and Social Democrats, on the role of the national bourgeoisie, etc., a number of parties developed stereotyped strategies and occasionally made mistakes in their guidance of socialist construction in the People's Democracies or in their leadership of the labour movement or the national liberation movement. The arbitrary policy of *diktat* associated with the cult of personality infringed Marxist–Leninist principles on relations between Communist parties and did serious harm to the whole Communist movement. It held back creative developments in the immediate problems of the international working-class movement and the national liberation movement, and it isolated the Communist parties from the mass of the workers.[24]

The theoretical and political views implied in this criticism are a long way from the analysis put forward in this book,[25] but the very fact of their public expression shows the extent of the regression which affected the great majority of Communist parties during the Cominform period.

After 1947, the general development of the Communist movement outlined in the first chapter of this volume became a general decline, with a few rare exceptions. The main exception, the Chinese revolution, was of historic importance. Another exception was the national revolutionary war of the Vietnamese Communists, with no direct help except from the Chinese Communists. Within Western capitalism, only the Italian Communist Party was able to keep its members and its influence. Apart from these three cases, it is hard to find a Communist party which did not decline during this period. The other 'giant' of Western Communism lost almost half its members. The Communist parties in power in the satellite states emerged from this period severely shaken, as the crises of 1956 very soon showed. Nor was the Soviet Union unaffected.

The disappointment of the hopes for renewal latent since the end of the war led to unprecedented political apathy. Even in China, the development of the party in the years after the victory followed a markedly regressive course as compared with its previous one. But, whereas in the capitalist world the deterioration of the Communist movement took place visibly, in the 'socialist' countries it remained hidden – until the Twentieth Congress – behind the façade of the bureaucratic dictatorial state and the mystification of the real development by propaganda.

The real progress made in industrialization and economic reconstruction made it possible to conceal the accumulating contradictions and bottlenecks. There was, in short, a general, world-wide regression in the Communist movement. Observed from the standpoint of the present, it appears in its true significance; it was not a conjunctural phenomenon, but the beginning of the irreversible historical decline of the Communist party of the Stalinist type. The ultimate causes are contained in the history of this party, but in this period – as in each of the earlier and subsequent periods – they took on their own particular form.

On the general political plane, the main cause of this setback outside the frontiers of the 'socialist camp' seemed to be the offensive of the reactionary forces led by the new aspirant to the position of world policeman. In fact the explanation of this offensive – its very possibility and its varying degrees of success in the different countries – is to be found ultimately in the policy of concessions to the Anglo-American coalition and the 'anti-Fascist' bourgeoisies practised in the previous period. This policy weakened the enthusiasm which had developed in the mass movement as part of the victory over Fascism and undermined from within what capacity for revolutionary action still remained in the Communist parties. The path of electoralism, of parliamentary cretinism, of illusions about the permanence of the 'grand alliance', in other words the path of class collaboration on a national and international scale, disarmed the movement and demoralized the groups of new militants who had joined it in the years of the resistance and the liberation. This is the reason for the lack of opposition to the offensive of American imperialism and the national bourgeoisies – underground from 1944–5 to 1947, open afterwards – except in the field of day-to-day economic demands.

The only two Communist parties in industrial capitalism which could perform the main role in this field better than Social Democracy were those of France and Italy. For this reason they managed to retain most of their influence within the working class, even though the French party, as we have seen, lost many of its militants. They had shown that they were not the party of the revolution, but on the other hand they had shown that they could be useful to the working class in its struggle for its day-to-day interests.

In all the other 'advanced countries' the Communist parties once more became little marginal groups, powerless by the side of the big Social Democratic parties and the reformist trade-union federations. Even in West Germany the reformed Communist party was no more than a shadow of what it had been in the distant past.[26] In the United States the Communist Party, reduced to its smallest size ever after Browder's expulsion (when a large group of militants left the party), became the victim of McCarthyite repression amid the indifference of the great majority of workers. The Spanish Communists were forced to break off their guerrilla struggle, which had found neither sufficient following nor sufficient support among a population demoralized by the terrible defeat of 1939, the terror which followed and the new 'treachery of the democracies'. The tragedy of the Greek Communists has already been described.

In 1947 the United States formed the Rio de Janeiro pact with the Latin American oligarchies as the start of a general anti-Communist offensive in Latin America. The majority of the Communist parties, which, influenced by the policy of the 'grand alliance' – accentuated in some by the influence of the Browder line – had practically abandoned any anti-imperialist struggle in the preceding years, were forced underground and were unable to organize effective resistance. Almost all went through internal crises which further increased their political impotence.[27] In Indonesia, Burma, Malaya and the Philippines the Communist parties were influenced by the Chinese experience, but had not assimilated it. They embarked on armed struggle without sufficient preparation, and with the further disadvantage that the opportunist policy of subservience to the national bourgeoisie which they had followed in the previous period had placed them in an unfavourable position. The armed movements were crushed or forced to take refuge in isolated areas, where they kept up a long drawn-out guerrilla struggle.

The Communist Party of India was shaken in this period by fierce internal struggles between the right and left wings. The right-wing opportunist faction which had predominated in the earlier period had made the party an appendage of the national bourgeoisie, while the sectarian leftist groups made no distinctions within the bourgeoisies and had failed to understand the Chinese lesson of the revolutionary potential of the peasant masses.[28] The Japanese Communist Party was similarly weakened by internal struggles and in addition became a victim of the repressive measures introduced by the American occupiers during the Korean war.

In the internal organization of the Communist parties the Cominform period was marked by the growth of bureaucratic centralism and the development of ideological uniformity. It was a sort of second 'Bolshevization' of the parties, carried out in the name of the fight against Titoism, as the first had been carried out in the name of the fight against Trotskyism. Purges were standard practice. There were few parties which did not experience crises in their controlling bodies, in addition to the effect on the lower ranks. Internal political activity became more than ever a matter of routine, stifling the breath of fresh air which had penetrated the parties during the years of the resistance and the liberation. The guiding principle of this second 'Bolshevization' was the same as the one which had dominated the first – to force the movement into monolithic solidity under the leadership of Moscow's 'Marxism'. This solidity was threatened at the time – as the Yugoslav heresy showed – by national and nationalist movements which had been strengthened by the war and the dissolution of the Comintern. The Cominform acted as a political and organizational instrument in the struggle against these tendencies.

Another, specifically ideological, instrument was the cult of Stalin. The proportions to which this phenomenon grew no doubt indicated the extreme point of the abandonment of Marxism and its replacement by a sort of fideism accompanied by pragmaticism and practicism; they were also related, however, to the practical function of the cult as a means of curbing centrifugal tendencies. The parallel development of cults of national Communist leaders was a more complex phenomenon. It was a guarantee of the monolithic unity of each party around a leader loyal to

Stalin, but at the same time it was an obscure expression – unconscious in some cases and less unconscious in others – of the national or national-ist reaction to the cult of Soviet rule. (The Stalin cult was the per-sonification of another, more deeply rooted, cult of the Moscow leadership which continued after the condemnation of the first and found a new personification in the picturesque Nikita.)

The critical assessment of the activity of the Cominform which was quoted on p. 591 admitted that 'the arbitrary policy of *diktat* . . . held back creative developments in the immediate problems of the inter-national working-class movement and the national liberation move-ment'. 'Held back' here is a euphemism in relation to the complete sterility in the field of 'creative developments' which characterized the Cominform period. In this respect it cannot be said that there was a worsening; the previous situation simply persisted. The results of the situation, however, became an increasing weight, since during this time the world, radically transformed by the war, continued to develop and create ever more complex problems.

Confronted with the problems of the new proletarian revolutions and the rebellion of the peoples oppressed by colonialism, with the spread of monopoly state capitalism and the struggle of the workers in this new stage of capitalism, the Communist movement continued to brandish the formulae and clichés of the past. There was no research, no real dis-cussion and no new ideas. At the very most, old reformist and pacifist ideas were slightly touched up and revived. The internal organization of the parties prevented anyone from putting forward the mildest sugges-tion for change. And if a suggestion chanced to emerge – a difficult process given the hardening of Communist brains after two decades of ideological uniformity – it was killed at birth. Only the Great Theorist was recognized as having the ability – and the right – to put forward new ideas. (A number of economists, historians and philosophers in Eastern Europe paid heavily for their timid transgressions of this rule.) In 1950 the Great Theorist became an authority on linguistics, in the process 'enriching' the Marxist theory of base and superstructure. In 1952 he tackled 'the economic problems of socialism', in the process giving his diagnosis of the present state and prospects of capitalism.

The theoretical vacuity of these last contributions of Stalin's is well enough known for us not to need to waste much time on them. It will be enough to note that Stalin applied to the new situation a schema of world revolution which he derived from the doctrine of 'socialism in one country'. Starting from the premise that the building of socialism had been completed in the Soviet Union, Stalin maintained that it was perfectly possible to build Communism within the confines of Soviet territory in the same way, even if capitalism and imperialism continued to exist in the rest of the world (outside the 'socialist camp').[29] And, with the help of the USSR, the complete construction of socialism would also be possible in the People's Democracies of Europe and Asia. According to Stalin their rate of industrial development was such that 'it will soon come to pass that . . . these countries will . . . be in no need of imports from capitalist countries'.[30] Trade with the Soviet Union would meet all their needs.

At the same time, capitalism was moving rapidly towards its grave. The main capitalist countries 'are trying to offset these difficulties with the "Marshall Plan", the war in Korea, frantic rearmament and industrial militarization. But that is very much like a drowning man clutching at a straw.' Stalin's grounds for this conclusion were the following: 'The economic consequence of the existence of two opposing camps was that the single all-embracing world market disintegrated, so that we now have two parallel world markets, also confronting one another.' While the 'socialist world market' would steadily expand, 'the sphere of exploitation of the world's resources by the major capitalist countries will not expand but contract . . . their industries will be operating more and more below capacity'. This would provoke an exacerbation of the contradictions between these countries and make wars between them inevitable, while a war between the capitalist and socialist blocs would prove to be daily more difficult.

The end of this triumphal development of socialism and Communism within the 'camp' led by the USSR, and of the steady regression of capitalism within the 'camp' led by the United States, would be followed naturally and inevitably by the world-wide victory of socialism. The main problem to be solved in order to ensure this irresistible historical development was, therefore, to prevent the capitalist powers — giving way to 'outbursts of fury', as Suslov put it, at their growing weakness – from attacking the 'socialist camp' and so interrupting its triumphant march towards Communism. To guarantee a 'stable and prolonged' peace, which was inconceivable without a 'stable and prolonged' compromise between the two super-powers, consequently became the primary aim of the Communist parties.

It was a logical result of this that the struggle for a socialist revolution in the capitalist countries should be relegated to second place, and in particular subordinated to the supreme consideration of not endangering world peace. The main thing was that the Communist parties in every country should unite all the supporters of peace as a wall against any warlike inclinations on the part of the United States against the Soviet Union, and all the supporters of national independence as a means of deepening the contradictions between the capitalist powers. These two tasks were not to be made more difficult by the advocacy of internal social and political goals which were unacceptable to the patriotic, democratic or pacifist sections of the various bourgeoisies. This explains why Stalin, in his last advice to the Communist parties (in his speech to the Nineteenth Congress of the Soviet Communist Party in October 1952), made no reference to the struggle for socialist goals in capitalist countries. To the Western Communist leaders attending the congress he said, 'If you wish to be patriots and become the leading force in your countries, you must raise the banner of national independence and national sovereignty, of bourgeois democratic freedoms and peace.'[31] The banner of socialism was to be left prudently furled.

EPILOGUE

In universal history, the actions of men have results which differ
from what they plan and achieve, from their immediate knowledge and intentions. They achieve their aims, but there is produced at the same time something hidden within them, which
their consciousness was not aware of and which was not included in their calculations.

HEGEL

With the death of Stalin the Communist movement entered its historical
decline, the stage of general crisis. This will be the subject of the next
two volumes of this book – in the second the period between the
Twentieth Congress of the CPSU and the Sino-Soviet split and in the
third the present period. We shall begin our analysis of this stage with a
general survey of the internal contradictions of the Soviet regime in the
Stalin period, since it was these contradictions, brought to a critical
point by the disappearance of the great charismatic leader, which produced the first serious disturbance at the centre of the Communist
movement. The shock-waves of that disturbance broke down ideological, political and organizational barriers in the regimes of the 'socialist camp', in Communist parties outside the 'camp' and in relations
between states and parties. Latent conflicts and centrifugal tendencies
were released. Myths and dogmas were shattered. Doubt, even anguish,
entered people's minds. The partial and peripheral crises merged with
the crisis of the Soviet centre to form a single general crisis of the whole
Communist movement.

In this first volume it did not seem essential to make a general analysis
of the development of the Soviet regime under Stalin in view of the fact
that the crisis of the Communist movement began, historically, at its

periphery. As we have seen, its first sign was the failure of the Communist International, both in the colonial and in the capitalist world. It next showed itself in the European Communist movement's powerlessness to bring the catastrophic crisis of the capitalism in the 1940s to a revolutionary conclusion, and later in the break with Yugoslavia and the degradation of the People's Democracies (reflected in the unbelievable mirror of the trials). At the same time Stalin's regime established and consolidated itself within the Soviet frontiers by implacably destroying all obstacles in its path, both the reactionary opposition of the kulaks and the revolutionary opposition of the Bolshevik old guard. This regime took shape and developed as a totally new social system, new not only to history but also to the theoretical predictions of Marxism. Neither capitalist nor socialist, it was based on the exploitation of the main means of production by a new type of social class which began to grow up out of the elements capable of taking on the most useful and most urgent functions in a ruined and starving country, the organization and control of the economy. Believing subjectively – at least for a time – that it was building socialism and embodied the dictatorship of the proletariat, that it was putting Marxism into practice, this new ruling class became the real beneficiary of the means of production, immune to any intervention or control by the mass of the workers, and gradually acquired the subjective characteristics of a dominant class.

This regime, born out of the destruction of the Soviet democracy of 1917, showed itself able to develop the forces of production, pull the country out of its economic and cultural backwardness and industrialize it at rates without precedent in the history of mankind. At the end of the 1940s – as the Twentieth Congress recognized – the socio-political structures had already come into contradiction with the level reached by the productive forces and with the needs of their further development. The notoriously ruthless character of the struggle between cliques for the succession – the only way of solving the problem of the succession in a political system which lacks any kind of democracy, in which the dictatorship is not hereditary and in which the conditions for revolution are not yet ripe – cannot be completely explained by personal ambitions. A fundamental cause of this struggle was the contradiction just mentioned, which had reached a certain degree of seriousness and interacted with other conflicts and tensions, not only within the Soviet state but throughout the 'socialist camp' and the Communist movement.

The dialectic of the struggle for power in this situation itself produced Khrushchev's 'secret report', a brutal revelation – in spite of the mystifications which it deliberately contained – of the underlying nature of the system. What had until this point been regarded by Communists as slanders invented by the bourgeoisie and by 'traitors' was now officially confirmed by the new General Secretary. It was now revealed that in the 'home of socialism' power was not – and had not been for a long time – in the hands of the workers, nor even in the hands of the party which claimed to represent them, but in those of an all-powerful dictator, served by an ever-present police force, whose chief methods of government were political crime and ideological manipulation of the masses. It was now revealed that the campaign against the Yugoslav revolution had been a disgraceful invention concocted by Stalin and his police, as had been the trials in the People's Democracies, from which it could be deduced that it was not the workers who held power in these either, nor again the parties which claimed to represent them, nor even the national dictator, but the new Russian autocrat and his political police. It was now revealed that the general policy of the Communist movement had not been decided by the member parties, nor even by the 'leading party', because the highest organs of the latter (the Congress and Central Committee) were manipulated at the whim of the master of the Kremlin and his clique of assistants, themselves in turn controlled by the inevitable secret police.

And so it went on. The 'secret report' admitted (or at least a reading of it allowed the deduction of) this central fact: in every area of Stalin's world – states, parties, ideology, politics, economy, culture – the secret police had the last word. Stalin was the supreme head, but at the same time the victim, of an enormous police machine.

Until this time the influence of the Soviet regime had spread throughout the Communist movement which had grown up around it, not so much for what it was as for what it claimed and seemed to be. It was able to impose its dogmas and models on the movement, and subordinate it to its national policy, because in the eyes of revolutionaries throughout the world it was the first embodiment of socialism and the highest point of

Marxist thought. It was able to appear as such because the elimination of specific historical forms of oppression and exploitation – the capitalist and feudal forms – and the quantitative successes in industrialization and education were a genuine liberation when compared with the old Tsarist world. The real achievement of liberation was for a time – with the help of the mystifying ideology which the regime itself produced by adapting 'Marxism' for this purpose – to act as a screen for the new forms of human alienation, oppression and exploitation, which, in some respects, represented a regression from the forms familiar under 'advanced' capitalism. Once again, the movement of history showed itself to be much more complex and contradictory than the most clear-sighted of theoretical predictions had envisaged.

This view of the development of the Soviet regime, of its appearance and its reality, has been constantly present throughout the foregoing analysis of the first historical manifestations of the crisis in the Communist movement, and we have tried to make clear, as the analysis required, the main sources of the various factors in the crisis of the movement and in its defeats and failures. These include belief in the socialist content of the Soviet regime and its use as the model of the socialist state and the revolutionary party, the canonization of its ideology as the definitive truth of Marxism, and the basis of the tactics, strategy, programme and policies of every Communist party, and the subordination of the world strategy, first of the Comintern and later of the Communist movement, to the international policy of the Soviet state.

But, beginning with the events of 1953–6 (the denunciation of Beria and the first revelations about the methods of the secret police, the rising of the Berlin workers, the 'rehabilitation' of Yugoslavia, the 'secret report', the Polish and Hungarian Octobers, the first armed intervention by Stalinist imperialism against a people in revolt), beginning with these events, the Soviet regime began to appear, more and more each day to the whole Communist movement, not as it had seemed to be hitherto, but as it really was. It is true that the new ideological excuses (the use of Stalin as a great scapegoat, the explanation of his absolutism by the 'cult' and of the 'cult' by his absolutism, the claim that the mind-bending reality described in the 'secret report' had left untouched the 'socialist essence' of the regime and the scientific essence of its 'Marxism'), in spite of their clumsy ineptitude, did satisfy many Communists, thereby showing how far their ideological formation had lost contact with living Marxism. Others regarded these arguments as a first, imperfect self-criticism which could open the way for a regeneration of the movement. But a new reality had burst in, and its immense demystifying power, destructive of all dogmas and myths, could not be stopped by any subjective barriers. Until now the failures, the defeats and the impotence of the Communist parties had always been explained – when no 'objective factors' were available – by their imperfections in relation to the Soviet model, insufficient 'Bolshevization', theoretical backwardness in comparison with the ideal theoretical level of the Soviet party, and so on. From now on, little by little, the view gained ground that the weaknesses from which the Communist parties and the movement as a whole suffered had the opposite cause, their resemblance to the Soviet model.

In this way the crisis of the Soviet party became the mirror in which the crisis of each Communist party and the crisis of the international Communist movement were reflected. This explains why the second volume of this work begins with the general analysis mentioned above, which will take us up to the Twentieth Congress, the historical precursor of the general crisis of the Communist movement.

We shall end the first volume of this study by bringing together various points which are in our view essential for a general understanding of the historical origin of the crisis in the Communist movement and its course in the Comintern period and the decade between the dissolution of the International and the death of Stalin.

1. As Chapter 2 ('The Crisis of Theory') showed, the constitution of the Comintern, its political platform, its organizational characteristics and its strategic and tactical views were decisively conditioned by the Leninist theory of the Russian revolution and of world revolution. But the course of events in advanced capitalism very soon disproved Lenin's hypotheses on the degree of maturity and the immediate course of the world revolution. The whole course of subsequent history showed more and more clearly that this refutation was an indication of gaps and

mistaken assumptions in Lenin's theoretical model of Western capitalist society. It showed clearly that it had now become an objective necessity to rethink the whole question of socialist revolution in this type of society.

This objective necessity was not, however, admitted or allowed for by the forces grouped around the Comintern except in a limited form and primarily for tactical reasons. The failure of the revolution in advanced capitalism was viewed as something temporary – due primarily to the 'treachery' of the Social Democratic leaders – which did not constitute an objection to the predictions of Marxist theory, either in its classical orthodox form or as interpreted by Lenin. At the same time the initial victory of the revolution in a backward, semi-capitalist and semi-feudal country, on the edge of the vital area of the capitalist system, was interpreted as an absolute proof that the Márxist theory of revolution as interpreted by Lenin had reached the highest degree of scientific perfection. The Soviet system was a practical model of the dictatorship of the proletariat, and Lenin's strategy and tactics offered a model of strategy and tactics for all their Communist parties which required only to be adapted to their respective national conditions. Even this adaptation, however, depended only partly on the national parties; the Executive Committee of the Comintern, in other words the Bolshevik centre, had the final decision. In short, the truth of the Russian revolution became the truth of revolution in every latitude, with no more than a few minor adjustments.

Being in possession of this universal truth, the Comintern opposed other tendencies and groupings within the working-class movement with 'Bolshevik intransigence'. It did not stop at barring them from membership, but also did much to make collaboration or discussion with them impossible. Just as the mirage of international civil war was dissolving, and a more or less peaceful coexistence was becoming established between the Soviet state and the capitalist states, a climate of civil war built up within the working-class movement. The Comintern might have promoted a fruitful interchange between the experience and ideas of the Russian revolutionaries on the one hand and the Western working-class movement on the other. Instead it became a barrier, not only against the reformist tendencies, though this was already bad enough, since these embraced the majority of the proletariat and only a genuine connection with these masses could give substance to the ideological and political struggle against reformism, but also against revolutionary tendencies of anarchist or anarcho-syndicalist types, and even against a number of trends which had genuine Marxist roots, such as Luxemburgism, or Ordine Nuovo and others which grew up on the left of Social Democracy. Rosa Luxemburg's criticism of the Russian revolution and the Bolshevik model of the party were far-sighted; her warning of the serious consequences which would follow for the international Communist movement from an insistence of forcing Bolshevism on to it as its model was prophetic. Both, however, like her ideas on strategy and tactics in the German situation and Gramsci's first theoretical work, were rejected *en bloc* or passed over in silence.

The result was that the disturbing questions raised by the real movement of history for Lenin's theory of revolution, and for Marx's theory, went unanswered. Even worse, they went unrecognized. The dazzling fact of the October revolution helped to obscure the theoretical crisis which had been revealed. Natural enthusiasm for the proletariat's first victory in history blinded or considerably weakened, except in a very few cases, the critical faculties of revolutionary Marxists. Nevertheless, the canonization of the new orthodoxy did not take place without resistance within the Comintern, particularly on the question of the nature of the party and the acceptance of Russian leadership. This resistance was, however, overcome without much difficulty thanks to the prestige of the Bolshevik leaders, and especially of Lenin, and as a result of the extraordinary powers the 'world party's' system of organization gave to its leading organs. But once Lenin was gone the 'Marxist–Leninist' orthodoxy very quickly degenerated into a dogmatism without precedent in the history of Marxism, and became an alienating ideology expressing and serving the interests of the new dominant class produced in the course of Stalinist industrialization.

2. One of the foundations of the new orthodoxy was a petrified view of capitalism which was fundamentally economistic and catastrophic in content.

In the 1920s, while a degree of freedom of thought and discussion still existed in the Comintern and the Bolshevik party, the problems raised by the building of socialism stimulated important discussion and research among Soviet theoreticians. Though to a lesser extent, the same thing happened within the Comintern in relation to colonial problems. In both cases, but especially in the first, it became quite clear that the problems involved were new ones, which had hardly been touched on by the classics of Marxism. This work continued until, here as in other areas, Stalin imposed his sterilizing ideological uniformity. But for the problem of capitalism there was not even this creative phase. It was taken for granted that on this subject the essential discoveries had been made by Marx, or, as regarded monopolies and imperialism, by Lenin. The position was made worse by a tendency to give both Marx's legacy and Lenin's analysis a dogmatic interpretation in terms of economism and catastrophism. According to this interpretation, the structures of monopoly capitalism formed an insuperable obstacle to the development of the productive forces, and the economic mechanism of the system was therefore doomed, within a relatively short period, to an inevitable collapse which would provoke the revolution, most probably as the consequence of a new imperialist war.

It is well known that some of Marx's expressions and analyses seem to postulate a structural limit beyond which the capitalist dialectic cannot go: 'Centralization of the means of production and socialization of labour at last reach a point where they become incompatible with their capitalist integument. This integument is burst asunder.'[1] Marx's theory of revolution as a whole, however, does not allow an economist–catastrophist interpretation of his ideas. Nevertheless this is how they were interpreted at the time of the Second International, not only by Kautskyan orthodoxy in its beginnings but also by the theoreticians of the left.

Lenin's analysis, too, even if in certain features it is a creative development of Marxism, does not completely escape the effects of this ancestry. For example, when Lenin characterises imperialism as a parasitic, putrified capitalism, a capitalism in decay, and in particular when he sums up the 'economic essence' of imperialism in the concept of 'capitalism in its agony',[2] is he not taking up the idea that the concentration of capital and the socialization of labour have already reached the limiting point of incompatibility with the 'capitalist shell' which

Marx seemed to have predicted? Imperialist war was only the expression of this fact in the form of catastrophe. And was it not this theoretical perspective of Lenin's which led him to regard the 'objective conditions' of world revolution as fully ripe, even to see the world revolution as having begun with the Russian revolution? A whole series of statements by Lenin at this time support this view, notably the documents of the first four congresses of the Communist International, in which Lenin took part or whose proceedings he endorsed. The Fourth Congress reaffirmed the description of capitalism made by the Third Congress, of which it gave the following summary:

> The Third World Congress, after an investigation of the world economic situation, could confidently assert that capitalism, after the fulfilment of its mission of developing the forces of production, now stands completely in opposition, not merely to the necessities of the present historical development, but even to the satisfaction of the most elementary human requirements ... Capitalism today is in a period of deterioration The collapse of capitalism is not inevitable.[3]

The first three congresses all gave the same diagnosis of irreversible collapse. The first referred confidently to

> the total incapacity of the ruling classes to continue to guide the destinies of the peoples ... the inability of finance capitalism to rebuild the ruined economy ... the impossibility of restoring capitalism on the old foundations ... the fatal general crisis affecting the circulation of commodities in the capitalist system ... the impossibility of a return, not just to free competition, but also to the rule of the trusts, cartels, etc.

The second asserted that, 'Europe is being ruined, and the whole world with it. On the basis of capitalism there is no salvation.'[4] According to the Third Congress, 'The curve marking the productive forces is going to decline from its present artificial level. The expansions are going to be short-lived and of a speculative nature.' If it did prove possible to restore the capitalist equilibrium, it would be 'under conditions of economic exhaustion and barbarity in comparison with which the present state of Europe might be regarded as the height of well-being ... A higher standard of living is utterly incompatible with the present state of the capitalist system.'⁵ The capitalist world was in its death-throes, and tottering once more towards world war. The essence of the Leninist International's view of capitalism was that the fundamental and inherent contradictions had reached a point of complete incompatibility with the functioning of the system. This was the specific content given in this period to the concept of 'the agony of capitalism'.

It is true that statements can be found in Lenin's writings which appear to contradict this view. As long as the proletariat is not in a position to give it the *coup de grâce*, the bourgeoisie can always find an escape; the decay of capitalism does not mean that production may not increase in a particular branch or in a particular country even if the opposite is happening in other branches of the economy or other countries. These fluctuations are explained by the 'law of unequal development'. But in Lenin the contradiction *is* only apparent. All these fluctuations take place within the last stage at which the fundamental contradiction of the system is assumed to have emerged. In whichever direction they go, the fluctuations can only exacerbate it. This explains, according to the Third Congress, why

It is an undoubted mark of our time that the curve of the capitalist evolution proceeds through temporary rises constantly *downwards*, while the curve of revolution proceeds through some vacillations constantly *upwards* ... These vacillations are going to accompany capitalism in its agony, as was the case during its youth and maturity.⁶

In 1924, when the new cycle of expansion in the capitalist economy was already under way, the Fifth Comintern Congress's resolution on the world economic situation insisted that the crisis was continuing in the form of a chronic industrial crisis in the big capitalist countries and an agrarian crisis throughout the world: 'The opinion of the Social Democratic theoreticians (Hilferding) that capitalism has surmounted the post-war crisis and is entering a boom is unfounded.'⁷ A few months later, a plenary session of the executive of the Comintern had to recognize the existence of expansion, but described it as a 'relative stabilization' of capitalism. The underlying view remained unchanged. The programme adopted by the Sixth Congress contained the following passage:

The epoch of imperialism is the epoch of dying capitalism. The world war of 1914–18 and the general crisis of capitalism which it unleashed ... prove that the material prerequisites of socialism have already matured in the womb of capitalist society; they prove that the capitalist shell has become an intolerable restraint on the further development of mankind ... The capitalist system as a whole is approaching its final collapse.[8]

The economic crisis of 1929 was seen in this light. Many writers praise the Comintern for predicting the crisis, but in fact very few of the economic analyses of the Comintern since its foundation did not predict the imminence of a large-scale crisis. Given the cyclic characteristics of capitalist development, it was a prediction which was bound to be fulfilled one day. But the successful prediction for 1929 led to no positive political effect because it was still embedded in the great mistake, the product of the concept of 'capitalism in its agony', of regarding the world economic crisis as the 'final crisis' of the system, so many times announced and so long awaited. This, with other factors connected with the domestic and foreign policy of the Kremlin, produced the ultra-leftist line of the Comintern in this period. The main features of this line were its underestimate of the danger of Fascism, dizzying sectarianism with regard to Social Democracy (which was defined as 'social Fascism'), the adventurist tactics forced on the Chinese Communist Party (which had previously been told to follow Chiang Kai-shek) and its absurd line during the initial stage of the Spanish revolution (1930–33).

In Lenin, the economist and catastrophist aspects noted above were balanced by the comprehensive character of his theory of revolution, in which political factors, the party and the class struggle retained a clear primacy. They were controlled by his dialectical approach to the examination of any problem, his capacity for correction to meet the requirements of political action, always on the basis of a specific examination of a specific situation (even if some important features of Lenin's view contained a tendency which was detrimental to this dialectical approach). All this will be discussed later. As Leninism became a set of dogmas in the theory and practice of the Comintern, each of its parts began to acquire an autonomous existence and ceased to be treated as an element in a dialectical whole. This happened to the economist-catastrophist element. The 'economic laws' of capitalism were manipulated as though they transcended the class struggle, and were 'objective forces' inevitably determining the course of history. In particular, the 'law' of the fall in the rate of profit and the 'law' of the increasing pauperization of the working class were used in abstraction from the contrary tendencies to which Marx drew attention. In the Comintern's analyses, the 'law' of the unequal development of capitalism took on universal demonstrative force. It was used both to 'prove' the possibility of the complete construction of socialism in the U S S R and as an adequate explanation of the economic growth of a particular capitalist country – in spite of the 'agony' of capitalism' – or the stagnation of another. It could also be used to pick out 'the weakest link' at any conjuncture, to show the danger of a new war and predict the alignment of adversaries.

Until the victory of Nazism, the economist–catastrophist outlook performed the ideological function – in the pejorative sense of 'ideological' – of reconciling the Comintern's basic strategic premise with the real situation. According to this premise, the world revolution would soon resume its course.

The real situation however was marked by a slackening of the class struggle in European and American capitalism which was reflected in the spectacular growth of Social Democracy and the reformist trade unions, and the other side of this was a very sharp decline in the membership and influence of the Comintern. The economist–catastrophist view made it possible to interpret this political and social development as a superficial phenomenon beneath which the action of the 'economic laws' was still pushing capitalism inexorably towards the edge of the 'final crisis'. This reinforced the credibility of the future of the Russian revolution, and justified the existence of the Comintern as an ultra-centralized and semi-militarized world party, ready to lead the approaching world revolutionary war.

3. As was to be expected, the view of capitalism based on economism and catastrophism, and the mechanistic methodology inherent in it, had a negative effect on the Comintern's strategic and tactical discussions on the revolutionary struggle in the advanced capitalist countries. Without doubt, this is a main cause of the Comintern's inability to influence the

proletariat of the vital centres of capitalism, such as the United States and Great Britain. It also explains its inability to attract the decisive proletarian forces in another crucial centre, Germany, in spite of the solid foothold the Comintern had possessed there and the weakness of German capitalism following the defeat and the revolutionary storm of 1918. In other words, it is the source of its inability to find a common language with the great mass of the proletariat in developed capitalism, and forms of action and organization adapted to their needs.

The economist-catastrophist vision also goes a long way to explaining why the Comintern interpreted the phenomenon of Fascism as the morbid expression of the incurable weakness of capitalism, a last struggle in its 'agony', and the New Deal as another vain attempt to overcome its structural contradictions. This vision, which, as has been mentioned, inspired the ultra-left and sectarian line of the years up to Hitler's coming to power, later acted as ideological camouflage for the line of class collaboration which was introduced at the period of the popular fronts, and reached its culmination in the period of the 'grand alliance'. The theory of imminent economic catastrophe continued to dominate the Communist movement until the end of Stalin's reign, and did not even disappear then. Stalin's 'economic writings' of 1952 are a new attempt to give it theoretical form.

These theoretical premises were the basis for permanent and essential features of Comintern tactics. In the first place, they determined the significance attributed to the struggle for 'elementary' economic demands which is summed up in the following passage from the tactical theses adopted at the Third Congress:

> The essence of the revolutionary character of the present period consists in the fact that the most modest living conditions for the proletariat are incompatible with the existence of capitalist society. As a result of this, the struggle for the most modest demands takes on the proportions of a struggle for Communism.[9]

Through all the Comintern's political shifts, this view remained one of the tactical principles of its action. The Comintern regarded the 'struggle for the most modest demands' not only as the first link in the process of the growth of class-consciousness and organizational unity in the widest groups of the working class, but also the most effective means of accelerating the collapse of the capitalist productive mechanism. It would also check the influence of the reformist leaders. This was proved by the following argument: if the capitalists, in the 'agony' of their 'system', could not give way to even the 'most modest' economic demands of the workers, the reformist leaders – clear agents of the bourgeoisie – would be objectively unable to encourage or lead any real struggle for economic demands.

In practice, Social Democracy was the main beneficiary of the economic struggle up to 1929, while the Comintern, even during the years of the great world crisis, suffered a serious loss of membership.[10] Only the French party after the popular front, the Czech party for a short time and the Italian party after 1945, were able to gain anything from competition with Social Democracy and the reformist unions on this ground, and then only at the cost of themselves adopting a reformist outlook. This experience nevertheless does not prove that the struggle for economic demands in the period we are studying here was of no importance for revolutionary action against capitalism. It shows, quite simply, that it did not have the significance attributed to it in the economist–catastrophist view. Below a certain quantitative limit, it not only remained perfectly compatible with the functioning of the system, but it was even an important force in its technological and organizational development. To go beyond that limit required a degree of class-consciousness and revolutionary politicization which the struggle for 'the most modest demands' alone could not create, since successes in this struggle swelled, rather than reduced, reformist illusions. For a different result, the economic struggle would have had to be made part of a political and ideological campaign based on the contradictions and problems, some new, some old, which were growing in importance in the existence of the masses in proportion as the fight for 'a crust of bread' lost its original dramatic character. But the vision of capitalism in its 'agony', which was essentially economic, led to an underestimate of this new range of problems, the central core of which can be summed up as the problem of political and social democracy.

Bourgeois democracy, which the mass of workers regarded as their conquest from the moment that it allowed for the legal existence of workers' organizations, the legality of the strike, universal suffrage, etc., could (and still can) be used in a revolutionary way, but at the same time it constitutes one of the main sources of reformism, both on the ideological and political level and on that of the struggle for everyday demands. This effect cannot be neutralized by an abstract denunciation of the formal aspects of this democracy, but only by a practical struggle for real democracy in all aspects of social life.

The Comintern not only underestimated this problem, but until its Seventh Congress it took a fundamentally abstract and negative attitude to it. On the programmatic level, it contrasted bourgeois democracy with proletarian democracy of the Soviet type. The particular model it recommended, however, had difficulty in arousing enthusiasm among the mass of workers formed in reformist (or anarcho-syndicalist) unions and Social Democratic parties, who had been informed – not always sympathetically, of course – about the developments taking place in 'Soviet democracy' by their own organizations. The masses of workers in the West found it hard to understand how the militarization of the unions, the suppression of political freedoms – not only for the bourgeoisie but also for the proletariat – and the hierarchical and Taylorist organization of production represented a form of democracy superior to the formal democracy of the bourgeoisie, which gave the workers at least some legal opportunities of defending their living conditions. Until its switch of line at its Seventh Congress, the Comintern always called for the formation of 'soviets' as soon as it judged that a revolutionary situation had developed in a particular country. But this abstractly administered advice, lacking any connection with the specific forms taken by the mass movement under the pressure of traditional experience, did not once have practical effects in the capitalist countries. Effective action would have required a different political strategy, which included a constant effort to develop forms of proletarian democracy in every area of the mass struggle, and particularly at work and in the unions. The Communist parties would have had to be themselves the bearers of the new democracy, in the forms of their links with the masses, in the way they worked out their policies and in their internal organization.

Given its theoretical and organizational bases, its narrow rejection of the experiences and movements in Europe which went furthest towards developing proletarian democracy in the actual process of the struggle against capitalism, the Comintern could not even imagine a strategy of this type. After the Seventh Congress, following the requirements of the defence of the USSR and the struggle against Fascism, the Comintern and its sections took their stand in defence of democracy, but bourgeois democracy. This was the basis on which the Communist parties succeeded in reforming their links with the mass of the workers, and, in a few rare cases, in becoming dominant parties within the working class. All this, however, was the beginning of the neo-reformist trend which was to gather strength and expand within the framework of the 'grand alliance'.

The view of capitalism as in its 'agony' and the corresponding interpretation of Fascism, mentioned above were also used as an excuse for allowing the Communist parties to slide on to the ground of bourgeois democracy, parliamentarism and legalism. It was now argued that the survival of capitalism was incompatible with the preservation of bourgeois democracy, and therefore that the defence of this democracy – like the defence of the immediate economic interests of the masses – was inevitably leading the system as a whole towards its end.

4. Around the middle of the 1920s, Comintern orthodoxy was 'enriched' by the introduction of the doctrine of socialism in one country. This had a similar ideological function to the economist–catastrophist view, namely to increase the credibility of both the future of the Russian revolution and the inevitability of world revolution, although in fact it was an expression of the Stalinist fraction's suspicion of the latter. This suspicion was expressed in Stalinist doctrine's tendency to make the Russian revolution independent of world revolution, though preserving the interdependence of the two 'in the last instance'.

What was being claimed by this theory was that socialism could be completely constructed in Russia even if the revolution did not take place in the advanced capitalist countries, though this revolution was still admitted to be necessary as an ultimate guarantee of the security of 'full socialism' in Russia against any foreign attack. On this basis the doctrine of socialism in one country was combined in the text of the Comintern with the expectation of world revolution (that is, until the shift of 1934, in which this expectation disappeared from the texts). This new element, however, entails a revision of essential aspects of the theory of world revolution, in both its Leninist and Marxian versions. We shall do no more here than give a schematic summary of the main points of this revision.

(*a*) Stalinist doctrine introduced the postulate – which contradicted the assumptions about the material conditions of socialism which were fundamental to Marx's method – that socialism could be completely constructed within a single region and did not require the area of the whole world. After the Second World War Stalin claimed that even Communism could be constructed within the frontiers of the U S S R. In both cases these were abstract propositions, lacking any serious theoretical basis and imposed in an authoritarian manner. Quite apart from this, the empirical evidence of 'full socialism', which was supposed to have been already achieved in the Stalin period, supported Marx's views. The substance of the problem will not, however, be discussed here; apart from what was said in Chapter 2, this aspect of Stalin's revision will be left for the second part of this study.

(*b*) Marx and Lenin held that the main advance of world revolution would take place in the developed capitalist countries. In their view, the various types of revolution on the periphery of the capitalist system could be very important and help the proletariat to revolutionary victory in the vital centres of the system, but only this final victory could create the economic and political conditions necessary for the establishment of a full socialist society. (The first comprehensive theory of the role of peripheral revolutions in the dialectic of the world revolution was produced by Lenin, with his experience of the Russian revolution and the first colonial revolutions, but there are also analyses in Marx which point in the same direction.)

Until Lenin's death the place and function of the Russian revolution within the world revolution was always seen in this way, and the building of a socialism within the frontiers of the Soviet Union was regarded as a task which could not be carried to completion and produce a real socialist society without combining with the revolution in the developed capitalist zone. The task of the Soviet Union was to go as far as possible in this direction as long as the proletariat in capitalism had not taken power, and at the same time to give this proletariat as much help of every sort as possible to help them to reach that goal.

The doctrine of socialism in one country brought a radical change in conceptions of strategy. The construction of socialism in the USSR became – according to the Sixth Congress of the Communist International – 'the international engine of the proletarian revolution ... the most important factor in world history ... the essential factor in the international liberation of the proletariat'. The contradiction between the USSR and the capitalist world became 'the new fundamental contradiction' determining the progress of the world revolution. To put it another way, as Ponomarev has recently done, the construction of socialism in the USSR was built up as 'the decisive front in the revolutionary struggle of the international working class', its 'most important international task'.[11] In other words, the first task of the Comintern was no longer the revolutionary struggle to overthrow capitalism in its vital centres, but the preservation of the Soviet state from all outside attacks while it built 'full socialism'.

(*c*) In the view of Marx and Lenin, the international organization of the revolutionary proletariat could not, from its very essence, be subordinated to any national interest. This was the spirit in which the Communist International was conceived. Soviet power was regarded as a force totally subordinate to the interests and demands of the world revolutionary struggle, as a unity of the Communist International, not a power above it. (In its first years, the Red Army took an oath of loyalty to the International.) In practice, as has emerged in the course of this study, the Communist International was from the very first subordinated to the leaders of the Soviet state and, in spite of the genuine internationalism of Lenin, Trotsky and other Bolshevik leaders, a separation grew up between theory and actual practice. Nevertheless Lenin saw the danger inherent in this subordination, which also contradicted his whole conception of internationalism; this can be seen in his speech at the Fourth Congress of the Comintern, criticizing the resolution on the tasks of the International for being 'too Russian'.

Under Stalin this subordination was not only increased in practice; it was also given a theoretical basis in the doctrine of socialism in one country. Once the construction of socialism in one country had been defined as the decisive front of the world revolution, once it had become the first task of the International to defend this goal from foreign threats, it became logical and inevitable that the activity of the International should be controlled by those who had the direct responsibility for the construction of socialism in the USSR.

(*d*) The Stalinist revision as a whole made the 'Marxist–Leninist' theory of revolution even more determinist than it had become under the influence of the economist-catastrophist outlook. For the new view, if capitalism in its 'agony' could not guarantee a substantial, long-term development of the productive forces, and if, on the other hand, these forces could grow without restriction in the USSR and create the material base for 'full socialism', the moment would inevitably come when the relation of forces in the world as a whole would tip finally in favour of socialism, even if the proletariat of the capitalist countries had not yet been able to make its revolution. In the end its revolution would fall like a ripe fruit from the tree of socialism in one country.

5. While this attitude, as illusory as it was optimistic, became the basis of Comintern strategy, a different, and this time very realistic, attitude was emerging unnoticed in the relations between the Soviet state and the capitalist world.

Marx (and Lenin too) had presumed that the victory of the revolution in any of the capitalist countries would – given the arrangement of the world economy, the character of the advanced productive forces and the system of international relations – be incompatible with the continued existence of capitalism in the other countries of the same type; a struggle to the death would inevitably follow. There can be no doubt that this prediction rested on solid foundations. We need only imagine what would have happened if the proletarian revolution had been successful in Germany in 1918. Would the Entente powers have limited themselves to an intervention analogous in proportion to their intervention against the Russian revolution? Would they not have mobilized a maximum of economic and military power to crush it? At the start, the Bolsheviks took this view of the fate of the Russian revolution, and the intervention by the Entente powers seemed to prove them right. This is the source of the accent of incredulity and surprise which can be heard in their first reactions to the situation of more or less peaceful coexistence which followed immediately on the defeat of counter-revolution at home and intervention from abroad. This is the source of their fear that a new intervention on a much larger scale might take place at any moment. The mobilization of the workers internationally and other political factors are only a partial explanation for the failure of this intervention to take place. The real reason, without any doubt, was that Tsarist Russia was a long way from having the same importance in the world economy as the main capitalist countries. The mechanism could go on functioning perfectly without this 'part', and there might even be a bonus in the shape of an opportunity of trade with the vast new state corporation now making its entry on the world stage.

On the other hand, the capitalist powers could not accept a Soviet Russia which 'fomented' socialist revolutions beyond its frontiers. They could not accept a Russia which not only gave theoretical, political and material assistance to the revolutionary movement in the capitalist world, but also, by creating a social system which made real progress towards the economic, political and cultural liberation of the working people, gave an explosive example to the world proletariat. This also explains part of the incredulity of Lenin and his comrades at the possibility of lasting coexistence with the capitalist world; for them Soviet Russia was before anything else the driving force of revolution in the world as a whole.

In this respect the doctrine of socialism in one country, as we have shown, introduced a fundamental change of attitude. It provided a theoretical possibility of eliminating the element of incompatibility from the relations of the Soviet state with capitalist states, since it asserted that the revolution in the advanced capitalist countries was no longer the necessary condition for the construction of socialism in the USSR. Of course, to transform this possibility into a reality it was necessary for the Soviet leadership to abandon proletarian internationalism and retreat into its 'national socialism'. It was also necessary that this 'national socialism' should cease to be the explosive example we have described.

The international bourgeoisie adjusted its attitude to the Soviet state according to the development of that state and its policies. The industrialization of Russia made no difference to the essential economic interests of the bourgeoisie, and might even open up possibilities of profit. In addition, the destruction of Soviet democracy and the limitation of the political and trade-union rights of the workers gave bourgeois and Social Democratic propanganda excellent arguments with which to discredit not just the Soviet regime, but also revolutionary Marxism and the very idea of revolution and socialism, in the eyes of the majority of workers. To the degree that this process became firmly established and the Soviet example provided less and less inspiration for large sections of the Western working-class movement, bourgeois politicians and ideologists concentrated their efforts on making the Soviet leaders abandon their claim to foment revolution outside their frontiers. Bukharin, at the end of 1927, caught the tone of the world bourgeoisie perfectly when he made Chamberlain say, 'We have no objection at all to trading with you, but would you mind winding up the Communist International?'[12]

Until Hitler's accession to power the Soviet leaders rejected this demand of the world bourgeoisie. The new dominant class had not yet fully emerged. In the internal struggle for power and in the achievement of its main economic aims, forced collectivization and industrialization by equally forced stages, the Stalinist fraction needed to be able to wrap itself in the ideology of world revoluton. Again, while the tacit alliance with a Germany burdened by the treaty of Versailles was still in being, the Soviet leaders regarded their frontiers as relatively safe, even if they made use of the threat of aggression for motives of domestic or foreign policy. The result was that the construction of socialism in the USSR was presented openly as the driving force of the world revolution and the Communist International as its main instrument. The theory of world revolution corrected and revised in the way we have seen was given its most coherent – and most dogmatic – formulation in the programme adopted by the Sixth Congress of the Comintern. This theory was to give rise to a *praxis* totally inoperative in both the capitalist and the colonial worlds. It led to disaster in China and finally to disaster in Germany, but at least it kept the sacred flame alight. These are the heroic and ultra-sectarian years of the Stalinist Comintern.

The year 1934 was a historic turning-point. In the USSR it was the year of the great terror which consolidated Stalin's dictatorship and, with it, the formation of the new dominant class. Abroad a reversal of alliances was undertaken. The United States and European capitalism became potential allies of the USSR in the face of the danger from Hitler. The year 1935 saw the Franco–Soviet pact, the first military agreement between the Soviet state and a capitalist state. The construction of new alliances required concessions, and Stalin, as the subsequent course of his policy showed, did not limit himself to tactical concessions. He went further and further along the path which was to lead him, at the expense of the world revolutionary movement, to sacrifice all that was required – and more than was required – on the altar of the 'interests of the USSR', already identified with the interests of the new privileged class. The first step was the shelving of the theory of world revolution. This programme, so solemnly proclaimed at the Sixth Congress, was replaced by a universal programme of anti-Fascism, peace and democracy. (The type of democracy was no longer specified.) The 'construction of socialism in the USSR' was no longer presented as the driving force of world revolution and became that of world democracy and the ultimate guarantee of peace. Nothing would have been less opportune at that moment than a proletarian revolution in the 'democratic' Europe which was the potential ally of the USSR.

This is why, when proletarian revolution broke out in Spain in 1936 and seemed to be developing in France, the Comintern consistently tried to push the Spanish revolution back into the framework of bourgeois democracy and to block any possible materialization of the revolution in France. This meant rejecting, without even exploring it, the possibility which arose in 1936 of giving the struggle against Fascism and the danger of war a revolutionary turn. The Soviet state's aid to the Spanish Republic, like the great movement of solidarity with it, was kept within the limits compatible with the new direction of the Kremlin's foreign policy. As early as the Seventh Congress, the dissolution of the Comintern was under consideration, but it was retained to assist in the application of the new policy of the popular front, the world Communist movement's great shift towards reformism. Its revolutionary prestige could still be used to mask the abandonment of revolution and to control the forces which, subjectively, had not yet abandoned it. This abandonment of revolution was a conscious act on the part of the Stalinist clique, but not as yet on the part of the vast majority of the militants and organizers of the Comintern.

After the brief interlude of the Nazi–Soviet pact, with its grotesque disinterment of old schemas now emptied of all content – the only function of which was to disguise Stalin's aim of reaching a lasting agreement with Nazi Germany – the theoretical and practical abolition of the initial revolutionary aims of the Communist movement was to reach its fullest development during the years of the 'grand alliance'. The dissolution of the Comintern was the symbol of this. The Communist International was not abolished because it was thought to be – as it indeed was – an unsuitable system for organizing and controlling the international revolutionary struggle; this was the reason given in the 1943 resolution, but the real reason was the abandonment of interest in revolution. The Communist International was not abolished because this was the necessary condition for the defeat of Germany, but because it was the necessary condition for the division of the world between the Stalinist state and its capitalist allies. It was not abolished to facilitate revolutionary action by the Communist parties in their respective countries, but to facilitate their reformist action within the framework of bourgeois democracy. It was not abolished because it was in a crisis but because, in spite of its crisis, it still symbolized proletarian revolution.

The whole policy of the Communist parties – with the exception of the few which were beginning to revolt against Moscow's leadership – was determined by the aim which Stalin set himself (as is proved by documents of unquestionable authority) from the time of his very first negotiations with the other two great powers, the division of Europe and the world into 'spheres of influence'. This entailed the Communist parties rejecting in advance any attempt to transform the anti-Fascist war into a socialist revolution, a rejection which itself determined the fact that the Communist parties' policies did not encourage, but actively discouraged, the appearance of any such possibility. Their conception of the alliances, of the nature of the new anti-Fascist power and the ways in which it could be created, tended to place the most advanced forces of the resistance under the political and ideological control of the national anti-Fascist bourgeoisie and the 'valiant allies' of the USSR.

And then, in spite of everything, in spite of Stalin's compromises and the general line he imposed on the Communist movement, revolution became a fact in Yugoslavia and Greece and a possibility in France and Italy. In that final and irreversible collapse of Hitler's army, military superiority in Europe swung decisively to the side of the Soviet army. The left wing of the resistance reached the peak of its influence, bringing with it the great majority of the proletariat and large sectors of the petty bourgeoisie. The conjunction of these two factors – Soviet military superiority on the continent and the dominance of the radical wing of the resistance – now made possible, at the very least, the formation of advanced anti-Fascist bases under the leadership of working-class and left-wing petty bourgeois forces.

When this real opportunity appeared – a possible first stage in an original continent-wide revolutionary development in Europe – the instructions which came from Moscow and were supported by almost all the national Communist leaderships were designed to head off this possibility completely, to hold back the movement and foster the wildest illusions about the likely decisions of the 'Big Three'; they strengthened Anglo-American authority in the west and south of Europe and recognized the authority of the Gaullists in France and of the Christian Democrats in Italy. And when a revolutionary development was more than a possibility and became a reality, as in Greece, Stalin had no hesitation in facilitating British military intervention to crush the rising. (He did this not only through his well-known compromise with Churchill, but also through his pressure on the Greek Communist leadership to capitulate.)

The result was that the transformation of the anti-Fascist war in Europe into revolution came about only in Yugoslavia, where the Communist leaders had made this their aim from the beginning and had followed this policy consistently in spite of pressure from Moscow. It also took place in the countries occupied by the Soviet army, where the abolition of the old regimes was a necessary condition for the establishment of the Soviet defensive barrier. Revolutions of this sort involved the loss of barely recovered national independence, however, and power did not pass to the people, or even to the Communist parties – which were very much a minority in most of these countries – but to small groups subservient to Moscow.

The line of the Communist parties in the colonies and semi-colonial territories was adapted to the policy of the 'grand alliance' in the same way. The Latin American Communists had to collaborate with U S imperialism, the Indian Communists with British imperialism. And, as everyone knows, there would have been no revolution in China if the Maoist leadership had adopted the policy of 'national unity', on French or Italian lines, with Chiang Kai-shek, which Stalin demanded.

The Soviet Union had become a world power, a super-power, had pushed its strategic frontiers forward into the heart of Europe and was recognized and respected as an immovable reality by the capitalist states. On this basis, the U S S R settled firmly into the new *status quo*, and the search for a global arrangement with the other super-power became the main aim of its international policy. The 'cold war' was no more than a dangerous stage of this search, provoked by American imperialism's pretensions to world leadership. It did not represent an anti-imperialist or revolutionary shift in Stalin's attitude. The same is true of the setting-up of the Cominform, the real purpose of which was to make it easier to control the satellites and to mobilize the Communist movement as an instrument for putting pressure on the White House to accept the compromise sought by the Kremlin.

While in the East the great Chinese revolution opened the period of revolt in the Third World, in the West the prospect of socialism was relegated to theory – if the term still has any application in the Communist movement – to a distant and uncertain future, and the decisive factor in bringing it about became 'economic competition' between the two systems, which was destined to be crowned by the victory of Soviet 'Communism'. Revolution became a disturbing, and almost undesirable, possibility; the main task was to preserve the *pax Sovieto-Americana*. On the level of theory, official Marxism was completely transformed into a rigid system of dogmas and stereotyped formulas; on the political level it became a narrow empiricism with a reformist content. Thus, at the end of Stalin's reign, the abandonment of living Marxism and of revolutionary theory and practice reached a much more advanced stage than in the old Social Democratic orthodoxy, and the Communist movement could have taken over Bernstein's formulation from the end of the last century: 'Social democracy must have the courage to free itself from the phraseology of the past and be willing to appear as it now is in reality, a party of democratic and social reforms.'

But the reformism which now made its appearance differed from the old in a number of important features. First, its emergence was primarily determined by the subordination of the Comintern to Soviet foreign policy and by the task assigned to the Comintern as part of that subordination, namely, the defence of the USSR. During the period of the popular fronts the requirements of this task had coincided with the needs of the anti-Fascist struggle, but only on condition – given the Stalinist leadership's view of what was meant by the defence of the USSR – that this struggle did not constitute a threat to the bourgeois system in states which were or might be allies of the USSR. More bluntly, the struggle against Fascism had to be approached in a spirit of class collaboration. This requirement persisted after the Second World War because the main aim of Stalin's policy, even during the 'cold war', was to reach a lasting arrangement with the United States and its satellites. But this fundamental characteristic came into increasing contradiction, as time passed, with the internal requirements of neo-reformist policies in each country.

Secondly, the reformist *praxis* in which the Communist parties now began to engage continued to be reconciled with a socialist perspective – just as the 'ultra-revolutionary' policy of the previous period had been – by means of the doctrine of socialism in one country (after the war, 'socialism in a number of countries' or 'in the socialist camp') and the economist–catastrophist view which, as has been mentioned, continued to be maintained until the death of Stalin. Subsequently, faith in this socialism received a mortal blow from the 'secret report', the denunciation of the 'trials', the Hungarian rising, the Polish October and the rest. The picture of capitalism at the last limits of its productive capacity was also severely shaken by the spectacular development of European, American and Japanese capitalism. With its ideological foundations so severely shaken, Communist neo-reformism now began to look for a doctrinal basis closer to that of traditional reformism.

Thirdly, the new reformism differed from the traditional version in the model of society to which it claimed to aspire, which continued to be that of Stalinist Russia. It followed from this that any groups which allied themselves with the Communist parties, all those who contributed to the arrival of this 'socialism', were digging their own graves as tendencies, groups or parties distinct from the Communist Party. The Moscow trials of the period of the Popular Fronts and the trials in the People's Democracies after the war were a constant check on potential fellow-travellers. During the Stalinist period this was the most vulnerable side of the Communist parties' new line. After the Twentieth Congress each day made it clearer that without repudiating the Stalinist model of 'socialism' the policy of neo-reformism would remain a dead end.

The last feature which distinguished the new reformism from the old was the type of party which supported it. When the switch began, the sections of the Comintern had reached – by means of 'Bolshevization' and a succession of purges – a high degree of ideological and organizational uniformity, on which the Seventh Congress congratulated them as an expression of their 'maturity'. This enabled them to take the new path without serious problems and to assimilate the new militants who joined during the resistance and the liberation. The organizational system of the Communist parties made the new reformism more effective in certain respects, and, together with ideological uniformity, made an internal struggle for a revolutionary line more difficult than in Social democratic parties. But these characteristics of the Communist parties, especially ideological uniformity and the absence of internal democracy, also came into contradiction with the policy of alliances implied by the new line.

To sum up, it can be said that the growth of 'Communist' neo-reformism, which was already visible in the period studied in this book and developed further after that, was marked by a movement in the direction of traditional reformism. This tendency is one of the most telling general signs of the crisis in the Communist movement.

6. Chapter 2 has already tried to show that the objective starting-point of the crisis in the Communist movement is the fact that at the time the Communist International was created, contrary to what Lenin thought, the objective conditions for the socialist revolution had not developed in advanced capitalism, and that the International was nevertheless devised to act in these non-existent conditions. (It should be

pointed out that the term 'objective conditions' here includes the general state of consciousness of the proletariat in the West in this period; not to include this would mean giving the term a purely economic content. It may also be noted that the most striking sign of the 'under-development', in this sense, of the revolution in Western society is the empirical fact that the imperialist war – the first general crisis of the capitalist system – only very slightly loosened the hold of reformism on the working-class movement, in spite of the enormous sacrifices of all kinds imposed by the war on the masses.) The Comintern, conceived as the headquarters and advance unit in an immediate assault on world capitalism, found itself confronted with a radically different task, to win the mass of the proletariat over to a revolutionary policy in non-revolutionary conditions, Logically, this task would have required a complete reorganization of the International, but, as was said above, this was not even considered. To explain this it is not enough to return to the factor noted in point 1 of this summary, the dazzling prestige of the October revolution. We must start from the Leninist view of the Party and the difference between this view and Marx's.

Marx's writings contain no systematic theory of the proletarian party, but his views on this subject, taken in connection with his militant activity, first in the Communist League and later in the First International or the German Socialist Party, form a coherent and significant whole. Marx's idea of the proletarian political party is a corollory of his conception of the Communist revolution as the self-emancipation of the working class. According to Marx, no outside force – charismatic leader, conspiratorial group, political party – can replace the revolutionary 'maturity' of the working class. The Communist revolution will be made by that class or it will not take place. According to Marx's theory of revolution, this maturity can only be produced by the practice of the class struggle, which is forced on the proletariat by its inevitable situation in capitalist relations of production. The experience of this struggle teaches the proletariat the need for organization and solidarity. It shows them their common interests and their common enemy, and gradually transforms them from 'class in itself', a set of individuals, to a 'class for itself', aware of the radical antagonism which exists between it and the capitalist system. The theory developed by intellectuals of bourgeois origin who 'join the revolutionary class', and 'have raised themselves to the level of comprehending theoretically the historical movement as a whole',[13] contributes to the growth of this awareness, but is not its cause. For Marx it is revolutionary activity which creates consciousness and consciousness in its turn extends and clarifies that activity. Between these two aspects of the same activity there exists the dialectical interaction defined in the third thesis on Feuerbach.

Marx had lived through the decline of the revolutionary spirit which followed the defeat of proletarian efforts in the revolutions of 1848, and had watched the English working class become 'bourgeois'. He was well aware that the process of the 'maturation' of the proletariat as a revolutionary class was not simply linear, but on the contrary deeply contradictory, marked out by advances and setbacks, illusions and disappointments, a permanent struggle between the dominant bourgeois ideology and the emerging proletarian ideology. But Marx believed that because of the nature of capitalist contradictions this process would lead, in the end, to the maturation of the proletariat as a revolutionary class. It was this process which he regarded – as he wrote in 1860 – as the formation of the proletarian party 'in the large historical sense of the term', the proletarian party which 'everywhere springs up spontaneously from the soil of modern society'[14] and in which Marx included all the forms (political, cultural, trade union) taken by the 'self-activity' of the proletariat. In other words, Marx saw the proletariat as forming the revolution party *as a class*, not as an entity distinct from the class and certainly not above it. This view cannot be called 'spontaneist' in the normal sense of the term, since while the process comes into being spontaneously, determined by the objective situation of the proletariat in capitalist society, it follows from its nature that consciousness should become more and more important. It entails that consciousness should more and more determine the subsequent stages and give them an organized character by defining more and more precisely their goals and the means needed to reach them.

Working-class political parties in the usual sense are for Marx partial and temporary – 'episodic' is his word[15] – expressions of the proletarian party in the large historical sense of the term, in the same way as the unions or other forms of working-class organization. Marx regarded the role of trade unions as very important – though he sharply criticized their tendency to 'economism' – while on many occasions he expressed reservations about working-class political parties. In 1869 he wrote: 'All political parties whatever, without exception, only arouse the enthusiasm of the mass of workers for a period, momentarily, while the unions win mass support permanently. Only the unions are capable of forming a real workers' party and setting up a barrier to the power of capital.'[16] This comment, and others like it, does not imply an underestimate of the political dimension of the class struggle – Marx was continually calling on the unions to politicize their activities and consider the question of power. It is Marx's warning against the separation of the economic and social aspect of the class struggle from the specifically political aspect, and a warning against the natural tendency of political groups to separate themselves from the class, and lead and mould it according to their own group views and interests.

In the course of his activity as a militant, Marx fought on several occasions against these tendencies. In 1850 he attacked the members of the Communist League, who, 'not content with organizing the revolutionary proletariat' and 'profoundly contemptuous of the more theoretical activity which consists in explaining to the workers their class interests', devoted themselves to 'anticipating the development of the revolutionary process and artificially precipitating the crisis'. They were, added Marx acidly, 'the alchemists of the revolution, fully sharing the old alchemists' confusion of ideas and the obstinacy which goes with the obsessive ideas'.[17] In 1873 he criticized the Bakuninists for regarding themselves as 'the privileged representatives of the *idea* of revolution', 'setting themselves up as a general staff' and taking it upon themselves to impose on the International, by conspirational and dictatorial means, a 'unity of thought and action' amounting to 'dogmatism and blind obedience', to the '*perinde ac cadaver* of the Society of Jesus'.[18] In 1870 Marx and Engels protested against the opportunist tendencies which were beginning to appear in the leading circle of the German Socialist Party, and in particular against the idea that 'the working class is not capable of liberating itself'.[19]

Many more examples could be cited to show that Marx and Engels systematically opposed any group, of 'left' or 'right', which attempted to substitute itself for the real movement of the working class, to dictate policies to it or impose theory on it. Marx never saw the activity of Communists, that is, of those who shared his theoretical views, as the activity of a party external to the working class, endowed with a privileged function of leadership in the Leninist sense. The *Communist Manifesto* proclaims:

The Communists do not form a separate party opposed to other working-class parties.

They do not set up any sectarian principles of their own, by which to shape and mould the proletarian movement . . .

The immediate aim of the Communists is the same as that of all the other proletarian parties: formation of the proletariat into a class, overthrow of the bourgeois supremacy, conquest of political power by the proletariat.

Communists are not 'a separate party', but a 'section' of the working-class movement, 'the most resolute' section. 'Theoretically, they have . . . the advantage of clearly understanding the line of march, the conditions, and the ultimate general results of the proletarian movement', which means that 'they always and everywhere represent the interests of the movment as a whole'.[20]

It is true that this theoretical 'advantage', and the 'representation' of the interests of the movement as a whole, carry within them the possibility of, and even a tendency to, separation from the class as a whole, a possibility of contradiction with the first principle that the Communists are not 'a separate party' and do not assume the right to mould the movement by 'sectarian principles'. This danger is all the greater since the theory which gives the Communists this 'advantage' requires a level of scientific development which the proletariat cannot produce by itself under the conditions of capitalism; it is supplied by intellectuals drawn, with a few exceptions, from the dominant classes and the bourgeoisie. This is the source of the possibility of a dictatorship of 'science' over the proletarian movement, and gives the theoreticians as a group a greater chance of winning a monopoly of real control. It was to guard against this danger that Marx insisted on a genuinely democratic party organization, with election and permanent control of the leaders by the militants, and a struggle against any cult of authority or leaders. In his polemic against the Bakuninists Marx declared himself clearly against any sort of hierarchial organization with an authoritarian internal structure and an official orthodox doctrine. He defended the legitimacy of theoretical and political differences within the International and its sections, and complete freedom of discussion in press, assemblies and congress.[21] At the same time he rejected the imposition of any 'party' criterion in scientific research.[22] Science could not impose its conclusions on the working-class movement, nor could the institutions in which the movement was embodied set themselves up as authorities over science.

To sum up, Marx's view of the proletarian political party is extremely flexible, sensitive and open: democratic in the least formal and most radical sense of democracy. Its actual form at any particular moment must be a function of the formation of the proletarian political party 'in the large historical sense'. In Marx's view, the real agent in historical action, in the revolution, is the class. The proletarian political party can never replace it in this role; it must be its instrument and under its control. Each time the particular form taken by the party – whether the Communist League or the First International – seemed to Marx and Engels to be entering into contradiction with the real movement of the class, Marx and Engels did not hesitate to suggest its disappearance. The political party is not the 'leader' of the class, in the Leninist sense; it is the theoretical and practical mediation between the scientific understanding of the class struggle and social development – itself liable to constant correction as a result of the real movement – and the autonomous action of the proletariat. Its mission is not to take over the leadership of the class, but to help it to lead itself. As Rosa Luxemburg said, arguing with Lenin and faithfully reflecting Marx's thought, 'social democracy is not connected with the organization of the working class; it is the actual movement of the working class.'[23]

With the entry of capitalism into the stage of monopoly and imperialism, a development began within the working-class movement which seemed to contradict Marx's predictions about the development of the proletariat into the revolutionary class. Under the pressure of the struggles of the proletariat, capitalism showed itself capable of conceding substantial improvements in the living conditions of most workers. The previous advances of anti-capitalist consciousness seemed to die away or even be reversed, and give way to a spirit of accommodation and reformism, which spread among large sections of the working class. Doctrinal revisionism, which was both a reflection and a source of this tendency, justified this abandonment of the revolutionary perspective with genuflections to the spontaneity of the working-class movement.

Orthodox Marxism reacted by exalting the role of the theory of 'scientific socialism', which it presented as the source of the proletariat's socialist consciousness. Kautsky made his famous statement: 'Socialist consciousness is something introduced into the proletarian class struggle from without and not something that arose within it spontaneously.'[24] It is a statement which, if taken literally, is incompatible with Marx's view. (And it is significant that Kautsky does not support this statement with a passage from Marx, which he would certainly have done if any such passage had existed, in vew of the importance of the problem and the context in which he made the statement.) The qualification 'if taken literally' is relevant because a reading of the document which contains this passage shows that Kautsky uses the term 'socialist consciousness' as the equivalent of 'socialist doctrine', that is, the scientific theory of capitalism and socialism. Lenin takes over Kautsky's ambiguous expression in *What Is To Be Done?* has the same confusion of concepts in his own argument and, much worse, makes it the foundation of his theory of the revolutionary party.

The reason for this view of Lenin's is not simply the fact that at the time he wrote *What Is To Be Done?* he regarded Kautsky as the highest authority in Marxism, but also because the history of the penetration of Marxism into Russia and its spread, together with the political context in which Lenin worked out his theory of the party, pushed him in the same direction. This was the period in which Marxism was beginning to gain a hold in Russia, and make numerous converts among young revolutionary intellectuals looking for new paths after the failure of 'The People's Will', the movement which marked the Russian proletariat's first real entry on the political scene with the strikes of 1896. Just as in the previous period the populist intelligentsia found its mass base in the muzhiks, the Marxist intellectuals of the last two decades of the nineteenth century – like the young Marx in 1843 – regarded the workers who were beginning to be produced by the late-developing Russian capitalism as the 'material weapons' of their new philosophy. They 'introduced' among the workers the 'socialist consciousness' which the practice of the class struggle had not yet had time to awaken, even in embryonic form. This empirical fact seemed to Lenin to be confirmation of Kautsky's theory. Stressing even the idealist background of the theory, Lenin could say: 'In Russia, the theoretical doctrine of Social Democracy arose altogether independently of the spontaneous growth of the working-class movement; it arose as a *natural and inevitable outcome of the development of thought* among the revolutionary socialist intelligentsia.'[25]

Furthermore, Lenin's view of the political and social context – a view which was soon confirmed by events in the shape of the 1905 revolution – made the political and organizational preparation of the revolutionary forces, and particularly of the proletariat, a matter of urgency. In this situation, the 'cult of spontaneity', represented most notably by the 'economist' Marxists, seemed to him little short of criminal. Lenin was also convinced that he possessed the Marxist key to the Russian revolution. All this helps to explain the violence and intransigence of his attacks on any opinion which deviated by as much as a millimetre from what he regarded as the revolutionary Marxist line. It also helps to explain his tendency to exalt the role of theory and organization, and his total condemnation of any concession to spontaneity.

According to Lenin, 'the *spontaneous* development of the working-class movement ... leads to its subordination to bourgeois ideology', because the class struggle in itself produces only 'trade-unionism', and

trade-unionism means the ideological enslavement of the workers by the bourgeoisie. Hence, our task, the task of Social Democracy, is to combat spontaneity, to divert the working-class movement from this spontaneous trade-unionist striving to come under the wing of the bourgeoisie, and to bring it under the wing of revolutionary Social Democracy.[26]

To those who accused his group of 'setting up their programme against the movement like a spirit hovering over formless chaos', Lenin replied: 'But what else is the function of Social Democracy if not to be a "spirit" that not only hovers over the spontaneous movement, but also *raises* this movement *to the level of "its programme"*?'[27] Lenin says that the direction taken by the working-class movement will depend on the outcome of the struggle between socialist ideology (worked out by Marxist intellectuals and brought by them to the working-class movement) and bourgeois ideology (with its 'Marxist' variants), which has enormous power, being both the older ideology and one of the many instruments of the state and the ruling classes. This is an idea which can be found in Marx, but with the important difference that he regards the working-class movement as tending spontaneously towards socialist ideology, with the proletariat as the central agent in the ideological struggle. For Marx theory also has a function in the struggle, but this is to contribute to the formation of the revolutionary consciousness of the proletariat, not to replace the real motive force, the proletariat's revolutionary activity.

In contrast, in Lenin's writings, the proletariat appears as the *object* in the ideological struggle between the Marxist theoreticians and the bourgeois ideologists. And to the degree that it is also an agent, its tendency is 'to come under the wing of the bourgeoisie'. Lenin also sees a need for a powerful instrument which will be able to keep the weapon of revolutionary theory sharp for use both against the ideology of the bourgeoisie and against the ideology spontaneously secreted by the working-class movement, an instrument which will be able to reverse the tendency of this spontaneity. This is the instrument which will implement the famous Leninist maxim, 'Without revolutionary theory there can be no revolutionary party.' The precise content of this maxim, in its context in *What Is To Be Done?* is as follows: The Revolutionary movement has to be created *on the basis of* theory, on principles, a policy and plan worked out in advance by the Marxist intellectuals who are the custodians of 'scientific socialism'. This powerful instrument is the party as seen by Lenin. Confronted with the cult of spontaneity, Lenin introduced into the history of Marxism orthodoxy, the bearer of socialist consciousness, the organizer and leader of the working class and the decisive instrument of the revolution.

If Lenin borrowed the fundamental theoretical principle of his conception of the party – that it should be the bearer of a socialist consciousness external to the class – from Kautsky, he also derived the organizational principle partly from his admiration for 'the magnificent organization that the revolutionaries had in the seventies, and that should serve us as a model'. This is only one source; there was also a German one, as we shall see. In Lenin's view, the Social Democrats had 'the duty of creating as good an organization of revolutionaries as the Zemlya i Volya had, or, indeed, an incomparably better one'.[28] Lenin did in fact follow this model, but also improved it. His central figure was the same, the professional revolutionary, with, apart from a few exceptions, the same social origin as the professional revolutionaries of the seventies, the intelligentsia. In spite of Lenin's insistence on the need to transform advanced and educated workers into professional revolutionaries (by taking them out of factory work), the results remained insignificant, especially as regards the leading group. (At the time of the October revolution the central committee of the Bolshevik party included only one worker.) This was a logical result, given the theoretical level required by the party for entry into the leading group and the average cultural level of the Russian proletariat.

The general organizational blueprint for the party was similarly taken from the populist model of the seventies, which Lenin, adapting Plekhanov's analysis, described as follows: 'At that time there was a well-organized and splendidly disciplined centre; around it there were the organizations, of various categories, which it had created; and what remained outside these organizations was chaos, anarchy.'[29] Lenin proposed a similar structure for the Marxist party: a central organization of professional revolutionaries with organizations of 'non-professional' revolutionaries around the centre and subordinate to it. The whole structure was to be strictly centralized, hierarchical and disciplined. To leave no doubt about the type of organization he had in mind, Lenin used military language: 'The thing we need is a military organization of agents . . . our "tactics-as-plan" consist in . . . demanding that all efforts be directed towards gathering, organizing and *mobilizing* a permanent army.' The task of this 'army' would be to 'lay effective siege to the enemy fortress' and prepare the assault; they would be 'troops' who, when the moment came to attack, 'will not be overwhelmed by the masses, but will take their place at their head'.[30]

In its organizational principles, the type of organization envisaged by Lenin resembles that of the enemy, which Lenin described as a 'purely military, strictly centralized organization ... led in all its minutest details by a single will'.[31] One of the main instruments of this enemy organization was the political police, and Lenin claimed that the mass of the workers were incapable of fighting effectively against the political police because 'the struggle against the political police requires special qualities; it requires *professional* revolutionaries ... trained professionally no less than the police'.[32]

This attitude easily gives the impression of an attempt to transplant into the running of the party the autocratic and bureaucratic principle which pervaded the Tsarist political system. So strong was this feeling among the leading Russian Marxists of the early years of this century that most of them – from Plekhanov to Trotsky – made it an explicit part of their polemic against Lenin. But Lenin could reply with solid arguments, based on an analysis of the period in which the Social Democrats had worked by rule of thumb, with no central leadership or plan. It was easy for him to show that democracy in the party was impossible under the Tsarist police regime. The type of organization he advocated did correspond, quite clearly, to particular demands of the revolutionary struggle under Tsarism. The organization of professional revolutionaries, supported by the subsidiary organizations of 'non-professional' revolutionaries, was an effective instrument for carrying to the spontaneous movement, to the unstructured working-class organizations, to the student movement and the peasants, the political line worked out by Lenin, and for introducing into this 'chaos' the beginnings of a national organization. It was an effective instrument for subordinating the workers' movement and the revolutionary movement as a whole to the leadership of the party which was the possessor of theory and consciousness, and had a precise plan and aims. This explains why Lenin was supported by a considerable group of the Russian Marxists, in spite of the hostility of important figures.

Besides this, Lenin's revolutionary genius, his ability to make a detailed analysis of a particular situation, led him to make corrections to

the norms and ideas of *What Is To Be Done?* when the revolution of
1905 showed that the spontaneous movement of the masses did not
inevitably tend to 'take refuge under the wing of the bourgeoisie', and
was capable of enormous revolutionary initiatives. In his writings of
1905 and later, Lenin stresses the great importance of these initiatives.
In November 1905 he went so far as to say, 'The working class is
instinctively, spontaneously Social Democratic.'[33] (Such language is,
however, rare in the later period, nor did Lenin go on to correct his view
that the spontaneous movement can create no more than a trade-union
consciousness and tends to be dominated by the bourgeoisie.) Following
on the limited political freedom extorted from the government by the
revolution, Lenin proposed some democratization of the internal organization of the party, and the Tammerfors Conference adopted the principle of 'democratic centralism'. The practical effect of this resolution
was, however, largely limited by political conditions.

It would be wrong to interpret these corrections as a fundamental
revision of the view of the party put forward in *What Is To Be Done?*,
One Step Forward, Two Steps Back and other writings of this period.
The essential relation between the party and the class remains unchanged. The party is still the custodian of theoretical truth and consciousness, understood in the sense given them by Kautsky, which Lenin
never rejected. The class cannot become the revolutionary class without
the party's leadership – in the strongest and most immediate sense of the
word 'leadership' – and only if the party gives the class a socialist consciousness and educates it politically. It is the party which controls the
class and not the other way round; it substitutes itself for the class each
time the class strays from the path laid down it by the party, and it is
always the authentic representative of the class even if the class does not
recognize it as its representative. What remains unchanged, in other
words, is the external character of the party's relation to the proletariat.
It is external to it in the origin of its title to leadership, which does not
derive from the class but from a theory developed outside it. It is
external in the way it is linked to the class, which is reflected in the
normal expressions, according to which the party, to be invincible, must
'base itself' on the class, 'establish links' with it, 'place it under the
leadership' of the party, and so on. The external character is also

reflected in the distinctions which Lenin insisted should be made between the party and the mass organizations of the working class, especially the unions. The difference followed from the subordination. All the mass organizations were to be under the leadership of the party and accept its authority. In Lenin's eyes, the soviets could not be genuine organs of working-class power unless they were placed under the authority of the party. The party, in other words, is the central agent of the revolution; the activity of the class is, at the most, secondary.

Secondly, the essential element of the organizational conception of the party also remained unchanged. In the Leninist conception of 'democratic centralism', 'centralism' always retained priority over 'democracy' (the Stalinist degeneration consisted in completely abolishing the second term) because it became associated with the extraordinary powers which, according to Lenin, were essential to the leading organs, with the exaggeration of the importance of leaders, their permanence and power, which enabled them to condition – overwhelmingly in normal conditions – the exercise of 'democracy' by the base and lower organs. Lenin was indignant at the action of the 'demagogues' who made the workers distrust 'all who bring them political knowledge and revolutionary experience from outside', and supported his argument with a reference to the German Social Democrats:

> Political thinking is sufficiently developed among the Germans, and they have acquired sufficient political experience, to understand that without the 'dozen' tried and talented leaders (and talented men are not born by the hundred), professionally trained, schooled by long experience, and working in perfect harmony, no class in modern society can wage a determined struggle.[34]

Lenin was to continue to admire the German Social Democrats' organization for the authority and stability of its leadership right up to the 'betrayal' of 1914.

Lenin did not think that the essence of his organizational views reflected specifically Russian conditions, though those conditions did give them some characteristic features, deriving basically from the struggle against the political police. Again following Kautsky, he declared that the fundamental differences over organization between Marxist orthodoxy and revisionism could be summed up in the formula 'bureaucracy versus democracy'. ('Bureaucracy' here means a centralized, hierarchical and professionally organized organization based on the specialization of members in the different activities of the party.)

Bureacracy versus democracy is in fact centralism versus autonomism; it is the organizational principle of revolutionary Social Democracy as opposed to the organizational principle of opportunist Social Democracy. The latter strives to proceed from the bottom upward, and therefore, wherever possible and as far as possible, upholds autonomism and 'democracy', carried (by the overzealous) to the point of anarchism. The former strives to proceed from the top downwards, and upholds an extension of the rights and powers of the centre in relation to the parts.[35]

Rosa Luxemburg in her criticism singled out this identification of revisionism (in theory and politics) with democracy (in organizational matters), and there can be no doubt that these criticisms of the best-qualified representative of revolutionary Social Democracy outside Russia were a faithful reflection of Marx's ideas.

Ultimately the structures and operation of the party as advocated by Lenin were nothing more than the organizational embodiment of the conception of the party as an external force dominating the class. They were a means of giving the party – in fact the leading group – independence and preserving its power of decision, not only to work out and put into practice specific policies, but also to work out theoretical orthodoxy. For this it was not enough for the party to have its own organization, distinct from that of the class, since the organization would have to have links with the masses and so be exposed to outside influences. In addition the organization had to be protected from 'spontaneist' ideology, and to ensure this the power of decision had to be concentrated in a small and particularly 'hard' core and, within this core, in the leader, who was regarded as the source of the group's cohesion. As early as 1904, Trotsky had summed up perfectly the logic of this conception of the party: the party tends to take the place of the class, the Central Committee that of the party and the leader that of the Central Committee.[36]

The Bolshevik victory of October 1917 canonized Lenin's theory of the party in the same way that the defeat of the German Spartacists and the Italian workers' councils discredited the ideas of Rosa Luxemburg and Gramsci, which were close to those of Marx. The Communist International was based totally on Lenin's theory, and the supra-national character it acquired reinforced and accentuated the external characteristic of the relationship to the party which were part of the Leninist model. The central body of professional revolutionaries (the Executive Committee of the International, the network of delegates and instructors, etc.) was a distant and mysterious world to the working-class movement of each member country. The loyalty owed by the professional revolutionaries of each national section to the central body as part of their work also kept them much more apart from their own working classes than was the case with the Bolshevik professionals.

The way in which the sections of the Comintern were established also reinforced this tendency. Whereas the Bolshevik party had been formed out of the originality of its national revolutionary movement, with a base of autonomous theoretical and political work, the formation of the Communist parties represented, to a greater or lesser degree, a break with the revolutionary traditions and experiences of their countries. Where the Bolsheviks' break with the Russian forms of opportunism was the result of a complex and prolonged process of ideological and political struggle, the Comintern and its sections broke with Western opportunism by the use of authoritarian and bureaucratic methods, symbolized by the 'Conditions' for membership.

This was the source of the exceptional difficulties experienced in most cases, by the new parties, in their efforts to become established in the working-class movement. If they nevertheless succeeded in staying in existence and in some cases – very few – acquired sizable memberships, this was because they embodied a revolutionary will which attracted the most radical groups of the proletariat, because they shared the prestige of the October revolution and – not least important – received financial support from the Soviet state. These last two factors, however, also helped to increase the dependence of each section on the controlling body established in Moscow, which controlled the funds and identified itself with loyalty to the October revolution.

In addition, the Bolshevik ruling nucleus of the Comintern regarded its theoretical authority as even less open to question than that of the Bolshevik group of 1903, since it had been validated by the great victory of 1917. Neither the resistance of the real movement of the world, and particular of the working-class organizations, to their ideas nor the refutation by the actual course of events of Lenin's theoretical model of the degree of maturity of the revolution in advanced capitalism shook their conviction that they possessed the key to the scientific interpretation of history. This course of events, in their view, could only be a superficial, episodic, deviation from the theoretical predictions which the strategy, internal structures and procedure of the Comintern had been designed to fit. There was no need to reform the new creation; quite the reverse – its ideological purity and organizational structures should be preserved at all costs against the time, not far off, when the world revolution would resume its progress and take on the predicted forms. For these reasons all the movements – and there were many in the early years in various sections of the Comintern – which fought for a degree of political and organizational independence from the Moscow centre were resisted with 'Bolshevik intransigence'. The new orthodox view of world revolution required the retention of the organizational forms of the 'world party', and these in their turn provided ideal protection for the new orthodoxy against the influences of the outside world, which were at this moment openly hostile. This led to a growing stress on the external character, the tendency to substitution, the rigid centralization and hierarchy inherent in the Leninist model of the party. The overall effect was an increasing split between the Comintern and the real world.

7. The groups within the Comintern which were struggling for autonomy found a natural ally in the opposition to Stalin's group within the Bolshevik party. This opposition proclaimed a struggle against bureaucracy and demanded respect for 'Leninist norms', the re-establishment of proletarian democracy, and so on, and therefore after Lenin's death the struggle of Stalin and his allies against Trotskyism and other oppositions within the Bolshevik party was naturally closely linked with the struggle against centrifugal tendencies within the Comintern. This did not exclude, however, indeed, it entailed, episodic alliances with either to defeat whichever seemed at any moment the more dangerous.

For this reason the struggle against the 'left' or the 'right' within the Bolshevik party cannot always be seen to be in step with the struggle against the 'left' or 'right' in a particular section of the International. These labels obscure the real nature of the struggle; though often accompanied by predetermined political positions, it was in fact the working-out of the conflict between the process of centralization in ideology and organization and the centrifugal tendencies. The winning of autonomy became the necessary precondition to the working-out of any policy, revolutionary or reformist, which could have an effect on reality. The policies dictated by Moscow had a peculiarly deadening quality: they were neither revolutionary nor reformist, but abstract and ineffective.

'Bolshevization' meant precisely this. Efforts to win autonomy were to be finally crushed in order to ensure the complete subordination of the Comintern to the Stalinist fraction, which was given an ideological justification by the doctrine of socialism in one country. This sharpened still further the contradiction between the Comintern and the demands of the revolutionary struggle in the different countries. The chapter on the dissolution of the Comintern showed that the arguments with which the executive of the Comintern justified the dissolution in fact admitted that the Comintern had foundered on the 'national factor'. This admission, however, was based solely on the organizational characteristics of the Comintern, and took great care to avoid saying either that these organizational characteristics were an inseparable part of the Leninist conception of the world party, or that the contradiction between the Comintern and the 'national factor' which resulted from this conception became markedly more acute when the Comintern became the unresisting tool of the Stalinist state.

In defence of their abandonment of any form of international revolutionary organization the liquidators of the Comintern pointed to this contradiction between the Comintern and the needs of the revolutionary movement at national level. In fact however, the experience of the Comintern did not prove that there is a contradiction between national requirements and any institutionalized or organized form of internationalism in theory or practice. It demonstrated no more than the failure of the Comintern form, the failure of an external form imposed on the international proletariat and subordinated to the needs of a national state. The failure of this experiment supports the belief that the expression of proletarian internationalism at all levels (theoretical, political, organizational) can only be the organic product of the international revolutionary movement accepted in its diversity. To this possibility Marx's ideas on the First International, which have already been mentioned, remain of great relevance.

The transformation of the Communist International into an alienated and alienating institution, at the service of the new ruling class which established itself on the ruins of the democracy of the soviets, was brought about by the successive elimination of groups, ideas or figures which were sources of conflict within it. This process did not succeed in 're-educating' all the early members of the International, and this is one of the main reasons for the rapid drop in membership. Those who could not be assimilated found themselves expelled or left voluntarily. New recruits entered an environment which was both more conditioned and more conditioning, but a similar process of selection took place among them. This is the source of the enormous fluctuation caused by the entry of members and their departure which all organs of the Comintern incessantly deplored.

Between 1921 and 1928 the Comintern lost more than half its members, which means, given the fluctuation just mentioned, that the great majority of the early militants had abandoned the International or been expelled. They included a sizable proportion of the leading groups in each country. The only member of later intakes who stayed were those whose degree of ideological alienation, unquestioning adherence to dogmas and leaders – nearly always associated with a strong spirit of sacrifice and aggressiveness – was sufficiently 'high'. At the moment of the switch to anti-Fascism the Communist International already possessed all the characteristics of what Marx meant by 'sect'. Marx's own description had referred to the mutualist Proudhonians, the Lassallians and Bakuninists, whom he called a sect which 'tries to assert itself against the real movement of the working class'.[37] Within the International, however, these characteristics were much more strongly developed; the Comintern's internal organization went much further in preserving dogma, making a cult of authority, mechanical discipline and a mania for secrecy.

It was this sect which took in and educated the wave of young people who entered the International in the years of anti-Fascism, and who, like previous intakes, saw in it the banner of October, the custodian of revolutionary Marxism. The new recruits entered the Comintern imbued with a hatred of Fascism and unlimited enthusiasm for the new world which seemed to be rising on the ruins of the Old Russia as one five-year plan followed another. In addition to their hostility to Fascism, the distinctive feature of these new Communists was their total lack of any critical spirit towards anything which carried the Soviet label, a disregard for theory – since all important problems were solved 'from above' – and what was known in party jargon as 'practicism'. Those who were interested in theory drew their basic nourishment from the works of Stalin. No one came to Lenin except through Stalin. Marx came a long way behind, in third place. It was this generation which provided the middle-rank organizers and many of the leaders in the period of the resistance, the liberation, 'national unity', the 'cold war', the People's Democracies, etc. This fact is fundamental to an understanding of the behaviour of most Communist parties after the dissolution of the Comintern.

After all this it is not surprising that the vast majority of Communists in the thirties should have accepted completely the official version of the Moscow trials. Their attitude was encouraged all the more by the coincidence of this acute phase of the Stalinist terror with the great propaganda campaign around the new constitution, which, Stalin claimed, set the seal on 'the epoch-making fact that the USSR had entered a new stage of development, the stage of the completion of the building of a socialist society and the gradual transition to Communist society.'[38] At the very moment that the terror struck Soviet society, Stalin was describing that society as a haven of freedom, whose citizens enjoyed 'freedom of speech, press, assembly . . . inviolability of person, inviolability of domicile and privacy of correspondence and the complete democratization of the electoral system.'

All these freedoms were genuine because they were not vitiated by the exploitation of man by man, but were based on 'socialist ownership of the means of production'. According to Stalinist propaganda, there was no contradiction between this perfect socialist democracy and the elimination of the most representative figures of the Bolshevik old guard since, as history showed, all revolutions have their renegades. Why should it be a matter for surprise that the greatest revolution in history should have the greatest number of 'fiends', 'lackeys of the Fascists' and agents of 'foreign espionage services', to use the scientific Stalinist terms? From the moment at which they became 'enemies of the people', the heroes of the October revolution were transformed, in Stalin's own words, into 'White Guard pigmies' and 'insects'.[39] In the eyes of the world's Communists, only professional slanderers, agents of the bourgeoisie or of Fascism, could cast doubt on Stalin's story. And not only in the eyes of Communists, but also in those of a great body of workers and anti-Fascists, who, while disagreeing about certain aspects of the Soviet regime, nervertheless regarded it as socialist. Could socialism be compatible with lies and crimes as monstrous as those denounced by the Trotskyites, bourgeois liberals, Social Democrats and reactionaries of every type? Communists did not just believe in the Stalinist account of the trials; it became an essential part of their ideological and political formation. Thanks to Stalin, the inspired leader, and to his unfailing vigilance and wisdom, the theory and practice of the working-class movement was being enriched with an understanding of new phenomena – the diabolic means to which the class enemy could resort in his efforts to halt the triumphant march of socialism – phenomena which Marx had not foreseen. Formed in this school, Communists were prepared in advance to 'understand', and 'interpret' to the newcomers who joined the parties in the heat of the victory over Hitler, the repetition of these phenomena in the years of the cold war, the transformation of the leading Communist cadres of the People's Democracies into as many new 'fiends' and agents of all the espionage services of imperialism.

The secret of the Stalinist party's enormous alienating power over successive generations of revolutionaries was its status as the embodiment of a great myth. This myth grew out of the event which, more than any other in the twentieth century, aroused the hopes and illusions of the proletarian masses and all progressive forces, the October revolution. According to the myth, there was being built in the Soviet Union the first society not based on the exploitation of man by man, the first society based on real equality and freedom. This great myth created another, that the Stalinist party was the unchallengeable bearer of revolutionary Marxism. For this reason, even when the crisis of the Stalinist party began to show itself, first in the Communist International and later in the national parties, in the process which has been analysed in this book, the crisis still could not enter its decisive stage until the great myth had been shattered. This is the historic importance of Khruschev's 'secret report'. Khrushchev's report begins the stage of general crisis in the Communist movement, which will be the subject of a subsequent book.

NOTES

5. Revolution and Spheres of Influence

1. Russian abbreviation for 'Communist Parties' Information Office', a body set up in September 1947.

2. The sources for these figures and those given below for Communist Party membership are, where no other indication is given, the book already mentioned in previous chapters, B. Lazitch, *Les Partis communistes d'Europe,* whose data are taken from official documents of the Communist movement, and a work compiled by a team of Soviet authors on the international labour movement and the national liberation movements and used as a textbook in the senior CPSU party school, *Istoria miezhdunarodnovo rabochevo i natsionalno–osvoboditelnovo dvishenia,* Misl, Moscow. The work is in three volumes, and we have used here the third, published in 1966, which covered the period 1939–55. This work will be cited as *History of the Revolutionary Movement (Misl).*

3. Hu Chiao-mu, *Thirty Years of the Communist Party of China,* pp. 76, 88 (for the 1937 and 1945 figures); Mao-Tse-tung, *Selected Works,* Vol. 4, Peking, 1961.

4. By country the increases are as follows:

Austria	16,000 (1935)	150,000 (1948)
Denmark	9,000 (1939)	75,000 (1945)
Norway	5,272 (1933)	45,000 (1946)
Sweden	19,000 (1939)	48,000 (1946)
Finland	1,200 (1944)	150,000 (1946)
Netherlands	10,000 (1938)	33,000 (1946)
Great Britain	17,746 (1939)	47,513 (1944)

I do not know the numbers of membership of the Belgian party before the war, but I do know that they were very low. In November 1945 the party had more than 100,000 militants.

5. See note 45, p, 17, below.

6. From Browder's report of 4 January 1944 to the Central Committee

of the North American Communist Party, as quoted in Jacques Duclos, 'À propos de la dissolution du Parti communiste américain', *Nuestra Bandera* (the journal of the Spanish Communist Party), 3 (1945), Toulouse, pp. 27–8. The report presented by Browder to the new Communist Political Association on 22 May 1944 contains passages such as this: 'We must learn to rise above old divisions and old prejudices, we must promote fraternization between old enemies. We must cross the old frontiers between the parties, we must go beyond the old class antagonisms. We must break down the old hostility between the supporters of the New Deal and the supporters of the old and build a unity stronger than that which has existed until now among American patriots' (*Nuestra Bandera* (1944), 7, Mexico, p. 33). Thanks to this ultra-reformist line, the Communist Political Association was able to increase its membership – according to information supplied by North American Communists, it reached a membership of almost 100,000 – and to exert some influence in some large unions. Browder's line was condemned by Moscow – for reasons which we shall see later – in April 1945, and the Communist Party was re-established in the following months, but a large number of the militants did not return to the party, which rapidly lost its positions in the unions.

7. *The Private Papers of Senator Vandenberg*, Gollancz, London. 1953, p. 219.

8. 'Secret' means that the meeting was not announced in advance, its discussions took place in the strictest secrecy and part of them were never revealed, except by participants who later fell out with Stalin or their own parties (the Yugoslavs and the Italian E. Reale). In early October a short communiqué was issued, announcing that it had taken place, and later the texts of certain reports, suitably revised and corrected, were published.

9. Dimitrov, *Œuvres choisies*, Éditions Sociales, Paris, p. 195.

10. *VIIo Congresso del Partito Communista Italiano* (resoconto), Cultura Sociale, 1951, p. 22.

11. *Histoire du PUF (Unir)*, 1, p. 236. (See Notes, Part 1, p. 47, note 18.) Marcel Cachin's letter to all his 'colleagues' in the Senate on 6 September contained the following passage: 'We repeat that the French Communists are and will be in the front line of the battle to crush the perpetrator of this criminal threat to peace [Hitler]. The Communist deputies liable for military service, led by Maurice Thorez, have already joined their units' (ibid., p. 237). The book describes the discomfiture produced by the German–Soviet pact within the party and among its closest allies. Pierre Cot, for example, stated in the press that Stalin 'had become an ally of Hitler ... Even workers complained to their Communist

comrades about the "Soviet betrayal" ' (ibid., p. 231).

12. Two more factors encouraged repression, the party's lack of preparation for underground activity after twenty years of legal activity in national and local politics, and later, after the defeat, the hope that because of the German–Soviet pact the occupation authorities would show a degree of tolerance towards the party's activities. In May 1941 the party produced a postcard which was to be sent to 'His Excellency Ambassador Otto Abetz', Hitler's official representative with the Vichy government, which carried the following printed text:

'Your Excellency,

'For opposing the war and insisting, from October 1939 onwards, that no peace offer should be rejected without being discussed in parliament, Communist deputies have been sentenced to hundreds of years in prison and treated as German agents.

'Among them, the following are imprisoned in the Maison-Carrée (Algeria) and threatened with deportation into the Saharan wilderness: [there follows a list of deputies, followed by another list of those] who are obliged to live in a state of illegality in order to carry out the mandate entrusted to them by the people [Thorez and the others, followed by a list of those in the Santé prison in Paris. The text continues] The Communist deputies count it an honour to have been against war after fighting for twenty years against the detestable Versailles Treaty, and opposing the occupation of the Rhineland and the Ruhr, actions for which they suffered imprisonment.

'This is a scandal and an injustice. Their liberation is urgent.

'Your Excellency, it is your duty to use all your powers to obtain their early release.

'Failing this, the people will rise and restore them to liberty.'

This text requires no commentary, but the most extraordinary aspect of the affair is that party militants and sympathizers were advised to sign these postcards with their names and give their addresses – still according to the *Histoire*. Signatories of this card paid with their liberty, and even their lives, for following this advice (ibid., p. 50).

Another example of illusions on the sympathetic attitude to be expected from the German occupation authorities was the attempt to publish *L'Humanité* legally. This is described in detail in the relevant volume of the history of the PCF (see Vol. 11, pp 24–8). The leadership of the PCF tried for a long time to hide this fact, right up to the recent publication of the history of the party in the resistance edited by a commission chaired by

Jacques Duclos, when it was at last admitted.

The authors of the *Histoire du PCF (Unir)* interpret these attempts to legalize *L'Humanité*, and other similar moves made by the party leadership at this period, as proof that 'the executive of the Communist International, misled by Stalin, hoped to see the Communist parties allowed to undertake legal activity in the countries occupied by Hitler's armies' (Vol. 11, p. 23).

13. *Histoire du PCF (Unir)*, 11, 59–61, 68. The official history of the PCF in the resistance (*Le Parti communiste français dans la Résistance,* Éditions Sociales, 1967), mentioned in note 12, does not mention this document, or a number of other documents and facts refered to in the *Histoire du PCF (Unir)*.

14. ibid.

15. *Histoire du PCF (Unir)*, 11, p. 60.

16. André Fontaine, *History of the Cold War: From the October Revolution to the Korean War, 1917–1950*, Secker and Warburg, New York and London, 1968, p. 195.

17. *Histoire du PCF (Unir)*, 11, pp. 134, 136. *Le Parti communiste français dans la Résistance* mentions that contacts between the party and representatives of de Gaulle were established as early as the summer of 1942, that is, very shortly after the de Gaulle–Molotov meeting, but the book does not indicate the importance of that meeting. De Gaulle's letter to the party leadership is published, but with the omission of the passage in which de Gaulle expresses his confidence that the party will show him the same 'loyal discipline' which operates in its own ranks. Nor is there any mention of Fernand Grenier's article in *L'Humanité*.

18. *Le PCF dans la Résistance*, pp. 234–6.

19. See Jacques Fauvet, *Histoire du PCF* (already referred to in previous chapters), 11, pp. 127–8. According to this version, the party finally entered the government without securing the slightest formal compromise between de Gaulle and itself, and *Le PCF dans la Résistance* implicitly confirms this claim by its silence about any compromise, which would certainly have been mentioned if it had existed (see pp. 237–8).

20. *Le PCF dans la Résistance*, pp. 241–2.

21. *Le PCF dans la Résistance* (pp. 286–328) contains a detailed account of the national rising which shows clearly that a large part of the territory of France was liberated by the action of 'the mass of the people, armed and unarmed' (p. 329). Eisenhower compared the contribution of the French resistance fighters to the efforts of the allied forces which landed in Normandy to the action of fifteen divisions. This military equivalence, however, takes into account the armed actions of the resist-

ance only in coordination with the allied offensive. It does not consider the cumulative effect on the morale and strength of the occupiers of the four years of action by the partisans and political activity, which increased in geometric progression. Nor does it reflect the effect of the massive political rising which followed the landings.

22. On what the PCF stood for on the eve of the liberation, Jacques Fauvet says that it was, 'of the resistance movements in France itself, the most powerful, the most persistent and the only one to cover the whole country' (*Histoire du PCF*, II, p. 59). And of the Liberation itself, André Fontaine says, 'power was in its reach in various parts of the country' (op. cit., p. 197).

23. De Gaulle, *War Memoirs: Unity*, Weidenfeld and Nicolson, London, 1955, pp. 292–3.

24. There is a reference to Duclos' speech in *L'Histoire du PCF(Unir)*, II, p. 246. The account given in this work, written by party militants who at this time occupied responsible positions and were far removed from any sort of 'leftism', makes it clear, beyond any ambiguity, that the mass of the party membership and the popular masses in general brought strong pressure to bear on the party leadership to give its policy an offensive character. A tendency was developing within the committees of liberation to insist on their role as organs of power. In October 1944 delegates from the committees of liberation of forty *départements* in the south of France met at Avignon and decided to invite local committees 'to call patriotic assemblies in the towns and villages at which the action programme of the National Council of the Resistance will be explained and worked out in detail to fit local conditions, and the composition and actions of the local committees will be submitted to popular ratification'. On 9 and 10 December the local committees of liberation of the Seine, at a meeting in the Hôtel de Ville in Paris, followed the initiative from the south with the proposal that the popular patriotic assemblies should prepare huge Estates General representing all sections of the population. Meetings of the Estates General took place later in Paris, but the movement died as a result of the party leadership's general line, which, as we shall see later, required the strict subordination of the committees of liberation to the central government.

25. *Histoire du PCF (Unir)*, II, pp. 247–51. According to the authors of this work, Thorez never refuted these allegations – and many others – from de Gaulle's memoirs.

26. M. Thorez, *Œuvres*, Vol. 20, pp. 181–2, 187–8.

27. De Gaulle explained his journey as follows: 'To obtain from the Communist Party the year's respite I needed to take the situation in hand,

I was obliged to go to Moscow and sign an agreement there' (quoted by Fauvet, op. cit., p. 148). As Fauvet very accurately remarks, this cannot have been the only explanation for the journey, but it was no doubt one of its main purposes. But I can find no evidence for Fauvet's view that Thorez, when he reached France, favoured increasing the power of the committees of liberation, and retaining the militias, etc., and changed his line only after de Gaulle's meeting with Stalin. In fact, as soon as he had reached France (and even before, in his statements on Radio Moscow), Thorez supported the abolition of the independent power which had arisen from the resistance and the liberation to make way for the restoration of the old bourgeois democratic state. His formula, 'One state, one police force, one army', which he launched immediately on his return, is a sufficiently eloquent proof of this (*Histoire du PCF (Unir)*, 11, p. 247). But prudence was necessary in the country, given the state of mind dominant both in the party and in the people. Thorez began by praising the role of the committees of liberation, but insisting at the same time that they should obey the organs of the new state. This was the argument of his speech to the meeting at the Vélodrome d'Hiver on 14 December 1944. He used the de Gaulle–Stalin agreement to harden this political line and give it the final, clear public form it took at the January meeting of the Central Committee.

28. On Benoît Frachon's reports, see *Histoire du PCF (Unir)*, 11, pp. 262–4.

29. See Thorez, *Œuvres*, Vol. 21, pp. 57, 100, 118, 127–9, and Vol. 20, p. 183.

30. Thorez, *Œuvres choisies* (1966), Vol. 2, p. 399.

31. Thorez, *Œuvres*, Vol. 22, p. 141.

32. This is the version given by Fauvet, *Histoire du PCF*, 11, p. 172.

33. De Gaulle, op. cit.

34. Thorez, *Œuvres*, Vol. 22, p. 105.

35. The authors of *L'Histoire du PCF (Unir)* give the following version of the negotiations between the PCF and the SFIO on the problem of unity between the two parties. In November 1944 the SFIO published a resolution containing the following statement: 'The Socialist Party solemnly renews the offer of unity already made to the French Communist Party during the underground struggle.' Shortly afterwards a 'committee of understanding' was formed, the main task of which was to draw up a memorandum to prepare the way for Socialist–Communist unity. The proposals of the Communist delegates to this committee showed a formal intransigence which contrasted with the concessions of principle which they accepted to stay on good terms with General de

Gaulle and take part in the government. They even insisted that the charter of unity with the Socialists should contain a paragraph giving unconditional approval to the position of the USSR and recognizing the supremacy of the Communist Party (Bolsheviks). In short, the Socialists were required to become Communists, faithful to the Soviet Communist Party and Stalin (op. cit., 11, pp. 254–5).

36. Thorez, *Œuvres*, Vol. 22, p. 207.

37. ibid., p. 132.

38. 40,000, according to the *History of the Revolutionary Movement (Misl)* see above, p. 1, note 2. The authors of this work refer to the crushing of the Algerian rising by the French imperialists without mentioning the presence of Communist ministers in the government.

39. Thorez, *Œuvres choisies*, Vol. 2, pp. 351–2. (The mention of Arles is an allusion to the Ninth Congress of the PCF, which was held in this town before the war.)

40. Fauvet, op. cit., 11, pp. 194–5. The attempt to make 'Vietnamese troublemakers' responsible for the war is mentioned in *L'Histoire du PCF(Unir)*, 111, p. 31. As everyone knows, the independence of Vietnam and the proclamation of the Democratic Republic over the whole territory of the country were the result of the victorious popular rising, led by the Communist Party, in August 1945. French colonialist aggression began, in effect, in the autumn of the same year. French troops, who had landed on the pretext of disarming the Japanese, reoccupied Saigon and forced the Republican authorities to take refuge in rural areas. During the whole of 1946 provocations and measures intended to restore the colonial regime followed rapidly. The shelling of Haiphong, which caused 6,000 deaths, marks the transition to open war.

41. See Fauvet, op. cit., 11, p. 195.

42. On 29 March 1947, in order to crush the national liberation movement in Madagascar, the French authorities provoked bloody clashes. The people replied with uprisings in a number of places on the island. The rising was brutally suppressed and several leaders of the liberation movement, including four deputies to the French parliament, were sentenced to death.

43. Thorez, *Œuvres*, Vol. 21, pp. 63–4 (report to the Tenth Congress, June 1945); *Œuvres choisies*, Vol. 2, p. 452; *Œuvres*, Vol. 23, pp. 10, 115.

44. Thorez, *Œuvres*, Vol. 23, p. 9. The quotation from Léon Blum is taken from Fauvet, op. cit., 11, p. 185. On the same page of Fauvet's book there is a reference to an article in the issue of *Cahiers du communisme* of 17 July 1946 criticizing the Socialists for giving priority to the demands of

'internationalism' in their approach to the German problem when 'in the present period the problems must first be solved from the French national point of view.'

45. Quoted by Fauvet, op. cit., II, p. 198.

46. Thorez, *Œuvres*, Vol. 23, pp. 121–2 (speech to the assembly of the Seine federation of the PCF).

47. Quoted by Fauvet, op. cit., II, p. 199.

49. Togliatti, *Le Parti communiste italien*, Maspero, Paris, 1961, pp. 109–10.

50. R. Battaglia, *Storia della Resistenza italiana*, Einaudi, Turin, 1955, p. 83.

51. See R. Battaglia and G. Garritano, *Breve storia della Resistenza italiana*, Editori Riuniti, Rome, 1965, p. 36.

52. Luigi Longo's report to the founding conference of the Cominform, in *Conferencia de información de los representantes de algunos partidos communistas*, Moscow, 1948, pp. 227–8. (This will be cited in future as *Cominform Conference 1947*.)

53. See, for example, Henri Michel, *Les Mouvements clandestins en Europe*, PUF, Paris, 1965, pp. 47–8. In his speech on the thirty-fifth anniversary of the PCI, Togliatti refers to this period in the following terms: 'In 1943, in March, the workers of Turin began to strike to defend themselves against terrible exploitation and fight the Fascist war policy. The movement, I remind you, was prepared, organized in all its stages and led by Communists, by the comrades who made up the internal centre of the party, here in Italy, led by Comrade Massola. This strike was one of the fatal blows dealt to the Fascist regime. When this regime finally collapsed, on 25 July, and we saw all the old foundations of the bourgeois state, including its military organization, also collapse, there began the largest movement of popular insurrection in the history of Italy. The people took the initiative, took the future of the country into their own hands. They organized, formed an army, chose leaders, fought to save their country from destruction and catastrophe. Oh yes, it was we who were in the lead then, out in front, we Communists, old fighters and new' (Togliatti, '35 années de lutte pour la liberté et le socialisme', *Cahiers du Parti communiste italien*, section pour l'étranger, 1956, pp. 14–15).

54. Togliatti, 'L'Italie en guerre contre l'Allemagne', *Pravda*, 12 November 1943. The text is taken from the *Selected Works* of Togliatti published in Russian by the Political Literature Publishing House,

Moscow, 1965, Vol. 1, p. 274. In his article Togliatti did not mention the fact that the three-power declaration on Italy contained a provision that as long as the war lasted all real power would be in the hands of the allied military authorities. The Italian people's right to elect its government democratically was deferred until victory.

55. Quoted by Pietro Secchia, 'Movimento operario e lotta di classe alla Fiat nel periodo de la Resistenza', *Rivista storica del socialismo*, 22 (1964).

56. Lelio Basso, in an article written in 1965, refers to a meeting in Milan shortly before the fall of Mussolini attended by representatives of the Communist, Socialist, Action and Christian Democrat Parties. 'I remember the embarrassment of Comrade Marchesi (a PCI representative) as he read a document devoted entirely to giving guarantees to the bourgeoisie against any disturbance of the social order (it was even concerned to soothe the industrialists by saying that the anti-Fascist government would compensate them for war damage), and I recall the Christian Democrat representative's naïve comment after listening to the document, "Now we Christian Democrats are farther left than the Communists!" ' (Lelio Basso, 'Il rapporto tra rivoluzione democratica e rivoluzione socialista nella Resistenza', *Critica Marxista*, July–August 1965).

57. From the time of the occupation of northern and central Italy by German troops there were three committees of liberation with national status, a northern one, one based in Rome and in theory the supreme authority but in practice unable to control the movement in the central area, and one in Naples.

58. Marcella and Maurizio Ferrara, *Palmiro Togliatti*, Éditions Sociales, Paris, 1954, p. 339. This book was revised and corrected by Togliatti himself, and compiled from conversations with him and PCI documents. Its contents must therefore be regarded as Togliatti's opinions on the events in question.

59. M. and M. Ferrara, op. cit., p. 340.

60. The account which describes former leaders of the PCI as offering some resistance to Togliatti's arguments comes from officials of the foreign section of the CPSU at a time when the Cominform had just been set up and the policy followed by the PCI had been criticized in Cominform meetings.

61. M. and M. Ferrara, op. cit., p. 350.

62. *Bol'shaya Sovyetskayta Entsiklopediya*, 19, p. 86. In the account of contemporary history used as a textbook in the CPSU higher party school, the matter is put with even greater precision: 'At the wish of the

Soviet government, the Consultative Committee for Italy (composed of representatives of the USSR, the United States, Great Britain and France) adopted a special resolution on the immediate formation by Marshal Badoglio of a government with representation from all the anti-Fascist parties' (*Noveishaya Istoriya*, Part 11, Moscow, 1959, p. 582).

63. A short account of the pressure brought to bear on Tito by Stalin will be found below, in the section on the Yugoslav revolution.

64. M. and M. Ferrara, op. cit., p. 362.

65. Togliatti, 'La politica di unità nazionale dei communisti' (speech made on 11 April 1944), *Critica Marxista*, July–October 1964, p. 24.

66. Togliatti, 'Avanti, verso la democrazia!' (speech of 24 September 1944), ibid., p. 74.

67. Battaglia and Garritano, op. cit., p. 192.

68. M and M. Ferrara, op. cit., p. 369.

69. M. and M. Ferrara, op. cit., pp. 369, 371–2.

70. M. and M. Ferrara, op. cit., p. 369 (my italics).

71. Togliatti, *Selected Works* (in Russian, see note 54), Vol. 1, p. 379.

72. See Battaglia and Garritano, op. cit., p. 189.

73. ibid., p. 91.

74. ibid., pp. 202–3.

75. Taking advantage of a hard winter, the enemy used large numbers of troops in an effort to isolate the partisan units in the high mountains and cut them off from their supply bases. The partisans decided to infiltrate through the enemy units and go down towards the plains. This tactic of *pianurizzazione* (from *pianura*, 'plain') gave very good results, and increased the forces available for armed struggle in the industrial centres and big factories.

76. Longo's report, *Cominform Conference 1947*, pp. 228–9.

77. ibid., p. 230.

78. *Noveishaya Istoriya*, p. 538.

79. Togliatti, 'Rinnovare L'Italia' (report to the Fifth Congress of the PCI), *Critica Marxista*, July–October 1964, p. 66.

80. The 'management committees' were formed by a decree of the national liberation committee for northern Italy just before the rising. They were bodies representing the workers, management staff and technicians, and their task was to run firms in collaboration with government commissioners and the owners. (See Longo's report cited above, note 76.)

81. *Rinascita*, 5–6 (May–June 1945) (my italics).

82. Togliatti, 'Rinnovare l'Italia', p. 99.

83. Marcella and Maurizio Ferrara, *Cronache di vita italiana (1944–1948)*, Editori Riuniti, Rome, 1960. The quotation is from the French translation of Chapters 7 and 8, which appeared in *Recherches Internationales*, 44–5 (1964), p. 205.

84. Togliatti was Minister of Justice from the liberation to the elections of 2 June 1946. The main problem of this ministry was the purging and punishment of Fascist activists. The party's policy on the matter, which was quite correct, was to concentrate efforts on the real culprits, the upper ranks. This was rarely possible, however, because the bourgeois forces and the allies used every means to sabotage the purge. Nor did the party put up much of a fight against this sabotage. Even a historian of Christian Democracy like Maurice Vaussard admits this: 'If the purge was superficial – and it was seriously so especially in the south – this must have been partly as a result of the presence and influence of the allied armies, of the opposition of right-wing liberal circles, but also to the extraordinary indulgence shown by the men appointed to carry out the purge, and in the first place Togliatti and Nenni themselves, who held the post successively. They probably realized that in spite of their wishes it would have been impossible to find better replacements in the posts thus made vacant. Successive amnesties did the rest and allowed the worst enemies of democracy, such as Prince Valerio Borghese or the diplomat Anfuso, one of the European leaders of the neo-Nazi movement, to re-emerge' (M. Vaussard, *Histoire de la Démocratie-chrétienne*, Éditions du Seuil, Paris, 1956, pp. 275–6).

85. Emilio Sereni, *Il mezzogiorno all'opposizione*, Einaudi, Turin, 1948, p. 60.

86. Togliatti, *Selected Works* (Russian), I, p. 463.

87. Vaussard, op. cit., p. 275. 'Tripartism' was the system under which governments were made up mainly of Christian Democrats, Communists and Socialists.

88. Vaussard, op. cit., pp. 274, 276.

89. Togliatti's biographers admit that the 'social content added to the constitution [was added] as a result of an agreement with part of the Christian Democratic party' (M. and M. Ferrara, *Togliatti*, 389).

90. The most 'advanced' social principles contained in the Italian constitution are the following: 'Italy is a democratic Republic, based on work' (Article 1); 'It is the duty of the Republic to remove economic and social obstacles which, by limiting in practice the liberty and quality of citizens, prevent the complete development of the human personality and the

genuine participation of all workers in the political, economic and social organization of the country' (Article 3); 'The worker has a right to payment in proportion to the quantity and quality of his work; in all cases this payment must be sufficient to ensure him and his family a free and dignified existence' (Article 36). According to Togliatti, these 'fundamental principles' written into the constitution 'mean a transformation of the old economic and political system of Italy' and 'Point to a path of development in the direction of socialism' (Togliatti, *Le Parti communiste italien,* p. 128).

It should be explained that this 'path of development in the direction of socialism' was approved by the party which represented mainly the upper Italian bourgeoisie and the Vatican six months after it had forced the Communist ministers out of the government. Examination of the various articles, and especially of the first, shows that this 'social content' rested – as was also the case with the Spanish constitution of 1931 – on an equivocation, in that the terms 'work' and 'worker' were used indiscriminately for the worker and the capitalist, the working peasant and the big landowner, and their respective 'work'. This ambiguity is brought out very clearly by a collection of essays on the Italian constitution published by Cahiers de la Fondation Nationale des Sciences Politiques, Paris, 1950.

91. Togliatti, 'Rinnovare l'Italia', pp. 115-17.

92. *Recherches Internationales*, 44–45, Paris, 1964, p. 228.

93. ibid., p. 227.

94. Quoted by M. and M. Ferrara, *Togliatti*, pp. 388-9.

95. E. Reale, *Avec Jacques Duclos au banc des accusés à la réunion constitutive du Cominform*, Plon, Paris, 1959, p. 4.

96. ibid., p. 135.

97. V. Dedijer, *Tito Speaks*, Weidenfeld and Nicolson, London, 1953, p. 304.

98. The brief analysis which follows of the policy of the Yugoslav Communists and Stalin's intervention is based mainly on Kardelj's report to the founding meeting of the Cominform on the activity of the Yugoslav party (*Cominform Conference 1947*, pp. 41–69), Dedijer's book (*Tito Speaks*), and Ferenc Fejtő, *Histoire des démocraties populaires*, Éditions du Seuil, Paris, 1969, I, pp. 66-9. I have also taken account of the Soviet version as represented by the textbook mentioned in note 2, p. 1, above. The Soviet version contains no mention of Stalin's intervention to change the revolutionary line of the Yugoslavs' policy at this period, though it implicitly admits that that policy was right.

It is interesting to note that No. 44–45 of *Recherches Internationales*, which appeared in 1964 and was devoted to the period between the liberation and the beginning of the 'cold war', contains essays on France, Italy, Hungary, Bulgaria, Czechoslovakia and the rest, but not a line about Yugoslavia. The French Communist Party prefers not to remember the example of the Yugoslav people's revolutionary struggle at the time of the liberation. The contrast with the policy followed by the PCF would be too brutal.

99. In his report (mentioned in the previous note), Kardelj describes how, as early as the end of 1941 and the beginning of 1942, the headquarters of the partisan forces began to select the best units and the best men and put them into tactical brigades, not tied to a particular area but capable of being fitted into a single plan of operations. These brigades later became divisions and army corps. By its discipline, military experience, fighting power and military methods, this revolutionary regular army was quite separate from the partisan formations, although these continued to play a very important role. The combination of the two forms of struggle was one of the characteristics of the Yugoslav revolutionary war. The Yugoslav people were facing an enemy no less strong than in France or Italy. The Germans always used strong forces, including Italian, Bulgarian and other foreign troops, the armed forces of the various puppet authorities in the pay of the occupier, and Mihailović's Chetniks.

1. Dedijer, *Tito Speaks*, p. 178.
2. ibid., p. 179.
3. ibid., p. 207.
4. ibid., p. 208.
5. Fejtő, op. cit., p. 79; Dedijer, op. cit., pp. 220–24.
6. The account of the meeting between Stalin and Tito comes from Dedijer, op. cit., pp. 232–5. On the allocation of 'spheres of influence' in the Balkans, see p. 17, note 45, below.
7. Dedijer, op. cit., p. 237.
8. Fejtő, op. cit., p. 83.
9. Quoted by Basile Darivas, 'De la résistance à la guerre civile en Grèce', *Recherches Internationales*, 44–45 (1964). Churchill's telegram is reproduced on p. 268 of the journal. It is interesting to note that this PCF journal quotes Churchill's evidence that Stalin had left him 'a free hand in Greece' without making the slightest objection to its accuracy.

10. The Eighth Congress of the Greek Communist Party made the following list of errors made in 1944 and the beginning of 1945:

'(1) *The Lebanon agreement* in May 1944, by which we made unacceptable concessions which materially assisted the British imperialists and the rich Greek oligarchy to restore the old system and prevent the Greek people from deciding its future.

'(2) *The Caserta agreement*, which placed the Greek armed forces under the command of the British General Scobie.

'(3) The absence of political, ideological, organizational and military preparation by the party leadership for the *December battle* forced on us by the British imperialists and their servants.

'(4) *The Varkiza agreement*, which was an unacceptable compromise amounting to a capitulation to the British imperialists and Greek reaction.' (*Eighth Congress of the GPC* (in Greek), Paris, 1961, p. 99.)

11. Quoted by André Kedros, *La Résistance grecque*, Laffont, Paris, 1967.

12. See above, notes 95 and 98, for references to the book by E. Reale, Kardelj's report and Dedijer's books on Tito. Without mentioning the French and Italian Communist Parties by name, Kardelj's report, by defending the policy of the Yugoslav Communists, constitutes an implicit criticism of the other parties. There is basic agreement between this indirect criticism and the version of the direct criticism given by Reale's notes.

13. Kardelj's report, *Cominform Conference 1947*, p. 52.

14. Gomulka's report on the activity of the Polish party, *Cominform Conference 1947*, p. 79.

15. Dedijer gives the following account of the reactions of Duclos and Longo to the Yugoslav criticisms, which, as we have seen, were 'supported' by Zhdanov: 'Duclos and Longo reacted differently to the attitude of the Yugoslav delegation: Duclos was angry, and huffily refused to speak to anyone. After the meeting he withdrew into the park and sat on a bench alone, restlessly swinging his short legs, which did not reach the ground. Longo, on the contrary, asked for a meeting with the Yugoslav delegation to hear their criticism in more detail. As to the Italian party's war-time policy, he said, it had acted on Moscow's instructions' (*Tito Speaks*, p. 305).

16. See pp. 20–32.

17. See the sub-sections 'Stalin as Revisionist' and 'The People's Front Experience', above, pp. 71 ff. and 166 ff.

14

18. See the sub-section 'The Last Act', above, pp. 294 ff.

19. 'Notes et études documentaires' (*Documentation française*, 5 May 1951, p. 6). For Elliott Roosevelt's interview with Marshal Stalin of 21 December 1946, see the *Daily Mail* of 22 January 1947.

20. Nine-party statement, *Cominform Conference 1947*, p. 6.

21. Stalin, *War Speeches, Orders of the Day and Answers to Foreign Press Correspondents During the Great Patriotic War, July 3rd, 1941 – June 22nd, 1945*, Hutchinson, London, 1946, p. 112.

22. Zhdanov's report, *Cominform Conference 1947*, pp. 12–14.

23. *Cominform Conference 1947*, pp. 7 and 22.

24. Ministry of Foreign Affairs of the USSR, *Stalin's Correspondence with Churchill, Attlee, Roosevelt and Truman 1941–1945*, London, 1958, II, p. 202 (a personal and strictly secret message from Roosevelt to Stalin, received by Stalin on 1 April 1945). André Fontaine mentions this message of Roosevelt's (op. cit., p. 236).

25. When General de Gaulle reaffirmed his well-known position on the division of 'spheres of influence' which took place at Yalta, the State Department published a communiqué on 25 August 1968 claiming that at the Crimea Conference 'there had been no discussion, either direct or indirect, of spheres of influence'. *Le Monde* of 25–26 August 1968 tried to support the State Department's view by publishing the complete text of the Yalta agreements, which – like all the public agreements of the three great powers – include among their aims that of concealing from the peoples the reality of this 'division'. They do this both by ambiguous expressions when the text explicitly mentions some aspects of this 'division' and also by ignoring the secret agreements made during the Conference. An example of the first technique is the reference to Yugoslavia in the official text of the Yalta agreements, which states that the three great powers agreed to recommend Tito and Šubašić to put into immediate effect the agreement made between them (which has been mentioned above), but gives no hint that this agreement was forced on the Yugoslavs by secret pressure from Stalin on one side and Roosevelt and Churchill on the other, under the terms of the secret division of 'spheres of influence' in Yugoslavia agreed between Stalin and Churchill in October 1944. The same could be said about Poland and many other cases. What is strange is that Communists should read the official texts of Yalta or other 'Big Three' conferences in the same way as the State Department. And yet this is the approach of Sergio Segre, for example, in his essay in *Critica Marxista* of 4 May 1968, and E. Ragionieri,

in his preface to a book published in 1965 by Editori Riuniti which contains the official accounts of the 'Big Three' meetings at Teheran and Yalta.

26. Deborin, *La segunda guerra mundial*, Spanish edn, Moscow, 1961, p. 214.

27. Eden, *The Reckoning*, Cassell, London and New York, 1965, p. 296; cf. Fontaine, op. cit., p. 179.

28. *History of the International Working-Class Movement*, textbook of the CPSU higher party school (see above, p. 1, note 2), pp. 43–4.

29. See above, p. 321.

30. Fontaine, op. cit., p. 182.

31. Quoted by Pierre Broué, *Le Parti bolchevique*, Éditions de Minuit, Paris, 1963, pp. 433–4.

32. Trotsky, *The Revolution Betrayed*, Faber and Faber, London, 1937, p. 189.

33. Quoted by Broué, op. cit., pp. 434–5.

34. See p. 8, note 53, above, for Togliatti's description of the mass movement, the partisan movement and the crisis of the Italian state at this period.

35. See Fontaine, op. cit., p. 188. Stalin's joke is quoted in Churchill's *History of the Second World War*, Vol. 5, p. 72. The 'Father of the Peoples' did not realize how right he was.

36. Deborin, op. cit., pp. 371 and 399. Deborin bases his account on the memoirs of Cordell Hull, the Secretary of State at the time. According to Hull, at the Quebec Conference Churchill pleaded for the opening of a second front in the Balkans since 'a Soviet rush' into this area would threaten important 'English and North American interests' (Hull, *Memoirs*, Hodder and Stoughton, London, 1948, p. 1231.

37. Stalin, *War Speeches*, pp. 94–5, 111.

38. Editorial in *Nuestra Bandera*, journal of the Spanish Communist Party, 30 June 1944.

39. I. Maisky, 'Le Problème du second front', *Recherches Internationales*, 9–10, Paris, 1958, p. 239.

40. *Bol'shaya Sovyetskaya Entsiklopediya*, 7, p. 181.

41. Deborin, op. cit., p. 425.

42. Roosevelt's son records that the president expressed this view at the Cairo Conference, in a conversation with the British Prime Minister (22 November 1943) (Elliott Roosevelt, *As He Saw It*, Duell, Sloan and Pearce, New York, 1946, p. 156).

43. US Department of State, *The Conferences of Malta and Yalta*, Washington, 1959, pp. 539 ff.

44. Stalin, *War Speeches*, pp. 94–5.

45. The division of Europe into 'spheres of influence' was of course generally made with due regard for the diplomatic forms appropriate to the conditions of the Second World War; in other words, it was justified by reference to respect for the independence of nations, the right of peoples to decide their futures for themselves, and so on. On occasion, however, more direct language was used. The following is one example. It is Churchill's account of his conversation with Stalin on 9 October 1944.

'The moment was apt for business, so I said, "Let us settle about our affairs in the Balkans. Your armies are in Romania and Bulgaria. We have interests, missions and agents there. Don't let us get at cross-purposes in small ways. So far as Britain and Russia are concerned, how would it do for you to have ninety per cent predominance in Romania, for us to have ninety per cent of the say in Greece, and go fifty-fifty about Yugoslavia?" While this was being translated I wrote out on a half-sheet of paper:

Romania	
Russia	90%
The others	10%
Greece	
Great Britain	90%
(in accord with USA)	
Russia	10%
Yugoslavia	50–50%
Hungary	50–50%
Bulgaria	
Russia	75%
The others	25%

'I pushed this across to Stalin, who had by then heard the translation. There was a slight pause. Then he took his blue pencil and made a large tick upon it, and passed it back to us. It was all settled in no more time than it takes to set down.

'... After this there was a long silence. The pencilled paper lay in the centre of the table. At length I said, "Might it not be thought rather cynical if it seemed we had disposed of these issues, so fateful to millions of people in such an offhand manner? Let us burn the paper." "No, you keep it," said Stalin.' (Churchill, op. cit., VI, p. 19).

The discussion about the second front raised the question of the 'division' once more. The English insisted throughout the war on the opening of a second front in the Balkans, for easily intelligible reasons. The Soviets opposed this equally firmly, for just as understandable reasons. Both sides put forward arguments of military effectiveness, but the real issue was which zones would remain under the control of each side.

It should be emphasized that the Russians have never denied Churchill's version. André Fontaine points out (op. cit., p. 246) that the Russian edition of the secret correspondence between the 'Big Three' omits a message from Churchill to Stalin bluntly reminding the Russians of the division of 'zones of influence' in the Balkans agreed to in October 1944. The Russian edition does, however, include a message from Churchill to Stalin dated 28 April 1945, which included the following: 'I must also say that the course of events in Yugoslavia is not such as corresponds to the division of interests of our countries in the proportion of 50:50.' Stalin's reply makes no objection to this complaint of Churchill's.

46. Stalin, *War Speeches*, p. 111.

47. See above, p. 380.

48. See Fontaine, op. cit., p. 220.   It was in the interests of the Labour opposition to exploit the events in Greece, with an eye to the approaching elections. After beating Churchill, Labour followed the same policy in Greece. The American leaders were already preparing to get the British out of Greece in order to take their place.

49. On the eve of the liberation EAM (the National Liberation Front) had more than 1,500,000 men and women organized in its ranks. Describing the fighting in Athens, Fontaine says: 'ELAS was only a hairsbreadth from victory. . . At Christmas [Churchill] himself landed in Athens, unaware that by so doing he himself guaranteed the defeat of the ELAS rising. ELAS had in fact planned to blow up the Hotel Great Britain on that day – it was the seat of the Anglo-Greek military staff and of Papandreou's "government", whose authority extended at most a few hundred square yards outside that building. A general attack was to follow in order to take advantage of the confusion created by the explosion.

ELAS renounced its plan because of Churchill's presence and because he had agreed to confer with ELAS representatives' (op. cit., p. 216). What really destroyed EAM was the eagerness of the leaders of the Greek Communist Party to find a compromise with Churchill, thus adapting to Stalin's policy.

50. According to the Soviet historians, the German plan was to take the port of Antwerp, an essential supply base for the allied armies, and cut off and destroy the most important of these armies, so making the Allies' planned offensive impossible.

51. *Stalin's Correspondence with Churchill etc.*, I, p. 295.

52. Guderian, *Panzer Leader*, Michael Joseph, London, 1952, p. 393.

53. Deborin, op. cit., p. 425. Soviet historians, logically enough, use secret documents and the memoirs of the main British and American participants in these events the evidence of which confirms that these were in fact the Allies' aims. The Soviet historians, however, use these sources only as confirmation. The real basis of the analysis of the Soviet official history is facts and actions witnessed by Stalin and the Soviet leaders during the war, and the interpretation then given to these facts and actions in the light of the class interests represented by the British and American leaders. Take for example one of the most representative presentations of the official point of view, Deborin's book, which we have frequently cited, written in collaboration with Major-General I. Zubkov. (References are to the Spanish edition.)

On pp. 337ff. there is an analysis of the Allies' operational plans for 1942 in North Africa, Italy and the Balkans. This shows that a simple examination of the American press made it possible to see behind these plans the interests of the monopolist groups of the two countries. On p. 344 we find mention of 'the support of the United States for French reaction, the lackeys of Nazi Germany', in North Africa after the landings. On p. 350 there is a reference to Walter Lippmann's 1943 articles in which the idea of an 'Atlantic community' as an instrument of the United States' world domination was launched. The open protection given to France by the London and Washington governments, on the basis of information publicly available at the time is noted on p. 354. On p. 395 the control set up by the allied military authorities in the liberated areas of southern Italy is described as a colonial system. On p. 399 it is explained that the Soviet delegation at the Teheran Conference opposed British plans for a landing in the Balkans because their real aim – as Deborin has explained on pp. 337 ff. – was 'to impose on these peoples the colonial rule of British imperialism and re-establish the anti-Soviet *cordon sanitaire*'. The passage quoted in the text about the Allies' real aims in the Normandy landings comes from p. 425. On pp. 474 ff. there is a very sharp criticism of British intervention in Greece, which records that 'the occupation of Greece by British troops aroused deep indignation in democratic opinion throughout the world'. (We may note in passing one significant detail. Deborin quotes no evidence – and he would certainly have done so if he could – of the way in which this general indignation was reflected in the Soviet press or Soviet official documents.)

54. Stalin must have known about the transport of troops into Greece by Italy's allies, for there was a Soviet military mission in Athens close to the headquarters of the British expeditionary force.

55. Deborin, op. cit., p. 485.

56. Deborin, op. cit., p. 481.

57. Engels, 'The Question of What is Really Happening in Turkey'.

58. See above, p. 378.

59. F. Fejtő, op. cit., 1, p. 57, gives the following details of the 'rapid and brutal Sovietization' of eastern Poland immediately after its occupation by Soviet troops in 1939: suppression of all Polish, Ukrainian, Byelorussian and Jewish political parties; the arrest of thousands of Socialists and members of the Agrarian Party; the deportation of 1,200,000 Polish citizens, in addition to the 250,000 soldiers of the Polish army taken prisoner and interned. The Polish deportees were released after the German attack on the USSR, but 200,000 of them had disappeared. Some of the political leaders released in 1941 were rearrested, among them two of the principal leaders of the Jewish Socialist Party, the *Bund*, Henryk Erlich and Victor Adler. These two leaders had sought refuge in eastern Poland when the west was occupied by the Nazis. In 1941 they accepted a suggestion from the Soviet government that they should form a world Jewish anti-Fascist committee, and sent a draft constitution to Stalin. After the evacuation of Moscow in October 1941 they were sent to Kuibychev to wait for Stalin's answer. On 3 December they were arrested and executed.

60. op. cit., pp. 56–7, gives details of the importance of the Polish resistance connected with the government-in-exile. On 1 August 1944, in accordance with the instructions of the government-in-exile, the resistance launched the Warsaw rising, in the obvious intention of liberating the capital and setting up its own authority before the arrival of the Soviet troops, who were very close. During the rising the Soviet troops arrived on

the opposite bank of the Vistula, on the outskirts of Warsaw, and did no more than shell the Germans, without making any attack, though an attack in combination with the resistance rising, might have defeated the Germans. The people of Warsaw were forced to surrender among the ruins of their city after two months of fighting. The Soviets have justified their passivity on technical grounds.

61. *Stalin's Correspondence with Churchill, etc.*, I, p. 347.

62. ibid., II, p. 202; Fontaine, op. cit., p. 236.

63. *Stalin's Correspondence with Churchill, etc.*, II, p. 206.

64. Quoted by Fontaine, op. cit., p. 239.

65. *Stalin's Correspondence with Churchill, etc.*, I, p. 331. The resistance had also been harshly put down in Belgium during the winter of 1944–5.

66. See K. S. Karol, *Visa for Poland*, MacGibbon and Kee, London, 1959, p. 82.

67. This was Point 3 of the protocol. The plan was later abandoned.

68. See Fontaine, op. cit., p. 243.

69. Quoted by Robert Murphy, *Diplomat Among Warriors*, Collins, London, 1964, p. 259.

70. See above, pp. 412–13. In his message of 12 May to Truman, Churchill argued that 'it would be open to the Russians in a very short time to advance if they chose to the waters of the North Sea and the Atlantic' (Fontaine, op. cit., pp. 243–4).

71. *The Times*, 10 August 1945.

72. Statement by Stalin to a *Pravda* correspondent (*Nuestra Bandera* 5 (1946)).

73. 'Interviews du maréchal Staline (1945–1951)', *La Documentation française*, 5 May 1951, pp. 3–7.

74. Dedijer, op. cit., p. 331; Djilas, op. cit., London, 1969, p. 141.

75. Mao Tse-tung, op. cit., IV.

76. 'Interviews du maréchal Staline (1945–1951)', p. 4.

77. The 'events' of May 1968 in Paris brought the problem up again. *L'Humanité* had to reply to a letter from a Communist who argued that revolution had been possible in 1944–5, but that the party had given way because of Stalin's opposition and fear of American intervention. (See Marcel Veyrier's article in *L'Humanité* of 24 January 1969.) Sartre discussed the matter in his interview with *Der Spiegel*, published as a pamphlet by Didier (Paris, 1968) under the title, *Les Communistes ont peur de la révolution*. According to Sartre the reason for the Communists' giving

way in 1944–5 was simply that 'their aim was not to start a revolution' (p. 14).

The question was also touched upon in Italy, though in far too marginal a way, in the discussion of the national popular front policy which took place in the journal *Critica Marxista* during the year 1965. Lelio Basso, who is anything but an extremist, admitted that the Yalta agreements made a socialist outcome difficult, and went on: 'But between socialism and the "restoration" which followed 1945 there was an infinite range of solutions, and I still think that among them the working-class movement could have found one which would have allowed it to make considerable progress, if it had not accepted, before and after the resistance, in order to safeguard anti-Fascist unity, a series of compromises which made the restoration easier' (*Critica Marxista,* July–August 1965, p. 17).

78. The French Communist Party document which discusses this question most thoroughly is that adopted by the political committee on 3 October 1952 in connection with the case of André Marty and Charles Tillon (*Cahiers du Communisme,* 10, 1952). The dispute with these two party leaders stemmed from difference about the policy followed during the resistance and in the period after the liberation. The main point was that Marty and Tillon (the latter had been one of the military leaders of the resistance) felt that the party had followed an opportunist policy and had not taken advantage of the opportunities offered to it. The PCF leadership suppressed this discussion by its usual methods, and used scandalous slanders against Marty, who was expelled fom the party. Tillon remained a member, but was politically annihilated. The political committee's document includes the following: 'Charles Tillon recently said at a meeting in Drancy that it was ridiculous to accuse us of wanting to take power on 28 May last when we could have taken it in 1944 but did not in order to keep our undertakings. Charles Tillon implied in this statement that the party had given unspecified undertakings without the knowledge of the working class and the people, instead of explaining the truth, which is that the necessary conditions for a take-over of power by the working class were not present in 1944.'

The political committee gave the following explanation:

'In August 1944 the war was not yet over. A reversal of alliance was possible, to produce a front of capitalist powers against the Soviet Union. If they had been given an excuse, the Americans who had come to France as fighters at the last minute, for fear that the Soviet army would advance too far west, would not have hesitated to make an alliance with Hitler in Europe and Japan in Asia in order to range all the forces of international capitalism against the country of socialism.

'In France itself, in spite of the considerable growth of its influence, the party would soon have been isolated if it had taken any other course than that of continuing the war against Hitler, and the only result would have been a bloody failure. De Gaulle would have been given an excuse to use the British and American armies to crush the working class, and come to terms with Pétain and continue the sinister work of the Gestapo.

'The wise and farsighted policy of the party did not allow this. Communists are revolutionaries, not adventurers.' Further on, we find, 'Their attitude towards the Soviet Union is the touchstone of Communist parties, both as regards proletarian internationalism and a logical policy of national independence.'

There is no need to answer these arguments here, since this is the purpose of this book, but one or two of the political committee's polemical methods may be noted.

(*a*) It presents the problem as one of taking power in August 1944, but no one would have worried if it had waited until April 1945, when the danger of a reversal of alliance had disappeared and the attempt could have coincided with the great rising in northern Italy. But what the party should have begun to do in August 1944 was to strengthen and extend the formidable mass movement produced by the liberation: in other words, prepare the conditions for a seizure of power at the right moment.

(*b*) It presents the problem as if the dilemma were either to seize power or to continue the war against Germany. But, assuming that a seizure of power was possible, why would it have meant the end of the war against Germany and not its transformation into a popular, revolutionary war for the defence of the new power and the final defeat of Hitlerism? And, above all, was there no other way of continuing the war against Hitler than that taken by the party leadership in placing itself under the authority of de Gaulle and the Americans, disbanding the armed forces of the resistance and reducing the committees of liberation to a purely decorative role?

(*c*) It presents the suggestion of a reversal of alliances as if an alliance between Roosevelt and Hitler and Japan and between de Gaulle and Pétain was a quite straightforward operation in the situation of 1944–5. It sees only the danger of the party's isolation and not that of the isolation of the Americans and de Gaulle.

The party unconsciously reveals the key to its policy in the remark,

'Their attitude towards the Soviet Union is the touchstone of Communist parties.' It was, if not the Soviet Union, at least Stalin, who forbade Thorez to explore the least of the revolutionary possibilities brought into being by the liberation.

79. See above, 8, note 53.

80. Quoted by the American historian, Joseph R. Starobine, in his essay 'Origins of the Cold War: the Communist Dimension', *Foreign Affairs*, July 1969, p. 685.

81. See Trotsky, *The Third International after Lenin*, Pioneer Publishers, New York, 1936, pp. 68–73.

82. See his *Stalin*, Chapter 12. In his last book, *The Unfinished Revolution* (OUP, London, 1967), Deutscher says, 'An international civil war, with tremendous social revolutionary potentialities, unfolded within the world war. Stalinism, however, went on clinging to conventional security, *raison d'état*, and sacred national egoism. It fought the war as a "Fatherland War", another 1812, not as a European civil war. It would not confront Nazism with the idea of international socialism and revolution. Stalin did not believe that that idea would inspire his armies to fight, or that it could infect and disintegrate the enemy's armies, as it had done during the wars of intervention. Moreover, he prompted the various Communist-led resistance movements in Europe to fight solely for national liberation, not for socialism' (p. 73).

83. Deutscher, *Stalin*, Penguin Books, Harmondsworth, rev. edn, 1966, p. 549.

84. Pavlenko and V. Kniajinsky, *International Relations after the Second World War*, Institute of World Economy and International Relations of the USSR Academy of Sciences, 1962 (in Russian). The passage quoted is from Chapter 13, published in *Recherches Internationales*, 44–45 (1964), p. 57.

6. The Cominform

1. H. Ripka, *Le Coup de Prague*, Plon, Paris, 1949, pp. 33f. In the elections of May 1946, which were regarded by all the Czechoslovak political parties and the Western governments as completely normal and free, the Communist Party won 38 per cent of the votes in Czechoslovakia as a whole. In Bohemia–Moravia it won more than 40 per cent. Out of 300 deputies, there were 115 Communists, 55 National Socialists (Beneš), 47 members of the Populist Party and 36 Social Democrats. A variety of

small groups shared the remainder. In July 1946 a new government was formed under the leadership of Gottwald.

The parliamentary representation gave no more than a partial idea of the relation of forces. During the liberation new governing bodies had been set up at local and regional level. These bodies were known as national committees, and included, as well as representatives of the various political parties, representatives of the unions and other organizations; they were legalized by the Beneš government even before its establishment in Prague. In 1946–7 the three regional presidents of the national committees were Communists. 128 of the 163 district national committees, and 6,350 of the 11,512 local national committees, were headed by Communists. Add to this the fact that the party controlled the Ministry of the Interior, the workers' militia, the bulk of the army and, in any case, the military leaders, and that it dominated the unions and other mass organizations, and it will be seen that Ripka's statement accurately represents the facts. (Details of the elections and the national committees are taken from the report of Slansky, the General Secretary of the Czech Communist Party, to the founding of the Cominform in September 1947.)

2. Quoted by F. Fetjö, *Histoire des démocraties populaires*, p. 107, from an essay by Raskosi in 1952, published in the theoretical journal of the Hungarian Communist party.

3. ibid., p. 108.

4. ibid., p. 107. 'Politically, the Soviet authorities showed themselves as liberal and tolerant in Hungary as they were harsh economically. The course of events gave the impression that, regarding Hungary as a country outside their security zone, they wanted to give proof of their willingness to respect the Yalta arrangements, arrangements which they felt unable to apply in either Romania or Bulgaria' (ibid., p. 106). Things changed quickly after these elections as relations between the Soviet and United States governments deteriorated. In December 1946 the leaders of the Smallholders' Party were accused of plotting against the regime. When the party's parliamentary group, which held 57 per cent of the necessary votes, refused to waive the parliamentary immunity of their General Secretary, Bela Kovacs, the Soviet military authorities intervened directly and arrested him in February 1947 on a charge of 'conspiracy against the security of the Red Army'. See ibid., p. 194.

5. Stalin, *Interview between J. Stalin and Roy Howard, March 1, 1936*, Moscow, 1936, p. 7.

6. Fejtő, op. cit., p. 127.

7. According to estimates quoted by Fejtő, Romania had paid the USSR $1,000m. in reparations and had a further $950m. to pay. In Hungary, 65 per cent of the country's overall production in 1946 was destined for reparations payments. For other details of this problem and the setting-up of joint companies, see Fejtő, op. cit., pp. 136–7, 154–7. A more detailed and specialized study is Jan Marczewsky, *Planification et croissance économique des démocraties populaires*, 1, PUF, Paris, 1956, pp. 218–32.

8. On the Czech–Polish dispute about Teschen, see Fejtő, op. cit., p. 114; on the problems of Hungarian minorities in Slovakia and of Transylvania, see ibid., pp. 116–17, 127–8.

9. Tito was a little-known leader at the beginning of the war. His attitude is sufficiently explained by the fact that he led the party and the liberation struggle on the spot, with no more contact with Moscow than radio links. He was to some extent influenced by his previous experiences, the disputes he had taken part in within the Comintern and his knowledge of the situation in the USSR. The biography of Tito by Dedijer is very interesting from this point of view, in spite of its regrettable traces of a 'personality cult'.

10. When he took the leadership of the government in 1946 Dimitrov said, 'Our immediate task is not the achievement of socialism or the introduction of a Soviet system, but the consolidation of parliamentary democracy' (quoted by Fejtő, op. cit., p. 126).

11. Quoted by a Chervenkov, a leader of the Bulgarian Communist Party, in his report to the founding meeting of the Cominform, which is included in the collection of documents of this meeting published in Moscow by Foreign Languages Publishing House, Spanish version, p. 185.

12. Dimitrov, *Informe al V. Congreso del Partido*, 19 December 1948, published under the title *La Bulgaria de hoy* by the Spanish Communist publishers Nuestro Pueblo. See p. 52.

13. Thorez, *Œuvres*, Vol. 23, p. 133.

14. Fejtő, op. cit., p. 180.

15. ibid., p. 179.

16. See ibid., 1, Chapter 4.

17. Taken from the official text of Zhdanov's report, published with the statement of the nine parties and the reports of their representatives in *Cominform Conference 1947* (see above, p. 8, note 52). All the references and quotations which follow are taken from this. Italics added.

18. The text of Vishinsky's speech is that of *Mundo Obrero*, a Spanish Communist Party paper published in France, 25 September 1946 (italics added).

19. Message to the US ambassador in Moscow, 9 May 1948 (*The Times*, 11 May 1948).

20. See above, p. 431.

21. On 13 May the Soviet press published an open letter from Henry Wallace to Stalin listing the questions on which Wallace felt it essential to reach agreement. Stalin replied in a signed statement on 17 May which paid lavish tribute to Wallace's letter, describing it as 'the most important document' of the recent past among those which sought 'to strengthen peace, normalize international cooperation and guarantee democracy'. Stalin said that the programme suggested by Wallace could form the basis for an agreement. The State Department had independently, and before Wallace's initiative, explored Soviet intentions, a step which led to an exchange of notes between 4 and 19 May in which the governments in Moscow and Washington accused each other of being responsible for international tension and showed the extent of their differences. Stalin's statement and the Soviet notes reflect Moscow's strong desire to reach a general agreement. This account is based on the texts published in *Mundo Obrero*, 13, 20 and 27 May 1948.

22. See *History of the Revolutionary Movement (Misl)*, Part 2, p. 421, note 2.

23. Resolution of the CGT confederal committee, 14 November 1947.

24. See the SFIO publication *Le Populaire*, 24 December 1947.

25. See J. Fauvet, *Histoire du Parti communiste français*, II, p. 212.

26. The official *Histoire du Parti communiste français* (Paris, 1964) implicitly recognizes that the party took this attitude and admits its negative effects: 'Part of the strikers wanted the movement to end. The strike gradually turned into a strike of minorities, *which led to sectarian errors. Insistence on continuing the movement* led to the isolation of the CGT miners, who returned to work after a strike lasting eight weeks' (p. 519, italics added).

27. Quoted by Fauvet, op. cit., II, p. 212.

7. The Yugoslav Breach

1. See F. Fejtő, op. cit., I, p. 194.

2. ibid., p. 209. See also the article by Amber Bousouglou, 'Comment la Tchécoslovaquie passe du régime parlementaire à la démocratie populaire', *Le Monde*, 23 February 1968.

3. Speech by Gottwald to the national constituent assembly, 10 March 1948 (taken from the Spanish version of *Nuestra Bandera*, 25 (1948), p. 247).

4. *XXe Congrès du PC de l'Union soviétique*, Cahiers du Communisme, Paris, 1956, p. 260.

5. Taken from the Spanish version published in *Nuestra Bandera*, 19 (1947). The passages quoted are from pp. 608 and 614.

6. *Meeting of the Information Bureau of the Communist Parties in Hungary in the Latter Half of November 1949*, published by the journal *For a Lasting Peace, For a People's Democracy*, Moscow, 1950, pp. 17 and 69.

7. See Fejtő, op. cit., pp. 202–3.

8. *Le Figaro*, 12 February 1948. At the time Groza was president of the Romanian council of ministers.

9. The account given here is based mainly on the correspondence between Stalin and Tito of March–May 1948. This was published by the Yugoslavs in various languages, including English. The English edition is *The Correspondence between the Central Committee of the Communist Party of Yugoslavia and the Central Committee of the All-Union Communist Party (B)*, Belgrade, 1948. Another translation of the correspondence was published by the Royal Institute of International Affairs as a pamphlet, *The Soviet-Yugoslav Dispute*, London and New York, 1948. The latter also includes the text of the 1948 Cominform resolution condemning Yugoslavia, and the Yugoslav pamphlet includes an account from the Yugoslav point of view of how the dispute arose. The text of the correspondence given here is that of the Yugoslav pamphlet, occasionally altered to bring out the meaning better where this was justified by the RIAI text and Claudin's French version (which was also published by the Yugoslavs). The alterations are in square brackets.

See also Dedijer, *Tito Speaks*, Djilas, *Conversations with Stalin*, and Fejtő, *Histoire des démocraties populaires*.

10. See p. 386 above.

11. Djilas, op. cit., pp. 97–100.

12. In his letter of 27 March 1948, after accusing the Yugoslavs of a series of hostile acts towards the Soviet civilian and military specialists who were in Yugoslavia (we shall come back to this), Stalin wrote, 'In the light

of these facts, the famous statement made by Djilas at a meeting of the Central Committee of the PCY in which he insulted the Red Army by claiming that Soviet officers were morally inferior to officers of the British army becomes completely intelligible. It is well known that there was no opposition to Djilas' statement from the members of the Central Committee of the PCY.'

13. See Fejtő, op. cit., pp. 85–6.

14. ibid., pp. 165–70.

15. See Jan Marczewsky, *Planification et croissance économique des démocraties populaires*, Bibliothèque de la Science Économique, Paris, 1956, I, pp. 227–9.

16. We have used the Spanish version of the final communiqué published in *Mundo Obrero* of 7 August 1947.

17. Quoted by Dedijer, op. cit., p. 323 (translation slightly altered).

18. The description of this Soviet–Yugoslav–Bulgarian meeting is in *Tito Speaks*, pp. 324–33. According to the Yugoslavs, Stalin pressed for the immediate setting-up of the Bulgarian–Yugoslav federation on the basis of the Bulgarian plan because he regarded it as a way of destroying the unity which had just been achieved by the federation of the Yugoslav peoples (ibid., p. 332). Earlier, Stalin had encouraged the Yugoslavs to 'swallow' Albania, but at the same time the Soviet secret service were intriguing against the Yugoslavs in Albania (ibid., pp. 320, 313).

19. At the meeting with the Yugoslavs and Bulgarians Stalin himself revealed that the Polish leaders had praised the Dimitrov–Tito plan (ibid., p. 326).

20. The quotation is from the Yugoslav 'blue book' published in 1951 containing a series of depositions about the activity of the Soviet secret services.

21. At a dinner for the Yugoslav leaders Stalin said that Togliatti was a theoretician who could write a good article, but was incapable of leading a nation. Thorez, too, had a serious weakness: 'Even a dog which doesn't bite bares its teeth when it wants to frighten someone. Thorez can't even do that much.' La Pasionaria was 'unable to pull herself together and incapable of leading the party in difficult circumstances'. Then Stalin said to Tito, 'Tito should take great care that nothing happens to him. I won't last much longer, but he will remain for Europe.'

During the Yugoslav delegation's stay in Moscow Kalinin died. On the day of the funeral Tito and the other Yugoslavs, like the rest of the foreign visitors, were placed to the left of the main stand occupied by Stalin and the members of the Politburo. 'Suddenly, just as the ceremony had begun, Stalin invited Tito to come up and stand with the Politburo. He was the only one to receive this honour. All the other foreign guests remained on the stand on the left (*Tito Speaks*, pp. 282–3, 285; translation adapted).

22. See Fejtő, op. cit., I, pp. 225–6.

23. See p. 491 and note 18 above.

24. These details and those which follow are taken from the Stalin–Tito correspondence referred to in note 9 above.

25. At this meeting of the Central Committee Ranković made a report on the activities of the Soviet secret services. Many of the agents recruited by the Soviets were members of the Russian émigré community which had settled in Yugoslavia after the October revolution, i.e., they, or their ancestors, were White Russians.

26. On 19 April Dimitrov passed through Belgrade on his way to Prague at the head of a Bulgarian delegation. Djilas went to greet him, and Dimitrov took advantage of a moment's privacy to say, 'Be firm!'. It was agreed that Dimitrov and the Yugoslav leaders should meet when Dimitrov returned. In the meantime came the Bulgarian Communist Party's reply supporting the Soviet Union. The meeting did not take place (Dedijer, op. cit., p. 360).

27. In May 1944 the Germans launched an elaborate operation in an attempt to destroy Tito's headquarters. The Yugoslav leader narrowly missed falling into the hands of a unit of paratroops, but managed to escape. The operation failed, and the partisan headquarters was able to save its archives and transmitters. The German attack was in no way the result of a crisis in the national liberation movement and its army, but rather the opposite, a desperate attempt by the occupiers to alter the situation. *Pravda* commented on 4 June: 'The failure of the attempt to capture Marshal Tito's headquarters is an open secret. The German attack was beaten off as a result of the heroic resistance of the Yugoslav army ... In Italy Kesselring needs reinforcements ... The Germans would have liked to release some of their divisions operating in Yugoslavia, but Marshal Tito has upset their plans. The Yugoslav front is holding down large numbers of German forces and is making any assistance to Kesselring impossible.'

28. See Dedijer, op. cit., p. 366.

29. The following is the main part of the resolution. The text is taken from *The Soviet Yugoslav Dispute*, pp. 61–70, which reproduces the

English text published in the Cominform journal *For a Lasting Peace, For a People's Democracy*, 1 July 1948.

Resolution of the Information Bureau Concerning the Situation in the Communist Party of Yugoslavia

'(1) The Information Bureau notes that recently the leadership of the CPY had pursued an incorrect line on the main questions of home and foreign policy, a line which represents a departure from Marxism–Leninism. In this connection the Information Bureau approves the action of the Central Committee of the CPSU (B), which took the initiative in exposing this incorrect policy of the Central Committee of the Communist Party of Yugoslavia, particularly the incorrect policy of Comrades Tito, Kardelj, Djilas and Ranković.

'(2) The Information Bureau declares that the leadership of the Yugoslav Communist Party is pursuing an unfriendly policy towards the Soviet Union and the CPSU (B). An undignified policy of defaming Soviet military experts and discrediting the Soviet Union has been carried out in Yugoslavia. A spy regime was instituted for Soviet civilian experts in Yugoslavia, whereby they were under surveillance of Yugoslav state security organs and were continually followed. The representative of the CPSU(B) in the Information Bureau, Comrade Yudin, and a number of official representatives of the Soviet Union in Yugoslavia, were followed and kept under observation by the Yugoslav state security organs.

'All these and similar facts show that the leaders of the Communist Party of Yugoslavia had taken a stand unworthy of Communists, and have begun to identify the foreign policy of the Soviet Union with the foreign policy of the imperialist powers, behaving towards the Soviet Union in the same manner as they behave towards the bourgeois states. Precisely because of this anti-Soviet stand, slanderous propaganda about the degeneration of the CPSU(B), about the "degeneration" of the USSR, and so on, borrowed from the arsenal of counter-revolutionary Trotskyism, is current within the Central Committee of the Communist Party of Yugoslavia.

'The Information Bureau denounces this anti-Soviet attitude of the leaders of the Communist Party of Yugoslavia, as being incompatible with Marxism–Leninism and only appropriate to nationalists.

'(3) In home policy, the leaders of the Communist Party of Yugoslavia are departing from the positions of the working class and are breaking with the Marxist theory of classes and the class struggle. They deny that there is a growth of capitalist elements in their country, and consequently a sharpening of the class struggle in the countryside. This denial is the direct result of the opportunist tenet that the class struggle does not become sharper during the period of transition from capitalism to socialism, as Marxism–Leninism teaches, but dies down, as was affirmed by opportunists of the Bukharin type, who propagated the theory of the peaceful growing over capitalism into socialism ...

'(4) The Information Bureau considers that the leadership of the Communist Party of Yugoslavia is revising the Marxist–Leninist teachings about the party. According to the theory of Marxism–Leninism, the party is the main guiding and leading force in the country, which has its own, specific programme, and does not dissolve itself among the non-party masses ...

'In Yugoslavia, however, the People's Front, and not the Communist Party is considered to be the leading force in the country. The Yugoslav leaders belittle the role of the Communist Party and actually dissolve the party in the non-party People's Front ...

'The leaders of the Yugoslav Communist Party are repeating the mistakes of the Russian Mensheviks regarding the dissolution of the Marxist party into a non-party mass organization. All this reveals the existence of liquidation tendencies in the Communist Party of Yugoslavia.

'(5) The Information Bureau considers that the bureaucratic regime created inside the party by its leaders is disastrous for the life and development of the Yugoslav Communist Party. There is no inner-party democracy, no elections and no criticism and self-criticism in the party ...

'It is a completely intolerable state of affairs when the most elementary rights of members in the Yugoslav Communist Party are suppressed, when the slightest criticism of incorrect measures in the party is brutally repressed ...

'The Information Bureau considers that such a disgraceful, purely Turkish, terrorist regime cannot be tolerated in the Communist Party.

'(6) ... Instead of honestly accepting this criticism and taking the Bolshevist path of correcting these mistakes, the leaders of the Communist Party of Yugoslavia, suffering from boundless ambition, arrogance and conceit, met this criticism with belligerence and hostility. They took the anti-party path of indiscriminately denying all their mistakes, violated the doctrine of Marxism–Leninism regarding the attitude of a political party to its mistakes and thus aggravated their anti-party mistakes.

'Recently after the Central Committee of the CPSU(B) and fraternal parties had criticized the mistakes of the Yugoslav leaders, the latter tried to bring in a number of new leftist laws ... The Information Bureau considers that since these leftist decrees and declarations of the Yugoslav leadership are demagogic and impracticable in the present conditions, they can but compromise the banner of socialist construction in Yugoslavia.

'That is why the Information Bureau considers such adventurist tactics as an undignified manoeuvre and an impermissible political gamble ...

'(7) [This section condemns the refusal of the CPY to take part in the Cominform meeting.]

'(8) In view of this the Information Bureau expresses complete agreement with the estimation of the situation in the Yugoslav Communist Party, with the criticism of the mistakes of the Central Committee of the party, and with the political analysis of these mistakes contained in letters from the Central Committee of the Communist Party of the Soviet Union (B) to the Central Committee of the Communist Party of Yugoslavia between March and May 1948.

'The Information Bureau unanimously concludes that by their anti-party and anti-Soviet views, incompatible with Marxism–Leninism, by their whole attitude and their refusal to attend the meeting of the Information Bureau, the leaders of the Communist Party of Yugoslavia have placed themselves in opposition to the Communist parties affiliated to the Information Bureau, have taken the path of seceding from the united socialist front against imperialism, have taken the path of betraying the cause of international solidarity of the working people, and have taken up a position of nationalism.

'The Information Bureau condemns this anti-party policy and attitude of the Central Committee of the Communist Party of Yugoslavia.

'The Information Bureau considers that, in view of all this, the Central Committee of the Communist Party of Yugoslavia has placed itself and the Yugoslav party outside the family of the fraternal Communist parties, outside the united Communist front and consequently outside the ranks of the Information Bureau.

'. . . The Yugoslav leaders evidently do not understand or probably pretend they do not understand that such a nationalist line can only lead to Yugoslavia's degeneration into an ordinary bourgeois republic, to the loss of its independence and to its transformation into a colony of the imperialist countries.

'. . . The task [of the healthy elements inside the Communist Party of Yugoslavia] is to compel the present leaders to recognize their mistakes openly and honestly and to rectify them; to break with nationalism, return to internationalism; and in every way to consolidate the united socialist front against imperialism.

'Should the present leaders of the Yugoslav Communist Party prove incapable of doing this, their job is to replace them and to advance a new internationalist leadership of the party.'

30. See Dedijer, op. cit., p. 370. The Soviets have never denied this report, which was given to the Yugoslavs by someone who took part in the meeting, and the turn taken by the campaign against Tito is indirect confirmation of it.

31. Cf. Dedijer, op. cit., p. 373.

32. J. B. Tito, *Political Report of the Central Committee of the Communist Party of Yugoslavia, delivered at the V Congress of the CPY*, Belgrade, 1948, 136.

33. Speech by Khrushchev in Sofia, 3 June 1955, according to the text published in *Pravda* on 4 July 1955.

34. This is a translation from the complete Spanish version of the Soviet note published in *Mundo Obrero* of 25 August 1949. The passages quoted are the full description in the note of the way the 'Soviet citizens' arrested in Belgrade were treated. It can easily be imagined that if there is any bias in the description it is on the side of making the picture worse. The full cynicism of this Soviet government document is brought out by a comparison of the accounts by Artur London, Solzhenytsin, Ginsburg and others of the methods of Beria's police.

35. According to reports in the *New York Star*, deliveries of military supplies to Greece in the first half of 1949 included 152 planes, 7,000 bombs, 10,000 military lorries, 3,840 cannons and mortars, and 280 million rounds of ammunition (quoted by Zisis Zographos in his article, 'Quelques enseignements de la guerre civile en Grèce', *Revue Internationale*, 11, Prague, 1964).

36. *L'Esprit*, 2 (1950), contains an article by J.-M. Domenach describing conversations he had between 15 and 20 August 1949 with Greek

partisans who had fled to the Yugoslav part of Macedonia. According to the statements of these partisans, the elimination of Markos in October 1948 took place without consultation of the guerrillas. Only the leaders of the large units were told. It was not until two months later (December 1948) that a conference of the Greek party met. The guerrillas were later told that Markos was ill. The news that he had been eliminated for 'opportunism' spread gradually. The replacement of Markos by Zachariades had a demoralizing effect on the people's army. There was an impression that Zachariades' mission was to end the armed struggle.

The struggle against the 'Titoists' took on large proportions. Greeks of Macedonian origin fighting with the guerrillas (about 18,000) were removed from all important commands on suspicion of sympathizing with the idea of a Greater Macedonia linked with the people's republic of Macedonia in the Yugoslav federation. Zachariades gave orders that all contact between Yugoslavia and the Greek territory occupied by the partisans should be prevented. An officer of the frontier guard told Domenach that in April 1949 he had received a telegram from Zachariades' headquarters ordering him to fire on anyone who tried to cross the Yugoslav frontier. Zachariades was said to have ordered the closure of the frontier in the spring of 1949.

J.-M. Domenach's conclusions are that the Soviet leaders were afraid of the growth of a new Titoism in Greece, and also regarded the civil war in Greece as dangerous and inopportune. He thinks that it was for these reasons that the Soviet leaders gave the pro-Soviet Greek Communist leaders the order to reject any aid from Yugoslavia and end the civil war. In this way they achieved two things. They demonstrated their good faith to the Western foreign ministries and at the same time were able to denounce Tito's 'treachery' before the other Communist parties and world opinion.

37. Pierre Albouy, 'La Grèce et la démocratie', *La Pensée*, 29 (1950), p. 61.

38. Around 25,000 Greek resistance fighters fled to Yugoslavia. Many others (there are no detailed figures) fled to Albania. It is reasonable to suppose that the Yugoslavs on their side took action to deal with any threat from supporters of the Cominform.

39. We shall come back to this question later. The existing information, which reveals only partial aspects, comes mainly from Artur London's *On Trial* (Macdonald, London, 1970), Eugen Löbl's *Procès à Prague* (Stock, Paris, 1969) and various reports in the Czechoslovak press during

its brief period of freedom. On the Rajk trial there is Savarius Vincent (i.e. Bela Szasz), *Volontaires pour l'échafaud*, Julliard, Paris, 1963. The official version of the Rajk trial is published in the Blue Book *Rajk et ses complices devant le tribunal du peuple*, Éditeurs Français Réunis, Paris, 1949, of the Kostov trial in *Le Procès de Traicho Kostov et de son groupe*, Sofia, 1949, and of the Slansky trial in *Procès des dirigeants du centre de conspiration contre l'État, dirigé par Rudolph Slanski*, Orbis, Prague, 1953.

40. Fejtő, op. cit., 1, p. 254.

41. Quoted from the Spanish version of the indictment published in *Mundo Obrero* of 8 December 1949.

42. See Fejtő, op. cit., 1, p. 262.

43. Resolution of the central committee of the Polish Workers' Party, from the full Spanish version published in *Mundo Obrero*, 9 September 1948.

44. All quotations from the proceedings of this meeting are from the pamphlet referred to in note 6 above, pp. 76, 81–2, 80–81, 79, 95, 94, 28–9.

45. Figures rounded off. The information is taken from Fejtő and Lazitch's book on the Communist parties in Europe. These two historians use official Communist party sources.

46. Fejtő, op. cit., 1, pp. 246–7. *Literarni Listi* gave a figure of 30,000 detainees for Czechoslovakia (*Le Monde*, 31 March 1968).

47. A detailed account of the trials and purges is given in Fejtő, op. cit., 1, Part V, Chapters 3–6.

48. Costas Papaioannou, *L'Idéologie froide*, J.-J. Pauvert, Paris, 1967, p. 141.

49. Artur London, op. cit., pp. 294–5, 303 (translation slightly altered).

50. ibid., p. 304 (slightly altered).

51. Papaioannou, op. cit., p. 140.

52. 'Doubt everything.' The motto is one of the answers Marx gave in 1865 to a questionnaire prepared by his daughters. See *Memories of Marx and Engels* (in Russian), Moscow, 1956.

53. As mentioned in note 39, in spite of the confirmation and the information contained in *On Trial* and other first-hand reports, important aspects of the intervention of the Soviet secret services and Soviet party leaders remain unknown. London managed to discover, from his own interrogations and information supplied by other victims, that the investigation was led by Soviet officials. He quotes, for example, the disclosures

made to him by Alois Samec in 1956, after his rehabilitation. Samec was a former member of the International Brigade, and had collaborated for a while with the 'Soviet advisers'. 'The Russian advisers arrived in Czechoslovakia in the autumn of 1948, after the Rajk trial. They said we must have had some form of conspiracy against the state in our country, and that the enemies who wanted to overthrow the socialist regime had infiltrated every branch of the Party and the government.

'In accord with the instructions they gave us we arrested individuals who "might" have been acting against the state because of their jobs or their contacts. Only later did we look for evidence.

'One of the Soviet advisers, Borissov, ordered me to give him a copy of each report signed by the accused after the interrogations. When I pointed out that the Secretary-General of the party already received a copy of these reports he reprimanded me sharply and told me not to question his instructions.

'I also had dealings with other Soviet advisers, notably with Likhache and Smirno, who were gathering compromising information about everybody, particularly politicians in the highest places, including Slansky and Gottwald.' (p. 79)

The Czechoslovak policemen who actually carried out the interrogations sometimes let slip remarks which indicated the character of their superiors. For example: 'A man like Radek lasted three months. After that he confessed everything. You have resisted four months. Do you think that'll go on much longer?' (p. 145). London reasoned, correctly, that only a Soviet official could have given the Czech policeman this sort of information about Radek's resistance to 'interrogation'. Other references to this point will be found in London.

During the Czech 'spring' the Prague press revealed that Mikoyan had intervened personally at certain stages of the Slansky trial.

In Poland Soviet intervention was particularly cynical. At the same time as Gomulka, General Spychalski and other Polish Communist leaders were expelled from the party (November 1949), the Polish government, on the orders of Moscow, appointed as Defence Minister the Soviet Marshal Rokossovsky (Polish by origin, but educated in Russia and speaking Polish with a strong Russian accent). Rokossovsky surrounded himself with Soviet specialists and began a vast purge of the Polish army which culminated in the trial of generals and officers in August 1951. On the eve of the trial Molotov, accompanied by Marshal Zhukov, arrived in Warsaw and delivered a speech calling for an intensification of the struggle against 'right-wing nationalists and Titoists of every sort' (see Fejtő, op. cit., 1, p. 266).

54. See the book by a former official of the Italian Communist Party, Giulio Senica, *Togliatti e Stalin*, Sugar, Milan, 1961. Senica reports a secret meeting held in Moscow on 12–14 July 1953, at which the Italian party was represented by Pietro Secchia. The Soviets said that Beria had wanted to go too far in the direction of concessions to the West, and had planned to abandon the building of socialism in the German Democratic Republic and its transformation into a bourgeois state. As final proof of his role as an agent of the secret services of imperialism, they produced the letter which had been found on him at his arrest. This shows that the 'proofs' of Beria's treason were identical with those he himself had used to send thousands of Communists from the People's Democracies to prison or death.

55. Ignacio Gallicio, 'La lutte contre le titisme est un devoir révolutionnaire des communistes', *Nuestra Bandera*, 4 (1950), p. 176. The quotations given from Spanish, French, Chinese, etc. Communist leaders on this point do not mean that these parties distinguished themselves in the general anti-Titoist campaign. Responsibilities in this matter are general, and the quotations have been chosen for their representativeness.

56. Liu Shao-Chi, 'Internationalisme et nationalisme', *Pour une paix durable, pour une démocratie populaire*, 1 June 1949. This was the official organ of the Cominform.

57. Georges Cogniot, 'Redoublons de vigilance dans la lutte contre la clique de Tito', *Cahiers du Communisme*, 6 (1950), p. 47.

58. ibid., p. 48. The false report of the setting-up by the Yugoslavs of V2 launching ramps appeared in the Italian bourgeois press in 1948. The Communist press took it up for its own purposes later.

59. ibid., p. 49.

60. ibid., p. 50.

61. *Cahiers du Communisme*, 6 (1951), pp. 657–9.

62. *VII° Congresso del Partito communista italiano* (resoconto), 1954. This collection contains nearly fifty speeches from the Congress.

63. *Cahiers du Communisme*, 5 (1950), p. 29.

64. ibid., 6 (1951), p. 66.

65. *La Nouvelle Critique*, 25 (1951), p. 19.

66. *Mundo Obrero*, 8 December 1949. Monzon was at the head of the party's organization in France and Spain during the Second World War.

He was arrested at the end of the war by Franco's police and spent many years in prison. After the Twentieth Congress Dolores Ibarruri wrote him a personal letter admitting that the accusations made against him were false, but he was never rehabilitated publicly. For Comorera, the former General Secretary of the PSU of Catalonia, there is a pamphlet published by friends of his in an effort to defend his memory, *Aportació a la historia política, social e nacional de la classe obrera de Catalunya*, Paris, 1969.

67. PCF political bureau document, 3 October 1952, *Cahiers du Communisme*, 10 (1952), p. 953. André Marty wrote a book in which he denounced the falsity of the slanderous accusations made against him by the political bureau and explained his political position (*L'Affaire Marty*, Éditions des Deux Rives, Paris, 1955).

68. *Histoire du PCF (Unir)*, 111, pp. 98–100.

69. ibid., pp. 63–4.

70. See David Caute, *Communism and the French Intellectuals*, Deutsch, London, 1964. On pp. 175–87 Caute describes the reactions of French Communist intellectuals and the non-Communist left intelligentsia at the time of Titoism and the trials.

71. See Caute, op. cit., p. 186.

72. *Pravda*, 21 December 1949.

73. *Cahiers du Communisme*, May 1950, p. 24.

74. *Les Lettres Françaises*, 24 March 1953.

75. The names of nine distinguished doctors were mentioned in the 13 January announcement. Among them was Vinogradov, who had been a medical expert at the trial of Bukharin in connection with the 'assassinations' of Gorky, Peshkov, Kuibyshev and others. Five of the doctors admitted to working for American intelligence through the Jewish organization 'Joint'. Three confessed to being agents of the Intelligence Service. Shortly after Dr Lydia Timashuk was decorated for her help in unmasking the killer doctor-spies. The Soviet press presented her as a national hero. The 4 April announcement mentioned thirteen names, including six which had not been on the 13 January list. The fate of the two doctors who had been on the January list but had disappeared from the April one is unknown. It is possible that they died under torture, or that they were agents of Beria's, like Dr Timashuk.

The suggestion of the various kremlinologists who have studied the affair (Leonard Schapiro, Harrison Salisbury, Wolfgang Leonhard) is that in the last months of his life Stalin was preparing a new and even larger

purge. Molotov's wife was arrested and deported from Moscow in connection with the accusation against the doctors, and so were two sons of
Mikoyan's. All the senior leaders felt threatened and Stalin himself felt
threatened by everyone. The affair of the doctors may have been intended
as the first stage of a fierce struggle in the highest spheres of the 'leading
party' which took an unexpected turn with the death of Stalin (in circumstances which have still not been completely explained). Krishna Menon,
the well-known Indian minister, who met Stalin shortly before his death,
reported that the dictator scribbled wolf's heads on a piece of paper and
told his visitor that the Russian peasant was very familiar with wolves, his
old enemies, and knew how to kill them, but the wolves knew about killing
too. See also Pierre Broué, *Le Parti bolchevique*, pp. 460–62.

76. Mayer Azev was an *agent provocateur* in the pay of the Tsarist
police who managed to become the leader of the Russian terrorists for
four years (1904–7). The police prevented most of the plots at the last
minute, but let some of them go ahead in order to justify their severity
against the revolutionaries in the eyes of public opinion. In January 1953 a
French Communist writer used this historical precedent to argue that
there was nothing surprising about the trials in the People's Democracies
(*La Pensée*, 46 (1953)).

77. *Cahiers du Communisme*, 8–9 (1953), p. 25.

8. *The East Takes Over*

1. Mao Tse-tung, *Selected Works*, IV, Peking, 1961, pp. 157–8. All the
quotations from Mao which follow, unless otherwise indicated, are taken
from the Peking English-language edition of his *Selected Works*.

2. The 'new democracy', defined by the CPC programme as an intermediate stage between the Kuomintang regime and socialist construction,
cannot be considered a stage of capitalist development, even if the capitalist
private sector continued to exist within it. The Central Committee's report
to the Eighth Congress of the CPC (September 1956) said: 'The establishment of the People's Republic of China signifies the virtual completion of
the stage of bourgeois-democratic revolution in our country and the beginning of the stage of proletarian-socialist revolution: the beginning of
the period of transition from capitalism to socialism' (*Eighth National
Congress of the Communist Party of China*, 1, Peking, 1956, p. 19).

3. The Soviet declaration of war on Japan and offensive against the
Japanese army in Manchuria, immediately after the United States had
dropped atomic bombs on Japan, must have had the same effect.

Nevertheless, as will be seen, the influence of the Soviet victories in the Second World War on the Chinese revolution was contradictory. On the one hand, they were a check on intervention by American imperialism, but on the other Stalin took advantage of the strength and prestige he derived from these victories to try and force the CCP to capitulate to the Kuomintang, to smooth the way for the wide-ranging agreement he wanted with the United States.

4. According to Guillermaz, *A History of the Chinese Communist Party 1921–1949*, Methuen, London, 1972, p. 305, the Soviet Union sent about 300 officers and technical staff under the command of General Cherbachev. This included Soviet E-5 and E16 aircraft and pilots.

5. Quoted by André Fontaine, *History of the Cold War From 1917 to the Korean War*, p. 369.

6. Wang Ming was in fact the main leader of the party before Mao took over the position. He was the Comintern's agent. After his replacement by Mao he returned to Moscow, which he left for Yenan at the beginning of 1938. With other leading party figures, he opposed Mao's policy, suggesting that greater concessions should be made to the Kuomintang, that the party's military units should be totally integrated into the Kuomintang army, its discipline respected, etc. He thought that only the Kuomintang was capable of leading the war of resistance against Japan. In other words, his political positions, a reflection of Moscow's, resembled those of the European Communist parties – except the Yugoslav – during the resistance period: 'national unity' under the leadership of the anti-Fascist bourgeoisie. See Hu Chiao-mu, '*Trente Années du Parti communiste en Chine,* Peking, 1957, pp. 72–3; Guillermaz, op. cit., pp. 204 n. 3, 366–7. In the heat of the current Sino-Soviet polemic, *Kommunist,* the main journal of the Soviet Communist Party, has confirmed that Wang and other leaders were attacked at this period for defending the views of the Comintern and the Soviet party (see the issue of June 1968, 'Some Questions in the History of the CPC').

7. In his report to the Seventh Congress of the CPC, Mao said, with reference to this period: 'There was actually no serious fighting on the Kuomintang front during those years. The sword-edge of Japanese aggression was mainly directed against the Liberated Areas' (*Selected Works*, III, p. 268).

8. No available document of the CPC contains any mention of Soviet military aid in this period, or in the later period of the war against Japan. There can be no doubt that, if there had been such aid, the Soviets would

not have failed to use it as an example in the *Kommunist* article mentioned in note 6.

9. *Kommunist,* June 1968, pp. 93–108.

10. This description by Guillermaz (op. cit., p. 330), which is based on very detailed documentation, coincides with the official versions produced by the CPC.

11. *Selected Works,* II, p. 107. The military organization set up by the CPC during the war against Japan was a very complex and diversified system. It included the Eighth Army and the New Fourth Army, organized on the basis of divisions, regiments and companies and enjoying large operational autonomy, with no restriction to a specific area. There were also territorial units which operated exclusively within a specific area within the provinces occupied by the Japanese and popular militias, armed mass organizations, generally equipped with very rudimentary weapons and locally based. At the time of the Seventh Congress (spring 1945) the People's army in the strict sense totalled 910,000 men and the popular militias 2,220,000. At that time the Liberated Areas had a total population of 95 million. The frontier region of Shensi-Kansu-Ninghsia (Yenan), where Mao's headquarters had been set up and which was outside the territory occupied by the Japanese, made up no more than a small part of the Liberated Areas. The largest part was in provinces theoretically controlled by the invaders or by the Kuomintang regime.

12. See *Trente Années du PCC*, pp. 68–9.

13. To supplement what was said in note 8, it may be noted that Mao insisted many times in speeches and articles on the lack of foreign aid. See, for example, Vol. IV of his *Selected Works*, and in particular his speech to a meeting of party activists in Yenan on 13 August 1945 (ibid., p. 22): 'During the past eight years the people and army of our Liberated Areas, receiving no aid whatsoever from outside and relying solely on their own efforts, liberated vast territories and resisted and pinned down the bulk of the Japanese invading forces, and practically all the puppet troops.' ('Puppet troops' means those of the Chinese 'collaborators'.)

14. See the American Blue Book, *United States Relations with China,* Washington, 1949, p. 73.

15. Quoted in Fontaine, op. cit., p. 375. (Hopkins was Truman's chief adviser on foreign affairs.)

16. See Herbert Feis, *The Chinese Tangle*, University Press, Princeton, 1953, p. 140.

17. See Fontaine, op. cit., p. 375.

18. On 10 August 1945 Chu Teh, the commander in chief of the People's Army, invited the Japanese troops and the Chinese armies of the pro-Japanese regimes to lay down their arms. Almost all the Japanese troops ignored this call and obeyed the orders of the 'Supreme Allied Command' (SCAP) – i.e. the Anglo-American high command – which had instructed them to surrender only to Chiang Kai-shek's troops and had made them responsible for the maintenance of order during the interregnum. As a result of this the bulk of the Japanese military equipment came into the possession of Chiang Kai-shek's troops, adding to what the Americans had sent, which had been enough to equip thirty-nine divisions with the most up-to-date weapons. This information is taken from Guillermaz, op. cit., p. 378, who also says that no previous Chinese government had possessed such a quantity of modern powerful military equipment. A rough estimate put at 199 the number of Chiang Kai-shek's divisions at the end of 1945. In addition he had 500 aircraft. Throughout the civil war the Communists never had any operational aircraft.

The value *in situ* of the industrial equipment removed by the Soviets from Manchuria was estimated by an American commission at $858m., and its replacement cost at $2,000m. The Soviet action, says Guillermaz, 'implied that the Russians intended to impose their economic cooperation on the future occupants of this region, which was vitally important to the economy of Siberia' (p. 379).

About the towns which the Soviets could have handed over to the People's Army, or which they could have made it easier for them to occupy, Guillermaz notes: 'Had the Communists occupied the large towns in these areas – Peking, Tientsin, Tsingtao, T'aiyüan and Kalgan – to speak of North China alone – this would have given them a valuable card to play off against the government, and caused considerable stir in the world as a whole' (p. 376). But the Sino-Soviet agreement 'gave explicit acknowledgement ... of the Nanking government's sovereignty over Manchuria' (p. 379). Guillermaz adds that 'the Russians had intended to leave Manchuria gradually in October and November, leaving the way open to the Chinese Communists. At the request of the central government, which had not finished its plans for the complete reoccupation of the area, they agreed to delay their departure until the following April' (p. 380). In other words, the Soviet army protected the towns of Manchuria from the threat of falling into the hands of the Chinese Communists until the arrival of Chiang Kai-shek's troops in American ships and aircraft.

19. Quoted by Dedijer, op. cit., p. 331. At this meeting with the Yugos-

43

lav and Bulgarian Communist leaders Stalin tried to force the Yugoslavs to stop helping the Greek uprising, on the pretext that it was bound to fail. His line, in essence, was, 'I can admit my mistake about China, so you should be able to admit your mistake about Greece.' The possibility cannot be excluded, however, that Stalin wanted to indicate – and wanted the Americans to know – that he had nothing to do with the policy followed by the Chinese Communists.

20. See Mao Tse-tung, op. cit., IV, p. 54.

21. Taken from *Mundo Obrero* (January 1946), which was reproducing the version given in the Soviet press. Marshall's mission to China should of course be seen against the background of this aim which the 'Big Three' shared. American and Soviet policy in China naturally had different aims, but both favoured the 'national unity' solution. This solution would allow the fight for influence to be continued without the international complications which civil war might involve.

22. Quoted by Fontaine, op. cit., p. 383.

23. Mao Tse-tung, op. cit., IV, p. 275. General Scobie was the commander of the British expeditionary force which crushed the Greek resistance in 1944.

24. ibid., III, p. 295.

25. ibid., III, p. 323.

26. ibid., V, pp. 54, 56. The CPC's policy in the period immediately preceding the Japanese capitulation is described in Mao's report to the party's Seventh Congress. The line of the united national front against Japan was translated into the plan for a coalition government including all the political forces and tendencies which would support the programme of 'new democracy' worked out by the party. In this programme bourgeois–democratic measures (agrarian reform on the principle 'land to the tiller', etc.) stood side by side with others which were 'socialist factors', as Mao called them, the establishment of a state sector in the economy (based mainly on the nationalization of foreign capital and that of the *comprador* bourgeoisie) and of a cooperative sector. The socialist character of these measures resulted from the fact that the state would be under 'the control of the proletariat'. In other words, this meant in practice that it would be under the control of the CPC. Of course a coalition government and programme of this sort was completely unacceptable to the Kuomintang, even if it did contain some progressive elements who might support such ideas.

During the negotiations begun after the capitulation of Japan, Mao made a number of concessions, the most important of which provided for the formation of a coalition government of which, in spite of strong CPC representation, the party would be a minority as against the Kuomintang. In fact the concession was more apparent than real. Mao was inflexible on the questions of the party's control of its armed forces and of the extent of revolutionary power in the Liberated Areas. The Kuomintang leadership, naturally, could not accept this. That is why the break was inevitable.

27. See above p. 21, note 75, and the relevant text. During the cultural revolution various references were made to the capitulationist tendencies of a number of party leaders in this period, but Stalin's intervention in the matter was not mentioned.

28. See above, p. 21, note 73.

29. Mao Tse-tung, op. cit., III, 54. On 4 May 1919 a student demonstration took place in Peking in protest against the Paris Peace Conference's decision to transfer to Japan Germany's rights over the Chinese province of Shantung. This event gave its name to a political and intellectual movement of opposition to the *ancient régime* and the old ideas which had been developing for a number of years and acquired a more radical character and a broader base after this demonstration.

30. Extracts from Liu Shao-chi's report are included in H. Carrère d'Encausse and Stuart Schram, *Marxism and Asia,* Allen Lane The Penguin Press, London, 1969, pp. 259–61, from which this and subsequent quotations are taken.

31. From an article by E. Zhukov, 'Questions of the National and Colonial Struggle after the Second World War' in the Soviet economic journal *Voprosy Ekonomiki,* 9 (1949): extracts in Carrère d'Encausse and Schram, op. cit., pp. 265–7.

32. G. V. Astafiev, 'From a Semi-Colony to a People's Democracy', *Krizis Kolonial'noy Sistemy,* Moscow, 1949: extracts in Carrère d'Encausse and Schram, pp. 267–9.

33. Carrère d'Encausse and Schram, pp. 269–73.

34. See, for example, the articles by Robert Guillain in *Le Monde,* 20–28 December 1949, under the general title 'La Chine sous le drapeau rouge'.

35. Marius Magnien, *Cahiers du Communisme,* March 1950, p. 57.

36. 'On the People's Democratic Dictatorship', 30 June 1949, reproduced in *Selected Works,* IV, pp. 422–3.

37. Mao's tactical skill was helped by the fact that during the anti-

Japanese war and the Second World War the contradictions between his policy and Stalin's did not have a serious effect on Soviet interests. These contradictions might have taken on a hostile character after the capitulation of Japan if the spirit of Yalta could have survived in relations between Washington and Moscow. However, the rapid worsening of relations between the two super-powers removed some of the sharpness in the differences between Mao and Stalin.

38. This information is taken from the textbook used at the CPSU higher party school, *History of the International Working-Class Movement and the National Liberation Movement*, Vol. 3, p. 250.

39. From the article mentioned in note 35, 'The Victory of Stalin's Policy in China'.

40. *La Politique étrangère soviétique, textes officiels (1917–1967)*, Moscow, 1967, pp. 131–4. The recognition of the 'independence' of Outer Mongolia was recorded by an exchange of notes between Vishinsky and Chou En-lai.

41. F. Fejtő, *Chineen URSS, la fin d'une hégémonie*, Plon, Paris 1964, p. 93, quotes the following story from S. Bialer, 'I Chose Truth', *East Europa*, July 1956: 'At a very important meeting of the Central Committee of the Soviet Communist Party in July 1955, when Molotov was opposing the *rapprochement* with Yugoslavia, Mikoyan made a sharp attack on the views of the old chief of Stalin's diplomacy. In the course of this he quoted the words of Mao Tse-tung during the Peking talks of 1954 [between Khrushchev and Mikoyan on one side and the Chinese leaders on the other]; Mao had strongly criticized the joint companies, calling them "a form of Russian interference on the economic life of China". Mikoyan spoke of the shame he had felt at hearing talk of the arrogant behaviour of Soviet experts abroad.'

42. *La Politique étrangère soviétique*, pp. 135–6. The comparison with the credits granted to Poland is taken from Fejtó, *Chine–URSS*, p. 73.

43. 'Nouvelles Considérations sur l'expérience historique de la dictature du prolétariat', Paris, 1957, p. 10. This is a French version, published by the French Communist Party, of an article in *Jemminjipao* (*The People's Daily*), 29 December 1956.

44. In Lin Piao's report to the Ninth Congress of the CCO (April 1969) and in many other texts from the Cultural Revolution, Liu Shao-chi is used as a scapegoat for the sins of Stalin not only during the anti-Japanese war and in the third revolutionary civil war (1946–9), but also in the period

between the seizure of power and Stalin's death. Without attempting to establish wha: truth there is in the criticism of the political positions attributed to Liu (and they cannot be accepted as they stand as long as Liu has not been given an opportunity to defend himself in public), we may be certain that they coincide exactly with the political line which Stalin tried to impose on the CPC in these different periods. This is a convenient place to note that the charges made against the former president of the People's Republic of China in this report, that he was an enemy agent, a traitor to the working class, and had been a lackey of imperialism since the time of the first revolutionary civil war, resemble in every feature the accusations made by Stalin against Trotsky, Bukharin, Zinoviev and the rest.

45. See Fejtő, *Chine–URSS*, pp. 88–9.

9. *The New World Balance*

1. The congress met in two sections, the delegates from the Soviet Union and the People's Democracies in Prague, having been refused visas by the French authorities, the others in Paris.

2. *Bol'shaya Sovyetskaya Entsiklopediya*, 2nd edn, Vol. 13, p. 456.

3. ibid., Vol. 13, p. 458.

4. ibid., Vol. 41, p. 23.

5. ibid., Vol. 13, p. 456.

6. See the illustration in the *Bol'shaya Sovyetskaya Entsiklopediya* between pp. 456 and 457.

7. Stalin, *Derniers Écrits (1950–1953)*, Éditions Sociales, Paris, 1953, pp. 125–6.

8. See the article by Luis Carlos Prestes, General Secretary of the Brazilian Communist Party in the Cominform journal, *For Lasting Peace, for People's Democracy* (5 June 1953).

9. M. Suslov, 'Defence of Peace and the Fight Against the Warmongers', *Meeting of the Information Bureau of Communist Parties in Hungary in the Latter Half of November 1949*, Moscow, 1950, p. 21.

10. *Cahiers du Communisme*, 5 (May 1950), pp. 49–50, 53.

11. *VII congresso del Partito Communista Italiano*, Rome, 1954, pp. 21–2, 32 (emphasis added).

12. See Fauvet, *Histoire du PCF*, II, pp. 242–3.

13. Suslov, 'Defence of Peace', p. 32. The other quotations are from pp. 51, 52, 43 and 47.

14. See *La Nouvelle Critique*, 50 (1953), p. 131. References to Tog-

liatti's speeches and writings are to the Russian edition, Moscow, 1965, I, p. 560.

15. See *La Pensée*, 44 (September–October 1952), p. 4.

16. *For Lasting Peace, for People's Democracy*, 18 February 1965, quoting an interview of Khrushchev by the American journalists W. R. Hearst, J. Kingsbury Smith and F. Connif on 5 February 1955. The Cominform paper quotes Khrushchev as saying: 'The Soviet Union did not want to act to the detriment of its allies in the struggle against Hitlerism. It was known that five years ago the United States was less highly mobilized than now. If the Soviet Union had wanted to attack the West, it should, according to the viewpoint of those who considered that an attack should be made at the moment most advantageous to the attacker, have done so at that time.'

17. There is a connection between this 'theory' and Stalin's 'theory' that the class struggle would inevitably become more acute in the Soviet Union and the People's Democracies as further progress was made in the building of socialism. Apart from their complete lack of scientific value, the theories share a utilitarian character. Stalin's theory was used, and of course continues to be used, to justify, among many other reactionary actions, repression against Communists and other citizens opposed to the bureaucratic and autocratic (or, at present, bureaucratic and leaderless) regime. It was (and still is) used to mystify the struggle between progressive and conservative tendencies within the regime, labelling the formed 'anti-socialist' and latter 'socialist'. Suslov's theory (really Stalin's, since Suslov was only a mouthpiece) was used during the 1950s to justify the line Stalin imposed on the Communist parties, the abandonment of the struggle for socialism, the campaign against Tito, the trials, etc. Its outline reappears today in the justifications of the 1968 invasion of Czechoslovakia, just as it previously justified the sending of tanks into Budapest.

18. See Fontaine, *History of the Cold War from 1917 to the Korean War*, pp. 359–65.

19. See Fontaine, *History of the Cold War from the Korean War to the Present*, Secker and Warburg, London, 1970, pp. 9–10; Fejtő, *Chine-URSS, la fin d'une hégémonie*, p. 77.

20. Fontaine, *History of the Cold War from the Korean War to the Present*, pp. 9–10.

21. Stalin, *Derniers Écrits*, pp. 80–81.

22. ibid., pp. 124–5.

23. ibid., p. 190.

24. *Istoriya mezhdunarodnovo rabochevo i natsionalnosvobitelnovo dvisheniya* ('History of the International Workers' and National Liberation Movement'), III, Moscow 1966, p. 592. It should be remembered that this work, which had already been quoted several times, is used as a textbook in the CPSU higher party school, which gives it a special authority in the official orthodoxy.

25. This is a condemnation of Stalin's dogmas in the name of the dogmas of the Twentieth Congress on the non-inevitability of wars, the peaceful road to socialism, the anti-imperialist role of the national bourgeoisies in the poor countries, unity with social democrats, etc. New and old dogmas – which had the same methodological ancestry in improvization and pragmatism – both served the same strategic aim, the consolidation of 'peaceful coexistence' by a stable and prolonged compromise – the 'stable and prolonged peace' of the Cominform's pacifist campaign – with American imperialism. This accounts for the paradox of this version, quoted above for its criticism of the Cominform: at the same time as its 'activity' was severely condemned, its 'general line' was described as totally correct. Moreover, in the case of the Cominform, as in the case of other more important problems, Stalin was used as a scapegoat for various unpleasant consequences of previous policies, just as the 'cult of personality' became the magic formula for explaining all mistakes. In this way the need for critical, Marxist, analysis of the underlying causes, contained in the very nature of the Stalinist system, both in the 'socialist' states and the Communist movement, was avoided. This made it easy to carry on with policies and methods very similar to those of the past.

26. The following are some details of the development of the Communist parties of Western Europe during the Cominform period.

Italian Communist Party

1947: 1,889, 505 members

1952: 2,093, 540 members

1946: 19 per cent of the votes (at parliamentary elections)

1953: 22·7 per cent of votes

French Communist Party

1946: 1,034,000 cards distributed, 804,229 members
1954:   506,250 cards distributed

(After 1946 the PCF published only the figure for party cards distributed by the Central Committee to the federations, and not the number of cards actually taken up by members. Given the difference which existed in 1946 between these two figures, it is reasonable to assume that in 1954 the number of militants was under 400,000.)

1946: 28.6 per cent of votes at parliamentary elections
1956: 25 per cent.

1947: In this year the party press had a combined circulation of 2,770,000, out of the total circulation of 11,000,000 for the daily press. (In this year the PCF had over 30 provincial daily and weekly papers.)

1952: Press circulation down to 900,000. (The party lost a series of provincial publications and the circulation of *L'Humanité* fell.) the total circulation of French daily papers is still 11,000,000.

Small Legal Communist Parties in Europe

	Active members		% of votes			
Austria	150,000 (1948)	28,000 (1951)	1945:	5·4	1953:	5·4
Belgium	100,000 (1945)	14,000 (1954)	1946:	12·7	1954:	3·5
Denmark	75,000 (1945)	21,000 (1953)	1945:	12·5	1953:	4·3
Finland	150,000 (1946)	50,000 (1952)	1945:	23·5	1951:	21·6
Gt Britain	47,513 (1944)	34,801 (1953)	1945:	0·4	1955:	0·1
Netherlands	53,000 (1946)	16,000 (1955)	1946:	10·5	1952:	6·2
Norway	45,000 (1945)	13,000 (1953)	1945:	11·9	1953:	5·1
Sweden	48,000 (1946)	28,000 (1953)	1944:	10·3	1952:	4·3
Switzerland	13,500 (1945)	8,000 (1953)	1947:	5·1	1951:	2·7
W. Germany	no figures		1949:	5·7	1953:	2·2

(Most of the above information is taken from Branko Lazitch, *Les Partis communistes d'Europe*. That on the French Communist press is from Annie Kriegel, *Les Communistes français*.)

27. According to Soviet historians all the Latin American Communist parties together had a membership of 500,000 in 1947 (*Istoriya mezhdunarodnovo ... dvisheniya*, III, 385). In 1964 they had no more than 300,000 (Ponomarev, *Le Mouvement révolutionnaire international de la classe ouvrière*, Moscow, p. 359). If we allow for the fact that, according to the former source, a great advance was made after 1956, we can get some idea of the dramatic decline of the Latin American Communist movement during the Cominform period.

During the whole of this period there were internal crises in the parties. In 1953 the Reinoso 'fraction' was expelled from the Chilean Communist Party after being accused of spreading anarcho-syndicalist views. In 1955 the Uruguayan party expelled its General Secretary, Gomez Chiribao, on a charge of nationalism. The Communist Party of Venezuela expelled the 'fraction' led by the former General Secretary Fuenmayor. In 1952 the Colombian Communist Party took action against a group accused of left deviationism.

By far the most serious crisis was that in the Argentinian Communist Party, whose leadership under the domination of Codovilla had always been outstanding for its anxiety to imitate the European Communist parties. This aping led it to classify Peronism as Fascism and to call for Popular Front tactics against it. The best member of the leadership, Juan José Real, criticized this policy and suggested a new strategy based on alliance with the anti-imperialist tendencies within Peronism, which had an influence on the vast majority of the working class. Juan José Real and other militants were expelled and the Codovilla clique organized a disgraceful slander campaign against them.

It was at this time (1948) that the Colombian civil war broke out, as a result of the assassination of the Liberal leader Gaitain. The Colombian Communist Party took an active part in the civil war, which lasted until 1958.

I will attempt a detailed study of the problems of the Latin American Communist movement and its historical development in a later book.

28. A bitter factional struggle took place during these years in the Communist parties of South and South-East Asia, over the questions of armed struggle and attitudes to the national bourgeoisie. As we have seen, the strategy of the Chinese Communist Party was to encourage an alliance with the anti-imperialist sectors of the national bourgeoisie while at the same time always preserving the independence and control of the revolutionary forces. Stalin's policies at the beginning of the 'cold war' pushed these parties into sectarian positions on this problem, as a result of the influence on the national bourgeoisie of American strategy's anti-colonialist propaganda. In addition, Mao's strategy of armed struggle had always been marked by tactical caution, and had been careful to avoid any premature attempts at an uprising. The left-wing tendencies which developed in the South and South-East Asian Communist parties under the influence of the Chinese revolution were not always so cautious about embarking on armed struggle, and attempted it without sufficient preparation. They also attacked the national bourgeoisie as a block.

29. In 1946 Stalin for the first time expressed the view that 'Communism in one country is perfectly conceivable, especially in a country like the Soviet Union' (interview in the *Sunday Times*, 17 September 1946).

30. Stalin, *Economic Problems of Socialism in the USSR*, Moscow, 1952, p. 36. On the same page Stalin claimed: 'The experience of this cooperation shows that not a single capitalist country could have rendered such efficient and technically competent assistance to the People's Democracies as the Soviet Union is rendering them.'

31. Stalin, *Derniers Écrits*, p. 188.

Epilogue

1. Marx, *Capital* (Moore-Aveling translation), 1, London, 1970, p. 763.

2. Cf. Lenin, *Collected Works*, Vol. 22, London and Moscow, 1964, p. 302, which translates 'moribund capitalism'.

3. *Resolutions and Theses of the Fourth Congress of the Communist International, Held in Moscow Nov. 7 to Dec. 3 1922*, Communist Party of Great Britain, London, n.d., pp. 23–4.

4. *Manifestes, thèses et résolutions des quatre premiers congrès mondiaux de l'Internationale communiste, 1919–1923*, Paris, 1969, pp. 19, 20, 25, 31, 74 (translated from the French).

5. *Decisions of the Third Congress of the Communist International . . . July 1921*, Communist Party of Great Britain, London, n.d., pp. 81, 90, 91; cf. *Manifestes . . . des quatre premiers congrès*, pp. 87, 91, 94.

6. *Decisions of the Third Congress*, pp. 95–6.

7. Jane Degras, ed., *The Communist International (1919–1943): Documents*, OUP, London, 1956–65, II, p. 114.

8. Degras, op. cit., II, pp. 472, 481.

9. *Manifestes . . . des quatre premiers congrès*, p. 100.

10. The membership of the Communist International (not counting the USSR) fell from 445,300 in 1928 to 318,176 in 1931. See Chapter 3 above.

11. On the language of the Sixth Congress, see Notes, Part 1, p. 15, note 56. The quotations from Ponomarev are taken from his article on the anniversary of the Communist International in *La Nouvelle Revue Internationale* (February 1969).

12. See Notes, Part 1, p. 17, note 74.

13. Karl Marx and Friedrich Engels, 'Manifesto of the Communist Party', *Selected Works in Three Volumes*, Moscow, 1969, p. 117.

14. Marx and Engels, *Works*, 2nd Russian edn, Vol. 30, pp. 400–401, 406. The same idea also occurs as early as the *Communist Manifesto*.

After describing the process by which the proletariat is transformed into a conscious class, the *Manifesto* goes on: 'This organization of the proletarians into a class, and consequently into a political party . . .' (Marx and Engels, *Selected Works in Three Volumes*, I, p. 117).

15. Marx and Engels, *Works*, 2nd Russian edn, Vol. 30, pp. 400–401.

16. Marx writing to Hamann, quoted in Kostas Papaioannou, *Les Marxistes*, p. 223. The second Russian edition of the works of Marx and Engels does not contain this text, on the pretext that it was altered by *Der Volkstaat*, the newspaper of the German Social Democratic Party (Vol. 16. p. 774). There is, however, no record of Marx's having disowned the version published in *Der Volkstaat*.

17. Marx and Engels, *Works*, 2nd Russian edn, Vol. 7, pp. 287–8.

18. ibid., Vol. 18, p. 342.

19. Marx-Engels, *Werke*, Vol. 19, Berlin, 1962, p. 161.

20. Marx and Engels, *Selected Works in Three Volumes*, I, pp. 119–20.

21. See the quotations on pp. 119–20.

22. In a letter to Lafargue of 11 August 1884, Engels defines Marx's position on this question as follows: 'Marx would protest against "the political, social and economic ideal" you attribute to him. A "man of science" has no ideal, but produces scientific results, and if he is in addition a party man he fights to put them into practice. But if one has an ideal one cannot be a man of science, because one has a position taken up in advance' (*Correspondance Engels–Lafargue*, I, Paris, p. 235 (original in French)).

23. Rosa Luxemburg, 'Centralisme et démocratie', in the pamphlet *Marxisme et dictature*, Paris, 1948, p. 21.

24. Quoted by Lenin in *What Is To Be Done?*, *Collected Works*, Vol. 5, p. 384.

25. Lenin, op. cit., Vol. 5, pp. 375–6 (my italics).

26. ibid., pp. 384–5.

27. ibid., p. 396.

28 ibid., pp. 474–5.

29. ibid., Vol. 7, p. 258.

30. ibid., Vol. 5, pp. 515, 510, 512.

31. ibid., p. 490.

32. ibid., pp. 450, 466.

33. ibid., Vol. 10, p. 32.

34. ibid., Vol. 5, pp. 462–3, 461 (translation slightly altered). In *One Step*

Forward, Two Steps Back, Lenin put the same ideas in different words: 'Now we have become an organized party, and this implies the establishment of authority the transformation of the power of ideas into the power of authority, the subordination of lower party bodies to higher ones' (ibid., Vol. 7 p. 389).

35. ibid., p. 396–7.

36. See Trotsky, *Nos Tâches politiques* (1904), Denoël–Gonthier, Paris, 1970, p. 121.

37. Quoted by Michel Lowy, *La Théorie de la révolution chez le jeune Marx,* Maspero, Paris, 1970, p. 175.

38. *History of the Communist Party of the Soviet Union. (Bolsheviks): Short Course.*

39. ibid.

INDEX

Action Party, 345; campaign against the King of Italy, 349; and the CLN revolution, 363; and the CNLAI, 346; membership in 1945, 362; opposition to new constitution, 367–9; and the partisan movement, 405; and the PCI on coalition government, 363; refusal to take part in new Bonomi government, 356, *See also* Italy

Africa, Communism in, 244

Albania, 491, 513, 514, 521; purge, 527

Alcala Zamora, Niceto, 212

Alexander, General Harold, orders to the CNLAI, 359

Algeria: Anglo-American troops in, 322; Communism in, 244; and Fascism, 294; repression (May 1945) in Constantine district of, 337; workers' and peasants' emancipation, 246

Algiers: consultative commission for Italy in, 351–2; French Communist deputies detained by Vichy state in, 322

American Federation of Labor, 310

American imperialism: and Chinese revolution, 574; condemnation of capitalism in Western Europe, 586; and defeat of revolution in Europe, 316, 392; new anti-Soviet strategy, 370; and Stalin's interpretation of Atlantic Charter, 399; taking-over of British imperialism, 381; world domination, 341

Anarcho-Syndicalists, Spanish: adaptation to Russian line, 232; apolitical and anti-state ideas, 219; expulsion from government, 233; and the Fascist danger, 219, 220; meaning of alliance with Republicans, 228; part in hypothetical Spanish Socialist Republic, 240; part in Spanish revolution, 225; and the PCE, 238, 240; repression, 218–19; resistance to 'people's anti-Fascist bloc', 213; and Spanish revolution, 211, 215; strategy, 214; vote for People's Front, 214

Anglo-American alliance: compromise with Germany, 439–40; over Europe and the Far East, 439–40; strategy for stopping revolution in Europe, 439–40

Anglo-Russian Trade-Union Committee, 153, 154

Anglo-Soviet alliance, Stalin's conditions for, 398, 400

Annam, workers' and peasants' emancipation, 246

'Anti-Comintern Pact', 40

Anti-Fascist alliance: of Communist

55

Bidault, Georges – *contd*
  Ruhr coal, 341, 342
Bielopolski (painter), 580
'Big Three': conference in Moscow,
  351-2, 376, 404; conference in
  Teheran, 376, 406, 407;
  demarcation of 'spheres of
  influence', 396, 397, 399, 414,
  558; Foreign Ministers' conference
  (December 1945), 432; permanence
  of secret agreement between,
  392; recognition of Yugoslav
  government-in-exile, 373;
  responsibility for formation of
  Italian government of 'national
  unity', 351; solemn declaration at
  Yalta, 424-5; splitting-up of
  Germany, 408; Tito's
  memorandum to, 376
Bismarck's Socialist Law, 119
Blanqui, Adolphe, 53
Bled Conference (July 1947), 489
Blum, Léon: on aid to Spanish
  Republic, 207-8, 227; call for
  split in trade-union movement,
  476; Comintern's criticism, 300;
  and devaluation of franc, 210;
  fear of civil war in France, 207,
  208; and Franco-Soviet Pact
  (2 May 1935), 188; and French
  Communists, 87, 171; as head of
  French Socialist–Radical
  government, 202; and the
  People's Front, 182, 200, 208;
  policy of non-intervention, 207,
  209; programme and French
  proletariat, 203-4; social
  legislation, 79
Bolshevik, 95
Bolshevik party: Central Committee
  (23 October 1917), 52; and the
  European socialist idea, 452;
  foundation, 105, 108; influence on

working masses, 57; and Lenin's
  'April Theses', 440; monolithism,
  118, 121; and the October
  revolution, 108, 633; and
  proletarian democracy, 150, 524-5;
  and the Russian Federal Soviet
  Republic, 106; Tito's clash with,
  515; victory (October 1917), 637-8
Bolsheviks: attitude towards
  Germany, 130-31, 136;
  experience of years 1917-20, 437,
  442; influence on world
  revolution, 92-3, 130; purges and
  trials in Moscow against, 124;
  responsibility in the ECCI, 113;
  and the Russian revolution, 106
Bolshevism: and national and
  colonial problems, 253;
  opposition to Stalinism, 87; as
  seen by Trotsky, 120; Tsarism
  and, 253; and unity in a
  revolutionary party, 123
'Bolshevization': of the Communist
  parties, 141, 594, 602, 624;
  definition, 640
Bonomi: expulsion from Socialist
  Party, 353; government of
  'national unity', 353, 355, 359;
  new government, 356; resignation,
  356; and the *rinnovamento sociale*,
  353-4
Borba, publication of Cominform
  resolution, 506
Bordiga, 165, 344
Borodin, 280
Bosnia, 376
Bourgeois democracy: Anglo-French,
  234; Comintern's temporary
  alliance with, 261, 262;
  Comintern's view on, 612; and
  Communist reformist action, 620;
  Dimitrov's statement on, 300;
  and Fascism, 192, 234; French,

Censorship of the press, 118, 119

CFLN, *see* French Committee for National Liberation

CGT, *see* Confédération Générale du Travail

Chamber of Deputies, French, 181, 200

Chamberlain, Joseph, and the Comintern, 88

Changchun, 556

Changsha, 290, 291

Chauvinism, Great-Russian, 255, 256, 259, 260

Checa, Pedro, 221

Chen Tu-hsiu, 276; reaction to Kuomintang's anti-Communist measures, 280; removal from Comintern, 283

Chetniks, 373, 374; British suppression of aid, 378; Soviet military aid, 376; and Yugoslav Communist Party, 445

Chiang Kai-shek: American military aid, 558; and Chinese Communist Party, 272, 279, 314, 555; *coup d'état*, 273, 274, 279, 281, 282; fifth campaign against 'Red bases', 284, 292; as head of army of Kuomintang, 271; and 'Northern Expedition' (1926), 271, 280; offensive against Chinese People's Liberation Army, 431, 558; 'Sino-Soviet treaty of friendship and alliance', 556, 557; and USA, 427-8, 431, 550, 555; and Yalta agreement, 429-30

Chicago Tribune, 403

China: agrarian revolution, 286-7, 288-9, 559, 560; American intervention, 468, 550; American search for agreement with Moscow, 427-8; 'Big Three' agreement, 431; civil war, 468, 469, 470, 558; and Comintern, 244, 251; democratic revolution, 50; economic situation after Mao's victory, 568; events of 1930, 292; independence, German and Japanese threat, 191; intervention of the USSR in armed struggle for socialism, 311; introduction of Communist or Soviet system, 276, 277; and Japanese invasion (1937), 244, 560; membership in Comintern, 271; as part of imperialist camp, 467; role of peasant masses, 286; and the Socialist revolution, 67, 248; and the Tsars, 407; unification and independence, 271; USA's wish to dominate, 472; war with Japan, 29, 292; working class, 268. *See also* Chinese Communist Party; Chinese People's Liberation Army; Chinese people's revolutionary war; Chinese revolution; People's Republic of China.

Chinese Communist Party: and absence of military aid from Soviets, 552, 555; and the adjustment of Communism to level of peasant country, 264; and the agrarian revolution, 273, 281, 293, 550; alliance with Kuomintang, 272, 276, 277, 278, 280, 281, 552-3; American pressure, 558; analysis of Communist defeat, 273-4, 275; breach with Stalinist monolith, 314; as champion of national independence, 293, 560; and the Cominform, 466, 563; debt to Stalin, 570, 571; defeat (1927), 245, 273, 274, 275, 292; expansion,

Index

Communist Parties – *contd*
German Pact (August 1939), 301;
fight against Titoism, 594;
Finnish, *see* Finland (Communist
Party); French *see* French
Communist Party; German, *see*
German Communist Party;
importance of peace for, 597;
Indian, *see* Indian Communist
Party; Indonesian, *see* Indonesia
(Communist Party); influence
among intellectuals, 545;
intellectuals in, 268; Italian, *see*
Italian Communist Party;
Japanese, *see* Japan (Communist
Party); Latino-American, 294,
580, *see also* Latin America
(growth of communist parties);
Mexican, 249; 'nationalization' of,
314; in People's Democracies, *see*
People's democracies (Communist
parties in); and preservation of
peace of Soviet policy, 186–7;
purges in, 594, 624; reasons for
failure of, 602; and reformism,
623–4; resurgence of national
feelings in, 313; revolutionary
potential after Nazi defeat, 394,
401; Russia, *see* CPSU;
Scandinavian, 243, 478, *see also*
Sweden, Communist Party,
Norway (Communist Party); seen
as parties of peace, 189–90;
shelving of socialist revolution,
620; Spanish, *see* Spanish
Communist Party; subordination
to Stalin's strategy, 434; Swiss,
see Switzerland (Communist
Party); Syrian, 20, 467; theoretical
weakness, 96; Third Congress
resolution about, 70; Titoist
agents in, 543; Turkish, *see*
Turkey, Communist Party in; of

the USA *see* United States of
America (Communist Party); and
USSR renewed prestige; Western,
270, 540–51, 576
'Communist Political Association',
310
'Communist totalitarianism', 427
Communist Workers' Party
(KAPD), 132 *See also* German
Communist Party; Germany
Communists: justification of Stalin's
theses and decisions by, 312;
number beyond Soviet frontiers
at the end of 1945, 307
Comorera, 543
Confédération Générale du Travail
(CGT): anti-strike policies, 341;
opposition to general strike in
France, 333; politization of 1947
strikes, 475–6; on reconstruction
in France, 329–30; reformed
underground, 323; and the
upsurge of the working class, 202
Conference of the nine parties, *see*
Cominform (conference of the
nine parties)
Conference of the Three
Internationals (Berlin, 2–5 April
1922), 146, 148, 149–50; Lenin
and, 150; and the workers' united
front, 146, 149, 150
Congress of Industrial Workers, 310
Congress Party of India: position in
war between Britain and Germany,
400; struggle for India's
independence, 400
Congress of the Peoples of the East
(Baku, September 1920), 246,
247
Congress of Soviets: the Czech
fiction used as example at, 483;
and Stalin's repression of
autonomization, 255–6

66

proletarian political parties, 629; on world revolution, 51, 63

Entente powers: and German crisis, 136; and German revolution, 616–617; intervention in Russian revolution, 616–17; and Nazi attack on USSR, 586; and Social Democrats, 183

Ercoli (pseudonym of Togliatti), 44, 90

Espionage, and Rajk trial, 517–18, 519, 524

'Eurocentrism': Comintern and, 245–6, 249, 252, 258; Lenin and, 50–51; Trotsky and, 82; among Western Marxists, 258, 259

Europe: decline of Communist parties, 112–13; colonial policy, 250; and Communism, 307; social and political agitation (1919–20), 166; socialist revolution, 133, 186, 247; and Stalin's ideas on, 398

Executive Committee of the Communist International, 112, 638; and Chinese CP alliance with Kuomintang, 281; decentralization, 114; dissolution of Comintern statement, 19, 21, 44; Enlarged Plenums (December 1921 and February 1922), 145; German insurrection (October 1923), 138–140; and KPD, 140–41, 144, 159; and Kuomintang, 272; Ninth Plenum (February 1928), 155; Plenary session, 607; Plenum (December 1921), 146; Presidium: meeting of December 1928, 161; of February 1930, 290; of 15 March 1943, 19, 22, 27–30, 32–3; resolution on China (June 1930), 290, 291; right to expel

parties, 113; Seventh Plenum (November–December 1926), 281; Sixth Enlarged Plenum, 144, 278–279; and Spanish revolution, 211; Tenth Plenum, 157–9; Text of Presidium Resolution of 15 May 1943, 40–43; Thirteenth Plenum, 173; ultra-centralistic structure, 114; views on Social Democracy, 173; and workers' united front in Germany, 146

Factions, forbidding of: by Lenin, 118; by Stalin, 118; by Tenth Congress of Russian party, 134

Fajon, Étienne, 539–40, 541–2

Far East: Soviet conditions for common policy with the USA over, 473; US understanding with Moscow in, 427, 431, 563

Fascism: and capitalism, 100, 167, 191–2; Comintern's interpretation of, 610; Comintern's *volte face* on, 300; Communist parties and, 185; defeat, 453; definition, 192; German, 153, 157; Italian, 153, 171; monolithicity against, 122; racial and anti-working-class violence of, 168; reconstruction of monopoly capitalism, 80; resistance of Communist parties against, 151; in Roosevelt's policy, 192; Stalin on, 153–4; threat to bourgeois democracy, 152, 192; threat to Spanish Republic and proletarian revolution, 220; way to defeat, 303–4

Fauvet, Jacques, 201, 338

Fejtő, Ferenc, *Histoire des démocracies populaires*, 457, 517, 527

Index

Ferrer, 543

Figaro, Le, 336, 486

Finland: Communist Party, 309;
Soviet recognition of 'right of
self-determination', 254

Finnish Karelia, 339, 401, 408

First World War: imperialist
powers' alliance with Soviet
Union, 197; German and
Japanese imperialism threat,
191

Fischer, Louis, 1

Fischer, Ruth, 154

Fontaine, André, *History of the Cold
War*, 399

Force Ouvrière, setting-up,
476

Foster, William Z., 25, 26, 123, 192;
*A History of the Three
Internationals*, 23

Four-power conference, in Moscow,
1947, 338

Frachon, Benoît, 329

France: alliance with the Soviet
Union, 179, 186, 188; anti-
Fascism movement, 199, 200;
attitude towards Spanish Republic
during civil war, 235;
capitulationist policy towards
Hitler, 317, 318; Comintern and
the working class, 243;
Communist brake on revolution,
203; defeat of right wing (May
1932), 167; election victory of
People's Front, 170; explosion of
June 1936, 167, 170; frustrated
revolution, 316–43; German
occupation, 296, 299; 'Leagues',
199; military strength, 201, 206,
207; mutual-aid pact with
USSR, 186; opening of second
front, 408, 411; as part of
imperialist camp, 467; People's

Front, 127, 170, 181, 182, 200,
204–5; policy of rapprochement
with Germany, 154, *see also*
Locarno, Treaty of; position after
Second World War, 38, 437;
possibility of revolutionary
development, 440; relation
of forces, 364; Soviet Union
alliance with, 179, 186, 201,
207, 240; Stalin and British
bases in, 398; strikes and
nationalizations, 202–3; upsurge
of working class (1934–6), 199–
210; wave of strikes (autumn
1947), 475. *See also* French
Communist Party; French
Socialist Party; French Radical
Party; French imperialism;
People's Front (in France);
'Croix de Feu'

Franco, Francisco: coup, 207;
entry into Madrid, 242; military
aid to, 241; regime's survival
after disaster of the Axis, 410;
Roosevelt's letter to (8 November
1942), 409; and Spanish
capitalism, 236

Franco–Soviet Pact (2 May 1935),
179, 201, 207, 388, 402, 619; (2
December 1944), 329

French Committee for National
Liberation, PCF representation
in, 322–4; setting-up (June 1942),
322

French Communist Party: aid to
Republican Spain, 209; on
Algerian policy, 337–8; anti-
American campaign, 583, 592–3;
anti-Fascist struggle, 200, 209,
317–18; anti-Tito campaign,
533–40; breach from Stalinist
monolith, 314; campaign against
Socialists, 173, 174; and the cause

70

Index

Grenier, Fernand, 321–2
Grimm, Robert, 171
Groza, 486
Guderian, General, memoirs, 417
Gullo, 369

Haiti, and Atlantic Charter, 399
Hamburg, armed insurrection, 139, 140
Harbin, 556
Harriman, Averell, 451
Hebrang, 489, 501
Hegel, 598; on party discord, 121
Helmsman of Peace, 580
Henderson, Arthur, 148
Hernandez, Jésus, 543
Herriot, Édouard, 154, 179, 181
Hilferding, 52, 59, 98, 144, 607
Hindenburg, 127, 154
Hiroshima, 429, 430, 554
Histoire de la Résistance, 322
Histoire du PCF, 544
Hitler: entry into Prague, 142; and the KPD, 127, 142; threat to Soviet frontiers, 191
Hitlerite: aggression and Comintern, 122; bloc and Communists' tasks in, 28; entry into Paris, 207; party: elections of 1930, 160; elections of November, 1932, 165
Hitler–Hindenberg government, 164
Hitler–Molotov talks (November 1940), 297–8
'Hitlero-Trotskyites', 332
Hobson, J. A., 52, 59
Holland: colonial territories, 436; Communist Party, 243, 249, 309, 478; German occupation, 296; national defence, 189; as part of Imperialist camp, 467; Stalin and British bases in, 398
Holy Synod, Stalin's restoration, 25
Hopkins, Harry, 555

Hsiang Hsung-fa, 283
Hull, Cordell, 426
Humanité, L', 174, 179, 180, 202, 206, 210, 322; and Cominform resolution on Yugoslavia, 506
Hunan Report, 288–9
Hungarian Communist Party, 308, 455, 516; control of AVO, 456; purge, 527; setting up Cominform, 315; Twentieth Congress (1956), 516
Hungarian People's Democracy, *see* Hungary
Hungarian Workers' Party, *see* Hungarian Communist Party
Hungary: 'democratic national revolution', 460; 'exported revolution', 457, 458; links with Russia, 455, 458; misbehaviour of Soviet Army, 488; problem of Slovaks in, 458; secret Stalin–Churchill agreement, 419; Smallholders' Party repressed, 460, 480; Socialist Party, 484; Socialists' unification with Communist Party, 485; Soviet intervention, 414, 456; Soviet invasion of (1956), 516–17; Soviet Republic in, 210
Hurley, General, 555
Husak, Gustav, 528
Hydrogen bomb, 589

Ibarruri, Dolores (La Pasionaria), 207, 221
'Idealization': of the forties, 403; of the thirties, 403
ILP, and the 'Hunger March' on London (1934), 170
Imperialism: American, *see* American imperialism; Anglo-American, 395, 444, 523; Anglo-French, Soviet Union and,

270; British, 271, 381, 399, 425, 427; Chinese bourgeois democratic revolution and, 285, 286; Chinese bourgeoisie and, 286; and dying capitalism, 52, 608; French, 138; German, 439; Japanese, 271, 388; Lenin's view of, 605; role of bourgeois nationalists in struggle against, 260; struggle against, 250, 251, 266, 267

Imperialist states, contradictions between, 68

Imperialist system, revolutionary crisis in, 64

Independent Social Democratic Party, German, 142–3

India: and the Atlantic Charter, 399; bourgeois nationalists' fear of agrarian revolution, 266; and the colonial revolution, 266, 268; Communism, 248; spread of democratic revolution to, 50, 67, 248; struggle against British rule (1921), 250, 251, 400; working class, 268

Indian Communist Party, 309, 594; legalization by colonial authorities, 400; support of British imperialism against Germany, 400

Indochina, and Japan, 294

Indonesia, 251, 258, 268; adhesion to anti-imperialist camp, 467; Communist movement, 593; Communist Party, 249, 258

Intellectuals: in Communist parties, 1, 2, 268; revolution theory, 625–6

International Brigades: and the French Communists, 209; and the Spanish Republic, 231

International labour movement, and Stalin's international strategy, 240

International Working Men's Association, 119

Internationale, abolition, 25

Internationals: the bourgeoisie and the, 150; First, 16, 42, 43, 629, 641; Foster and the, 23; Fourth, 79–80; Second, 16, 17, 49, 50, 62, 80, 146, 154, 157, 166, 245, 249, 303, 337, 604; and setting-up of new parties, 103; in Stalin's speeches, 90; Third, 16, 17, 18, 56–7, 80, *see also* Comintern; Two-and-a-half, 145, 146

Iran: Soviet withdrawal from Northern, 432; Yalta talks about, 424

Isolation, as condition for survival of Soviet society, 452

Italian Church: and the Concordat in new constitution, 368; PCI's concessions to, 368

Italian Communist Party, 96, 160; anti-Fascism, 344; attack on German imperialism, 345; campaign against the King and Marshal Badoglio, 349; campaign against Titoism, 540; and Christian Democrats, 359–9, 366, 367; and the Cominform resolution against Yugoslavia, 536; concessions to the Church, 368; expansion, 308, 310, 362, 442; Fifth Congress resolution, 396; growing prestige, 352; influence after the war, 32; initiative in general strike in German-occupied territory, 346–7; justifications for abdication, 443–444; and 'national unity', 352, 367, 404, 407, 444–5, 447, 448, 453, 581; part in new Bonomi government, 308, 356, 453; and

Index

Marx, Karl: 46, 53; on capital, 193;
Capital, 101; conception of
revolution, 54, 61; conception of
revolutionary party, 120;
criticism of Bakuninists, 627, 629;
Eighteenth Brumaire, 199;
Eurocentrism of, 50; influence of
German crisis on, 101; *Manifesto*,
54; motto, 532, 548; proletarian
internationalism, 641; proletarian
political parties, 625–6, 629;
reservations on working-class
parties, 627; socialist revolution
and, 46–8, 244–5; and Stalin,
72; trade unions, 626–7;
working-class movement, 632;
Working Men's International
Association, 42; workers'
movements, 119–20, 625; world
socialist revolution theory, 51,
63, 76, 221, 222, 605, 625–6
Marxism: adaptation to Spanish
revolution, 221, 222; Bolshevik
version, 93; crisis, 62;
dogmatization, 95, 622; Fascism
and, 193; in France, 243; fusion
with Chinese reality, 288 (*see also*
Hunan Report); progressive
sclerosis of, 92–102; and
revolutionary struggle in colonies,
244; 'Sinification', 564, 565;
theory of 'scientific socialism',
630; US impermeability to, 310
Marxism–Leninism: and
'Browderism', 381; degeneration to
dogmatism, 604; doctrine on
People's Democracies, 460–61;
party training and, 532, 533;
purge and purity of, 529;
Spanish Caballerist and Anarcho-
Syndicalists and, 225; theory of
revolution, 616; Yugoslav
Communists and, 503, 515

Marxist–Leninist Party: and French
proletariat, 204; leading role in
dictatorship of proletariat, 484;
subordination to Comintern, 221;
and Trotskyism, 222
Maslarić, 524
Maslov, 154
Mehring, Franz, 93
Melnikov (Soviet historian), 297–8
Mensheviks: 57, 105, 149; and
Bolshevik Party, 108, 109, 253;
in Georgia, 254. *See also* Russian
revolution
Menshevism: and Chinese
revolution, 285; and Yugoslav
Communism, 503
Merrheim, 148
Metropolitan Sergius, 25
Mexico, 427
Meyer, Alfred G., 69
Middle class: collaboration with
working class, 194, 195; 1936
radicalization of in France, 200;
role in victory of German
Fascism, 195; and Seventh
Comintern Congress, 194–5
Mihailović, Col. Draza: 373, 374;
resigns from Defence Ministry,
378; Soviet military aid to, 376,
400–401; Tito's move towards,
373, 374; US relations with, 472
Mikoyan, A., 483
Moch, Jules, 476
Molotov, V.: discussion with de
Gaulle (May 1942), 321, 336, 400;
dispute with PCF over Germany
and Saar, 340; meeting with
Kardelj, 491; signature of pact
with Germany (August 1939),
295; speeches to Supreme Soviet,
295–7; on Stalin, 545–6; talks
with Hitler (November 1940),
297–8; on zones of influence, 471

Index

Monde, Le, 486
Mongolia, Outer, 571
Mongolian People's Republic, 241
Monolithicity: definition, 117;
failure, 123; against Fascism and
war, 122; Trotsky on, 120
Monzon, Jesus, 542, 543
Morocco, 244, 294
Moscow, 491
Moscow Conference (October 1943),
351, 376; and Atlantic Charter,
404
'Moscow Trials': and Bukharin,
516; and Communist Parties' new
line, 624; seen as historical
necessity, 312, 642–3; and
Kretinski, 532; Spanish view,
241; and Trotsky, 503, 516
Moulin, Jean, 324
Mrazović, 524
Mukden (Shenyang), 556
Mundo Obrero, 227, 234, 235, 236
Munich Agreement, 210, 236, 295,
339
MUR (Mouvement Uni de la
Résistance), 323
Muslims, of Central Asia, 253, 256,
257, 258
Mussolini, Benito: British
agreement with, 236; fall, 345–7,
352, 367–8, 441, 447; and Italian
Communist Party, 345, 447; and
Italian Labour movement, 133;
and Italian ultra-Left, 165
Mutual Aid Pacts, and Italian
'volunteers' in Spain, 236. *See
also* Pacts
Muzhiks, 631

Nagasaki, 429
Nanchang, 290, 291
Nanking, 272, 273, 290, 291, 550,
559

Naples, 349
National Council of the Resistance
(French), 323–4, 326, 334–5
National Liberation Front (EAS),
309
National liberation movements in
colonies, 62, 584; Comintern
policy, 242–71; and policy of
diktat, 595; role of bourgeois,
260–63; role of working class,
262–3; way towards Communism,
265; and world revolution, 66
National Socialist Party (Czech),
482
'National Unity', 561, 563, 622;
French Communist Party, 331,
407, 444–5, 446, 447, 453; Italian
Communist Party, 352, 367, 404,
407, 444–5, 447, 448, 453;
justifications for policy, 453; and
masses, 402; as step towards
People's Democracy, 462
Nationalism, 313–14, 389
NATO, 577, 585
Nazi Party, 127
Nedić, 376, 500
Negrin, Juan, 227; ideological and
political concessions, 236; and
the Nin case, 241; 'thirteen
points', 236
Nekrich, Alexander, 297
Nenni, P., 171
'Neo-capitalism' and the New Deal,
168–9
NEP, *see* New Economic Policy
Nesković, 524
Netherlands, *see* Holland
Neue Zeit, Die, 119
New Deal, 81, 168–9, 610. *See also*
USA
New Economic Policy, 134, 135;
and Russian revolution, 252
New York Times, 23, 24, 401, 403,

81

Purić, Bozidar, 378

Quai d'Orsay, 178
Quebec Conference, 411
Quislings, 444

Radek, Karl, 137, 140, 149; and
Bolshevization, 141; and
proletarian democracy, 150, 151
Radicals, French, *see* French Radical
Party
Rajk, Laszlo, 503, 505, 512, 515,
516, 517, 525, 527, 531, 534
Ramadier, Paul, 341, 342
Ranković, 497, 499, 510, 517, 524
Rapallo, Treaty of, 176, 252; and
Germany, 130, 131, 183; USSR
and, 135, 176
Rakosi, 499
Raynaud, Henry, 333
Reale, E., 381
Red Army: collaboration with
Reichswehr, 130; drive against
Chiang Kai-shek, 289, 292;
misbehaviour in Yugoslavia,
487–8; oath of loyalty to
Comintern, 615; occupation of
Georgia, 149, 254; operations in
China, 290–91; presence in
Eastern Europe, 456; and Warsaw,
133, 246
'Red bases', 283, 284, 289, 290
'Red Lazarus', 474
Reformism: in colonial exploitation,
59, 60; and Communist parties,
623–4; of parties of Second
International, 103; Lenin's
underestimation, 58, 59, 61; of
Marxist Party, 103
Reformist parties, 147–9
Reichswehr, 130, 139
Renault strike, 341
Resistance: 621; and De Gaulle,

327, 447; French, 303, 325, 334,
335, 383, 447; Greek, 318, 379,
380, 415, 449; Italian, 358–61;
Yugoslavian, 318, 325
'Republic of Salo', 355
Revisionism, 637
Revolution: in advanced countries,
61; agrarian, 266–7; Asian, 308;
Austrian (1918), 316; Chinese, *see*
Chinese revolution; in Eastern
Europe, 32; European, 61, 325,
573; French, 32, 372, 385, 387;
German (1918), 131, 137, 316;
Greek, 32, 513; Hungarian Soviet,
56; Italian, 32, 372, 385, 387;
Lenin's three types of, 51; Persian,
269; proletarian, 55–7, 619;
Russian (1905–7), 49, 52, 104,
115, 131, 456, 602, 634–5 (*see also*
October revolution); Spanish, *see*
Spanish revolution; Trotsky's
theory of permanent, 78; Turkish,
269; world, *see* World revolution
Reynaud, Paul, 209
Rhineland, 398
Rhodes, Cecil, 59
Ribbentrop, J. von, 301
Ridgway, General, 583
Rio de Janeiro Pact, 593
Ripka, H., 456
Risorgimento, 441
Rodino, 351
Romania: and the 'exported
revolution', 457; Communist
Party in, 308, 455, 458; and
democratic national revolution,
460; links with Russia, 315, 455,
458; repression of bourgeois
parties, 480; secret Stalin–
Churchill agreement on, 419;
Soviet penetration into, 414, 458,
521; and Yugoslavia, 486
Rome, liberation of, 355

Serrati, G. M., 248

SFIO, 333; and the French
Communist Party, 334

Shanghai: Chinese Communist Party
leadership in, 284; liberation of
March 1927, 272; liberation of
January 1949, 559; proletarian
insurrectionary strikes, 291;
workers' and peasants' revolt, 272,
288, 550

Shelley, Percy Bysshe, 2

Shirinya, K. K., 175, 178

Siberia, Soviet opposition to
deportation to, 282

Silesia, 407

Sinkiang, 571

Sino-Soviet railway company, 424

Sino-Soviet treaty (14 August 1945),
556, 557, 560–61

Sino-Soviet treaty (February 1950),
568, 571

Slansky, Rudolf, 522, 527, 528;
trial, 528, 529

Slav unity slogans, meaning in
Prague and Sofia, 457–8

Slezkin (Soviet historian), 299

Slovak Democratic Party, 482

Slovenia, 488

Slovenian Carinthia, 493

Slovakia: Hungarian minorities in,
458; repression of bourgeois
parties, 480

Smallholders' Party, in Hungary,
457, 460

Social Democracy: alliance with
Communist parties, 172, 221, 310;
collaboration with American
policy, 583; Comintern's attack
on, 149, 300, 608; development of
left-wing tendencies, 169, 311;
Dimitrov's statement on, 300; in
the Entente countries, 183; factors
explaining the rise of, 230; in fight

against Fascism, 152, 171, 172;
and the German Communists, 87,
147; growth, 609, 611; illusions of
the masses about, 382; influence
on working-class movement, 38,
79; Lenin's view, 631–2, 633, 637;
the proletariat and, 131, 137, 147,
148, 149; and referendum of 9
August 1931 in Germany, 163–4;
reformism, 623; Russian *volte-face*
on, 302; and social Fascism, 152,
158; Stalin on, 153; and world-
wide anti-Soviet drive, 190

Social Democratic Party, German,
115, 127; campaign against the
KPD, 129; and the censorship of
the press, 118–19; collapse, 172;
dissolution by Hitler, 122; at
elections of 1930, 160; left-wing,
139, 154, 155, 156–7; position in
factories (1930), 160

Social Fascism: and the Comintern,
213, 300; danger, 162, 163, 175;
difference from Fascism, 157

Socialism: advance, 576, 582;
definition, 46; French road to,
335; in one country, 46, 47, 71, 74,
77, 83, 613, 615, 616, 617, 640;
union with Communism, 174,
178; world-wide victory, 596

Socialist revolution: in advanced
capitalism, 48; attack on proletarian
democracy, 149–50; 'backwardness'
in, 69; capitalist contradictions
and, 69; and collapse of the KPD,
127; crisis of capitalism in Europe
and, 127; failure, 603; in France,
206; inter-nationalism, 458; law of
uneven development of
capitalism and, 73–4; obstacles to
European, 450, 452; in one
country only, 46, 47, 387, 596;
and Russian revolution, 49;